Interaction of Butanedioic and Hexanedioic Acid Bis-Hydrazides with Selected Essential and Hazardous Elemental Ions

Vasilissa

Interaction of Butanedioic and Hexanedioic Acid Bis-Hydrazides with Selected Essential and Hazardous Elemental Ions

First Edition July 2025

Written by Vasilissa

TABLE OF CONTENTS

CHAPTER- 1

INTRODUCTION

1.1 Significance of Chemical Speciation Studies:

Chemical speciation of metal ions in aquatic environments is one of the most important topics in the fields of environmental chemistry, analytical chemistry, Pharmacology, toxicology and geochemistry. The term "Chemical species" was defined[1] in "IUPAC Recommendations-2000" as "a specific form of an element defined as to isotopic composition, electronic or oxidation state, and/or complex or molecular structure". Chemical speciation is "the distribution of an element amongst defined chemical species in a system". Speciation analysis is "the analytical activity of identifying and /or measuring the quantities of one or more individual chemical species in a sample".

Speciation is generally determined through analytical data acquisition methods that measure free metal ion and/ or free ligand and/or free hydrogen ion concentration(s) in conjunction with thermodynamically based predicted models. Vigorous mathematical algorithms are used to refine the predicted model and to get the best-fit model that accounts for all the species in solution, satisfying all the mass balance equations and probed data. Species concentration distribution against pH of the solution, which relies on the local equilibria assumption and on experimentally determined formation constants, is then generated.

Metal ions are essential for many structural and functional components of the body. Metal toxicity may occur due to essential metal overload or exposure to heavy metals from various anthropogenic sources. The toxic effects of trace metal ion pollutants strongly depend on their distribution among the ligands present in biological or environmental systems[2]. It is well known that the toxicity of a metal in natural or biological systems is determined by the activity of the particular metal species causing the toxic effect and not by the total soluble metal concentration. For example, although arsenic at low levels is assumed to be a poison for humans, it is evident that even higher concentration of arsenic in marine food is harmless as the species containing arsenic are non-toxic. Therefore, the total concentration of toxic metal is not a measure of its toxicity. In fact nature of the species containing the toxic metal ion determines its (1) mobility (2) bioavailability, (3) toxicity, (4) biological, chemical and physical activity and (5) lifetime, fate and metabolism. It is therefore essential that toxicological studies should always consider the chemical species present rather than the elemental constituent in order to create meaningful data with respect to risk assessment.

Chemical speciation is also required to understand the metal ion centred specificity and selectivity of biological reactions. Complexes with metal ions play an important role in numerous biological reactions, especially in those with metal–activated enzymes and substrates. The reaction mechanism involves the formation of an enzyme–metal ion substrate species, which probably occurs in biological fluids that contain several ligands as well as different metal ions. Action of metal ions in biological systems is intimately connected with the selective formation of complexes with numerous complex-forming molecules like amino acids, peptides, proteins, carboxylic acids, organic phosphates and nucleic acids. These various complexing species compete for the metal ions, as the total ligand concentration is far greater than the metal ion concentration. This leads to the formation of mixed ligand complexes, in which a metal ion is simultaneously bound to two or more different ligands.

The extent to which a ligand binds a particular metal ion depends on many factors. Therefore, the design of a complexing agent as a drug to eliminate excess or toxic metal ions introduced by environmental pollution needs a thorough understanding of the mixed ligand equilibria. The information expected from such a study includes, i) the number and nature of species present in solution, ii) extent of formation of each species as a function of pH and iii) various forms of the ligand (or drug) present at physiologically important temperature, ionic strength and pH. Since conditions in natural systems vary greatly in terms of composition, ionic strength, solvent and temperature, which affect the nature and extent of formation of various species, it is necessary to use a different set of species every time a new system is examined.

Stability constant of a metal complex has long been employed as an effective measurement of the affinity of a ligand for a metal ion in solution. It plays a key role in 1) assessing the metal-ligand binding strength in solution, 2) understanding the solution equilibrating process, 3) screening appropriate complexing agents, and 4) providing practical guidance for ligand/ drug design[3]. Determination of reliable values of formation constants has gained immense importance in analytical chemistry in general and understanding the metal transport in living systems, in particular. The selection of suitable chelating agents for sequestering toxic metal ions depends on the formation constants of the resulting complex species.

Molecules possessing several binding sites in their structures are known as polytopic ligands. These molecules are of recent interest[4] as they allow the creation of well-ordered extended complexes containing different cations. The multi metal-centred nature of these ligands allows other interactions outside the coordinative such as hydrogen and halogen bonding[5]. They have been used in various applications such as creation of metal organic frameworks and monitoring guest exchange. Some of these ligands and their metal complexes possess useful properties, for instance antimicrobial/ antifungal activity[6] and capacity for DNA binding. Some units of the ligands like phospholes act as unique building blocks for tailoring azahelicene derivatives that can be assembled on metal centres. These ligands are also used for selective extractions of cations and anions[7].

Biochemically, there is a need of non-toxic polytopic ligands that are efficient at sequestering metal ions with high atom efficiency. This has been the basis of our emphasis on the study of interaction of polytopic ligands with metal ions for their probable use in sequestration of offending metal ions. Dihydrazides are found to act as ditopic ligands[8] that can accommodate two metal ions in different coordination pockets. Dihydrazides are capable of forming symmetric and asymmetric bimetallic complexes in addition to mononuclear species. The presence of two metal ions in the same species separated by a flexible part of the molecule leads to several interesting applications like, (i) creation of supramolecular structures to mimic metalloproteins[9] and to understand their structure-reactivity relationship, (ii) specific and selective catalysis[10, 11], (iii) sequestering of toxic metal ions and other biological and industrial applications (iv) DNA binding, etc. *In vitro* and *in vivo* tests proved dihydrazides to be non-genotoxic[12]. Food and Drug Administration (FDA) approved[13, 14] the use of dihydrazides as cross linkers for coatings on plastics used for food package that is not in direct food contact. In view of the number of important factors connected with the multinuclear complexes, a detailed study of the driving forces leading to their formation has recently come more and more into foreground of interest. In this connection the author had taken up a speciometric study on the interaction of some ditopic ligands and amino acids with selected essential and toxic metal ions. The ditopic ligands selected for the study were aliphatic dihydrazides derived from succinic and adipic acids.

1.2 DIHYDRAZIDES as ditopic ligands:

Dihydrazides belong to a group of nitrogenous organic compounds that find extensive application in chemical analysis, synthetic chemistry, agriculture and chemotherapy. These compounds are useful curing agents for epoxy resins, chain extenders for polyurethanes, and excellent crosslinking agents for acrylics. The growing commercial and biological applications increased the importance of this class of compounds. Dihydrazides are represented by the general formula,

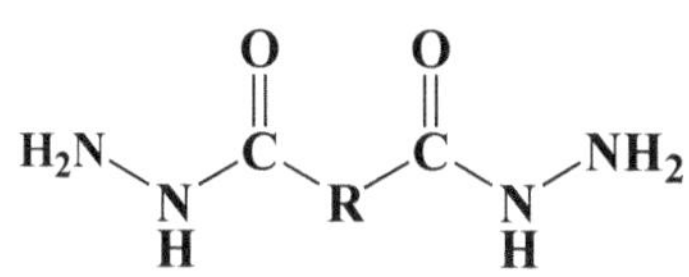

Figure 1.1: General structure of a Dihydrazide molecule

In the case of aliphatic dihydrazides, the 'R' group can be of any length. The most common are, dihydrazides derived from oxalic, malonic, glutaric, succinic, adipic, azelaic, sebacic, icosanedioic acids etc. Dihydrazides are synthesized by condensation reaction of hydrazine with corresponding diesters[15-16]. Although hydrazine is a suspected carcinogen, the safety of dihydrazides has been well established. Adipic acid dihydrazide was approved by the FDA (U.S. Food and Drug Administration) for indirect food contact when used to cure epoxy resins[14].

Dihydrazides of succinic and adipic acids have been widely used for coatings of epoxy resins and in varnishes. They are also used as nickel corrosion inhibitors[17-18]. Further, they are employed as latent hardeners, curing agents, and cross-linkers in many industrial products including semiconductors[19-20]. Hydrazides display antimicrobial, antifungal, antibacterial and anti-tubercular properties[21-22], based on their tendency to form metal chelates.

Dihydrazide contains two hydrazide groups and each hydrazide group is known to exist either in ketonic or enolic form.

Figure 1.2: Keto-enol tautomerism of dihydrazides

Depending on the pH the terminal amino groups of the neutral ligand may be protonated. These ligands may lose protons from enolic form either at higher pH or on interaction with metal ions. Hence, there is a chance of formation of a variety of coexisting mononuclear and binuclear species in protonated, unprotonated and deprotonated[8, 23] forms. The formation of binuclear species has special significance. The presence of two metal ions in the same species separated by some distance not too far, leads to several interesting and important applications including unusual magnetic properties[24]. Depending on the degree of flexibility of the molecule between the two coordination sites there is a possibility of formation of coordination polymers[25] with supramolecular architecture. They can be used to mimic metalloproteins and to study the structure- reactivity relationships[9]. The metal centres are found to act synergistically in catalysing reactions [10,11,26,27].

The structural formulae of the dihydrazides used in the author's investigation, i.e. succinic acid dihydrazide (SADH) and adipic acid dihydrazide (AADH) are shown in Figure 1.3.

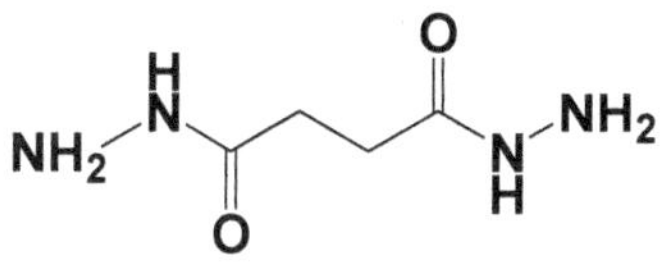

a. Succinic acid dihydrazide

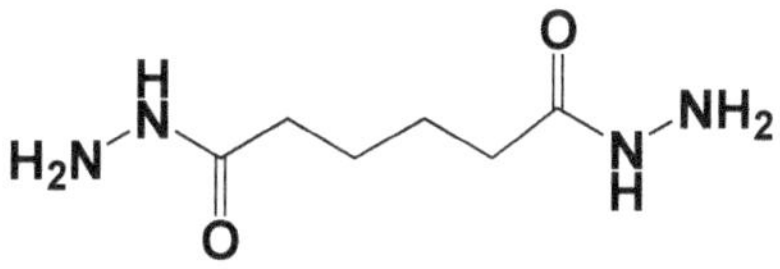

b. Adipic acid dihydrazide

Figure 1.3: Structures of Dihydrazides

Miminoshvili[28], in 2009, published a review on the structural aspects of the transition metal, mono- and di- hydrazide complexes based on the physicochemical studies reported by a number of investigators. It was concluded that, irrespective of the chemical nature of the transition metal ion, the hydrazide group is always present in the inner coordination sphere. Metal ions are coordinated by carbonyl oxygen and terminal amino group nitrogen of hydrazide moiety. Mono hydrazides act as bidentate ring forming ligands while dihydrazides perform the symmetric or asymmetric bis-bidentate rings forming function.

Nickel (II), cobalt (II), manganese (II) cadmium (II) and magnesium (II) tetrafluoro- borate complexes of the dihydrazides of succinic, adipic, oxalic, malonic, phthalic, and terephthalic acids were synthesized and characterized by Patel and Adeniyi [29a-d]. These complexes were characterized by elemental analysis, magnetic susceptibility measurements, electronic and infrared spectral studies. The formed complexes are of the type $(ML_n)(BF_4)_2$ where M is the metal ion, L is the dihydrazide and n=1.5 or 2 or 3. They suggested that in all the species the bonding of the dihydrazide is through any two of the carbonyl, amino and amide groups. Magnetic and electronic spectral data indicated an octahedral geometry with the tetrafluoroborate anion in the outer sphere.

Nagano et al.[30] and Paul et al.[31] in their study of metal complexes of monocarboxylic acid hydrazides suggested that the coordination cites are carbonyl oxygen and amino nitrogen. Dutta et al.[32] instead, suggested amide nitrogen atoms as the bonding centres in their study of metal (Mn^{2+}, Fe^{2+}, Co^{2+}, Ni^{2+}, Cu^{2+}, Zn^{2+}, Pd^{2+}, Ag^{+}, Cd^{2+}, and Pb^{2+}) complexes of malonic acid dihydrazide. This tendency of bonding through amide nitrogen atoms in preference to carbonyl oxygen was explained by these authors[33] in their further study on metal complexes of succinic and malonic acid dihydrazides with Co^{2+}, Ni^{2+}, Cu^{2+}, and Pd^{2+}. The inductive effect of the amino group, without leading to delocalization, renders the carbonyl group poorer in electron density. Some of its electron density is distributed to amido nitrogen in between, leading to the bonding through amide nitrogen atoms.

Gogorishvili et al.[34] synthesized bivalent metal chloride, nitrate, sulphate and isothiocyanato complexes of adipic acid dihydrazide (L) and characterized by various physicochemical methods. The study indicated the formation of MLX, MLX_2 and ML_2X_2 (M = Co^{2+}, Mn^{2+}, Cu^{2+}, Ni^{2+}, Fe^{2+}; X = Cl^-, NO_3^-, SO_4^{2-}, NCS^-) type of complexes. The stability of the bond of dihydrazide with the central metal ion was attributed to the ring formation.

Srivastava et al.[35] synthesized [Cp_2ZrL] and [$CpZr(LH)_2Cl$] type of complexes by reacting dicyclopentadienylzirconium (IV) dichloride with aliphatic dihydrazides (LH_2) derived from oxalic, adipic and succinic acids in basic medium. They suggested that in 1:1 (M: L) type of complexes the ligands act as bidentates bonding through the two deprotonated amido nitrogens. On the other hand, in the case of the ML_2 type of species the deprotonated donors may be from the same or different ligands.

Thermal and infrared spectral studies conducted by Tsitsishvili et al.[36], on the synthesized complexes of cobalt with dihydrazides (LH_2) of malonic, succinic, glutaric, and adipic acid revealed that the dihydrazides act as bidentate ligands either in neutral or deprotonated anionic (L^{2-}) form.

The crystal and molecular structure study of Mn(II) sulphate complex, $MnL_2.SO_4.4H_2O$ with malonic acid dihydrazide (L) showed that malonic acid dihydrazide acts as a bis-bidentate ligand[36], bridging through NH_2 and O groups at each end to form 5-membered rings. $Mn(L)(NCS)_2.H_2O$ (I) and $Mn(L)_2(ClO_4)_2$ (II) (L= succinic acid dihydrazide) were prepared and characterized by single crystal structural analysis by Zhorzholiani et al.[37] Compound I is a dimer and compound II is a polymer. In both the complexes dihydrazide acts as a bidentate bridging ligand.

Kharitonov et al.[38] prepared succinic acid dihydrazide (L) coordination compounds with transition metal ions Mn^{2+}, Fe^{2+}, Co^{2+}, Ni^{2+}, and Cu^{2+}. The complexes are of the type, (a) $MLCl_2.nH_2O$ (M= Mn^{2+}, Ni^{2+}), (b) $ML_2Cl_2.nH_2O$ (M= Mn^{2+}, Fe^{2+}, Co^{2+}, Ni^{2+}, Cu^{2+}), (c) $ML_3Cl_2.H_2O$ (M= Co^{2+}, Ni^{2+}), and (d) $ML_3.SO_4.2H_2O$ (M= Co^{2+}, Ni^{2+}). These complexes were characterized by infrared spectral and thermal decomposition studies. Type (a) species are found to be either dimers or polymers in which the ligand is a tetradentate bridging through NH_2 and O groups. In other types of species with metal to ligand ratios 1:2 and 1:3 some of the hydrazide groups form chelate cycles and the remaining acts as monodentates.

Krivis et al.[39] in a polarographic study on cadmium complexes of succinic and adipic dihydrazides observed that there is no drop in pH of the dihydrazide solutions when titrated with Cd^{2+} solution. This indicates that the neutral form of dihydrazide participates in complexation as there is no release of protons.

Iron complexes of malonic acid dihydrazide and phthalic acid dihydrazide in 1:2 (metal to ligand) ratio was prepared by Hammad, et al.[40] The complexes were studied by magnetic susceptibility measurements and infrared, electronic and mössbauer spectroscopy. The Fe atom is coordinated octahedrally in the complexes. Fe (III) is reduced to Fe (II) in the malonic acid dihydrazide complex and Fe (II) is oxidized to Fe (III) in the phthalic acid dihydrazide complex.

Eight coordinate Uranium(VI) complexes of malonic and phthalic acid dihydrazides (LH_2) were synthesized and characterized by Kumari et al.[41], using elemental analysis, electrical conductance and spectral (IR and electronic) measurements. The complexes are of the type $UO_2L(LH_2)(H_2O)_2$ where the ligands act as bidentates, coordinating through secondary amide nitrogen atoms. LH_2 being the neutral form of the dihydrazide and L is the deprotonated form.

Gogorishvili et al.[42] prepared and characterized $MnL_2.(NCS)_2.H_2O$ (L = malonic acid dihydrazide) complex by reacting manganese thiocyanate with acid dihydrazide. The ligand acts as a bidentate bonding through amino nitrogen and oxygen. The complex was also found to be polymeric with octahedral environment about each manganese atom. Polymeric cobalt(II) thiocyanate complexes with bridging dihydrazide (succinic acid dihydrazide, glutaric acid dihydrazide, adipic acid dihydrazide, nonanedioic acid dihydrazide and sebacic acid dihydrazide) groups were also reported by the same authors[43]. The complexes were characterized by infrared spectral and DTA studies.

Some "$MLCl_2.H_2O$ and $CuL.SO_4.H_2O$" type of polymeric complexes of malonic, oxalic and terephthalic acid dihydrazides (L), where M= Cu^{2+}, Co^{2+} or Ni^{2+} were synthesized and characterized by Kumbhar et al. [44, 45] The chloride containing species are found to be octahedral and $CuLSO_4.H_2O$ type of complexes are sulphate bridged polymeric square planar.

Malonic, succinic and adipic acid dihydrazides are found to act as tetradentates in the complexes of Cd^{2+}, Zn^{2+} and Sr^{2+} synthesized by Machkhoshvili et al.[46] Malonic, succinic and adipic acid dihydrazide complexes of Mg^{2+}, Ca^{2+}, Ba^{2+}, Cd^{2+}, Mn^{2+}, Fe^{2+}, Co^{2+}, Ni^{2+} and Cu^{2+} were synthesized[47-49] and characterized by thermal decomposition studies, electrical conductance and infrared spectra. In all the complexes the ligands act as tetradentates and bridging.

X-ray diffraction studies of $ZnL.SO_4.3H_2O$[50] and $MnL_2.SO_4.4H_2O$[36], where L= malonic acid dihydrazide, indicated that L acts as a bis-bidentate; forming two five membered chelate rings each containing one metal atom. The complexes are polymeric and the ligand coordinates through carbonyl oxygen and amino-group nitrogen atoms.

Homo and hetero metallic complexes of adipic acid dihydrazide[25] with Co^{2+}, Ni^{2+}, Cu^{2+}, Zn^{2+}, Cd^{2+}, Hg^{2+}, Ag^{+}, Pd^{2+} and Pt^{2+} were prepared and characterized by elemental analysis, spectral (MS, ESR, HNMR and Electronic), thermal and magnetic measurements. The ligand behaves as a neutral bidentate or neutral/ binegative tetra-dentate.

Hetero binuclear complexes of the type $M.Hg(SCN)_4.L$, where L = malonic or oxalic acid dihydrazide and M= Zn^{2+}, Cu^{2+}, Ni^{2+}, Co^{2+} were synthesized and characterized by Narang et al.[51] using physicochemical methods. Both the ligands were found to act as bidentates. Some of these bimetallic complexes were tested against Escherichia coli, Klebsiella pneumonia bacteria and Aspergillus flavus, Penicillium Sp. Fungi, and were found to be active.

The structures of mixed ligand complexes of oxalic or malonic acid dihydrazide (L) and deprotonated amino acids (glycine, serine, glutamic acid and methionine) with transition metal ions Co^{2+}, Ni^{2+}, and Zn^{2+} were reported by Fridman et al.[52] The complexes are of the type MALX (A^-= deprotonated amino acid, L=dihydrazide and X= Cl^-, NO_3^-, or $1/2SO_4^{2-}$). The formation constants of these mixed ligand complexes along with those of adipic and succinic acid dihydrazides were also reported using spectrophotometric and pH-metric methods.

Seven and nine coordinate scandium, yttrium and lanthanum (nitrate and isothiocyanate) complexes of succinic and adipic acid dihydrazides were synthesized and characterized by Machkhoshvili et al.[53] IR and Raman spectra indicated the tetradentate and bridging nature of dihydrazides.

Tsitsishvili et al.[54] reported the formation of $MLX_2.nH_2O$ (M= Cu^{2+}, Co^{2+}, Ni^{2+}, Mn^{2+}; X= Cl^-, 0.5 SO_4^{2-}), $ML_2X_2.nH_2O$ (M=Co^{2+}, Ni^{2+}, Mn^{2+}; X= Cl^-, 0.5 SO_4^{2-}) and $M_2LX_4.nH_2O$ (M= Ni^{2+}, Co^{2+}, Mn^{2+}; X= Cl, 0.5 SO_4^{2-}) type of complexes with succinic acid dihydrazide (L).

Hg^{2+} complexes of oxalic and malonic acid dihydrazides were prepared and characterized by Narang et al.[55] Some of the complexes were found to possess antifungal and antibacterial activity. Cavier et al.[56] observed that molecules containing two hydrazide groups possess anthelmintic activity on Syphacia obvelata and Hymenolepis. Dihydrazides are non-toxic[57] and possess two hydrazide groups which are necessary for the anthelmintic activity.

Oxalic acid dihydrazide and its derivatives were found to exhibit good activity against influenza virus in chorioallantoic cultures[58]. Hydrazones derived from malonic and succinic acid dihydrazides complexed with metal ions of Fe(II) and

Co(II) were found to be active against bacteria[59]. The condensation of 2-acetyl-pyridine with dihydrazides of malonic and succinic acid resulted in novel ligands, which, on complexation with transition metals, were found applications in various chemical, biological and industrial systems. Co(III), Zn(II), Cd(II) and Fe(III) complexes with condensation derivatives of 2-acetylpyridine and the dihydrazides of oxalic and malonic acid showed significant cytotoxic activity against HeLa and B16 cell cultures *in vitro*[60, 61]. This activity was assumed to be due to the strong bonding of the binuclear complexes to DNA[62]. Co(II), Ni(II), Cu(II), Zn(II) and Cd(II) metal ion complexes of diacetyl salicylaldehyde and diacetyl benzaldehyde hydrazones of succinic, oxalic and malonic acid dihydrazides were found to have antifungal and antibacterial activity[63].

Hydrazones synthesized from succinic acid dihydrazide and furfuraldehyde/ 2-acetylthiophene/ 2-acetylfuran/2,6-dichlorobenzaldehyde/2,4-dichlrobenzaldehyde/ 3,4-dichlorobenzaldehyde were found to show an appreciable increase in the antimicrobial activity in comparison to hydrazides[64]. Acylhydrazones, obtained from succinic acid dihydrazide were found to be active against both gram positive and gram negative bacteria at less than 6 mg/ml concentration[65].

Some dihydrazides are studied for their corrosion inhibition. Malonic, succinic and adipic acid dihydrazides have been found to give the best performance as nickel corrosion inhibitors. The theoretical and electrochemical studies confirmed that the adhesives of these dihydrazides effectively inhibit the corrosion of nickel[66]. The reaction products of dihydrazides of malonic and succinic acid with formaldehydes are used as adhesives in glues. They are employed as cross-linking agents of the urea-formaldehyde resins[67].

Molecular recognition and self-assembly may be used with reactive species in order to pre-organize a system, for a specific chemical reaction. It may be considered a special case of supramolecular catalysis. Non-covalent bonds between the reactants and a template hold the reactive sites of the reactants close together facilitating the desired chemistry. This technique is particularly useful for situations where the desired reaction conformation is thermodynamically or kinetically unlikely, such as in the preparation of large macrocycles. This pre-organization also serves purposes such as minimizing side reactions, lowering the activation energy of the reaction, and producing desired stereochemistry. After the reaction has taken place, the template may remain in place, be forcibly removed, or may be "automatically" decomplexed. The template may be as simple as a single metal ion or may be extremely complex. Malonic acid dihydrazide and its metal complexes play a role as precursors for the synthesis of hydrogen bonded supramolecules[68]. Being metals acting as templates, the complexes of dihydrazides of oxalic, succinic and adipic are used in the synthesis of macrocyclic compounds via cyclization. The macrocycles and their metal complexes mimic naturally occurring macrocyclic molecules in their structural and functional features and have rich chemical behaviour[69].

Majority of the studies reported in the literature on metal complexes of dihydrazides were therefore, aimed at the preparation and elucidation of their structures by physicochemical methods. Characterization of the complexes is often specific to an isolated/ precipitated single species and may not be relevant to the solution behaviour of the compound wherein a number of species coexist. Chemical modelling study in which the nature and extent of formation of all the species can be determined when a ligand interacts with metal ions in solution is an essential pre-requisite to understand their behaviour in biological and other systems. Studies on the solution equilibria of the metal complexes of dihydrazides are scanty. Relatively a few reports on the solution equilibria of dihydrazides with transition metal ions were found in the literature[39, 70-78]. Thus, the author has taken up a detailed speciation study on the proton-ligand and metal-ligand equilibria of SADH and AADH in aqueous medium. The metal ions included in the study were Ca^{2+}, Mg^{2+}, Pb^{2+}, Hg^{2+} and Cd^{2+}.

1.3 SIGNIFICANCE OF SPECIATION STUDIES of essential and toxic trace metal ions:

Depending on the function with respect to the human body, metal ions are classified mainly into three categories *viz.* essential, non-essential but medicinally useful and toxic. Essential metal ions play specific roles in many vital biological reactions. Many enzyme catalysed biochemical reactions involve the participation of specific and selective metal ions. Without an appropriate metal ion, a biochemical reaction catalysed by a particular metalloenzyme may not take place or occurs very slowly. These essential metal ions may be bound by main-chain amino and carboxyl groups of amino acids. Specific binding is achieved by the amino acid side chains, particularly the carboxylate groups of aspartic and glutamic acid, and the ring nitrogen atom of histidine. Other side chains that bind metal ions include (i) Tryptophan (ring nitrogen), (ii) cysteine (thiol), (iii) methionine (thioether), (iv) serine, threonine, tyrosine (hydroxyl groups) and (v) asparagine and glutamine (carbonyl groups, less often amino groups).

Metal ions are generally positively charged and act as electrophiles, seeking the possibility of sharing electron pairs with atoms of the ligand so that a bond or electrostatic interaction is established. Metal ions compete with protons for the active sites of the ligands. Metal ions, however, often have positive charges greater than one, and have a larger ionic volume so that they can accommodate many ligands at the same time around them. In addition, at biological pH the hydrogen ion concentration is low while that of the metal ions may be relatively high.

At biological pH, trace metal ions involve in many vital biological reactions. Some elements are highly toxic and others are considered as essential, but may become toxic at higher (example Cu^{2+}, Ni^{2+}, etc.) concentrations. Essential metal ions like Mg^{2+}, Ca^{2+}, Zn^{2+}, Cu^{2+}, Fe^{2+}, etc. are homeostatically controlled. Toxic metal ions such as Pb^{2+}, Hg^{2+}, Cd^{2+} Al^{3+}, As^{3+}, etc. are not homeostatically controlled and may interact with the biological molecules that are involved in the use and control of essential metal ions. The toxicities and environmental behaviour of metal ion pollutants strongly depend on their speciation and distribution among the ligands present[79].

Calcium and Magnesium are most abundant intracellular cations in the human body that work synergistically on not only the bones and nervous system but also on the muscles. Despite the important involvement of Ca^{2+} and Mg^{2+} in biological systems, relatively little is known about their structural chemistry due to the fact that these ions do not seem to form stable covalent bonds. On HSAB scale, both Ca^{2+} and Mg^{2+} are hard Lewis acids and prefer hard ligands with low polarizability, oxygen being the most preferable coordinating atom followed by nitrogen. Crystallographic studies have shown that carbonyl and carboxyl groups are the most common bonding sites[80-82]. Both Mg^{2+} and Ca^{2+} are more likely to form ionic bonds rather than covalent. Ca^{2+} ion is larger than Mg^{2+} and is therefore more suited for binding by large multi-dentate anion ligand groups. Mg^{2+} possesses a higher charge density, prone to form stronger electrostatic bonds, favours sixfold octahedral coordination, whereas Ca^{2+} is most commonly found coordinated by seven or eight ligands.

Toxic metals comprise a group of minerals that have no known function in the body and, in fact, are harmful. Today, mankind is exposed to the highest levels of these metals in recorded history. This is due to their industrial use, the unrestricted burning of coal, natural gas and petroleum, and incineration of waste materials worldwide. They get into the human food chain from the environment. Once they enter the human system they disturb the biochemical processes and become a major cause of illness, aging and even genetic defects. Toxic metal ions can bind to proteins in lieu of essential metal ions, thereby altering the biological function of the target molecule. Heavy metal ions in particular Pb^{2+}, Hg^{2+} and Cd^{2+} act as effective enzyme inhibitors. They have an affinity for sulphur containing donor atoms of cysteine, methionine amino acid residues present in protein part of the enzyme. Heavy metal ions exert toxic action by attacking –SH group of an enzyme, thereby inhibiting enzyme action.

Pb^{2+} belongs to the borderline category and can interact with both hard and soft donors. Pb^{2+} blocks entry of Ca^{2+} into nerve terminals and impairs normal calcium homeostasis in cells, which is essential for their function. Lead replaces zinc in heme enzymes, particularly, δ-aminolevulinic acid dehydratase inhibiting its activity. Lead inhibits the activity of ferrochelatase by replacing the iron. This enzyme is needed to incorporate iron into the haemoglobin molecule. Divalent lead provides a complicated structural story because of the "inert-pair effect" which involves the inertness of the two 6*s* electrons on Pb^{2+} towards removal or participation in a covalent bond formation or hydrogen bonding. This is ascribed to a relativistic effect, causing the 6s orbital to contract, so that the energy required to remove or interact with this lone pair of electrons is increased. The presence of this lone pair of electrons can cause a non-spherical charge distribution around the Pb^{2+} and there may be an identifiable gap in the ligand arrangement around the metal ion.

With a filled d-shell of electrons, Cd^{2+} biology resembles that of Zn^{2+} regarding the flexibility in coordination and the lack of redox chemistry. Thus, the only valence slate important for biology is cadmium (II). It displays a variety of coordination geometries based on the balance of electrostatic, covalency and size factors. Four and six are the most common coordination numbers existing in tetrahedral and octahedral configurations. Cd^{2+} replaces Zn^{2+} biochemically and is toxic to aquatic biota. The crystal ionic radius (109 pm) of Cd^{2+} is significantly larger than that of Zn^{2+} (88 pm), increasing the potential of cadmium to adopt higher coordination numbers. This leads to slightly longer bond lengths in its coordination compounds relative to Zn^{2+}. Cadmium ions also bind in calcium-binding sites of proteins in *vitro* because the ionic radius of Ca^{2+} (114 pm) is quite similar to that of Cd^{2+} (109 pm). It interferes with calcium and vitamin D metabolism in the kidney. Interactions between cadmium and calcium in bone may result in disorders of bone metabolism. Cd^{2+} is a softer Lewis acid and has slightly lower stabilities in complexes with oxygen and nitrogen ligands and higher stabilities with sulphur containing ligands. Metallothionein, a low molecular weight protein that binds zinc and copper interacts with cadmium. The coordination geometry of the Cd^{2+}-amino acid complex is generally octahedral with the involvement of the amino and carboxylate groups in metal binding. The terminal amino group and the subsequent carbonyl-O atom are the primary binding sites for Cd^{2+}-peptide complexes. In group 12 of the periodic system of the elements, cadmium is between zinc and mercury. It shares some properties with the essential element zinc, its lower atomic weight neighbour and with the toxic element mercury, its higher atomic weight neighbour.

Mercuric ion (Hg^{2+}) is one of the most stable inorganic forms of mercury. It is electronically equivalent in a VSEPR (Valence Shell Electron Pair Repulsion) sense to Pb^{2+} without the lone pair of electrons on it. The structural chemistry of Hg^{2+} is dominated by its tendency to form linear complexes. Mercury is toxic at such low levels that it leaves a very small margin to humans and causes acute and chronic toxicity. On HSAB scale Hg^{2+} is a soft Lewis acid and prefers to bond with soft bases. The cell killing activity is related to its high affinity for protein thiols. Mercury redistributes easily when new ligands become available.

Therefore, by complexing with appropriate ligands, these toxic metal ions can be excreted out of the body. For clinical use, in order to facilitate excretion in urine, the chelating agent needs to be water soluble. If the complex is lipid soluble it may cause a redistribution of toxic metal ions, which is not beneficial to the patients. The probable use of an exogenous ligand can be decided on the basis of its speciation with both essential and toxic metal ions. The prediction of metal chelate equilibria in biological or environmental systems is based on the use of stability constants in chemical speciation calculations. Several characteristics of metal ions including ionic size, coordination number, hard & soft acid-base nature, geometric factors etc. affect the stabilities of the formed species. The nature of the bond between a metal ion and a ligand may vary from purely electrostatic to almost covalent. Therefore, the selection of a compound to eliminate any excess or toxic metal ions introduced by environmental pollution needs a thorough understanding of the speciation of the interested metal ion in the presence of biological and exogenous ligands.

1.4 AMINO ACIDS as chelating agents:

Knowledge of the interaction between amino acids and essential/ toxic metal ions is of significance for a possible understanding of the biological activity of these metals. When an exogenous ligand in the form of a drug or a pollutant enters the biological stream, there is a chance of formation of a ternary species containing amino acid residue, exogenous ligand and the metal ion of interest. As a prelude to understand the fate of the metal ion in such a complex situation, it is essential to have knowledge of the nature of the interaction between the selected metal ions and amino acids.

Amino acids are the chemical units that build proteins and are therefore commonly known as the 'building blocks". They are required for the synthesis of neurotransmitters, structural proteins, enzymes and some hormones[83-90]. Among more than three hundred known amino acids, only twenty of them serve as building blocks of proteins. All the twenty amino acids commonly found in proteins are alpha- amino acids; i.e., the amino group in each is a substituent on the carbon atom alpha to the carboxyl group. These amino acids combine to create several types of proteins found in the biological systems. Out of twenty, nine are essential amino acids and the remaining belongs to non-essential category as they are produced by the body itself. The general structure of α-amino acid is shown in Figure 1.4.

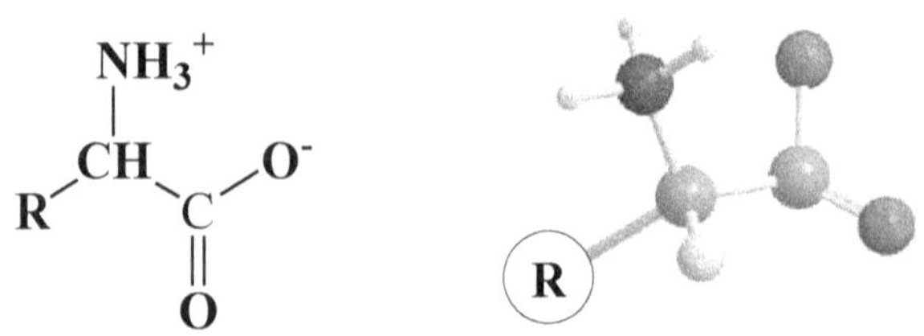

Figure 1.4: General structure of α-amino acids

Amino acids are also classified on the basis of polarity and charge of their R-groups. The non-polar aliphatic class includes glycine, alanine, leucine, isoleucine, methionine and valine. Phenylalanine and tryptophan have aromatic side chains and are relatively hydrophobic. The polar uncharged class includes asparagine, cysteine, glutamine, proline, serine and threonine. The acidic amino acids are aspartate and glutamate and the basic ones are arginine, histidine and lysine. The study of the interactions between metal cations and amino acids is of fundamental relevance to understand the naturally occurring metalloprotein chelation as well as human and environmental toxicology[91]. The amino acids included in the present study are glycine, L-histidine and L-aspartic acid.

Glycine:

Glycine is the simplest amino acid and is the only amino acid that is not optically active. It is a sweet tasting non-essential amino acid that was first isolated in 1820 from gelatine. Glycine can be manufactured by the body from serine and threonine, so its dietary intake is not essential. It is required to build protein in the body and synthesis of nucleic acids, the construction of RNA as well as DNA, bile acids and other amino acids in the body. It is further found to be useful in aiding the absorption of calcium in the body. It helps in retarding degeneration of muscles since it helps to supply extra creatine in the body. It is also found in fairly large amounts in the prostate fluid and may, for this reason be important in prostate health. Glycine is also used by the nervous system and its function as an inhibitory neurotransmitter makes it important to help prevent epileptic seizures and it is also used in the treatment of manic depression and hyperactivity. Foods rich in protein such as fish, meat, beans, and dairy products contain good amounts of glycine. The zwitter ionic form of glycine (Figure 1.5) is the most stable form in solution.

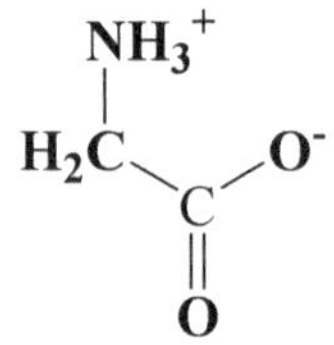

Figure 1.5: Zwitter ion form of glycine

Glycine generally acts as a bidentate ligand with most of the metal ions forming mono, bis and tris complexes having stable five membered chelate rings bonding through the amino nitrogen and carboxylate oxygen. Protonated complexes may also be formed in which glycine acts as a mono-dentate bonding through only the carboxylate oxygen.

L-Histidine:

L-Histidine is an essential amino acid that is required for the production of histamine[92, 93]. Histidine cannot be formed from other nutrients, and must be in the diet to be available to the body. L-histidine is required by the body to regulate and utilize essential trace minerals such as copper, zinc, iron, manganese, and molybdenum[94, 95]. L-Histidine is essential in forming many metal bearing enzymes and compounds [96, 97]. Metals such as zinc, copper, and nickel are transported by binding with L-histidine, and such binding appears essential for rapid excretion of excess metal. The transport properties of copper (II) –L-histidine led to its application in the treatment of Menkes disease, a fatal genetic neurodegenerative disease.[98-99]

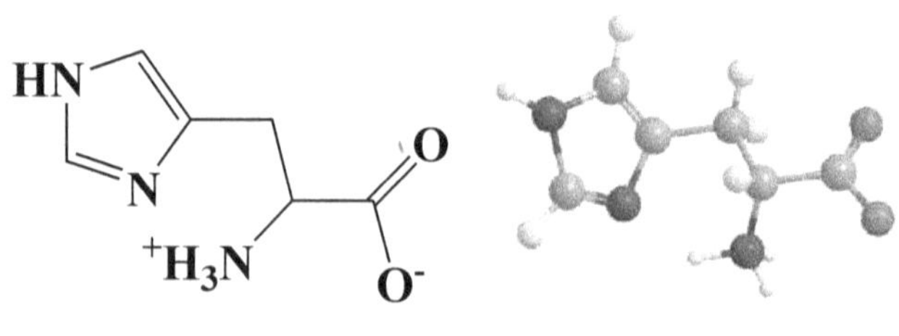

Figure 1.6: L-Histidine Structure

Histidine (Figure 1.6) contains a heterocyclic ring (imidazole) that has a pair of non-bonded electrons that are not involved in resonance. It exists in both protonated and unprotonated forms at physiological pH. This is one of the reasons for histidine to be an important component of many enzymes and often found in active sites when the donation or abstraction of a proton is needed.

Among the amino acids, L-histidine is one of the strongest metal coordinating ligands and plays an important role in the binding of metal ions by proteins. It has three potential metal-binding sites, namely the carboxylate oxygen, the imidazole imido nitrogen and the amino nitrogen. The imidazole nitrogen of histidine residues often provides the primary means by which the metal ions are bound to proteins. It has an exceptional ability to bind metal ions as mono, bi or tridentate. As a bidentate histidine form a six membered ring bonding through imidazole nitrogen and α-amino group or a five membered ring bonding through carboxylate oxygen and amino nitrogen. Coordination may also occur from all the three and thus generally it may also show tridentate behaviour forming adjacent six and five membered rings.

L-Aspartic acid:

Aspartic acid is a dicarboxylic amino acid. The presence of the second carboxylate group makes the molecule very hydrophilic. It is a nonessential amino acid generally found in proteins, and acts as an excitatory neurotransmitter in the central nervous system. The main food sources of aspartic acid are sugar cane, sprout seeds, oat flakes, avocado and asparagus. Aspartic acid exists in two configurations, L- and D-. The biological role of D-aspartic acid is much less compared to that of L-aspartic acid (Fig. 1.7).

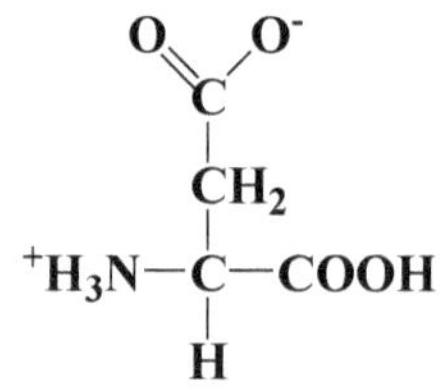

Figure 1.7: Structural formula of L-Aspartic acid

Aspartic acid is an ambidentate ligand. It can act as a,

- monodentate, bonding through either of the carboxylate oxygens,
- bidentate bonding through (i) α-carboxylate oxygen and amino nitrogen forming a five membered ring or (ii) side chain carboxylate oxygen and amino nitrogen forming a six membered ring or (iii) both the carboxylate oxygens and
- Tridentate bonding through all the three centres.

The multidentate nature of the ligand leads to the formation of protonated species in addition to simple complexes.

In literature, there are a number of reports on the stability constants of metal complexes of Glycine, L-histidine and L-aspartic acid in solution[100-105]. The stability constants were determined by several investigators, under different experimental conditions, using different methods of data acquisition. The data were analysed using a variety of numerical and graphical methods. The literature survey indicates that there is a wide spread in the formation constants of both proton-ligand and metal-ligand complexes. The use of activity and concentration scales for hydrogen ion in potentiometric methods may be one of the reasons for the inconsistency observed in the formation constants. As stoichiometric or concentration formation constants are highly dependent on experimental conditions like ionic strength, temperature, etc., the author has redetermined the formation constants of proton-ligand and metal-ligand species of the amino acids of interest under the conditions identical to binary systems of dihydrazides and ternary systems.

1.5 PURPOSE OF THE PROPOSED STUDY AND ADAPTED METHODS OF ANALYSIS:

Chemical speciation study is critical for understanding the nature and extent of formation of species of interest in biological, environmental, analytical and industrially important systems. It is crucial in assessing bioavailability, transport and fate of the species of interest to understand their physiological activities or to estimate the risk to humans and ecosystems. The design of a drug molecule to eliminate toxic metal ions needs an understanding of the nature and extent of formation of various species containing drug molecule, biologically active ligands and metal ions. Speciation is generally determined through analytical methods in conjunction with mathematical models. These models rely on mass balance and thermodynamics to determine the concentration of each species that contains a given component. Chemical speciation is usually predicted with thermodynamic expressions, because the reactions involved take place in the bulk aqueous phase and are generally rapid.

Metal complexes of hydrazides have been found to have therapeutic activity and this is one practical reason for the continuing interest in these compounds. In the field of hydrazide chemistry, a special place is held by dihydrazides for several reasons:

- Dihydrazides are ditopic ligands and the presence of two coordinating units connected by bridges of varying degrees of flexibility may yield supramolecular architectures such as double helices, grids, racks or coordination polymers.

- The coordination of a metal ion by one unit may induce changes in the coordinative properties of the other unit. It is particularly interesting to observe that there are cases where, in the same complex, two structurally identical units have different coordination modes, thus generating complexes where the metal ion is symmetrically or asymmetrically coordinated.
- The presence of two coordinating units in the appropriate positions may yield better or stronger coordinating properties than those of a sole coordinating unit.
- Depending on the pH of the solution, dihydrazide (L) may exist in diprotonated (LH_2^{2+}), mono-protonated (LH^+), unprotonated (L) and deprotonated (LH_{-1} and LH_{-2}) forms. The protonation is at the terminal $-NH_2$ groups and deprotonation at higher pH is due to the neutralization of enolic protons. Therefore, the ligand may be bound to metal ions in any of these states of protonation, thus enabling the properties of its complexes to be modulated by the degree of deprotonation. The extent of such modulation may be increased in systems where more than one ligand unit is present.

The ditopic nature of dihydrazides and their existence in different protonated forms in solution may lead to the formation of bimetallic (homo and hetero) symmetric/ asymmetric species in different states of protonation/ deprotonation in addition to mono-metallic simple, bis and tris species. Further, it is interesting to see the effect of variation of $(-CH_2)_n$ chain length between the two hydrazide units on the stabilities of the formed species. Despite the importance of dihydrazides in chemical speciation, only a few studies on solution phase speciation that too with some transition metal ions were found in the literature. No solution phase studies on Ca^{2+}, Mg^{2+}, Pb^{2+}, Hg^{2+} and Cd^{2+} complexes of dihydrazides were found in the literature. Although there are reports on the synthesis and characterization of metal complexes of some dihydrazides in solid state, they are specific to isolated single species and may not be relevant to the solution behaviour where in a number of species coexist. Therefore, it is worthwhile to have a detailed understanding of the chemical speciation of dihydrazides metal complexes in solution. As these ligands are biologically significant, a study of ternary systems containing dihydrazide, amino acid and an essential / toxic metal ion throws light on their behaviour *in vivo*.

As described above, the primary aim of the speciation study is to calculate the concentrations of all the species present in solution including the free metal ion(s) and free ligand(s) at any given experimental point or pH under the specified experimental conditions. Consider a system containing a metal ion and two ligands (L and X) involved in the formation of a generalized species, represented by the equilibrium,

$$m\mathrm{M} + l\,\mathrm{L} + x\mathrm{X} + h\mathrm{H} \rightleftharpoons \mathrm{M}_m\mathrm{L}_l\mathrm{X}_x\mathrm{H}_h \quad \ldots\ldots\ldots\ldots (1.1)$$

The overall formation constant is given by,

$$\beta_{mlxh} = \frac{[\mathrm{M}_m\mathrm{L}_l\mathrm{X}_x\mathrm{H}_h]}{[\mathrm{M}]_i^{\,m}.[\mathrm{L}]_i^{\,l}.[\mathrm{X}]_i^{\,x}.[\mathrm{H}]_i^{\,h}} \quad \ldots\ldots\ldots\ldots\ldots\ldots (1.2)$$

Where, $[M]_i$, $[L]_i$, $[X]_i$ and $[H]_i$ are the free concentrations of metal, ligand-L, ligand-X and hydrogen ion respectively at i^{th} experimental point. Different species in solution possess different values of stoichiometric coefficients *m, l, x* and *h.* Positive value of h indicates protonated species and a negative value indicates either deprotonated or hydroxylated species. The overall formation constants for all the species (with various *mlxh* values) present in the solution are to be determined from the experimental data. Potentiometric methods using ion selective and/or glass electrode are found to be superior compared to other methods like spectrophotometry, polarography, conductometry etc.

Bjerrum[106] titration technique as modified by Calvin and Wilson[107-109] is still the main method in use today, though the accuracy and precision of the measurements have greatly increased. A solution containing a metal ion and ligands in a medium of constant ionic strength is first acidified using a strong mineral acid to the point where the ligands are fully protonated. This solution is then titrated, often by means of a computer-controlled auto-titrator, with a standard solution of carbon dioxide-free base. The concentrations, or activities, of the hydrogen ion and/ or metal ion are monitored by means of suitable probes.

In a solution containing a metal ion and two or more ligands, there is a possibility of formation of a number of species in addition to simple mono-nuclear unprotonated species. Further, if the ligands possess more than one associable/ dissociable proton, there is also a possibility of formation of protonated simple and mixed ligand complexes. The classical procedures for the evaluation of formation constants fail in such complex systems wherein several species coexist. Therefore, one has to resort to modern computational methods based on the nonlinear least squares algorithms.

At present there are several computer programs[110, 111] that facilitate the extraction of parametric information from potentiometric titration curves. The ACBA-program developed by Arena et al.[112], for example, is particularly useful for the potentiometric titrations of acids and bases (weak and strong). This program calculates the formation constants and concentrations of various proton-ligand species in solution using volume of base or acid *vs*. pH or emf data. It also refines electrode parameters simultaneously using nonlinear least-square procedures. Other important programs used for the refinement of formation constants using potentiometric data are POT[113] and LETAGROP[114] by Sillen and co-workers, SCOGS[115] by Sayce, PSEQUAD[116] by Nagypal, BEST[117] by Martell, SQUAD[118] by Leggett, SPECFIT[119,120] by Mayer et al. The MINIQUAD group of programs, including Miniquad[121], Miniquad-75[122], Superquad[123] and Hyperquad[124] developed by Gans and co-workers yield best-fit estimates of the formation constants from potentiometric and spectrophotometric data.

Most of these algorithms are based on the minimization of error square sum between the experimentally determined quantities and the corresponding calculated ones using the predicted values of the formation constants. The refinement is performed iteratively starting with the guess estimates of the formation constants. The values of the formation constants obtained by graphical procedures are normally taken as the initial or guess estimates. The computer based algorithms generate a vector of shifts to the estimated formation constants and free concentrations. The modified constants after applying the shifts are then used as the initial estimates for the next cycle. Several computations and checks throughout the iteration procedure may lead to rejection of some or all the postulated species from the refinement model. If the chosen model is a true representation of the system and the initial estimates of formation constants are not far from the true values, the iteration will converge in a finite number of cycles. The procedure is repeated for different chemical models and the best-fit model is selected based on the statistical parameters. Using the formation constant in the best-fit model these programs calculate the species (concentration) distribution diagrams as a function of pH. From potentiometric titrations it is practically impossible to propose structures for the species except in very simple cases, in which knowledge of analogous systems can be of help. However, when UV-VIS measurements are used in spectrophotometric titrations to study equilibria, spectra of the individual species are also obtained besides stability constants and can be used to discuss the structure of the complexes in solution.

The presence of different ligands in the same coordination sphere of a metal ion, may lead to higher stabilities of mixed-ligand complexes relative to binary that can be attributed to several factors. The selectivity and specificity achieved by nature in biological systems are certainly due to the formation of such higher order mixed-ligand complexes. The tendency towards ternary complex formation can be evaluated in various ways. Among many the $\Delta\log K$ given by the following equation, has been widely accepted and used for many years.

$$\Delta log\,K = log\,\beta_{ML_l X_x} - (log\,\beta_{M L_l} + log\,\beta_{M X_x}) \quad \ldots\ldots\ldots\ldots (1.3)$$

The advantages of $\Delta\log K$ formulation over other methods for comparing the stabilities of ternary and binary complexes have been reviewed by Sigel[125].

A perusal of the literature indicated that no sufficient work has been carried out on the acid-base and complex equilibria of succinic and adipic acid dihydrazides in solution. In view of the multifaceted applications of dihydrazides in biochemical processes, industry and synthesis, the author has taken up an in depth investigation on the (i) Speciation studies of the proton-ligand and metal-ligand systems of the succinic and adipic acid dihydrazides with some essential and toxic metal ions and (ii) Chemical modelling studies on the metal-dihydrazide-amino acid systems, to understand the nature of such interactions *in vivo*. Modern computational methods developed in our laboratory were used to test the sufficiency of the models obtained to represent the speciation in solution. The best-fit models were obtained using the Miniquad-75[122] program modified to run on a PC under MS-Windows environment. The species distribution diagrams were generated using HYSS[126] program.

1.6 REFERENCES:

1. D.M. Templeton, F. Ariese, R. Cornelis, L. Danielsson, H. Muntau, H.P.Van Leeuwen and R. Lobinski, "Guidelines for terms related to Chemical Speciation and fractionation of elements", *Pure Appl. Chem.(IUPAC)*, 72(8) (2000) pp. 1453–1470.
2. K.I.Popov and H.Wanner, "Stability constants data sources: Critical evaluation and application for environmental speciation" in Biogeochemistry of Chelating Agents, ACS Symposium series, (B. Nowack, J.M. Van Briesen Eds), 910 (2005) pp. 50-75, Washington DS.
3. A. E. Martell, "Determination and Use of Stability Constants", VCH Publishers, Weinheim, Germany (1988).
4. B. Kharusov, P. Elizondo Marti'nez, V. M. J.-Pe'rez, O. V. Kharissova, B. Marti'nez and Nancy Pe´ rez, "Review - Recent advances on ditopic ligands", *J. Coord. Chem.* 63 (1) (2010) pp.1–25.
5. C. Merkens, F. Pan and U. Englert, "3-(4-Pyridyl)-2, 4-pentanedione – a bridge between coordinative, halogen, and hydrogen bonds", *Cryst. Eng Comm. (Royal Society of Chemistry)*, 15 (2013) pp. 8153-8158.
6. R.M. Patil, "Synhetic, structural and biological properties of binuclear complexes with some Schiff bases", *Acta Pol Pharm [dlnm]*, 64(4)(2007) pp.345-353.
7. H. A. Miller, N. Laing, S. Parsons, A. Parkin, P.A. Tasker and David J. White, "Supramolecular assemblies from ditopic ligands and transition metal salts", *J. Chem. Soc., Dalton Trans.*, (2000) pp. 3773–3782.
8. L.D. Tsitsishvili, T.I. Tsutsunava and Yu Ya Kharitonov, "Complexes of cobalt with deprotonated dihydrazides", *Koord. Khim.* 8(5) (1982) pp.674-679.
9. A.K.Thomas, "Dinuclear metal complexes of bis-macrocycles", *Coord. Chem. Rev.*, 190-192(1999) pp.371-389.
10. E.K.Van den Beuken and B.L.Feringa, "Bimetallic catalysis by late transition metal complexes", *Tetrahedron*, 54(1998) pp.12985-13011.
11. H.Steinhagen and G. Helmchen, "Asymmetric two-center catalysis: Learning from Nature", *Angew. Chem. Int. Ed.*, 35(1996) pp.2339-2342.

12. EFSA Panel: B. Claudia, C. Laurence, C. Jean-Pierre, E. Karl-Heinz et al., "Scientific opinion on the safety assessment of the substance adipic acid dihydrazide for use in food contact materials", *EFSA Journal*, 13(1) (2015)3961: CAS No 1071-93-8.

13. M.T.Adrian, R.Xavier, F.Francesc and S.Angels, "The use of dihydrazides as latent curing agents in diglycidyl ether of bisphenol-A coatings", *Prog. Org. Coat.* 74(2012) pp.59–66.

14. FDA: "Final Report on the Safety Assessment of Adipic Acid Dihydrazide." *Int. J. Toxicol,* 13(3)(1994) pp.154-156, doi: 10.3109/10915819409140998

15. H. L. Yale, K. Losee, J. Martins, M. Holsing, F.M. Perry and J. Bernstein, "Chemotherapy of Experimental Tuberculosis-VIII: The synthesis of acid hydrazides, their derivatives and related compounds", *J. Am. Chem. Soc.,* 75(8) (1953) pp.1933-1942.

16. L. N. Volovelskii and G.V. Knorozova, "Synthesis of derivatives of the androstane series. III: Dihydrazones of 2-hydroxymethylene dihydro-testosterone and 2-hydroxymethylene-17 α-methyldihydrotestosterone", *Zh. Obshch. Khim*, 34 (1964) pp.343-347, CAN 60:68429; AN 1964:68429; (English): *J. Gen. Chem*., 34 (1964) p341.

17. M. A. Amin, H. Shokry, E. M. Mabrouk, "Nickel corrosion inhibition in sulfuric acid-electrochemical studies, morphologies and theoretical approach ", *Corrosion* (Houston, TX, United States), 68 (2012) pp.699-712.

18. M. Abdallah, M. El Nagar, H. E. Megahed, D. Radwan, E. M. Mabrouk, "Corrosion kinetics of nickel alloys in H2SO4 and the effect of dihydrazide derivatives as corrosion inhibitors", *Corrosion Prevention & Control,* 50 (2003) pp.173-180.

19. T. Bunichiro, O. Hideaki, Y. H. Chung and E. M. George, "New Curing System of Urea-Formaldehyde Resins with Polyhydrazides I. Curing with dihydrazide compounds", *MokuzaiGakkaishi,* 35 (1989) pp.455-459.

20. Hitachi Chemical Co. Ltd. Jpn. Kokai Tokhyo Koho, "Electrically conductive epoxy resin adhesives", JP59, 172 (1984) 571; *Chem. Abstr.* 105 (1986) 44290k.

21. M. L. Ciompi, A. Lucacchini, D. Segnini, M. R. Adu. Mazzoni, *Exp. Med. Biol*. 122b (1980) 395.

22. K. K. Narang and V. P. Singh, "Synthesis, Characterization, Thermal Studies and Biological Activity of Iron(III) Complexes with some Acylhydrazines", *Synth. React. Inorg. Met.-Org. Chem.*, 23 (1993) pp.971-989.
23. Bakir Jeragh, Ahmed A. El-Asmy, "Structure and spectroscopic studies of homo- and hetero-metallic complexes of adipic acid dihydrazide", *Spectrochim. Acta, Part A Molecular and Biomolecular Spectroscopy,* 125 (2014) pp 25-35.
24. Jayanthi Narayanan, Alejandro Solano-Peralta, Vıctor Manuel Ugalde-Saldivar, Roberto Escudero, Herbert Hopfl and Martha Elena Sosa-Torres, "New dinuclear cobalt(II) octaaza macrocyclic complexes with high oxidation redox potentials: Their crystal structure and unusual magnetic properties", *Inorg. Chim. Acta* , 361 (2008) pp.2747–2758.
25. Adrian-Mihail Stadler and Jack Harrowfield, "Bis-acyl-/aroyl-hydrazones as multidentate ligands", *Inorg. Chim. Acta,* 362 (2009) pp.4298–4314.
26. H. B. Jonasse and V. V. Ramanujam, "Binuclear complexes as catalysts", *J. Phys. Chem.,* 63 (3) (1959) pp.411-415.
27. C. J. McKenzie and R. Robson, "High turnover catalysis at bimetallic sites of the hydration of nitriles to carboxamides co-catalyzed by acid", *Chem. Commun.,* (1988) pp.112-113.
28. E.B. Miminoshvili, "Metal hydrazide complexes", *J. Struct. Chem*, 50 (2009) pp S168- S175.
29. (a) A. A. Adeniyi and K. S. Patel, "Dicarboxylic Acid Hydrazide Complexes of Magnesium Tetrafluoroborate", *Synth. React. Inorg. Met -Org. Chem*, 29:6 (1999) pp.1063-1075; (b) A. A. Adeniyi and K. S. Patel, "Dicarboxylic acid hydrazide complexes of manganese(II) tetrafluoroborate", *Synth. React. Inorg. Met -Org. Chem*, 23 (2) (1993) pp.185-198; "Dicarboxylic acid hydrazide complexes of cadmium(II) tetrafluoroborate", pp.199-211; (c) K. S. Patel and A. A. Adeniyi, "Dicarboxylic acid hydrazide complexes of cobalt(II) tetrafluoroborate", *Synth. React. Inorg. Met -Org. Chem*, 21 (9) (1991) pp.1351-1364 and (d) K. S. Patel and A. A. Adeniyi, "Dicarboxylic Acid Hydrazide Complexes of nickel (II) Tetrafluoroborate", *Synth. React. Inorg. Met -Org. Chem*, 21 (9) (1991) pp.1331-1350.
30. K. Nagano, H. Konoshita and A. Hirakawa, *Chem. pharm. Bull.* 12 (1964) p119.

31. R. C. Paul and S. L. Chadha, "Structure of donor-acceptor complexes-V: Infrared spectral study of Lewis acid complexes with hydrazides", *Spectrochim. Acta* 23A (1967) pp.1249-1256.

32. A. Dutta Ahmed, P. K. Mandal and N. Ray Chaudhuri, "Metal complexes of malondihydrazide", *J. Inorg. Nucl. Chem.* 28 (1966) pp.2951-2959.

33. Ahmed, A. Dutta, N.R. Chaudhuri, "Acid hydrazides as ligands-II: Metal complexes of dicarboxylic acid dihydrazides", *J. Inorg. Nucl. Chem,* 31 (8) (1969) pp.2545-2556.

34. P.V.Gogorishvili, L. D. Tsitsishvili and M. V. Chrelashvili, "Complexes of transition metals with adipic acid dihydrazide", *Perekhodnykh Redk. Metal,* (1970) pp.5-13; CAN 74:82616; "Complexes of transition metal sulfates with adipic acid dihydrazide", *Perekhodnykh Redk Metal,* (1970) pp.27-36; CAN 74:60339.

35. V. Srivastava, O.P. Pandey, S.K. Sengupta and S.C. Tripathi, "Aliphatic acid dihydrazide derivatives of dicyclopentadienylzirconium(IV) dichloride and their reactions with β-diketones. Formation of cyclic compounds", *J. Organomet. Chem.* 321 (1987) pp. 27-35.

36. T. O. Vardosanidze, A. E. Shvelashvili, A. N. Sobolev and M. A. Porai-Koshits, "Crystal and molecular structure of a manganese (II) sulfate complex with dihydrazide of malonic acid ($[Mn(CH_2(C(O)NHNH_2)_2)2SO_4].4H_2O$) ", *Zh. Neorg. Khim.* 30 (2) (1985) pp.364-367.

37. N. B. Zhorzholiani, A. E. Shvelashvili, A. N. Sobolev, T. O. Vardosanidze, and V. I. Sokol, "Synthesis and X-ray analysis of the manganese coordination compounds $Mn(DS)_nX_2.mH_2O$ (DS = succinic acid dihydrazide)", *Seriya Khimicheskaya,* 13 (2) (1987) pp.102-110.

38. Yu. Ya. Kharitonov, L. D. Tsitsishvili, T. I. Tsutsunava, T. M. Chumakova and M. G. Stoppe, "Coordination compounds of some metals with succinic acid dihydrazide", *Koord. Khim.* 8 (5) (1982) pp.666-673

39. A. F. Krivis, G. R. Supp and R. L. Doerr, "Stability constants of some dihydrazide complexes of cadmium", *Anal. Chem.,* 38(7) (1966) pp.936-938; "Polarographic Study of Some Hydrazide Complexes of Cadmium", 37 (1) (1965) pp 52-54.

40. H. A. Hammad, M. A. Mostafa, K. A. El Manakhly, M. M. Hussien, and M. M. El Okr., "Spectroscopic studies on some dicarboxylic acid dihydrazide-iron complexes", *Can. J. Appl. Spectrosc.,* 41 (4) (1996) pp.86-89.

41. V. Kumari, S. K. Suresh, K. Sushma and N. K. Ramesh, "Reactions of uranyl(VI) complexes of acid dihydrazides with β-diketones", *Transition Met. Chem.* (Dordrecht, Netherlands), 5 (1980) pp.85-87.

42. P. V. Gogorishvili, R. I. Machkhoshvili, L. D. Tsitsishvili, Yu. Ya. Kharitonov, A.E. Shvelashvili and T. I. Tsutsunava, "Complexes of manganese(II) thiocynate with acid dihydrazides", *Zh. Neorg. Khim* 22 (1977) pp. 3275-3279, CAN 88:57758.

43. P. V. Gogorishvili, R. I. Machkhoshvili, L. D. Tsitsishvili, A. E. Shvelashvili, Yu. Ya. Kharitonov and T. I. Tsutsunava, "Complex compounds of cobalt thiocyanate with some acid dihydrazides", *Koord. Khim* 2 (1976) pp.958-964, CAN 85:136411.

44. C. G. Kumbhar and N. Sadasivan, "Inorganic coordination polymers-III: Studies on metal-dihydrazide compounds", *Journal of Armament Studies*, 12 (1976) pp. 135-137. CAN 86:132710.

45. C. G. Kumbhar and N. Sadasivan, "Cobalt(II), nickel(II) and copper(II) complexes of oxalic, malonic and terephthalic dihydrazides", *Defense Science Journal* 32 (1982) pp.113-117. CAN 98:190534.

46. R. I. Machkhoshvili, Yu. Ya. Kharitonov and N. N. Vekua, "IR absorption spectra of zinc, cadmium and strontium complexes with malonic and succinic acid dihydrazides", *Redkikh Metallov,* 3 (1978) pp.63-67.

47. R. I. Machkhoshvili, N. N. Vekua, P.V. Gogorishvili, A. E. Shvelashvili, and Yu. Ya. Kharitonov, "Complexes of Group II elements with glutaric and adipic acid dihydrazides", *Koord. Khim*, 3 (1977) pp.22-28.

48. R. I. Machkhoshvili, Yu. Ya. Kharitonov, P. V. Gogorishvili and L. D. Tsitsishvili, "IR spectroscopic study of complexes of metals with adipic acid dihydrazide", *Koord. Khim,* 3 (3) (1977) pp.402-407.

49. R. I. Machkhoshvili, N. N. Vekua, P.V. Gogorishvili, Yu. Ya. Kharitonov and A.E. Shvelashvili, "Complexes of Group II elements with dihydrazides of malonic and succinic acids", *Koord. Khim,* 3 (3) (1977) pp.332-341; CAN 86:182220.

50. A. E. Shvelashvili, R. I. Machkhoshvili, E. B. Miminoshvili, B. M. Shchedrin, N. N Vekua, A. I. Kvitashvili and E. A. Mikeladze, "Study of the structure of compounds of zinc sulphate with malonic acid dihydrazide", *Zh. Neorg. Khim* 25(7) (1980) pp.1779-1783.

51. K. K. Narang and Meena Singh, "Complexes of Zn(II), Cu(II), Ni(II) and Co(II) tetrathiocyanato mercurates(II) with hydrazides and their biological activity", *Synth. React. Inorg. Met -Org. Chem*, 15 (6) (1985) pp.821-837.

52. Ya. D. Fridman, O. P. Svanidze, N. V. Dolgashova and P.V. Gogorishvili, "Mixed compounds of cobalt, nickel, and zinc with amino acids and carboxylic acid hydrazides", *Zh. Neorg. Khim* 19(12)(1974)pp.3304-3310; CAN 82:116894

53. R.I.Machkhoshvili, D.A. Gogitidze, R.N Shchelokov and O.Kh. Shamilishvili, "Scandium, yttrium and lanthanum complexes with hydrazides and isothiocyanato groups", *Zh. Neorg. Khim* , 33(6) (1988) pp.1408-1414; "Scandium, yttrium and lanthanum nitrate complexes with hydrazides", *Zh. Neorg. Khim* , (1988), 33(5) 1139-43.

54. L.D. Tsitsishvili, P.V. Gogorishvili and T.I. Tsutsunava, "Complex compounds of transition metals with succinic dihydrazide", *Perekhodnykh Redkikh Metal*, 2(1974) pp 145-151.

55. K.K.Narang, and Singh Meena Kumari, "Synthesis, characterization, IR spectra and other studies of some mercury(II) chloride, nitrate and thiocyanate complexes of organic acid hydrazides and hydrazones", *Synth. React. Inorg. Met -Org. Chem*,, 17(1) (1987) pp.57-78

56. R. Cavier and R. Rips, "Anthelmintic activity of a series of dihydrazides", *Therapie,* 21 (3) (1966) pp.743-751, CAN 65:41622.

57. R. Cavier and R. Rips, "Dihydrazides, a new class of anthelmintics", *J. Med. Chem.*, 8 (5) (1965) pp.706-708, CAN 63:75190.

58. L.Heinisch, Chr. Kuechler, and W.Kuechler, "Inhibition of viruses in vitro by semioxamazide derivatives", *Arzneimittel-Forschung*, 18(10) (1968) pp.1324-1328.

59. N. Rathor, S. C. Pandeya and R. C. Sharma, "Synthesis, characterization and antimicrobial activity of some hydrazones and their metal complexes", *J. Ind. Coun. Chem.*, 12 (1996) pp.19-23.

60. M. Lazić, S. Radulović, T. Todorović, D. Sladić, Ž. Tešić, K. Andjelković, *Mater. Sci. Forum*, 495 (2006) pp.513–518.

61. N. R. Filipović, A. Bacchi, M. Lazić, G. Pelizzi, S. Radulović, D. M. Sladić, T. R. Todorović, and K. K. Anđelković, "Synthesis, structure and cytotoxic activity evaluation of a dinuclear complex of Cd(II) with N′,N′2-bis[(1E)-1-(2-pyridyl) ethylidene] propane dihydrazide", *Inorg. Chem. Commun.*, 11 (2008) pp.47–50.

62. M. Vujčić, M. Lazić, M.Milenković, D. Sladić, S. Radulović, N. Filipović, K. Anđelković, "A comparative study of DNA binding and cell cycle phase perturbation by the dinuclear complex of Cd(II) with the condensation product of 2-acetylpyridine and malonic acid dihydrazide N',N'2-bis[(1E)-1-(2-pyridyl)ethylidene]propanedihydrazide", *J. Biochem. Mol. Toxicol.*, 25 (2010) pp.175–182.

63. Vinod P. Singh and Parul Gupta, "Synthesis, characterization and biocidal activities of some metal(II) complexes with diacetyl salicylaldehyde acyldihydrazones", *J. Coord. Chem.*, 59 (2006) pp.1483–1494 and "Synthesis and spectral studies of metal(II) complexes with succinic acid dihydrazones and their biological activity", *Pharm. Chem. J.*, 42 (2008) pp.196-202.

64. D. Kumar, Dharmendri and B. Anupama, "Synthesis, structural and biological significance of some new hydrazones derived from hydrazide", *J. Inst. Chem. (India),* 81 (6) (2009) pp.161-165.

65. H. B. Shivararna, G. Richard and S. Shalin, "Synthesis and antibacterial studies of a new series of 1,2-bis(1,3,4-oxadiazol-2-yl)ethanes and 1,2-bis(4-amino-1,2,4-triazol-3-yl)ethanes", *Eur. J. Med. Chem.,* 35 (2) (2000) pp. 267-271.

66. M. A. Amin, H. Shokry and E. M. Mabrouk, "Nickel corrosion inhibition in sulfuric acid-electrochemical studies, morphologies, and theoretical approach", *Corrosion (Houston, TX, United States),* 68 (8) (2012) pp. 699-712.

67. T. Bunichiro, O. Hideaki, Y. H. Chung and E. M. George, "New Curing System of Urea-Formaldehyde Resins with Polyhydrazides I. Curing with dihydrazide compounds", *Mokuzai Gakkaishi* , 35 (5) (1989) pp.455-459.

68. L. Mishra, B. Pathak and S. K. Dubey, "Aggregation of malonic acid dihydrazide with thymine and 2, 6-diaminopyridine in the presence of

copper(II) and zinc(II) chlorides: synthesis, characterization and molecular conducting properties", *Ind. J. Chem.,* 46 (2007) pp.48-53.

69. V. Srivastava, O.P. Pandey, S. K. Sengupta and S.C. Tripathi, "Aliphatic acid dihydrazide derivatives of dicyclopentadienylzirconium(IV) dichloride and their reactions with β-diketones. Formation of cyclic compounds", *J. Org. Metal. Chem.*, 321 (1987) pp.27-35.
70. Magdalena Woz´niczka, Ewa Szajdzinska-Pietek, Julia Jezierska, Beata Pasternak, Joanna Ga̧dek-Sobczyn´ska and Aleksander Kufelnicki, "The complexing properties of oxalodihydrazide, acethydrazide and formic hydrazide with Cu(II) in aqueous solution", *Inorg. Chim. Acta,* 455 (2017) pp.659–665.
71. Dunkana Negussa Kenie, P.Shyamala, A. Satyanarayana and K.M.M. Krishna Prasad, "Chemical speciation studies on the complexation of ditopic ligands: Interaction of malonic acid dihydrazide with some divalent transition metal ions in aqueous medium", *J. Indian Chem. Soc.*, 91 (2014) pp. 729-737.
72. A. Satyanarayana, Dunkana Negussa Kenie and P. Shyamala, "Speciation Study on the Interaction of Some Divalent Transition Metal Ions with Succinic acid Dihydrazide in Aqueous Medium", *Acta Chim. Slov.,* 60 (2013) pp 807–812.
73. G. V. Afanas'eva, T. I. Bychkova, V. G. Shtyrlin, A. R. Shakirova and A. V. Zakharov, "Composition, stability, and structure of Cu(II), Ni(II), and Co(II) complexes with adipic acid dihydrazide in aqueous and aqueous-ethanol solutions", *Russ. J. Gen. Chem.,* 76(5) (2006) pp 757-765.
74. S.V.V.S. Rao, J.S.V.M.L. Rao, A.R. Babu, D.M. Krishna and R.S. Rao, "Chemometric Investigation of Complex Equilibria in Solution Phase. Part-V. Correlation of Formation Constants of Manganese (II) or Zinc (II) Complexes of AADH/FAH with Co-solvent Characteristics", *J. Indian Chem. Soc.*, 73 (1) (1996) pp 9-19.
75. A. Ravindra Babu, J.S.V.M. Lingeswara Rao, D. Murali Krishna and R.Sambasiva Rao, "Acid-base equilibria of 2-furoic acid hydrazide and adipic acid dihydrazide in aqueous-organic media", *Anal. Chim. Acta* , 306 (1995) pp 297-300.
76. Babu, A. Ravindra; Krishna, D. Murali; and Rao R. Sambasiva, "Chemometric investigation of complex equilibria in solution phase II: sensitivity of chemical

models for the interaction of AADH and FAH with Ni(II) in aqueous medium", *Talanta,* 40(12) (1993) pp 1873-1882.

77. Babu, A. Ravindra and Rao R. Sambasiva, "Chemometric investigation of complex equilibria in the solution phase- Chemical models for the complexation of nickel(II) with adipic acid dihydrazide and 2-furoic acid hydrazide in water-N,N'-dimethylformamide and water-dioxane media. Correlation with solvent parameters", *J. Chem. Eng. Data,* 37(4) (1992) pp 526-531.
78. G. R. Supp, "Polarographic studies of some mono- and dihydrazide complexes of Zinc", *Anal. Chem.*, 40 (6) (1968) pp. 981-982.
79. K.I. Popov and H. Wanner, " Stability constants data sources: Critical evaluation and application for environmental speciation", PP 50-75; in Biogeochemistry of Chelating Agents (B.Nowack, J.M. Van Briesen Eds) ACS Symposium series Vol 910, Washington DS, 2005.
80. H. Einspahr and C.E. Bugg, "Calcium binding to α-amino acids: The crystal structure of calcium di-L-glutamate tetrahydrate", *Acta Crystallogr.,* B35 (1979) pp. 316 – 321.
81. H. Einspahr and C.E. Bugg, "Calcium-binding proteins and calcium function in health and disease", *Proc. Intern. Symp., Cornet Univ. Ithaca,* (1977) pp. 13-20, Elsevier, New York.
82. H. Einspahr, G.L. Gartland and C.E. Bugg, "Calcium-binding to α-amino acids: The crystal structure of calcium L-glutamate chloride monohydrate", *Acta Crystallogr.,* B33(1977) pp. 3385 - 3390.
83. D. Barrett, A. Tanaka, K. Harada, H. Ohki, E. Watabe, K. Maki and F. Ikeda, *Bioorg. Med. Chem. Lett.* 11 (2001) pp.479-482.
84. J.T. Kovalainen, J. A. M. Christians, S. Kotisaari, J.T. Laitinen, and P.T. Mannisto, *J. Med. Chem.,* 42 (1999) pp.1193-1202.
85. A El-Faham, A. M. El Massry, A. Amer and Y. M. Gohar., *Lett. Pept. Sci.*, 9 (2002) pp.49-54.
86. F. Polyak and W. D.Lubell, *J. Org. Chem.*, 63 (1998) pp.5937-5949.
87. Y. Okada, M. Tsukatani, H. Taguchi, T. Yokoi, S. D. Bryant and L. H. Lazarus, *Chem. Pharm. Bull.,* 46 (1998) pp.1374-1382.
88. G. Sun, N. J. Uretsky, L. J. Wallace, G. Shams, D. M. Weinstein and D. D. Miller, *J. Med. Chem.,* 39 (1996) pp.4430-4438.

89. P. R. Marsham, J. M. Wardleworth, F. T. Boyle, L. F. Hennequin, R. Kimbell, M. Brown, and A. L. Jackman, *Med. Chem.,* 42 (1999) pp.3809-3820.
90. Y. Xia, Z.-Y. Yang, P. Xia, K. F. Bastow, Y. Nakanishi and K.-H. Lee, *Bioorg. Med. Chem. Lett.,* 10 (2000) pp.699-701.
91. M. M. Shoukry and R. Koussini, *Bull. Soc. Chim. Fr.* 128 (1991) p465.
92. D. Voet, and J. G. Voet, "*Biochemistry*", 2nd edn, Wiley, New York, (1995).
93. Zhang M-Q, R. Leurs, and H. Timmerman, "Histamine H1-receptor antagonists, In *Burger's Medicinal Chemistry and Drug Discovery* (Wolf ME ed) ,John Wiley & Sons, Inc., New York, (1997) pp. 495–559.
94. F. Oakley, N. M. Horn, A. L. Thomas, "Histidine-stimulated divalent metal uptake in human erythrocytes and in the erythroleukaemic cell line HEL.92.1.7", *J Physiol.,* 561 (2004) pp. 525–534. Doi: 10.1007/BF00675792.
95. Y. El Khoury and P. Hellwig, "Infrared spectroscopic characterization of copper–polyhistidine from 1, 800 to 50 cm-1: model systems for copper coordination", *J Biol Inorg Chem* 14 (2009) pp.23–34. Doi: 10.1007/s00775-008-0421-4.
96. J. Rebek, "On the structure of histidine and its role in enzyme active sites", *Struct Chem* 1 (1990) pp.129–131. Doi: 10.1007/BF00675792.
97. P. G. Besant and P.V. Attwood, "Mammalian histidine kinases", *Biochim Biophys Acta* 1754 (2005) pp.281–290. doi:10.1016/j.bbapap. 2005.07.026.
98. B. Sarkar, *Chem. Rev.* 99 (1999) p.2535.
99. D. M. Danks, in: C.R. Scriver, A.I. Beaudet and W.S. Sly, D. Valle (Eds.), "*Metabolic Basis of Inherited Disease*", McGraw-Hill, New York, (1995) p2211.
100. A.E. Martell and R.M. Smith, "Critical stability constants Volumes 1 to 5", Plenum Press, NY and London, (1974-1982): Volume 1: Amino acids (1974), Volume 2: Amines (1975), Volume 3: Other Ligands (1977), Volumc 4: Inorganic Complexes (1976), Volume 5: First Supplement, (1982) and Volume 6: Second Supplement (1989).
101. L.D. Pettit, "Critical survey of formation constants of Histidine Phenylalanine, Tyrosine, L-Dopa and Tryptophan", IUPAC, *Pure & Appl. Chem.,* 56(2) (1984) pp 247-292.
102. T. Kiss, I. Sovago and A. Gergely, "Critical survey of stability constants of complexes of Glycine", IUPAC, *Pure & Appl. Chem.,* 63(4) (1993) pp 597-

638.

103. I. Sovago, T. Kiss and A. Gergely, "Critical survey of the stability constants of complexes of aliphatic amino acids", IUPAC, *Pure & Appl. Chem.,* 65(5) (1993) pp 1029-1080.

104. G. Berthon, "The stability constants of metal complexes of amino acids with polar side chains", IUPAC, *Pure & Appl. Chem.,* 67(7) (1995) pp 1117-1240.

105. O. Yamauchi and A. Odani, "Stability constants of metal complexes of amino acids with charged side chains- Part-I: Positively charged side chains", IUPAC, *Pure & Appl. Chem.,* 68(2) (1996) pp 469-496.

106. J. Bjerrum, "Metal ammine formation in aqueous solution: theory of the reversible step reactions", P. Haase and Son, Copenhagen (1941).

107. M. Calvin and K.W. Wilson, "Stability of chelate compounds", *J. Am. Chem. Soc.*, 67 (1945) pp. 2003 -2007.

108. H. M. Irving, H. S. Rossotti, "Methods for Computing Successive Stability Constants from Experimental Formation Curves", *J. Chem. Soc.* (1953) pp. 3397–3405.

109. H. M. Irving, H. S. Rossotti, "The Calculation of Formation Curves of Metal Complexes from pH-Titration Curves in Mixed Solvents", *J. Chem. Soc.* (1954) pp. 2904–2910.

110. D. J. Leggett, "The determination of Stability constants: A Review", *Am. Lab.*, 14(1) (1982) pp 29-35.

111. D. K. Nordstroml, N. Plummert, M. L. Wigleyt, J. Woleryj, W. Ball, E. A. Jenner, L. Bassett, A. Crear, T. M. Florence, M. Fritz, R. Hoffmang, G. Holdrejnr, M. Lafons, V. Mattigodr, E. Mcduff, F. Morelr, M. Reddy, G. Sposito and J. Thrailkilal, "A comparison of computerized chemical models for equilibrium calculations in aqueous systems', ACS Symposium Series, Volume 93, Chapter 38 (1979) pp. 857-892.

112. G. Arena, E. Rizzarelli, S. Sammartano and C. Rigano, "A non-linear leastsquares approach to the refinemnet of all parameters involved in acid-base titrations", *Talanta*, 26 (1979) pp. 1-14.

113. D. Dyrssen, N. Ingri and L.G. Sillen, "Pit-mapping - A general approach to Computer refinement of stability constants", *Acta Chem. Scand*, 15 (1961) pp. 694–696.

114. N. Ingri and L.G. Sillen., "High-speed computers as a supplement to

graphical methods, IV. An ALGOL version of LETAGROP-VRID". *Arkiv. Kemi,* 23 (1964) pp. 97–121.

115. I.G. Sayce, "Computer calculation of equilibrium constants of species present in mixtures of metal ions and complexing agents", Talanta, 15 (1968) pp. 1397-1411.
116. L. Zekany and I. Nagypal, PSEQUAD A comprehensive program for the evaluation of potentiometric and/or spectrophotometric equilibrium data using analytical derivatives", in "Computational methods for the determination of formation constants" by Leggett, Plenum, (1985).
117. R. J. Motekaitis and A. E. Martell, "Program PKAS: A novel algorithm for the computation f successive protonation constants", *Can. J. Chem.*, 60(2) (1982) pp. 168-173; Book: A. E. Martell and R. J. Motekaitis, 'Determination and use of stability constants", Wiley-VCH, Second Edition, 200 pages, (1992).
118. D Leggett, "SQUAD: Stability quotients from absorbance data" in the book "Computational methods for the determination of formation constants", Plenum, (1985).
119. H. Gampp, M. Maeder, C. J. Mayer and A. D. Zuberbühler, "Calculation of equilibrium constants from multi-wavelength spectroscopic data—I: Mathematical considerations". *Talanta,* 32 (1995) pp. 95–101.
120. H. Gampp, M. Maeder, C. J. Mayer and A.D. Zuberbühler. (1985). "Calculation of equilibrium constants from multi-wavelength spectroscopic data—II: Spec fit: two user-friendly programs in basic and standard` FORTRAN 77", *Talanta,* 32 (1995) pp. 251–264.
121. A. Sabatini, A. Vacca and P. Gans, "MINIQUAD- A general computer program for the computation of Stability constants", *Talanta,* 21 (1974) pp. 53–77.
122. P. Gans, A. Sabatini and A. Vacca, "An improved program for the computation of formation constants from potentiometric data", *Inorg. Chim. Acta,* 18 (1976) pp 237-239.
123. P. Gans, A. Sabatini and A. Vacca, "SUPERQUAD: An improved general program for computation of formation constants from potentiometric data", *J. Chem. Soc. Dalton Trans.,* (1985) pp. 1195-1200.
124. P. Gans, A Sabatini and A. Vacca, "Investigation of equilibria in solution.

Determination of equilibrium constants with the HYPERQUAD suite of programs". *Talanta,* 43 (1996) pp. 1739–1753.

125. H. Sigel and A. Sigel, "Metal Ions in Biological Systems", Vols. 12 & 13 (Marcel Dekker, New York, (1981).

126. L. Alderighi, P. Gans, A. Ienco, D.Peters, A. Sabatini and A. Vacca, "Hyperquad simulation and speciation (HySS): A utility program for the investigation of equilibria involving soluble and partially soluble species", *Coord. Chem. Rev.* 184 (1999) pp 311–318.

CHAPTER- 2

DATA ACQUISITION AND METHODS OF ANALYSIS

Complex formation is a fundamental process in biological, environmental and chemical systems wherein different metal ions and ligands coexist. The formation of a complex modifies metal species in solution, reducing the activity of free ion, changing solubility, mobility and toxicity. Therefore, it is well known that, the chemical or biological activity of a trace metal ion depends only on the nature of the species containing the metal ion but not on its total analytical concentration. In spite of the central importance of knowing the full speciation of an element to predict its behaviour in a system, it is generally not possible to determine both concentrations and compositions of several coexisting species using analytical methods alone. Therefore, the primary aim of the speciation study is to calculate the concentrations of all the species present in a solution including the free metal ion and free ligand at any given experimental point or pH under the specified experimental conditions. To achieve the goal, chemical speciation generally relies on utilising analytical methods in conjunction with modern, rigorous iterative mathematical algorithms to obtain a best-fit chemical speciation model that represents the system under study.

The extent of formation and the reactivity of a metal complex, mostly depend on its formation constant. Therefore, the equilibrium constant is a standard measure of the binding affinity of a ligand in coordinating a metal ion. Experimental determination of reliable formation constants of several coexisting species in a multi-metal, multi-ligand system needs a careful experimental design. The probed data that contain all the necessary information should be acquired with utmost accuracy and precision. Generally, complex formation reactions are measured in a solvent under controlled experimental conditions. Commonly used methods include potentiometry, Uv-Vis and fluorescence spectrophotometry, conductometry, polarography, paper electrophoresis, membrane permeation, affinity capillary electrophoresis and mass spectrometry[1-4]. Of these potentiometry, spectrophotometry and polarography have been found to yield substantially quantitative results compared to other methods[5-8]. This is due to the fact that measurements can be made in media of approximately constant ionic strength. In potentiometry, the change in activity of either the hydrogen ion displaced by the metal ion from the ligand or one of the free reacting components is measured by using an appropriate ion-selective electrode.

Chemical speciation studies of binary metal-ligand or multi-metal or multi ligand systems using pH-potentiometric technique requires an accurate probing of the equilibrium hydrogen ion activity in the experimental solution using a suitable electrode. The change in pH is normally measured as a function of the added ligand concentration or as a function of the concentration of base or acid added to a solution of constant initial concentrations of metal ion and ligand(s). Alternatively, simultaneous monitoring of the hydrogen ion and the metal ion may be done to yield more accurate results, if appropriate metal ion-selective electrode is available. Bjerrum[9], in his classical experiments, measured the hydrogen ion activity of several mixtures containing constant initial concentrations of an ammonium salt and metal ion and varying the concentration of alkali to determine the stability constants of copper(II)-ammonia complexes. Calvin and Wilson[10] adopted a titration technique in which, instead of measuring the pH of several solutions of constant volume, a mixture of strong acid, metal ion and excess of ligand was titrated with a strong alkali. This method of data acquisition is still the main method in use today; though the precision and accuracy of the measurements are greatly increased and modern computational methods are used for the analysis of data.

In the present study Calvin and Wilson titration technique was used as the analytical method for data acquisition. The acquired data for proton-ligand, binary and ternary metal- ligand systems were analysed using the Miniquad-75[11] program.

2.1 REAGENTS AND SOLUTIONS

All the solutions were prepared in triple-distilled and de-ionised water, through which nitrogen gas was passed for nearly an hour to expel any dissolved oxygen or carbon dioxide. A-Grade glassware was used throughout the experiment.

Succinic acid dihydrazide and adipic acid dihydrazide solutions:

Succinic and Adipic acid dihydrazides (SADH and AADH) obtained from Fluka Chemie, Buchs, Switzerland, were recrystallized from water and dried at 100°C. Solutions of ~0.05 mol dm^{-3} of SADH and AADH were prepared freshly in deionized water and 0.1 mol dm^{-3} hydrochloric acid, respectively just before their use.

Amino acid solutions:

Glycine, L-Aspartic acid and L-histidine (Merck, proanalysi') were recrystallized from 1:1 ethanol-water mixtures and dried in a vacuum oven. Aqueous solutions of the amino acids (~ 0.1 mol dm^{-3}) were prepared freshly before use in pH-metric titrations.

Metal ion solutions:

Aqueous solutions of (~0.1mol dm^{-3}) $MgCl_2$, $CaCl_2$, $Pb(NO_3)_2$, $HgCl_2$ and $CdCl_2$ (BDH. AR) were prepared and standardized by conventional complexometric titrations[12]. An overall 0.01 mol dm^{-3} of strong acid was maintained in all the metal ion solutions to repress hydrolysis[13]. The acid contents of the metal solutions were determined by titration with 0.1 mol dm^{-3} NaOH solutions after liberation of the H^+ ions by cation exchange[14].

EDTA solution:

E. Merck, proanalysi sample of EDTA disodium dihydrate was purified by precipitation from aqueous solution with methanol. The precipitate was filtered and washed with acetone and ethyl ether and finally air dried. Even though, EDTA is a primary standard substance, it is recommended[15] to establish the purity of the commercial sample by standardizing against the zinc solution. An approximately 5.0 x 10^{-2} mol dm^{-3} solution was prepared and standardized complexometrically with standard zinc (II) solution using Eriochrome Black-T as an indicator.

Sodium hydroxide solution:

A ~0.2 mol dm^{-3} stock solution of sodium hydroxide (Merck, GR) was prepared by first dissolving the required quantity in a small amount of CO_2 free water. The solution was made free of carbonates by allowing the concentrated solution to stand for a long time till any carbonate, if present, precipitated. It was then filtered, diluted with CO_2 free water, standardized against potassium hydrogen phthalate (Merck) and kept in a Pyrex vessel under nitrogen atmosphere. The solution was Gran-titrated to check the presence of any carbonates[16, 17].

Hydrochloric acid/ Nitric acid solution:

A ~0.2 mol dm^{-3} solution was prepared from analytical grade acid (Merck EMSURE®.) by successive dilutions. Its strength was determined by titrating with a standard solution of sodium hydroxide.

<u>Sodium chloride/ nitrate solution:</u>

An approximately 2.0 mol dm^{-3} solution of sodium chloride/ nitrate was prepared from a BDH, AR sample of the salt.

2.2 APPARATUS AND CALIBRATION:

2.2.1 Potentiometric Titration Assembly:

A Control Dynamics pH meter model APX 175 E/C in conjunction with a combination electrode (0-14 pH range) was used for pH measurements.

The electrochemical cell, in which a test solution surrounding a glass electrode is in electrical contact with a reference electrode through a salt bridge, can be represented as,

+ First reference half-cell (Internal to Glass-Electrode)	G	Experimental Solution	L	− Second reference half-cell (External)

Where, 'G' represents the glass membrane and 'L', the liquid junction between the test solution and the salt bridge. The measured potential of the cell is given by the equation,

$$E_{cell} = E_r' + E_r'' + E_j + E_g \qquad \ldots\ldots\ldots\ldots\ldots\ldots\ldots (2.1)$$

Where, E_r' and E_r'' are the potentials due to the reference electrodes that are independent of the composition of the experimental solution. On the other hand, the potential difference generated across the boundaries (E_j and E_g) depends on the activities of the species on either side of them, equation (2.1) can be written as,

$$E_{cell} = E_r' + E_r'' + E_j + (E_g^0 + RT/F \ln a_{H^+}) \quad \ldots\ldots\ldots \quad (2.2)$$

Where, E_g^0 represents the standard glass electrode potential (for unit activity of hydrogen ion) and a_{H^+} is the hydrogen ion activity in the experimental solution. If the changes in E_j are assumed to be negligible, equation (2.2) reduces to,

$$E_{cell} = E_{const.} + s. \log_{10} a_{H^+} \qquad \ldots\ldots\ldots\ldots\ldots (2.3)$$

Where, $E_{const} = E_r' + E_r'' + E_j + E_g^0$ and $s = 2.303.RT/F$ (Nernstian slope)

2.2.2 Errors affecting pH measurements with the Glass Electrode:

Over a long period of time (>15 hrs.), the pH of even a 0.05 mol dm^{-3} solution of potassium hydrogen phthalate changes up to ± 0.05 pH units due to the electro-thermal effect in the head of the glass electrode. Similar variations in pH were observed when measurements were made in bright-diffused daylight and near darkness. This effect, which is reversible, may be due to the photosensitivity of Ag/AgCl electrode employed as the internal reference electrode in the glass electrode[18]. These difficulties were surmounted by working in an air-conditioned room illuminated by an artificial light source of nearly constant intensity.

Sodium ion error comes about in basic medium because the potential of the glass membrane depends not only on the concentration of hydrogen ions but also on the concentration of other metal ions, notably the alkali metal ions, for example, Na^+ and K^+. Recasting equation (2.3) to account for the influence of sodium ion,

$$E_{cell} = E_{const.} + (s. \log a_{H^+}) + (k. \log a_{Na^+}) \qquad \ldots\ldots\ldots (2.4)$$

Where, k is a constant that describes the sensitivity of the glass membrane to sodium ions. Smaller the k is, the less susceptible the pH glass is to sodium error. When hydrogen ion concentration is high (acidic side), E_{cell} depends only on a_{H^+}. However, as the hydrogen ion concentration decreases (pH>11), the term "k. log a_{Na^+}" starts to become, the more important term. Therefore, the measured voltage does not change as much as it should for a given change in a_{H^+}, so the pH is lower than expected. Eventually, the error becomes so great that changes in the hydrogen ion concentration no longer affect the measured pH. At this point the concentration of sodium determines the cell voltage. Most general purpose glass electrodes on the market today have almost no sodium error up to a pH of 11. Above pH 11 the measured pH can be substantially less than the expected due to alkaline error. This interference is somewhat alleviated by using special lithium glass (high pH electrodes) with sites too small to fit either Na^+ or K^+. High pH glass electrodes are available which have practically no sodium error up to a pH of 12, and small error above this. In the present study, the author employed a 0-14 pH combination electrode that possesses practically no alkaline error below 12 pH.

It is also important that the sensor, solution and entire measurement cell should be at a constant uniform temperature. This requirement is important as the lack of uniformity in temperature is one reason for the change in isopotential point when the temperature changes.

A tip less double walled Pyrex glass vessel of 100 ml capacity fitted with a perspex lid, through which the combination glass electrode, gas inlet and outlet tubes and burette tip were admitted, was used for carrying out the potentiometric titrations. The temperature of the solution was maintained by passing water from a thermostat through the annular space between the walls of the titration cell. The experimental solution was earthed by means of a platinum wire sealed in a glass tube. In order to prevent the introduction of an earth loop, the pH meter, thermostat and magnetic stirrer were earthed to the same terminal. Purified nitrogen gas was passed through the experimental solution both before and during titration to expel carbon dioxide.

2.2.3 Equilibration and Calibration of Combination Glass Electrode

In order to obtain steady and reproducible results, newly acquired glass electrode was immersed in an aqueous potassium chloride solution for several days before use, according to the general procedure of electrode calibration and specific procedures provided with the electrode. At regular intervals the electrode was washed with distilled water and conditioned overnight in 0.1 mol dm^{-3} HCl. The electrode was then tested with aqueous buffers. This procedure was repeated until reproducible results were obtained. Before each titration the electrode was preconditioned for at least one hour in a solution of identical composition as that of the titrand. This practice results in a reasonably consistent and appropriate hydrogen ion activity in the outer layer of solvated gel in the glass membrane. The calomel electrode was cleaned and refilled frequently with a saturated potassium chloride solution.

May et al.[19] described two methods for the calibration of glass electrode, which did not require reference to conventional standard buffer solutions. The first method involves the linear least-squares analysis of the data obtained from a titration of strong acid *vs.* strong base, to obtain the values of "E_{const}" and "s" as shown in the equation (2.3). This procedure was prone to errors as the analysis was based only on the data collected in the pH ranges 2.30 to 2.90 and 10.8 to 11.3. Powell and Tayler[20] later commented that this method introduces error in the pH region 4.0 to 9.2.

The second method called internal calibration method involves the simultaneous determination of electrode parameters along with equilibrium constants. This method is also not free from errors, if data outside the calibration range is used for analysis.

For determination of equilibrium constants with the pH glass electrode, the IUPAC[21] recommendation requires electrode calibration in terms of hydrogen ion concentrations. Consider an equilibrium, in which a metal ion, ligand and proton form a complex,

$$mM + lL + hH^{+} \underset{}{\overset{\beta}{\rightleftarrows}} M_{m}L_{l}H_{h}$$

The thermodynamic overall formation constant, β_T should be expressed in activities rather than concentrations of all the components of the equilibrium, given by,

$$\beta_T = \frac{a_{M_mL_lH_h}}{(a_M)^m (a_L)^l (a_{H^+})^h} = \frac{[M_mL_lH_h]}{[M]^m [L]^l [H^+]^h} \cdot \frac{f_{M_mL_lH_h}}{(f_M)^m (f_L)^l (f_{H^+})^h} = \beta_S \cdot \frac{f_{M_mL_lH_h}}{(f_M)^m (f_L)^l (f_{H^+})^h}$$

Where, a_i, are the activities, f_i are the activity coefficients and β_S is the stoichiometric overall formation constant. Then,

$$\log \beta_T = \log \beta_S + \log \frac{f_{M_mL_lH_h}}{(f_M)^m (f_L)^l (f_{H^+})^h}$$

$$\log \beta_T - \log \beta_S = \log \frac{f_{M_mL_lH_h}}{(f_M)^m (f_L)^l (f_{H^+})^h} \quad \text{.......... (2.5)}$$

In a medium of constant ionic strength the thermodynamic overall formation constant will differ from that of stoichiometric by a constant term[22]. Values of β_S, determined under identical conditions are therefore comparable. This assumption leads to the conclusion that all the components of the equilibrium, including the free hydrogen ion should be measured in concentrations and not in activities. This is done by calibrating the glass electrode in terms of hydrogen ion concentration. The system should be calibrated using conditions as close as possible to those used in data acquisition.

Correction factor proposed by McBryde[23] and others[24, 25] to convert the pH meter dial reading into logarithm of the reciprocal of hydrogen ion concentration which accounts for the above calibration was used in the present electrometric titrations. The pH measured at any i^{th} experimental point in a pH-metric titration of a strong acid with a strong base under the selected experimental conditions differs from $-\log_{10} [H^+]_i$ by a constant offset term 'b' (correction factor) given by,

$$-\log_{10} [H_i^+] = b + pH_i$$
$$\text{or } [H_i^+] = 10^{-(b+pH_i)} = 10^{-b} \times 10^{-pH_i} \qquad \text{.............. (2.6)}$$

Where, pH_i is the pH-meter dial reading. Error in the determined value of 'b' introduces a systematic error that affects the accuracy of the calculated formation constants. The value of 'b' is not a constant but varies with electrode and experimental conditions. Even for a particular glass electrode it varies with use due to the changes in the surface properties of the glass. Therefore, the value of the correction factor must be determined for each set of potentiometric titrations.

The value of the offset or correction factor 'b' can be calculated by Gran method[16, 17] in which a strong acid of the initial volume V_0 and concentration $[H^+]_0$ is titrated pH-metrically with a strong base of initial concentration $[OH^-]_0$ under selected conditions of ionic strength, temperature, solvent, etc. A plot of $(V_0+V_i).\ 10^{-pHi}$ *vs.* V_i gives a straight line on the acid side, i.e. before equivalence point, with slope = $-\frac{[OH^-]_0}{10^{-b}}$, where V_i the volume of the base added at i^{th} experimental point, from which the value of 'b' can be calculated. Similarly, after the equivalence point, from the slope of the line of a plot of $(V_0 + V_i).\ 10^{pH_i}$ *vs.* V_i which is equal to $\frac{[OH^-]_0}{K_w 10^b}$, the ionic product of water K_w can also be calculated.

The values of the ionic product of water and correction factor can also be obtained by the analysis of strong acid-strong base titration data acquired under identical conditions to that of the proton-ligand or metal-ligand systems of interest by ACBA[26] or SUPERQUAD[27] or HYPERQUAD[28] programs making K_w and b as parameters.

In the present investigation, the author adopted a three layer method to calibrate the electrode system before each set of potentiometric titrations. Layer-1 includes the equilibration and calibration of electrode system using standard buffers as indicated in the first paragraph of this Section. Under the second layer the electrode offset and ionic product of water under the identical conditions to that of the systems under investigation were determined by Gran's graphical method. In layer- 3 these values were chosen as the initial estimates for refinement using SUPERQUAD program. Taking the ionization constants of Bates et al.[29] to determine the equilibrium hydrogen ion concentration, the calibration of the electrode system was checked in the pH region 2.0-7.0 by titrating acetic acid with sodium hydroxide. Protonated 2- amino ethanol was titrated with sodium hydroxide to test the calibration in the pH region 8.0-11.5. Titration of potassium acid phthalate with alkali further confirmed the linearity in the region 4.0-5.9 pH.

The values of the correction factor and ionic product of water, thus obtained were taken as constants in the analysis of the potentiometric data of the subsequent systems in that particular set of titrations.

2.3 ALGORITHMS OF CHEMICAL SPECIATION:

In a system containing a metal ion and a ligand, the compositions and stabilities of various species formed depend on the chemical properties of both the metal ion and ligand. Further, the nature of the complexes formed is also influenced by the external factors like characteristics of the solvent, temperature and ionic strength. The situation becomes much more complicated if a number of metal ions and complexing agents coexist in solution. Therefore, the mathematical description of a solution containing a large number of species is rather a complicated procedure. Simplified procedures using auxiliary/ secondary formation functions[9] fail if the complexity of the system increases. Modern computational procedures, in which the formation functions are replaced with original correlations, are useful to some extent in defining a system containing a metal ion and several complexing species.

Consider a system containing `N' equilibria and therefore, there are N formation constants of which NBV are to be determined. Let NMBE be the number of mass balance equations at each experimental point and NP, the total number of experimental points, then there will be NMBE x NP mass-balance equations. Out of NMBE free concentrations at each experimental point, if NEMF free concentrations are measured using appropriate electrodes, it leaves NC=NMBE–NEMF unknown free concentrations. This leads to NP x NC + NBV unknown parameters to be determined from a set of NP x NMBE mass balance equations.

In a system containing one metal ion and one ligand forming N complexes, the formation of jth complex can be represented as,

$$m(j)M + l(j)L + h(j)H \rightleftharpoons M_{m(j)}L_{l(j)}H_{h(j)} \qquad \ldots\ldots\ldots \; (2.7)$$

and the overall formation constant is given by,

$$\beta_{m(j)l(j)h(j)} = \frac{[M_{m(j)}L_{l(j)}H_{h(j)}]}{[FM_i]^{m(j)}.[FL_i]^{l(j)}.[FH_i]^{h(j)}} \quad \text{.......... (2.8)}$$

Where, FM_i, FL_i and FH_i are free concentrations of metal, ligand and hydrogen ion respectively at i^{th} experimental point. The mass balance equations for such a system at i^{th} experimental point are,

$$TMC_i = FM_i + \sum_{j=1}^{N} m(j).[M_{m(j)}L_{l(j)}H_{h(j)}] \quad \text{......... (2.9)}$$

$$TMC_i = FM_i + \sum_{j=1}^{N} m(j)\beta_{m(j).l(j).h(j)}.[FM_i]^{m(j)}.[FL_i]^{l(j)}.[FH_i]^{h(j)} \quad \text{..... (2.10)}$$

$$= FM_i + \sum_{j=1}^{N} m(j).C(j)_i \quad \text{................. (2.11)}$$

Where, $C(j)_i$ is the concentration of the jth complex at i^{th} experimental point. Similarly, the mass balance equations for the ligand and hydrogen ion are,

$$TLC_i = FL_i + \sum_{j=1}^{N} l(j).C(j)_i \quad \text{........... (2.12)}$$

$$THC_i = FH_i + \sum_{j=1}^{N} h(j).C(j)_i - [OH]_i \quad \text{............ (2.13)}$$

Where, TMC_i, TLC_i, and THC_i are the calculated total metal, ligand and hydrogen ion concentrations respectively and $[OH]_i$ represents the hydrogen ion concentration due to auto ionization of water.

In order to evaluate the stability constants of the metal complexes it is necessary to find a relationship between them and the experimentally determined variables. This relationship is often established through the definition of secondary concentration variables. It is from these variables that the stability constants are calculated. One of these secondary variables is, $\bar{n}$ -the average number of ligand molecules associated per mole of metal, which has been extensively used for the determination of stability constants of simple and mono-nuclear complexes in the absence of protonated and hydroxylated species. This function may be defined theoretically as,

$$\bar{n}_i = \frac{total\ bound\ ligand}{total\ metal} = \frac{\mathrm{TLC_i\text{-}FL_i}}{\mathrm{TMC_i}} = \frac{\sum_{j=1}^{N} j.\beta_{\mathrm{m(j)}\,l\mathrm{(j)}\,\mathrm{h(j)}}.[\mathrm{FL_i}]^{l\mathrm{(j)}}}{1+\sum_{j=1}^{N} \beta_{\mathrm{m(j)}\,l\mathrm{(j)}\,\mathrm{h(j)}}[\mathrm{FL_i}]^{l\mathrm{(j)}}} \quad \text{........ (2.14)}$$

If the values of $\bar{n}_i$ and $[FL_i]$ are obtained experimentally, equation (2.14) can be used to calculate the values of the formation constants.

The values of $\bar{n}_i$ and $[FL_i]$ can be evaluated experimentally using the Bjerrum[9] titration technique modified by Calvin and Wilson [10, 30, 31]. The following solutions are to be prepared for pH-metric titrations against a strong base.

a. 'VA' ml of strong acid of initial concentration 'A0' + 'x' ml of a strong electrolyte solution of concentration, 'X0' to maintain required ionic strength in a total volume 'V0' of the solution

b. Solution (a) + 'VL' ml of ligand solution of initial concentration 'L0'.

c. Solution (b) + 'VM' ml of metal ion solution of initial concentration 'M0'.

The three solutions are made up to a total volume of 'V0' using requisite volumes of solvent. Different ratios of ligand to metal can be maintained in various titrations by varying the volumes 'VL' and 'VM' of ligand and metal respectively. Then the resulting concentrations of acid, ligand and metal ion in a total volume 'V0' of solution are given by,

$$\mathrm{E^0} = \frac{\mathrm{VA\,.\,A0}}{\mathrm{V0}}, \quad \mathrm{TL0} = \frac{\mathrm{VL\,.\,L0}}{\mathrm{V0}} \quad \text{and } \mathrm{TM0} = \frac{\mathrm{VM\,.\,M0}}{\mathrm{V0}} \quad \text{....... (2.15)}$$

The solutions, (a), (b) and (c) are titrated against a standard solution of sodium hydroxide, of concentration, [BASE]. Typical pH-metric titration curves for solutions a, b and c are shown in figure 2.1. Now, let V_1, V_2 and V_3 are the volumes of base added to reach the same pH reading in the case of titrations (a), (b) and (c) respectively. Then, $(V_2\text{-}V_1)$ is a measure of the displacement of ligand curve relative to the acid curve and $(V_3\text{-}V_2)$ is a measure of the displacement of the metal + ligand curve relative to the ligand curve.

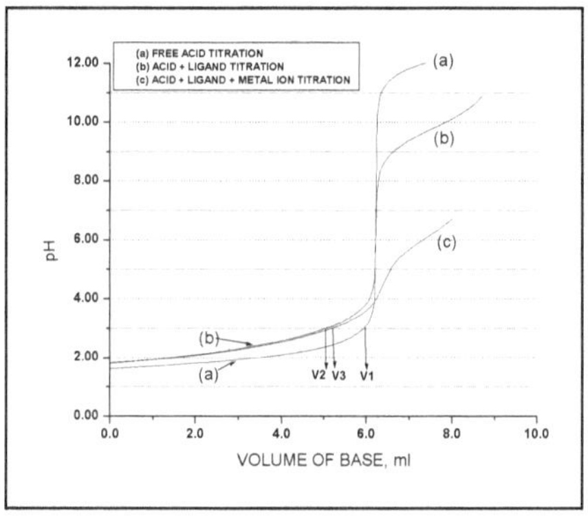

Figure 2.1: Typical Calvin-Wilson pH-metric titration curves

Then the values of $\bar{n}_H$ (average number of protons associated per mole of ligand) and $\bar{n}$ (average number of ligand molecules attached per mole of metal ion) at any ith experimental point can be calculated using the expressions,

$$\begin{aligned} \bar{n}_H &= y - \left[\frac{(E^0+[BASE]).(V_2-V_1)}{(V0+V_1).TL0} \right] \\ \bar{n} &= \left[\frac{(E^0+[BASE]).(V_3-V_2)}{(V0+V_2).TM0} \right] \end{aligned} \qquad \ldots\ldots\ldots\ldots\ldots\ (2.16)$$

where, 'y' denotes the number of ionizable protons of the ligand. Several such values of $\bar{n}_H$ and $\bar{n}$ at various pH values are obtained from the titration curves. The values of the protonation constants β_1^H, β_2^H... β_j^H of the ligand can be obtained from $\bar{n}_H$ *vs.* pH values using half $\bar{n}_H$ method or successive approximation method[30] etc. Then the values of pL at various experimental points can be calculated using the expression,

$$pL = -\log_{10}[FL] = \log_{10}\left[\frac{\sum_{j=1}^{NPL}\beta_j^H.(1/antilog\beta_j^H)^j}{(\text{TL0-}\,\bar{n}.\text{TM0})}\cdot\frac{\text{V0+V}_2}{\text{V0}}\right] \quad \ldots\ldots\ldots\ldots (2.17)$$

Where, 'NPL' is the number of proton-ligand species. Now a plot of $\bar{n}$ *vs.* pL gives a complex formation curve of the metal-ligand system.

A number of procedures, graphical and numerical have been suggested[32] to evaluate the metal-ligand stability constants from a set of $\bar{n}_i$ and FL_i values. This is possible because the secondary formation function $\bar{n}$ depends only on the values of the formation constants and free ligand concentrations. However, only relatively simple systems can be treated in such a linear fashion; for more complex systems, i.e., in which there is a formation of multi-nuclear, protonated and deprotonated species, this treatment of data can lead to erroneous results[33, 34]. However, these methods can be used to get approximate values of the formation constants of simple complexes which may be used as the initial estimates for refinement by modern computational algorithms. The important limitations of the graphical procedures are,

- Testing different chemical models to obtain a best-fit model is not possible.
- The reliability of the equilibrium constants obtained cannot be judged, as it is difficult to obtain good estimates of the errors involved.
- In complex systems it is unavoidable to use only a certain range of data resulting in the limitation of precision of the parameters.

- The primary data must conveniently be transformed into linear functions that can be plotted and this involves several assumptions restricting the reliability of the parameters.

The adoption of computer algorithms by solution chemistry enabled to extract as much reliable information as possible from experimental data. Several computer programs have been proposed for the evaluation of formation constants from potentiometric and spectrophotometric data. Many of these computer-based algorithms involve the minimization of error square sum between an experimentally determined quantity and the corresponding calculated one using the approximate or estimated values of the parameters. The values of the formation constants obtained from the graphical procedures are usually taken as initial estimates and working through the mathematics gives a correction factor which produces a lower sum of squares of the errors. In this way a vector of improved values of the parameters is generated and is used as the estimate for the next iteration. If the function is well behaved and the initial estimates are not very far from the final values, the iteration will converge in a finite number of cycles. The procedure will be repeated for different models and the best-fit model will be selected based on the statistical considerations.

The calculation of stability constants with the use of computer started with Sillen's LETAGROP program[35]. This program involves a specially developed technique called pit-mapping. The function chosen for minimization is the sum of squares of residuals in hydrogen ion concentration. The minimization by this algorithm is very slow and better ones have been developed which will converge more rapidly in spite of the poor initial estimates. Later SCOGS[36] and MINIQUAD[37] appeared and are still the most used programs. The program SCOGS is based on

Gauss-Newton method for the minimization of error square sum of the titration volumes. The calculation of shifts in the unknown formation constants, involves the partial derivatives being obtained numerically by incrementing the constants. The method of numerical differentiation is slow, lacks precision owing to the finite increments given in the differentiation and further, does not work well if bad values for increments are chosen. Both the programs SCOGS and LETAGROP suffer from the defects in Newton-Raphson or Gauss-Newton methods that they cannot distinguish between maxima, minima and saddle points. Thus, poor initial estimates of stability constants may lead to the sum of the squares tending to be maximized instead of minimized. In SCOGS this is reflected in producing extreme over shifts in the stability constants, a condition that requires arbitrary and unpredictable intervention in the program.

The parameters chosen for refinement in MINIQUAD[37] and MINIQUAD-75[11] are the formation constants, $\beta_{m(j),l(j),h(j)}$ as in LETAGROP while in SCOGS *log* $\beta_{m(j),l(j),h(j)}$ are employed. As the error square sum is almost a parabolic function of β the change of scale from β to $\log \beta$ transforms the error square sum into a highly non-linear, non-concave function, which is difficult to be minimized by any method. Hence, many of the difficulties experienced in the calculation of stability constants using the program SCOGS are due to the adoption of $\log \beta$ values instead of β s as variables.

The author employed the program MINIQUAD-75 developed by Gans et al.[11] for the refinement of proton-ligand and metal-ligand formation constants. This program minimizes the sum of squares of the residuals in mass balance equations for all the titration points.

If TME_i, TLEi and THEi, are the experimental total concentrations of metal, ligand and hydrogen ion, respectively at i^{th} titration point, then the residuals in the mass balance equations, f_i (M, L, H), ϕ_i (M, L, H) and ψ_i (M, L, H) may be represented as,

$$f_i (M, L, H) = TME_i - TMC_i \quad ...... (2.18)$$

$$\phi_i (M, L, H) = TLE_i - TLC_i \quad .... (2.19)$$

$$\psi_i (M, L, H) = THE_i - THC_i \quad .... (2.20)$$

Substituting the values of TMC_i, TLC_i and THC_i from equations, (2.11), (2.12) and (2.13) respectively,

$$f_i (M,L,H) = TME_i - FM_i - \sum_{j=1}^{N} m(j) \times C(j)_i$$

$$= TME_i - FM_i - \sum_{j=1}^{N} m(j) \times \beta_{m(j)\,l(j)\,h(j)} \times FM_i^{m(j)} \times FL_i^{l(j)} \times FH_i^{h(j)} \quad .... (2.21)$$

$$\phi_i (M,L,H) = TLE_i - FL_i - \sum_{j=1}^{N} l(j) \times C(j)_i$$

$$= TLE_i - FL_i - \sum_{j=1}^{N} l(j) \times \beta_{m(j)\,l(j)\,h(j)} \times FM_i^{m(j)} \times FL_i^{l(j)} \times FH_i^{h(j)} \quad .... (2.22)$$

$$\psi_i (M L H) = THE_i - FH_i - \sum_{j=1}^{N} h(j) \times C(j)_i + OH_i$$

$$= THE_i - FH_i - \sum_{j=1}^{N} h(j) \times \beta_{m(j)\,l(j)\,h(j)} \times FM_i^{m(j)} \times FL_i^{l(j)} \times FH_i^{h(j)} + OH_i \quad .... (2.23)$$

and U_i, the sum of squares of the weighted residuals at the ith experimental point is given by the equation

$$U_i = W_i . f_i^2 + W_i . \phi_i^2 + W_i . \psi_i^2 \quad .... (2.24)$$

Where, W_i is the weight applied. A statistically correct weighing scheme is possible only if good estimates of the elements of the variance-covariance matrix of the observations are available. If unit weights are assumed equation (2.24) becomes

$$U_i = f_i^2 + \phi_i^2 + \psi_i^2 \qquad \text{........... (2.25)}$$

$$U = \sum_{i=1}^{NP} U_i \qquad \text{.......... (2.26)}$$

Where, NP is the total number of titration points. The residuals f_i, ϕ_i and ψ_i are very nearly equal to zero only if FM_i, FL_i and FH_i along with the formation constants are accurately known. As `U' represents the sum of squares of deviations for all mass balance equations and for all experimental points, it can be represented as a product of two vectors, as shown in equation (2.27),

$$U = R^T \text{ x } R \qquad \text{........ (2.27)}$$

Where, `R' is a column vector whose elements are the residuals ($TXE_i - TXC_i$ ) and $R^T$ is the transpose of the matrix `R'. A gradient vector `g' (equation (2.28)) can now be defined such that its elements $g_i$ are equal to the partial derivatives of `U' with respect to each of the variable parameters i.e. unknown free concentrations at each titration point and unknown formation constants.

$$g = \begin{bmatrix} g_1 \\ g_2 \\ g_3 \\ g_4 \\ \cdot \\ \cdot \end{bmatrix} = \begin{bmatrix} \partial U / \partial FM_1 \\ \partial U / \partial FL_1 \\ \\ \\ \partial U / \partial \beta V_1 \\ \partial U / \partial \beta V_2 \\ \cdot \\ \cdot \end{bmatrix} \qquad \text{........ (2.28)}$$

For each point, the calculated total concentrations are only functions of the concentrations of free metal and free ligand at that point and of the formation constants. Thus, the derivatives of the components at a point with respect to the free concentrations at other points will be vanishing. Hence the matrix can be represented as

$$g = -2 . A^{T} . R \quad \text{.........} (2.29)$$

Where, the matrix 'A' is a design matrix, whose elements 'a_i' are the partial derivatives. When the estimated values of unknown parameters are identical with true values, the residual matrix (R) becomes a zero matrix and hence the elements of `g' also reduced to zero. If the functions are linear in unknown parameters, then the magnitudes of these parameters can be evaluated by solving a set of simultaneous equations. As these functions are non-linear, initial estimates of free metal, free ligand at each point (NC x NP) and of the unknown formation constants (NBV) which are very close to the true values are needed. In such a case, the elements of `R' and hence `g' are not equal to zero, but will have a small definite value. The elements of the `g' matrix can be expanded by Taylor's polynomial series truncated after the terms of first-degree. Therefore, the matrix `g' can be represented as

$$g = \begin{bmatrix} g_c \\ g_\beta \end{bmatrix} = - H . \begin{bmatrix} S_c \\ S_\beta \end{bmatrix} \quad \text{.........} (2.30)$$

Where, S_c and g_c are the `shift' and `gradient' vectors related to the unknown free concentrations at each titration point and S_β and g_β are those related to the formation constants. From equations (2.29) and (2.30) it follows that,

$$H . \begin{bmatrix} S_c \\ S_\beta \end{bmatrix} = - \begin{bmatrix} g_c \\ g_\beta \end{bmatrix} = 2 . A^{T} . R \quad \text{......} (2.31)$$

The elements of the 'H' matrix may be divided into two matrices 'Z' and 'C', the elements of the latter being second derivatives of functions. If one ignores the `C' matrix, then the method is referred as Gauss-Newton least-squares method and in that case `H' matrix is identical with that of `Z' matrix which in turn equal to $A^T. A$. The order of the matrix $A^T A$ is (NC.NP + NBV) x (NC.NP + NBV). Owing to its large dimension, the inversion of this matrix is not feasible with medium size computers. Taking advantage of the particular form of the $A^T A$ matrix, which contains a large number of zero elements, a new matrix `D' is found such that $[D^T. (A^T. A). D]$ will be strictly a block diagonal matrix.

$$D^T. (A^T.A). D= \begin{bmatrix} B_1 & B_2 \\ B_2^T & B_3 \end{bmatrix} = B \qquad ...... (2.32)$$

Now, B_1, B_2, B_3 are the matrix partitions of the symmetric normal equations matrix B. Then the whole problem is reduced to inversion of each block along the diagonal. Therefore, equation (2.31) can be represented as,

$$\begin{bmatrix} B_1 B_2 \\ B_2^T B_3 \end{bmatrix} . \begin{bmatrix} S_c \\ S_\beta \end{bmatrix} = - \begin{bmatrix} g_c \\ g_\beta \end{bmatrix} \qquad .... (2.33)$$

This can be rearranged to give equations, (2.34) and (2.35)

$$(B_3 - B_2^T. B_1^{-1}. B_2)\ S_\beta = - g_\beta + B_2^T. B_1^{-1}. g_c \qquad .... (2.34)$$

$$S_c = -B_1^{-1}. g_c - B_1^{-1}\ B_2.. S_\beta \qquad .... (2.35)$$

Equation (2.35) is solved after equation (2.34) and the shifts thus obtained are applied to the parameters. In MINIQUAD this represents one cycle and new values, thus obtained are used as initial estimates for the second cycle. In each cycle, only fractions of the shifts obtained are applied to the parameters, to make the refinement reliable. This linear optimization is not an efficient process and in extreme cases, significant reduction in error square sum may not be possible, as the shift vector becomes almost tangential to the iso-value contours.

This unreliability of convergence in extreme cases is rectified in the MINIQUAD-75 program, which is a hybrid program of two procedures 'A' and 'B'. Procedure `A' is a constrained least-squares method in which the free concentrations are calculated separately and are, therefore, optimal for every set of formation constants. This modification transforms a non-linear problem into a linear one and therefore, the convergence becomes fast and takes only a few cycles. In procedure `B' the Marquart parameter `λ' is introduced whose affect is to rotate the shift vector towards the direction of steepest descent. As solution approaches, the value of the Marquart parameter tends to zero. This makes the procedure 'B', a standard un-damped, un-constrained least-squares method with excellent convergence properties. Neither 'A' nor 'B' alone could give a fast and reliable convergence. In the MINIQUAD-75 program process `A' is repeated once after five cycles of B.

One of the advantages that have widely been publicized in recent computer programs is that, even wild constants far away from the true values will be converged. This has been found to be true for simple systems. However, Sylva and Davidson[38] observed the necessity of fairly good initial estimates for the stability constants. Otherwise the species that really exist may be rejected or may result in an ill-conditioned matrix. They argued that it was not the limitation of MINIQUAD-75 but a problem inherent in numerical analysis of mathematically complex systems. The required initial estimates of formation constants for proton-ligand and binary metal-ligand systems can be obtained using classical methods[30-32]. In the case of initial estimates for protonated complexes, simple algebraic methods proposed by Martell[39] and Alniami and Al-Saadi[40] help in rapid and reliable convergence. In the absence of any information, wild guess based on literature reports for similar systems is the only alternative, but a careful choice of optimization algorithm is necessary.

2.3.1 Input and Output of MINIQUAD-75 Program:

The input experimental data for MINIQUAD-75 include total millimoles of each reactant initially present in the titration vessel, concentration of the titrant in the burette, total initial volume, electrode offset and volume of the titrant *vs.* pH data. A suggested chemical model of the system containing the stoichiometric coefficients and log β values of all the species is to be submitted for refinement. The log β value of a particular species can be held constant or subjected to refinement by making the corresponding key either zero or one respectively. The output contains the refined formation constants along with their standard deviations and other statistics like some of the squares of residuals in the mass balance equations, chi-square, Hamilton R factor, skewness and kurtosis etc. Several models containing chemically plausible species are to be tested to select a best-fit model of the system under study.

2.3.2 Criteria for the Selection of a Best-Fit Model:

The validity and sufficiency of a chemical model that represents the system under study to qualify as a best-fit model of the experimental data, may be tested using,

1. The sum of the squares of residuals in mass balance equations 'U',
2. The standard deviations in the refined formation constants,
3. The χ^2 –test, and
4. "R' (the Hamiltonian R factor).

- The error square sum 'U" can be represented as,

$$U=\sum_{i=1}^{np}[(TMC_i-TME_i)^2+(TLC_i-TLE_i)^2+(THC_i-THE_i)^2]$$

i.e. ……… (2.36)

$$U=\sum_{i=1}^{np}(RM_i^2+RL_i^2+RH_i^2)$$

Where, RM_i^2, RL_i^2 and RH_i^2 are the residuals in mass balance equations

TME_i, TLE_i, THE_i are the experimental and TMC_i, TLC_i, THC_i are the calculated total concentrations of the metal ion, ligand and hydrogen ion respectively. The best-fit model should have a minimum value of error square sum 'U' compared to other models.

- The standard deviations in the formation constants of all the species refined must be low, i.e. <10% of log β.
- χ^2 –test, tests the distribution of errors against a normal one. The model may be rejected if χ^2 is greater than a specified value within the given confidence level.
- The value of Hamilton, R factor is represented by the equation,

$$R=\left[\sum_{i=1}^{NP}\{(Q_{exp}-Q_{cal})_i\}^2/\sum_{i=1}^{NP}\{(Q_{exp})_i\}^2\right]^{1/2} \quad \text{...... (2.37)}$$

Where, Q_{exp} and Q_{cal} are the experimental and calculated quantities. This value of R must be less than R_{limit} given by the equation,

$$R_{limit}=\left[\sum_{i=1}^{NP}e_i^2/\sum_{i=1}^{NP}(Q_{exp})^2\right]^{1/2} \quad \text{.......... (2.38)}$$

Where, e_i is the residual at i^{th} experimental point calculated from the estimates of the errors in all the experimental quantities using the error propagation rules[41]. A satisfactory fit is assumed if $R< R_{limit}$. The model may be rejected if on the introduction of a new species, the value of 'U' increases and/or if 'R' exceeds the limit.

- Kurtosis is the degree of peakedness of a distribution usually taken relative to a normal distribution. If this value is equal to 3.0, the distribution of residuals is normal (mesokurtic), i.e. neither very peaked nor flat–topped. A high value indicates that the distribution is peaked (lepokurtic) and a low value represents a flat-topped distribution called platykurtic.
- Skewness indicates the symmetry of the residual distribution curves. For a symmetrical or bell shaped curve skewness must be equal to zero. A *+ve* value indicates the presence of a longer tail towards right and a *–ve* value towards left.

Knowledge of the relevant equilibrium or stability constants allows the calculation of the concentrations of all the individual complexes for any given experimental conditions; the resulting set of concentrations is called the speciation of the system under study. Consider a system containing a metal ion M^{Z+} and a ligand L in equilibrium with the generalized species, $M_mL_lH_h$, with overall stability constant β_{mlh} (equations 2.7 and 2.8). For any individual component of the system, a variable, α_{mlh}, can be defined such that,

$$\alpha_{mlh} = \frac{[M_mL_lH_h]_i}{[TM]_i} \qquad \text{.................} \quad (2.39)$$

The variable α_{mlh} is the partial mole fraction of the component $M_mL_lH_h$ at i^{th} experimental point. Hence, it is possible to get a series of component distribution curves by plotting α_{mlh} versus pH. Therefore, α_{mlh} function (or $\%\alpha_{mlh}$) can be used to show at a glance the relative proportions of each of the species present in solution against pH. Species distribution diagrams can be generated using the output data of the Miniquad-75 program or using HySS2009 software[42].

The author conveniently modified the program MINIQUAD-75 to run on a personal computer under MS-Windows environment. The main program and subroutines DINP and STATS were also modified to suit the requirement. Calvin and Wilson titration technique was used for data acquisition. The initial estimates of the formation constants required for refinement by the Miniquad-75 program were obtained using classical procedures. Various chemical models containing plausible species depending on the nature of the ligand and metal ion were subjected to refinement. Simulated titration curves using the formation constants in the refined model were then generated using computer program SOPHD[43]. The algorithm of the program SOPHD, developed in our laboratory is based on the Gauss-Newton iteration technique. This program originally written for proton-ligand and binary metal-ligand systems was modified by the author to work even for ternary mixed ligand systems. The adequacy of a refined model can be tested by comparing the simulated titration curve with the experimental one. The simulated titration curves thus obtained were plotted along with the experimental ones to identify the regions of pH where they differ. The differences between the two curves indicate the presence of other species in addition to the assumed model. From the nature, position and extent of the deviation and also keeping in view of the chemical nature of the system under study, more suitable models can be predicted for the refinement. This procedure was repeated until best-fit models of the systems under study meeting the required statistical criteria were obtained.

2.4 REFERENCES:

1. Petit, V. Geertsen, C. Beaucaire and M. Stambouli, "Metal complexes stability constant determination by hyphenation of capillary electrophoresis with inductively coupled plasma Mass Spectrometry: The case of 1:1 metal-to-ligand stoichiometry," *J. Chromatogr. A*, 1216 (18) (2009) pp. 4113-4120.
2. B. B. Tewari, "Paper Electrophoretic Determination of the Stability Constants of binary and ternary complexes of copper(II) and cobalt(II) with nitrilotriacetate and cysteine," *J. Chromatogr. A*, 1103 (1) (2006) pp. 139-144.
3. M. Cirri, F. Maestrelli, S. Orlandini, S. Furlanetto, S. Pinzauti and P. Mura, "Determination of stability constant values of flurbiprofen-cyclodextrin complexes using different techniques," *J. Pharm. Biomed. Anal.*, 37(5) (2005) pp. 995- 1002.
4. R. Tauler, A. Smilde and B. R. Kowalski, "Multivariate curve resolution applied to second order data," *J. Chemom.*, 9(1) (1995) pp. 31-58.
5. S. Arhaland, "On the complex chemistry of the Uranyl Ion. The complexity of Uranyl Monochloroacetate. A comparative potentiometric and extinctiometric investigation", *Acta. Chem. Scand.*, 3 (1949) pp 783-808.
6. L. Sommer, V. Kuban and J. Havel, "Spectrophotometric studies of complexation in solution", *Chemia.* XI (1970) 4.
7. L. Sommer and P. Voznica, "Some Aspects of the contemporaneous analytical chemistry A personal view", *Chem. Papers*, 53 (3) (1999) pp 184-199.
8. K. Takacs-Novak, K. Y. Tam, "Multi-wavelength spectrophotometric determination of acid dissociation constants: a validation study", *Anal. Chim. Acta, 434* (2001) pp 157–167.
9. J. Bjerrum, "Metal ammine formation in aqueous solution: theory of the reversible step reactions", P. Haase and Son, Copenhagen, (1941, Reprinted:1957).

10. M. Calvin and K. W. Wilson, "Stability of chelate compounds", *J. Am. Chem. Soc.*, 67 (1945) pp 2003-2007.

11. P. Gans, A. Sabatini and A. Vacca, "An improved computer program for the computation of formation constants from potentiometric data", *Inorg. Chim. Acta.*, 18 (1976) pp 237-239.
12. . Schwarzenbach and M. Flascha, "Complexometric Titrations" Methuen, London (1957).
13. C. F. Baes Jr. and R. E. Mesmer, "The hydrolysis of cations" Oak Ridge National Laboratory (1976).
14. J. P. Birk, "Mechanism of the reduction of vanadium (V) by hexacyanoferrate (II) in acidic aqueous solution", *Inorg. Chem*. 9 (1970) pp 125-129.
15. F. J. Weltcher, "The analytical uses of ethylene diamine tetra acetic acid", D Van Nostrand Company INC, New York, (1957).
16. G. Gran, "Determination of the equivalence point in potentiometric titrations", *Analyst* 77 (1952) 661.
17. G. Gran, "Determination of the equivalence point in potentiometric titrations", *Acta Chem. Scand.* 4 (1950) pp 559-577.
18. D. D. Perrin and I. G. Sayce, *Chem. Ind.* (1966) 661.
19. M. Peter May, R. David Williams, W. Peter Linder and G. Ralph Torrington, "The use of glass electrodes for the determination of formation constants-I A definitive method for calibration", *Talanta* 29 (1982) pp 249-256.
20. H. K. J. Powell and M. C. Taylor, "A comment on the simultaneous determination of glass electrode parameters and protonation constants", *Talanta* 30 (1983) pp 885-886.
21. A. Braibanti, G. Ostacoli, P. Paoletlti, L. D. Pettit and S. Sammartano, "Recommended procedure for testing the potentiometric apparatus and technique for the pH-metric measurement of metal-complex equilibrium constants", *Pure Appl. Chem.*, 59 (12) (1987) pp 1721-1728.
22. H. Siegel, A. D. Zuberbühler, and O. Yamauchi, "Comments on potentiometric pH titrations and the relationship between pH-meter reading and hydrogen ion concentration", *Anal. Chim. Acta,* 255(1991) pp 63-72.
23. Mc Bryde, W. A. E, "The pH meter as a hydrogen-ion concentration probe", *Analyst* 94 (1969) pp 337-346.
24. G. R. Hedwig, and H. K. Powell, *J. Anal. Chem.* 43 (1971) 1206.

25. R. E. Jervis, and K. Neelakanthan, “On the measurement of low acidity (pHc) in acetone-water and 1-propanol-water”, *J. Inorg. Nucl. Chem.* 37 (1975) pp 531-535.
26. G. Arena, E. Rizzarelli, S. Sammartano and C. Rigano, “A non-linear least-squares approach to the refinement of all parameters involved in acid-base titrations.”, *Talanta* 26 (1979) pp1-14.
27. P. Gans, A. Sabatini and A. Vacca, “SUPERQUAD: an improved general program for computation of formation constants from potentiometric data”, *J. Chem. Soc. Dalton*, (1985) 1195-1200.
28. P. Gans, A Sabatini and A. Vacca, "Investigation of equilibria in solution. Determination of equilibrium constants with the HYPERQUAD suite of programs". *Talanta* 43 (1996) 1739–1753.
29. R.G. Bates, G.D. Pinching, E. Smith, “pH Standards of High Acidity and High Alkalinity and the Practical Scale of pH”, *J. Res. Natl. Bur. Stand.* 45 (5) (1950) pp 418–429.
30. H. M. Irving, H. S. Rossotti, “Methods for Computing Successive Stability Constants from Experimental Formation Curves”. *J. Chem. Soc.* (1953) 3397–3405.
31. H. M. Irving, H. S. Rossotti, “The Calculation of Formation Curves of Metal Complexes from pH-Titration Curves in Mixed Solvents”, *J. Chem. Soc.* (1954) 2904–2910.
32. F. J. C. Rossotti and H. Rossotti, “The Determination of Stability Constants”, McGraw–Hill (1961).
33. W. A. E. Mc.Bryde, “Constrints on the determination of stability constants for metal complexes. I. Bipyridyl and phenanthroline complexes”, *Can. J. Chem.*, 45 (1967) pp 2093-2100.
34. G. Schwarzenbach and E. Frietag, “Komplexone XIX. Die Bildungskonstanten von Schwer-metallkomplexen der Nitrilo-triessigsäure”, *Helv. Chim. Acta.* 34 (1951) pp 1492-1502.
35. N. Ingri and L.G. Sillen., "High-speed computers as a supplement to graphical methods, IV. An ALGOL version of LETAGROP-VRID". *Arkiv. Kemi.*, 23 (1964) 97–121.

36. I. G. Sayce, "Computer calculation of equilibrium constants of species present in mixtures of metal ions and complexing agents", *Talanta* 15 (1968) pp1397-1411.

37. A. Sabatini, A. Vacca and P. Gans. "MINIQUAD - A general computer program for the computation of Stability constants". *Talanta* 21 (1974) pp 53–77.

38. R. N. Sylva, and M. R. Davidson, "The Hydrolysis of Metal Ions. Part I. Copper (II)", *J. Chem. Soc. Dalton Trans*, (1979) pp 232-235, "Hydrolysis of Metal Ions. Part 2. Dioxouranium(VI), (1979)pp 465-471.

39. T. A. Bohigian and A. E. Martell, "New multidentate ligands. V. Transition metal chelates of Triethylenetetraminehexaacetic acid", *J. Am. Chem. Soc.* 89 (1967) pp 832-836.

40. N. S. Alniami, and B. M. Al-Saadi, "Thiosalicylic acid complexes of divalent zinc, cadmium, mercury and lead", *J. Inorg. Nucl. Chem.* 36 (1974) pp1617-1622.

41. H. H. Ku, "Notes on the Use of propagation of Error Formulas", *J. Res. Natl. Bur. Stand..*, 70C (1966) pp 263-273.

42. L. Alderighi, P. Gans, A. Ienco, D. Peters, A. Sabatini, A. Vacca, "Hyperquad simulation and speciation (HySS): A utility program for the investigation of equilibria involving soluble and partially soluble species", *Coord. Chem. Rev.* 184 (1999) pp 311–318.

43. R. Sambasiva Rao, A. Satyanarayana and P.V. Krishna Rao, "SOPHD- A computer program for the simulation of pH-metric data", *Proc. Summ. Simul. Conf.*, (1984) p 563.

CHAPTER- 3

ACID-BASE EQUILIBRIA OF DIHYDRAZIDES AND SELECTED AMINO ACIDS

As a prelude to the determination of formation constants of binary and ternary systems containing metal ions, dihydrazides and amino acids, the author has taken up a study on the proton-ligand equilibria of both dihydrazides and amino acids under similar experimental conditions. This is an essential prerequisite as the formation of a metal complex is also an acid-base equilibrium, where, there is a competition between the metal ion and proton for the binding site(s) of the ligand. This leads to the pH dependence of the formation of metal ligand species that can be monitored using a glass electrode. Hence, by following the changes in hydrogen ion concentration of a system containing a metal ion and ligand using Bjerrum's method of potentiometric titration and a knowledge of protonation constants of most anionic form of the ligand(s) could facilitate the speciation study of binary and ternary systems.

Dihydrazides selected for the study were, succinic acid dihydrazide (SADH) and Adipic acid dihydrazide (AADH). In spite of the biological importance of dihydrazides[1-5] there is a paucity of information in the literature on their solution equilibria.

3.1 DATA ACQUISITION:

Calvin-Wilson titration technique [6, 7] as described in Chapter 2 of the thesis was used for the study of protonation equilibria of SADH, AADH and amino acids in aqueous medium. Requisite volumes of hydrochloric acid (to give an overall concentration of 0.02 -0.05 $mol.dm^{-3}$), sodium chloride (ionic strength was maintained at 0.1 $mol.dm^{-3}$) and water in the presence and absence of ligand in a total volume of 50 cm^3 was titrated with ~0.2 mol. dm^{-3} sodium hydroxide. The concentration of the ligand was between; 0.004 to 0.015 $mol.dm^{-3}$ in different experiments. Freshly prepared solutions of ligands were used in all the titrations. After the addition of each aliquot (0.1ml) of sodium hydroxide, the pH meter dial reading was recorded at regular intervals of time until two successive readings do not differ by more than 0.01 pH units. The pH correction factor and ionic product of water were calculated by Gran method [8, 9].

3.2 PROTON - LIGAND EQUILIBRIA OF SUCCINIC AND ADIPIC ACID DIHYDRAZIDES:

Succinic and adipic acid dihydrazides belong to a group of nitrogenous organic compounds with general formula, R $(-CO-NH-NH_2)_2$ as shown in Figure 3.1. In the case of aliphatic dihydrazides R= $(CH_2)_n$, the value of n= 2 for SADH and n=4 for AADH.

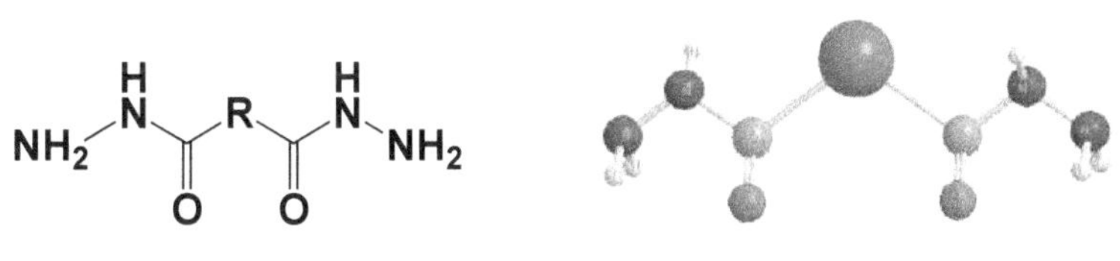

Fig.3.1: General formula of a dihydrazide

In the presence of an acid the neutral form of these ligands (L) may be protonated at the terminal $-NH_2$ groups forming mono-protonated (LH^{+}) and biprotonated (LH_2^{2+}) species. Hydrazides are also known to undergo keto-enol tautomerism and may also lose enolic protons in basic medium, leading to the formation of LH_{-1} and LH_{-2} type of deprotonated species.

Fig. 3.2: Keto-enol tautomerism of dihydrazides

Thus, the acido-basic equilibria of dihydrazides may contain LH_2^{2+}, LH^{+}, L, LH_{-1} and LH_{-2} type of species in solution. In literature, there are no reports on the proton-ligand equilibria of SADH. In the case of AADH, there are two reports on the protonation in aqueous-dioxane[10], aqueous-dimethylformamide[10] and aqueous-ethanol[11] media. These authors did not consider the deprotonation of AADH in basic medium. Therefore, the author has taken up a study on the proton-ligand equilibria of these ligands which is an essential pre-requisite for the determination of the formation constants of metal-ligand complexes. Preliminary experiments revealed that, addition of a drop of 0.1 mole dm^{-3} alkali suddenly raised the pH of both SADH and AADH solutions to about ~ 9.0. This indicates that these ligands do not possess any dissociable protons in the pH region below 9.0.

The pH metric titration data for SADH and AADH are shown graphically in Figures 3.3a and 3.4a respectively. Curve 1 represents titration of hydrochloric acid in the absence of ligand, while curve 2 represents the titration of acid + ligand with sodium hydroxide. The titration curves of both SADH and AADH (curve 2 in Figures 3.3a and 3.4a) are above that of free acid below a pH of ~5.0. This difference between the free acid and ligand curves in the lower pH region for both the ligands indicates the presence of proton associable centres in the ligands

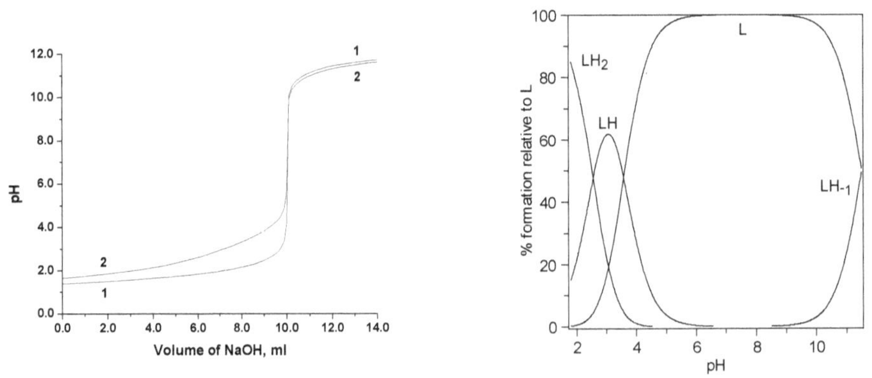

a. 1. Titration curve of free mineral acid
2. Titration curve for acid + SADH

b. Species distribution diagram

[SADH] = 0.00960 mol dm^{-3} [HCl] = 0.04039 mol dm^{-3} [NaOH] = 0.2016 $moldm^{-3}$
Temp.: 30.0 ±0. 1°C Total volume= 50.0 cm^3 I = 0.1 mol dm^{-3} NaCl

Figure 3.3: PROTON-LIGAND SYSTEM OF SADH

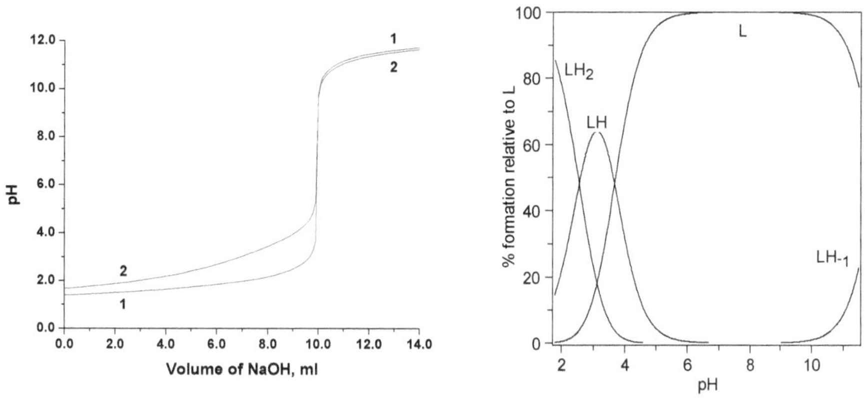

a. 1. Titration curve of free mineral acid
2. Titration curve for acid + AADH

b. Species distribution diagram

[AADH] = 0.0100 mol. dm^{-3} [HCl] = 0.04016 mol. dm^{-3} [NaOH]= 0.2016 mol. dm^{-3}
Temp.: 30.0 ±0. $1^{0}C$ Total volume= 50.0 cm^{3} I = 0.1 mol. dm^{-3} NaCl

Figure 3.4: PROTON-LIGAND SYSTEM OF AADH

On the basic side, i.e. above pH ~9.0, there is a significant lowering of the ligand titration curves relative to the free acid indicating deprotonation of the ligands. In between these two pH regions free acid and ligand curves coincide indicating the absence of other proton-ligand equilibria.

The titration data was first subjected to analysis by ACBA computer program[12], modified by the author to run on a personal computer. The formation constants obtained from ACBA program were taken as initial estimates for refinement by MINIQUAD-75 program[13]. The protonation and deprotonation equilibria of SADH are shown in Figure 3.5. The best-fit model obtained using the Miniquad-75 program (Table 3.1) contained three formation constants β_{011}, β_{012} and β_{01-1} corresponding to the formation of LH, LH_2 and LH_{-1} (charges are omitted for brevity) respectively.

The species distribution diagram of SADH (Figure 3.3b) indicates that the LH_2^{2+} form exists only below a pH of 4.0. The extent of its formation is ~84% (at ~1.8 pH) in the pH region of study. The species LH^+ which has a maximum of 62%

around a pH of 3.1 ceases to exist above ~6.0 pH. β_{011} and β_{012} are the formation constants (Figure 3.3) of mono and biprotonated forms of SADH respectively, the protonation being at the terminal nitrogen atoms of the two hydrazide groups.

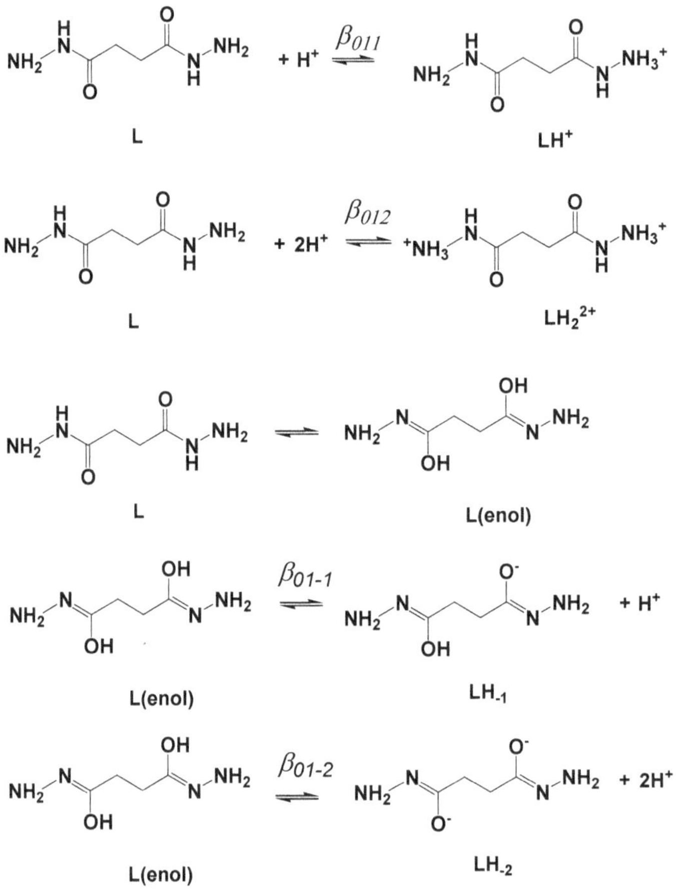

Figure 3.5: PROTONATION AND DEPROTONATION EQUILIBRIA OF SADH

Table 3.1: Best fit chemical model for acido-basic equilibria of succinic acid dihydrazide in aqueous medium. Temp. = 30.0 ± 0.1°C and ionic strength, $I = 0.1$ mol dm^{-3} (NaCl)

Species *mlh*	Log β_{0lh} (SD)	Number of experimental points analysed	Sum of the squares of residuals, U	χ^2
011	3.58 (2)	110	1.642 X 10^{-8}	12.34
012	6.14 (2)			
01-1	-11.91 (3)			

Up to ~99% of the ligand is in neutral form between 6.0 and 9.0 pH. In basic medium hydrazides are prone to lose a proton from the enolic form. As SADH contains two hydrazide groups, there is a probability of losing two enolic protons at higher pH. The formation constant, $\beta_{01\text{-}1}$ in the best-fit model corresponds to the deprotonation of one of the enolic protons leading to the formation of LH_{-1} species. This species appears in the solution above a pH of ~9.0 and represents 49% of the total ligand at a pH of 11.5. The formation constant, $\beta_{01\text{-}2}$ which corresponds to the deprotonation of the second enolic group leading to the formation of LH_{-2}, was not converged. This is because its equilibrium may lie well above the pH range of the study. However, in the presence of a metal ion the ligand may also lose the second enolic proton forming both deprotonated $M_mL_lH_{-1}$ and $M_mL_lH_{-2}$ type of species.

The best-fit model and the corresponding protonation and deprotonation equilibria of AADH are shown in Table 3.2 and Figure 3.6 respectively. The best-fit model for AADH (L) indicates the formation of LH_2^{2+}, LH^+, L and LH_{-1} species in aqueous medium. At lower pH (below ~3.0 pH), the biprotonated form, LH_2^{2+} of AADH dominates and with increase in pH, undergoes successive deprotonation to form the mono-protonated (LH^+) and neutral species (L). β_{011} and β_{012} are the formation constants (Figure 3.6) of mono and biprotonated forms of AADH from its neutral form.

Table 3.2: Best fit chemical model for acido-basic equilibria of adipic acid dihydrazide in aqueous medium. Temp. = 30.0 ± 0.1°C and ionic strength, I = 0.1 mol dm^{-3} (NaCl)

Species *mlh*	Log β_{0lh} (SD)	Number of experimental points analysed	Sum of the squares of residuals, U	χ^2
011	3.67 (3)	75	4.099 X 10^{-8}	11.92
012	6.24 (7)			
01-1	-12.03 (5)			

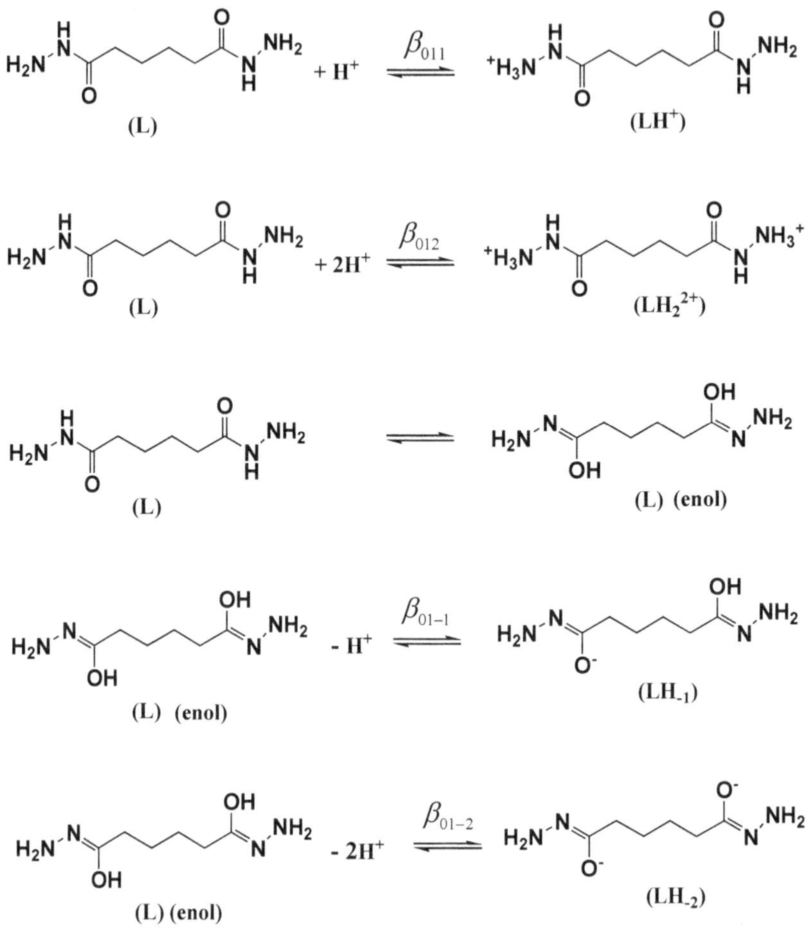

Figure 3.6: PROTONATION AND DEPROTONATION EQUILIBRIA OF AADH

The relatively high values of these formation constants compared to SADH indicate the increase in basicity of the ligand with increase in chain length of "R" group connecting the two hydrazide groups. The formation constant, β_{01-1} in the best-fit model corresponds to the deprotonation of one of the enolic protons leading to the formation of LH_{-1} species. The other, β_{01-2} which corresponds to the formation of LH_{-2}, is not observed as its equilibrium may lie well above the pH range of study. The species distribution diagram (Figure 3.4b) indicates that AADH exists in the protonated form below pH ~6.5, deprotonated form above pH ~9.0 and in neutral form between pH ~6.5 and ~9.0. The maxi mum percentage concentrations (with respect to total ligand) of LH_2^{2+}, LH^+ and L^- are 85% (1.8 pH), 64%(3.1pH) and 23%(11.5 pH) respectively in the pH region of study.

3.3 PROTON-LIGAND EQUILIBRIA OF AMINO ACIDS:

Equilibrium constants of acid- base equilibria of amino acids reported in literature were determined using different methods in various solvents and at specific conditions of temperature, ionic strength etc. Several databases are available that give the formation constants of proton-ligand and metal-ligand systems, including,

- The IUPAC Stability Constants Database, SC-Database and Mini-SC Database, 2006 and
- NIST (National Institute of Standards and Technology) -Critically Selected Stability Constants of Metal Complexes- Database Version 8.0 For Windows, R. M. Smith and A. E. Martell, (May, 2004)

Along with the formation constants, these databases give the experimental conditions and methods that can be used to adjust the values for different conditions.

Stability constants reported in the literature, mostly for amino acids and some of the other ligands, were critically surveyed and published by Martel et al.[14], Pettit[15], Kiss et al.[16], Sovago et al.[17], Berthon[18]and Yamauchi et al.[19]. Use of the values obtained either from data bases or critical surveys in speciation calculations at different experimental conditions can lead to a significant uncertainty. This may be attributed to the variations in experimental conditions and the use of classical/ graphical methods of formation constant calculations by earlier workers. Most of the classical methods ignore the possibility of formation of protonated and hydroxylated species in addition to the formation of simple mono-nuclear species. The formation constants obtained without considering these aspects are unreliable and associate with some systematic error. Also the methods used for adjusting the equilibrium constants to the required conditions of temperature and ionic strength introduce some uncertainty in the predicted values as experienced by several workers[20-22].

The protonation constants of glycine, aspartic acid and histidine, although available in literature, were, therefore, redetermined under the same experimental conditions of ionic strength and temperature used to study the binary and the ternary complexes.

3.3.1 Proton-ligand equilibria of Glycine:

Glycine is the simplest possible proteinogenic non-essential amino acid with the chemical formula NH_2-CH_2-COOH. It is amphoteric in nature and in aqueous solution, depending on the pH, can exist in three different forms (Figure 3.7) *viz.* the cationic (XH_2^+), the neutral or zwitter ionic (XH) and the anionic (X^-) forms. XH is the zwitter ionic form in which the amino group is protonated while the carboxyl group is deprotonated.

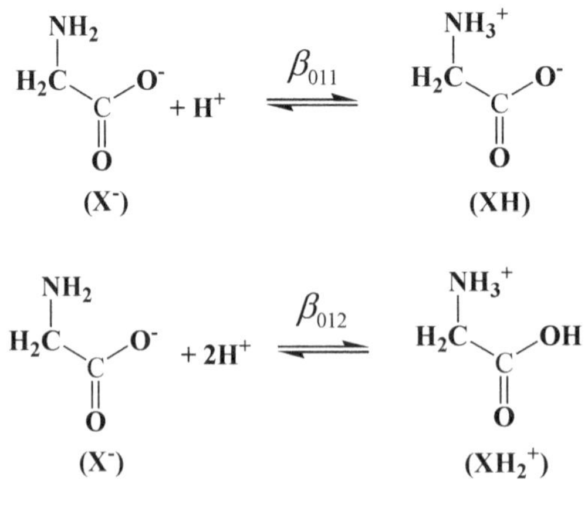

Figure 3.7: Protonation equilibria of glycine

The Calvin-Wilson[6, 7] potentiometric titration curves obtained for glycine are shown in Figure 3.8a. Curve 1 represents the titration of free acid in the absence of amino acid. The titration curve for acid + amino acid (curve-2) lies above that of the free acid in the region below a pH of ~ 4.0 indicating association of a proton to the ligand. Above ~7.5 pH, i.e. in the basic region, the titration curve of ligand is well below that of the free acid, indicating the dissociation of proton from the ligand. The difference at lower pH is due to the protonation of the zwitter ionic form of the ligand at the carboxylate group and at higher pH the lowering of the curve relative to that of free acid is due to the ionization of the $-NH_3^+$ group. Therefore the proton association and dissociation processes of the zwitter ionic form of the ligand (XH) are widely separated.

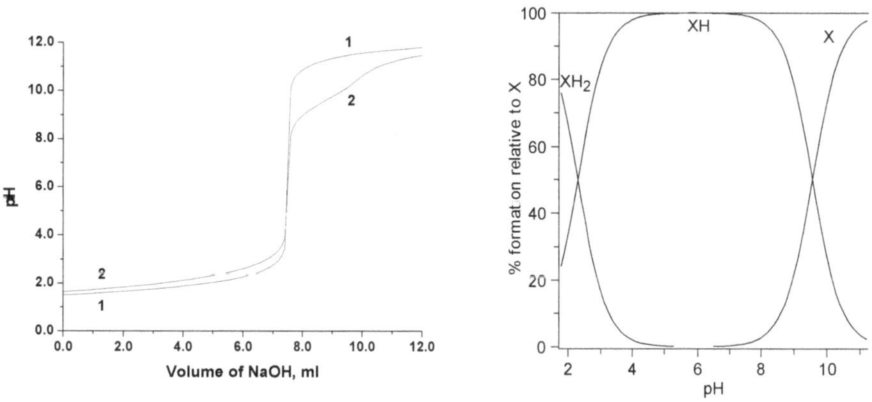

a. 1. Titration curve of free mineral acid
2. Titration curve for acid + Glycine

b. Species distribution diagram

[Glycine] = 0.0100 mol. dm^{-3} [HCl] =0.03099 mol. dm^{-3} [NaOH]= 0.2066 mol. dm^{-3}
Temp.: 30.0 ±0. 1^{0}C Total volume= 50.0 cm^{3} I = 0.1 mol. dm^{-3} NaCl

Figure 3.8: PROTON-LIGAND SYSTEM OF GLYCINE

The protonation equilibria of glycine (XH) can be expressed as,

$$X^- + H^+ \underset{}{\overset{\beta_{011}}{\rightleftharpoons}} XH$$

$$X^- + 2H^+ \underset{}{\overset{\beta_{012}}{\rightleftharpoons}} XH_2^+$$

The best-fit model obtained using Miniquad-75 program for glycine, is shown in Table- 3.3. The IUPAC recommended[14, 15] values for the protonation constants of glycine are 9.60 and 11.97 for $log\ \beta_{011}$ and $log\ \beta_{012}$ respectively at 25.0^{0}C and ionic strength between 0.1 and 0.2M. The observed values are in good agreement with the IUPAC and other literature values[17, 18] after allowing for changes in experimental conditions.

Table 3.3: Best fit chemical model for acid-base equilibria of glycine in aqueous medium Temp. = 30.0 ± 0.1°C and ionic strength, I = 0.1 mol dm^{-3} (NaCl)

Species *Mxh*	$Log\ \beta_{0xh}$ *(SD)*	Literature[14, 15] recommended values At 25.0 ^{0}C	Number of experimental points analysed	Sum of the squares of residuals, U	χ^2
011	09.56 (1)	09.60			
012	11.86 (2)	11.97	84	3.56 X 10^{-8}	6.86

(SD= Standard Deviation in the least significant digit)

The constant $log\ \beta_{011}$ is due to the protonation of the amino group of the most basic form of the ligand, to form a zwitter ion. The magnitude of the protonation constant is low, when compared to the corresponding amine and may be explained as due to the electron withdrawing effect of neighbouring deprotonated carboxylate group. The second protonation constant, $log\ \beta_{012}$ is due to the addition of one more proton to the ligand at the carboxylate group. Again, the relative decrease in magnitude of the constant to that of alkyl carboxylate is due to the strong withdrawing effect of the protonated amino group. The species distribution diagram for glycine is shown in fig. 3.8b. Nearly 75% of the ligand is in biprotonated form at 1.80 pH. The zwitter ion form dominates in the intermediate region i.e. between ~4.0 and ~8.0 pH. The deprotonated form of the ligand (X^-) exists only above 7.5 pH and increases monotonically above this point.

3.3.2 Proton-ligand equilibria of L-Histidine:

Among the amino acids, L-histidine is one of the strongest metal coordinating ligand which plays an important role in the binding of metal ions by proteins. Histidine has three potential metal-binding sites, namely the carboxylate oxygen, the imidazole imido nitrogen and the amino nitrogen. The imidazole nitrogen of histidine residue often provides the primary means by which the metal ions are bound to proteins.

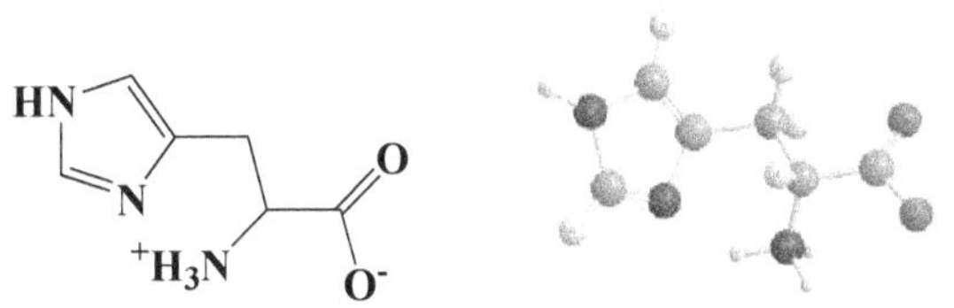

Figure 3.9: L-Histidine

Histidine belongs to a group of amino acids that contain one or more amino groups in the side chain. Because amine groups can accept protons, they are bases and these amino acids are considered as basic amino acids. In solution they can accept protons from water to become positively charged. In histidine in addition to the amino group, it is the double bonded nitrogen atom that accepts the proton and has a pK_a value in the physiological pH range, hence often is the only amino acid seen in biologically active sites when the donation or abstraction of a proton is needed. Structurally, it is possible that histidine (XH) can exist (Figure 3.10) in solution as XH_3^{2+}, XH_2^+, XH and X^-.

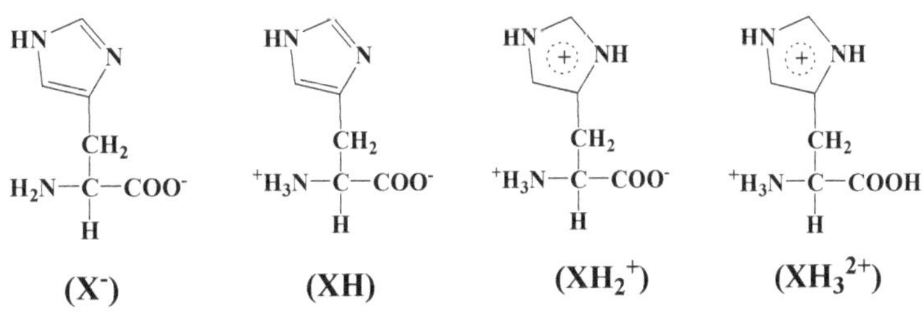

Figure 3.10: Fischer Projections of successive protonated species of L-Histidine

The first centre to protonate in the fully ionized histidinate anion (X^-) is the amino-nitrogen, followed by the pyridine-like imidazole-nitrogen of the side chain and finally the carboxylate group. Since these protonation reactions take place over a widely separated and accessible pH ranges, the formation constants (Fig. 3.11) can be determined comparatively accurately. At higher pH (>14), the pyrrole like proton may also ionize (forming an imidazolate side chain) to give a dianion (X^{2-})[15] which is of course out of the pH region in aqueous solutions.

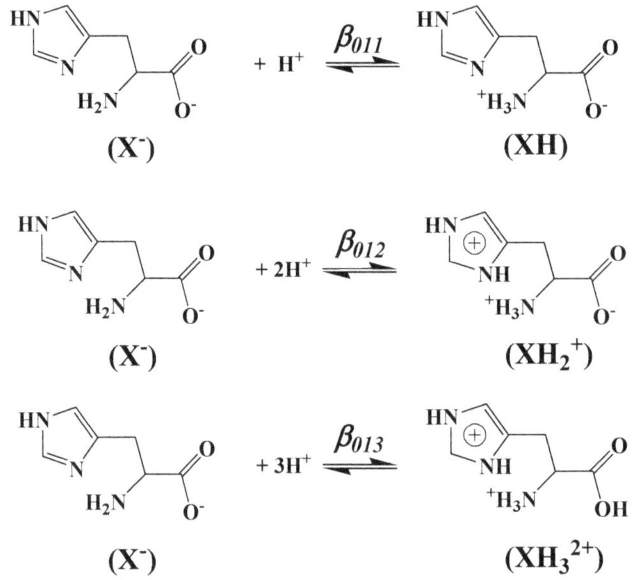

Figure 3.11: PROTON-LIGAND EQUILIBRIA OF L-HISTIDINE

The alkalimetric titration curves obtained, in the presence and absence of histidine are shown in Figure 3.12a. The titration curve for the acid+ ligand (curve 2) is above that of free acid (curve 1) up to a pH of ~ 7.0 indicating the initial association of the proton to the ligand. The wide difference between the curves indicates proton associations at more than one centre. The two buffer regions below ~7.0 pH correspond to the titrations of carboxylic and ring protons. The buffer region above pH ~7.0 indicates the titration of ammonium proton.

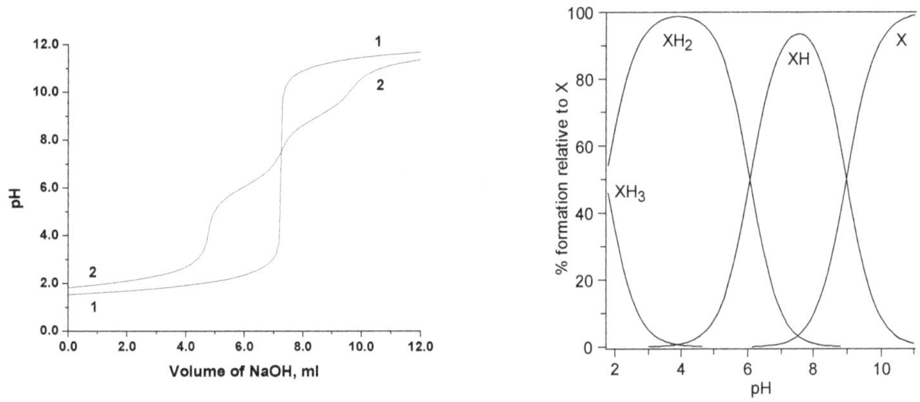

a. 1. Titration curve of free mineral acid
2. Titration curve for acid + Histidine

b. Species distribution diagram

[Histidine] = 0.0100 mol dm^{-3} [HCl] = 0.02944 mol dm^{-3} [NaOH]= 0.2030 $moldm^{-3}$
Temp.: 30.0 ±0. 1^0C Total volume= 50.0 cm^3 I = 0.1 mol dm^{-3} NaCl

Figure 3.12: PROTON-LIGAND SYSTEM OF L-HISTIDINE

The titration curve for the acid+ ligand (curve 2) is above that of free acid (curve 1) up to a pH of ~ 7.0 indicating the initial association of the proton to the ligand. The wide difference between the curves indicates proton associations at more than one centre. The two buffer regions below ~7.0 pH correspond to the titrations of carboxylic and ring protons. The buffer region above pH ~7.0 indicates the titration of ammonium proton.

The titration data of all the experiments with different concentrations of the ligand (0.004, 0.01 and 0.015 mol dm^{-3}) were analysed by the ACBA[12] computer program and the constants obtained were used as the initial estimates for the refinement using the MINIQUAD-75 program[13]. The best-fit chemical model thus obtained along with the statistical paramcters is shown in Table 3.4.

Table 3.4: Best fit chemical model for acido-basic equilibria of L-histidine in aqueous medium. Temp. = 30.0 ± 0.1°C and ionic strength, I = 0.1 mol dm^{-3} (NaCl)

Species *mlh*	Log β_{0lh} (SD)	Number of experimental points analysed	Sum of the squares of residuals, U	χ^2
011	08.95 (1)	102	4.021 X 10^{-8}	23.12
012	15.02 (2)			
013	16.74 (2)			

(SD= Standard Deviation in the least significant digit)

The results are in good agreement with the literature reports (Table 3.5) after allowing for the changes in experimental conditions and calculation methods.

Table 3.5: Some representative literature reports on the protonation constants of Histidine

S.No.	Experimental conditions		Log β_{011}	Log β_{012}	Log β_{013}	Reference
	Temp. ^{0}C	Ionic strength				
1.	37.0	0.10 M ($NaNO_3$)	8.80	14.55	16.65	23
2.	25.0	0.10 M (KCl)	9.11	15.19	16.96	24
3.	25.0	0.10M (KNO_3)	9.16	15.25	17.31	25
4.	25.0	0.10M (KNO_3)	9.12	15.17	16.60	26
5.	25.0	0.10M (KNO_3)	9.12	15.22	16.93	27
6.	25.0	0.10 M (KNO_3)	9.11	15.15	16.92	28
7.	25.0	0.10 M (KCl)	9.09	15.11	16.81	14, 29
8.	25.0	0.10-0.15M (KCl)	9.11	15.16	16.88	15

The species distribution diagram for proton-ligand equilibria of histidine is shown in Figure 3.12b. The fully protonated form XH_3^{2+} exists only below a pH of 4.0. This species lose the carboxylate proton and forms XH_2^+ which is a dominating species between 2 to 6 pH and represents nearly 99% of the ligand at 3.90 pH. Further increase in pH causes neutralization of the side chain proton resulting in the zwitter ionic species XH. The formation of the XH reaches a maximum of 93% of the total ligand around 7.5 pH. Above a pH of 9.0, the major species is the most anionic form of the ligand (X^-) and represents the total ligand concentration around ~11.0 pH.

3.3.3 Proton-ligand equilibria of L-Aspartic acid:

Aspartic acid (2-Aminobutanedioic acid) is an acidic amino acid with two –COOH groups, one on alpha carbon atom and the other on the side chain. It is a nonessential amino acid generally found in proteins and acts as an excitatory neurotransmitter in the central nervous system and also for hormone production and release. Biochemically, it plays an important role in the citric acid cycle.

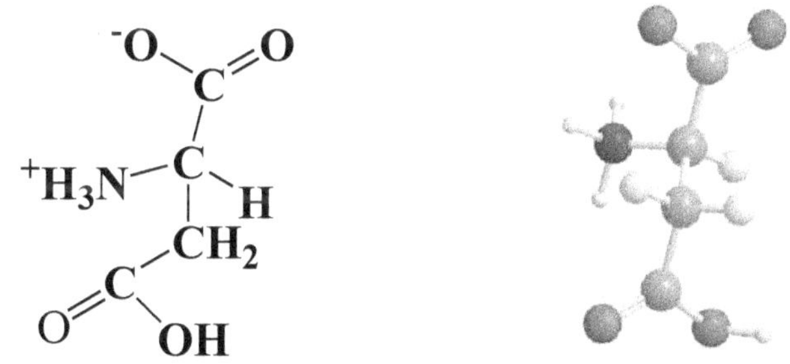

Figure 3.13: L- Aspartic acid (XH_2)

In aqueous solution depending on the pH, L-aspartic acid may exist (Fig. 3.14) in cationic (XH_3^+), neutral zwitter ionic (XH_2) or anionic (XH^- and X^{2-}) forms.

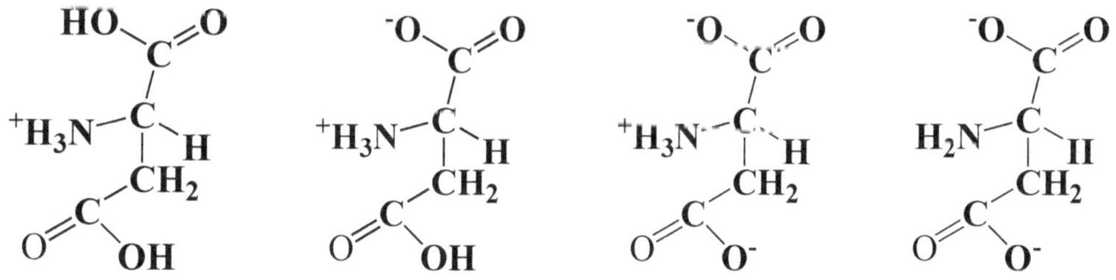

XH_3^+ XH_2 XH^- X^{2-}

Figure 3.14: Successive protonated species of L-Aspartic acid

At and above neutral pH the overall molecule is negatively charged. Due to the presence of negatively charged carboxyl group, it is found almost at the surface of proteins. The charged group can form ionic bond with various metal ions as well as dipole interaction with water which is important concept of solubility of amino acid in water.

The pH-metric titration curves of free acid (curve 1) and acid + ligand (curve 2) are shown in Figure 3.15a.

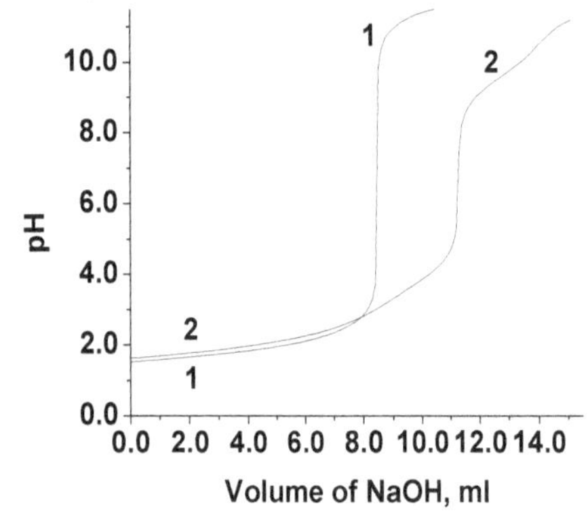

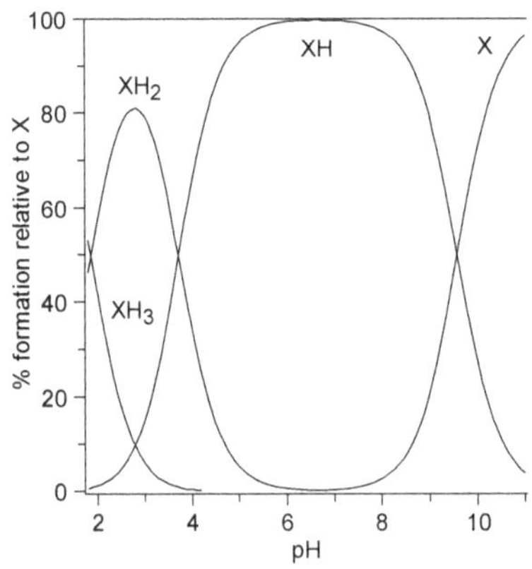

a. 1. Titration curve of free mineral acid
2. Titration curve for acid + Aspartic acid

b. Species distribution diagram

[ASP] = 0.0100 mol dm^{-3} [HCl] = 0.0300 mol dm^{-3} [NaOH]= 0.1773 moldm^{-3}
Temp.: 30.0 ±0. 1^{0}C Total volume= 50.0 cm^{3} I = 0.1 mol dm^{-3} NaCl

Figure 3.15: PROTON-LIGAND SYSTEM OF L-ASPARTIC ACID

The titration curve of the ligand possesses three buffer regions corresponding to the titration of the three protons associated with the cationic (XH_3^+) form of the ligand. The ligand curve is above that of the free acid in the lower pH region indicating proton association to the ligand. The experimental data were subjected to analysis by the Miniquad-75 program[13] and the best-fit chemical model obtained along with statistical parameters is shown in Table 3.6.

The obtained values are in close agreement with the IUPAC recommended values, with due consideration of the differences in experimental conditions. The formation constants obtained represent the equilibria;

Table 3.6: Best fit chemical model for acid-base equilibria of L-aspartic acid in aqueous medium. Temp. = 30.0 ± 0.1°C and ionic strength, $I = 0.1$ mol dm^{-3} (NaCl)

Species *Mlh*	*Log* β_{0lh} *(SD)*	Literature[14] recommended values At 25.0 ^{0}C	Number of experimental points analysed	Sum of the squares of residuals, U	χ^2
011	09.58 (2)	9.62	104	4.28 X 10^{-9}	6.37
012	13.30 (2)	13.32			
013	15.16 (2)	15.26			

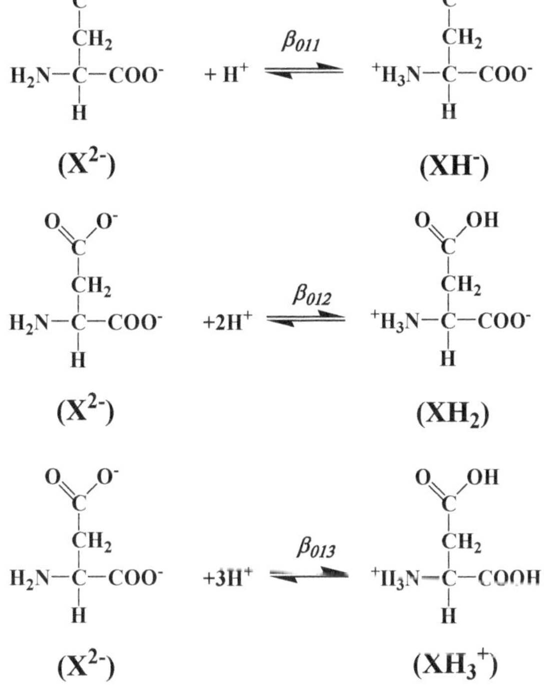

Figure 3.16: Proton-Ligand equilibria of L-ASPARTIC ACID

The formation constant β_{011} is due to the protonation of the amino group of the most anionic form of the ligand. β_{012} is due to the protonation of both amino and carboxylate group in the side chain of the molecule. β_{013} corresponds to the overall formation constants for the complete protonation of the most anionic form of the ligand.

The species distribution diagram indicating the percentage of formation of each species against pH is shown in Figure 3.15 b. The fully protonated form XH_3^+ exists up to a pH of ~4.0. With increase in pH it loses the 'α- carboxylic' proton leading to the formation of g neutral zwitter ion. The maximum extent of formation of XH_2 form is 80.6% at 2.83 pH. This species exists up to ~6.0 pH. The neutral form of the ligand, with increase in pH, loses carboxylic proton of the side chain forming anionic XH^- form of aspartic acid. Nearly 99% of the ligand is in this form between 5.8 to 7.8 pH. Further increase in pH leads to the formation of the most anionic X^{2-} form by the loss of the proton associated to amino group.

3.4 REFERENCES:

1. N.Vandana Jugran, Ashok Kumar Sharma, N. Jeetendra Singh, Veerma Ram, "Biological activities of hydrazide derivatives in the new millennium", *Int. J. Pharm.*, 2 (4) (2012) pp 100-109.
2. R.Narang, B.Narasimhan and B. Sharma, "A review on biological activities and chemical synthesis of hydrazide derivatives", *Curr. Med. Chem.*, 19(4) (2012) pp 569-612.
3. B.K. Kaymakçioğlu, E. E. Oruç-Emre , U. Seda and A. Dimoglo "Synthesis and characterization of novel hydrazide-hydrazones and the study of their structure-antituberculosis activity", *Eur. J. Med. Chem.*, 41(11)(2006) pp 1253-1261.
4. G. Verma, A. Marella, Md. Shaquiquzzaman, M. Akhtar, Md. Rahmat Ali and Md. Mumtaz Alam, "A review exploring biological activities of hydrazones", *J Pharm Bioallied Sci.*, 6(2) (2014) pp 69-80.
5. S. Rollas and Ş. Güniz Küçükgüzel, "Review- Biological activities of hydrazone derivatives", *Molecules,* 12(2007) pp 1910-1939.
6. H. M. Irving and H. S. Rossotti, "Methods for Computing Successive Stability Constants from Experimental Formation Curves", *J. Chem. Soc.* (1953) pp 3397–3405.
7. H. M. Irving and H. S. Rossotti "The Calculation of Formation Curves of Metal Complexes from pH-Titration Curves in Mixed Solvents", *J. Chem. Soc.* (1954) pp 2904–2910.
8. G. Gran, *Analyst,* 77 (1952) p 661.
9. G. Gran, Acta *Chem. Scand.,* 4 (1950) p 559.
10. A.Ravindra Babu, J. S. V. M. Lingeswara Rao, D. Murali Krishna, and R. Sambasiva Rao, *Anal. Chim. Acta,* 306(2-3) (1995) pp 297-300.
11. G.V. Afanas'eva, T. I. Bychkova, V. G. Shtyrlin, A. R. Shakirova, and A. V. Zakharov, *Russ. J. Gen. Chem.*, 76(5) (2006) pp757-765.
12. G. Arena, E. Rizzarelli, S. Sammartano and C. Rigano. *Talanta.*, 26 (1979) p1
13. P. Gans, A. Sabatini and A. Vacca., *Inorg. Chim. Acta.*, 18 (1976) p237.
14. A.E. Martell and R.M. Smith, "Critical stability constants Volumes 1 to 5", Plenum Press, NY and London, (1974-1982): Volume 1: Amino acids (1974), Volume 2: Amines (1975), Volume 3: Other Ligands (1977), Volume 4:

Inorganic Complexes (1976), Volume 5: First Supplement, (1982) and Volume 6: Second Supplement (1989).

15. L.D. Pettit, "Critical survey of formation constants of Histidine Phenylalanine, Tyrosine, L-Dopa and Tryptophan", IUPAC, *Pure & Appl. Chem.,* 56(2) (1984) pp 247-292.
16. T. Kiss, I. Sovago and A. Gergely, "Critical survey of stability constants of complexes of Glycine", IUPAC, *Pure App. Chem.,* 63(4) (1993) pp 597-638.
17. I. Sovago, T. Kiss and A. Gergely, "Critical survey of the stability constants of complexes of aliphatic amino acids", IUPAC, *Pure App. Chem.,* 65(5) (1993) pp 1029-1080.
18. G. Berthon, "The stability constants of metal complexes of amino acids with polar side chains", IUPAC, *Pure App. Chem.,* 67(7) (1995) pp 1117-1240.
19. O. Yamauchi and A. Odani, "Stability constants of metal complexes of amino acids with charged side chains- Part-I: Positively charged side chains", IUPAC, *Pure App. Chem.,* 68(2) (1996) pp 469-496.
20. R.F. Criscent, G.F.Laniak and R.L. Erikson, "Propagation of uncertainty through geochemical code calculations", *Geochim. Cosmochim. Acta,* 60 (1996) pp 3551-3568.
21. C.Ekberg and I. Lunden Burro, "Uncertainty analysis for some actinides under groundwater conditions", *J. Stat. Comput. Simul.,* 57(1997) pp 271-284.
22. F.H. Denison and J. Granier-LaPace, "The effect of database parameter uncertainty on uranium (IV) equilibrium calculations", *Geochim. Cosmochim. Acta,* 69(2005) pp 2183-2191.
23. Reda A. Ammar, Nawal A. Alarfaj and Maha F. El-Tohamy, "Potentiometric Study of 1, 2-Diphenylethylenediamine Palladium (II) Complex with Some Selected Amino Acids", *Int. J. Electrochem. Sci.,* 7 (2012) pp 1512 – 1521.
24. Y. Altun *and* F. Koseoglu, "Stability of Copper(II), Nickel(II) and Zinc(II) Binary and Ternary Complexes of Histidine, Histamine and Glycine in Aqueous Solution", *J. Solution Chem.,* 34 (2) (2005) pp.213-231.
25. M. J. Bojczuk, P. Kaczmarek, W. Bal and K. S. Kasprzak, "Determination of the stability constants and oxidation susceptibility of nickel(II) complexes with 2′-deoxyguanosine 5′-triphosphate and L-histidine", *J. Inorg. Biochem.* 99 (2005) p 737-746.

26. Piotr Kaczmarek, Wojciech Szczepanik and Małgorzata Jeżowska-Bojczuk, *Dalton Trans.*, (2005) pp 3653-3657.
27. Leslie D. Pettit and John L. M. Swash, *Dalton Trans.*, (1976) 588-594.
28. H. C. Freeman and R. P. Martin, *J. Biol. Chem.*, 244 (1969) p 4823.
29. B. L. Mickel and A. C. Andrews, *J. Am. Chem. Soc.* 77 (1955) p 1955.

CHAPTER- 4

CHEMICAL MODELLING STUDIES ON THE BINARY METAL ION-LIGAND SYSTEMS OF SUCCINIC AND ADIPIC ACID DIHYDRAZIDES AND AMINO ACIDS; GLYCINE, HISTIDINE AND ASPARTIC ACID

Many biological processes in some manner involve the use of metal complexes. These complexes are implicated in the storage and transport of metal ions and of active substances through membranes. Metal ions like Mg^{2+}, Ca^{2+}, Fe^{2+}, Zn^{2+}, Cu^{2+} and Mn^{2+} are essential and required for triggering a number of reactions in the human body. Magnesium and calcium are most abundant intracellular cations in the human body that work synergistically on not only the bones and nervous system but also on the muscles. Calcium builds bones and teeth and also helps to relieve from muscle cramps. Magnesium is the most abundant metal ion in the cells. The active form of RNA is dependent on the concentration of magnesium. The role of magnesium as a catalyst or activator in the production of ATP that supplies energy to cells is well-known.On the other side there are some metal ions which are toxic to the humanbeings. Lead is a well-known insidious poison. Mercury is poisonous even at very low levels and is deceptive. Often the symptoms are misleading and attributed to other causes. Cadmium replaces metal ions in essential biological reactions and is therefore toxic. Cadmium induced carcinogenesis may be antagonized by administering Mg^{2+} and Ca^{2+}. Biological systems in organisms employ homeostatic strategies for essential metals, and protective strategies for toxic metals at the cellular level. Most of these mechanisms involve the formation of a metal ion complex with the biologically occurring ligands such as amino acids and proteins. The ability of certain ligands to bind and release metal ions in some processes, and to oxidize and reduce in other processes makes them important in biological systems. Various mechanisms protecting against metal toxicity exist among different species, with several acting by accumulating metals in inert granules that either are excreted or retained for the lifetime of the organism. Other strategies involve complexing with stable metal-chelating proteins[1] such as MTs (cysteine rich,low molecular weight metallothionein proteins) and MT-like proteins that occur in eukaryotes (invertebrates, vertebrates and plants). But toxic metal ions bound to cellular constituents, DNA, iron channels and enzymes causes potential harm. The safest and simplest way to excrete toxic metal ions is in the form of simple or mixed ligand complexes using exogenous non-toxic ligands.Therefore, biochemically, there is a need of non-toxic polytopic ligands that are efficient at sequestering toxic metal ions with high atom efficiency.But, when external complexing agents in the form of drugs or pollutants are introduced into the biological system, they may interact with the essential metal ions. As a consequence, the biologically important metal ions may be depleted from the system, leading to various deficiency syndromes that are to be cured by the metal ion administration. The selected ligand should therefore form strong complexes with toxic and weak complexes with essential metal ions.

Polytopic ligands that contain multiple binding sites in their structures, enabling the formation of multi-nuclear complexes are of recent interest[2] as they allow the creation of well-ordered extended complexes containing different cations. They are usually N, P, O, and S containing organic molecules, and have been used in various applications such as monitoring guest exchange and the creation of metal organic frameworks. The multi-centred nature of these ligands allows other interactions outside the coordinate such as hydrogen or halogen bonding. The self-assembly processes of metal complexes of polytopic ligands into highly organized architectures (racks, ladders, grids, helicates, cages etc.) represent one of the most important topics in supramolecular chemistry. The various topologies of the metal arrays generate interesting optical, redox, magnetic or catalytic properties with potential applications in nanotechnology. Some possess useful properties, for instance antimicrobial/ antifungal activity and capacity for DNA binding. These ligands are also used for selective extractions of cations and anions. Polytopic ligands may also find application as non-toxic efficient sequestering agents of metal ions with high atom efficiency. These ligands can accommodate metal ions in different coordination pockets leading to the formation of multinuclear complexes. The formation of multinuclear species has special significance. The presence of more than one metal ion in the same species linked by small units of the ligand leads to several interesting and important applications. They possess unusual magnetic[3] and electrical properties and have been used as molecular switches[4], monitoring guest exchange and to mimic metalloproteins for understanding the structure- reactivity relationships[5]. The metal centres are found to act synergistically in catalysing reactions[6, 7].

Dihydrazides[8] are found to act as ditopic ligands that can accommodate two metal ions in different coordination pockets. Dihydrazides are capable of forming symmetric and asymmetric bimetallic complexes in addition to mono-nuclear species. *In vitro* and *in vivo* tests[9]proved dihydrazides to be non-genotoxic. Food and Drug Administration (FDA) approved[10] the use of dihydrazides as cross linkers for coatings on plastics used for food package that are in indirect food contact. Dihydrazides and their derivatives are found to be biologically active[11-15]. These ligands possess a large number of potential donor atoms and hence display versatile behaviour in metal coordination. The mode of coordination depends on the nature of the central metal ion, conformational flexibility of the ligand and also on the presence of other species capable to compete for coordination pockets. The role of dihydrazides as ditopic ligands in sequestering heavy metal ions is therefore, worth investigating. This involves a chemical speciation study of dihydrazide-metal ion systems in solution.

Speciation study is a well-known tool for the solution chemists to determine the nature of species formed by the metal ions with exogenous or biological ligands to access their beneficial or toxic effects on the biological systems.

When a metal ion is in contact with a ligand or several ligands as in biological systems, there is a chance of formation of a number of species depending on their relative concentrations and other environmental conditions. The activity of a metal ion or a ligand in a biological system depends strongly on the actual form of the species in which it exists but not on the total concentration. Therefore, chemical speciation study is a prerequisite to understand the bioavailability, toxicity, distribution, fate and transport of various species. It gives the required information regarding the nature and extent of formation of various species as a function of pH. Hence, in this chapter the results of the speciation study of the binary systems of ditopic ligands, succinic acid dihydrazide (SADH) and adipic acid dihydrazide (AADH) with Mg^{2+}, Ca^{2+}, Pb^{2+}, Hg^{2+} and Cd^{2+}in aqueous medium are included. These metal ions were selected as they are of great biological concern either as essential and physiologically desirable or toxic and require excretion. An extensive chemical speciation study of the amino acid- metal ion binary systems of Glycine, L-Histidine and L-Aspartic acid, under the same experimental conditions is also included. This is required as these amino acids were used as secondary ligands in the ternary systems.

Calvin-Wilson titration technique[16-19] as described in Chapter-2 of the thesis was employed for the study of the complex equilibria of the ligands. The data acquisition procedure involved titration of a mixture of hydrochloric acid/ nitric acid(0.02- 0.05 mole dm^{-3}), metal ion (~5.0 to 20.0 mmole dm^{-3}) and dihydrazide or amino acid (~10.0 mmole dm^{-3}) with standard sodium hydroxide solution (~0.2mole dm^{-3}). The ionic strength in a total volume of 50.0 cm^3 was adjusted to 0.1 mole dm^{-3} by the addition of sodium chloride/ nitrate solution. The temperature of the system was maintained at 30.0 ± 0.1^{0}C, by circulating thermostatted water through the annular space of the titration vessel. The metal to ligand molar concentration ratio was varied (1:1, 1:2 and 2:1) in different experiments. The reproducibility of the acquired data was checked by performing two to three independent titrations for each system. The number of data points used in the calculation of the stability constants varied between 90 to 160 depending on the metal ion and the ligand. In some of the titrations, the upper pH limit of accepting data for analysis was determined by the appearance of opalescence leading to precipitation indicated by a downward drift of the pH-meter dial readings.

In a system containing a metal ion and a ligand forming 'n' complexes, the formation constant of a complex can be represented as,

$$\beta_{mlh} = \frac{[M_m L_l H_h]}{[M]_i^m . [L]_i^l . [H^+]_i^h} \quad ......(4.1)$$

Where $[M]_{l,}[L]_i$ and $[H]_i$ are the free concentrations of metal, ligand and hydrogen ion respectively at i^{th} experimental point. Different species in solution possess different values of stoichiometric coefficients *m, l* and *h.* Positive value of h indicates protonated species and a negative value indicates either deprotonated or hydroxylated species. The potentiometric titration data obtained was subjected to analysis by Miniquad-75 program[20]. The stoichiometry and stability constants of the species formed in solution were determined by examining various chemically plausible composition models for the systems studied. The best-fit models were selected as described in Chapter-2, on the basis of U (sum of the squares of residuals in mass balance equations), standard deviations in formation constants and other statistics like χ^2 test which tests the distribution of errors against a normal one. Species distribution diagrams for all the systems under study were generated using HYSS[21] program.

4.1 SPECIATION STUDIES OFDIHYDRAZIDE-METALION BINARY SYSTEMS:

Several reports[8, 22-35]were found in the literature on metal complexes of dihydrazides. Most of these studies involve synthesis and structural elucidation of the complexes by elemental analyses, magnetic moments, molar conductance, and electronic, ESR, IR, and X-ray diffraction studies. Characterization of the complexes is often specific to an isolated/ precipitated single species and may not be relevant to the solution behaviour of the compound wherein a number of species coexist. Further, Isolation or precipitation of solid complexes from solution requires mixing of stoichiometric concentration ratios of metal and ligand in a suitable solvent often followed by various physical methods of precipitation, including refluxing, freezing, evaporating the solvent, etc. If the conditions are not selected carefully this may lead to a precipitation of a mixture of species. The physical methods of precipitation employed may even change the nature of the species. On the other hand chemical speciation study in solution phase gives the information regarding all the species of various configurations existing in solution under selected experimental conditions.

Literature reports on the metal–ligand complex formation equilibria of dihydrazidesin solution were, however, scanty. Only a few reports[36-45] on the metal-ligand equilibria of SADH and AADH in solution phase were found in the literature. No reports were found on the complexing tendencies of SADH and AADH in solution towards Mg^{2+}, Ca^{2+}, Pb^{2+}, Hg^{2+} and Cd^{2+}.

Supp et al.[36-38], in a polarographic study on cadmium and zinc complexes of succinic acid dihydrazide observed that there was no drop in pH of the dihydrazide solutions when titrated with a metal ion solution. This indicates that the neutral form of dihydrazide participates in complexation as there is no release of protons. Plots of half-wave potential gave curved lines, indicating the formation of successive complexes. Formation constants for Cd^{2+} and Zn^{2+} complexes were reported. Zinc complexes were found to be more stable compared to those of cadmium.

Chemometric investigation on the acid-base and binary adipic acid dihydrazide (L)- M^{2+} systems (M^{2+}= Ni^{2+}, Mn^{2+} and Zn^{2+})was carried out by Sambasiva Rao et al.[39-42] in water-dimethylformamide and water-dioxane media. The best-fit models indicate the formation of MLH, ML. ML_2H and ML_2type of species. The formation constants and their variation with percentage of co-solvent were reported.

Afanaseva et al.[43] studied the solvation and complexation of adipic acid dihydrazide (L) with Cu^{2+}, Ni^{2+} and Co^{2+} in aqueous and aqueous-ethanol mixtures by spectrophotometric methods. The formation constants of the species MLH, ML and M_2L (M= Cu^{2+}, Ni^{2+}, Co^{2+}) were reported. The ligand was found to act as a bidentate in MLH and ML and tetradentate in the M_2L type of complexes.

Satyanarayana et al.[44-45] investigated the interaction of succinic and malonic acid dihydrazides with Mn^{2+}, Co^{2+}, Ni^{2+}, Cu^{2+} and Zn^{2+} in aqueous medium by potentiometric method. Both the ligands were found to act as ditopic, leading to the formation of mono-nuclear and homo-binuclear species in different protonated, unprotonated and deprotonated forms.

Magdalena et al.[46]determined the protonation constants and formation constants of the Cu(II) complexes of oxalodihydrazide, acethydrazide and formic hydrazide in aqueous solution using potentiometric and spectrophotometric methods. Acetylhydrazide (L) exhibited the formation of CuLH, CuL_2H_2, CuL_2H and CuL_3H_3 species. Formic acid hydrazide (L), showed the formation of CuLH and CuL_2H_2 species, while oxalic acid dihydrazide (L) formed only $CuLH_2$ species. In the case of oxalic acid dihydrazide the study was hindered due to precipitation at low pH,i.e around 2.5-3.5 pH.

Svanidze et al.[47] spectrophotometrically determined the formation constants, pK_1 and pK_2 of Co^{2+} and Ni^{2+} complexes of Succinic, Malonic and Glutaric acid dihydrazides. The pK values are found to be in the range 1.5 to 2.0.

Chemical speciation studyof complex equilibria in aqueous systems using glass electrode as a probe in the potentiometric method of data acquisition involves the detection of the activity of the free hydronium ion that is in equilibrium with different forms of ligand and metal complexes. The dihydrazides of Succinic and Adipic acids contain two hydrazide groups separated by 2 and 4 units of -CH_2-groups respectively (Fig. 4.1). Each hydrazide group is capable of bonding through both carbonyl and terminal $-NH_2$ groups. At lower pH both the amino groups are protonated. Therefore, as discussed in Chapter 2 of the thesis, depending on the pH of the solutions, both SADH (L) and AADH (L) exist in biprotonated (LH_2^{2+}), mono-protonated (LH^+) and unprotonated neutral (L) species. Hydrazides are also prone to lose enolic protons at higher pH leading to the formation of LH_{-1} and LH_{-2} type of species. Metal ion bonding to the dihydrazide leads to release of protons from the protonated terminal $-NH_2$ groups. Metal ion promoted deprotonation of the ligand may also occur at higher pH.

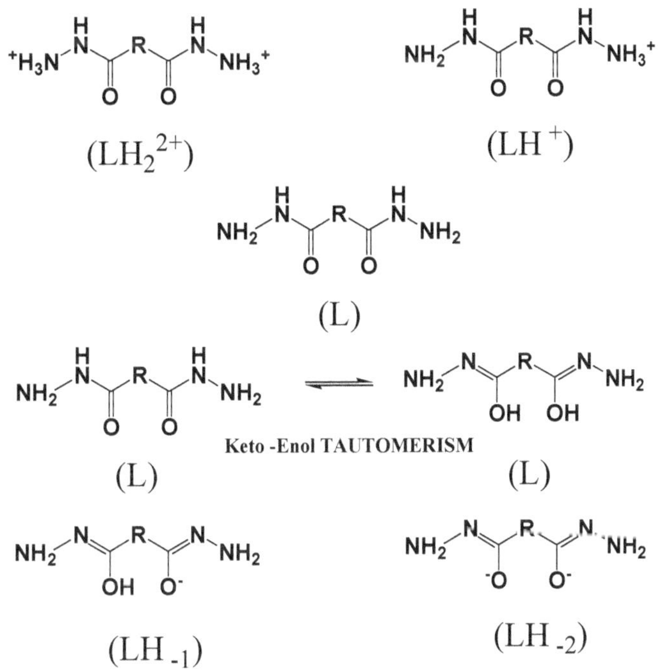

Figure 4.1: Protonated, unprotonated and deprotonated forms of dihydrazide
R= $\mathbf{(CH_2)_2}$ for Succinic acid dihydrazide and $\mathbf{(CH_2)_4}$ for Adipic acid dihydrazide

Therefore, depending on the relative molar concentrations of metal ion and dihydrazide, there is a chance of formation of several species like MLH, ML, MLH_{-1}, MLH_{-2} (for 1:1metal to ligand); ML_2H_2, ML_2H, ML_2, $ML_2H_{-n\ (n=1-4)}$ (for 1:2 metal to ligand) and M_2L, M_2LH_{-1} and M_2LH_{-2} (for 2:1 metal to ligand).Therefore, the various chemical speciation models selected for refinement using the Miniquad-75 program should contain all the above plausible species.

4.1.1 Succinic Acid Dihydrazide (SADH) - Metal ion systems:

The experimental data acquired for metal ion- SADH systems of 1:1, 1:2 and 2:1 metal to ligandmolar concentration ratios were first subjected to analysis by classical procedures[18, 19] to get the formation constants of simple mono-nuclear complexes. The stability constants of the simple complexes thus obtained were used to simulate the primary data using the computer program SOPHD[48] developed in our laboratory. The experimental and simulated titration curves were plotted together (Figs. 4.2a to 4.16a) to determine whether or not these species alone satisfy the experimental data. The difference between the two curves indicates inadequacy of the proposed model. Keeping in view of the position and extent of deviation between simulated and experimental curves suitable chemically plausible models including protonated and deprotonated species were prepared and subjected to refinement bythe Miniquad-75 program[20]. The stability constants obtained from classical procedures were taken as the initial estimates for simple complexes. The formation constant estimates for protonated and deprotonated species were calculated using the stability constants of simple complexes and the experimentally determined protonation/ deprotonation constants of the ligand SADH. As the metal ions are susceptible to hydrolysis, the formation constants of the corresponding hydroxylated species were also included in the models. Initial estimates of the hydrolysis constants were obtained from the literature reports[49-51].

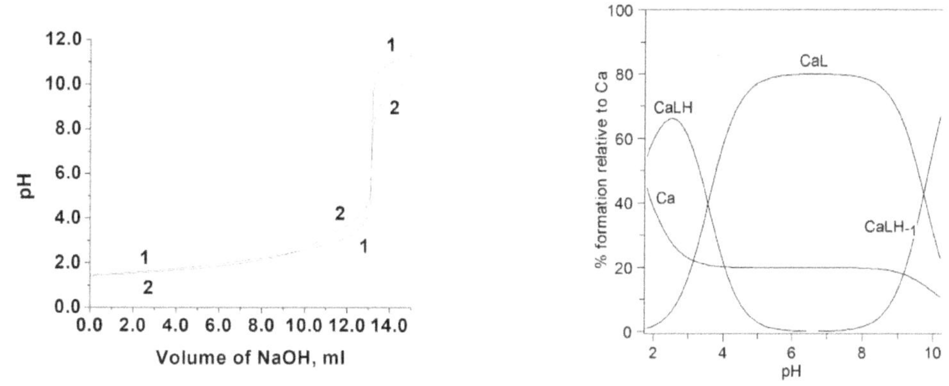

a. 1. Simulated titration curve
2. Experimental titration curve

b. Species distribution diagram

[SADH]= 0.01032mol dm^{-3} [Ca(II)] = 0.0100mol dm^{-3}

[HCl] = 0.05480 mol dm^{-3} [NaOH] = 0.2083 mol dm^{-3}

Total Volume= 50.0 cm^3 Temp= 30.0 ± 0.1°C I = 0.1 mol dm^{-3} NaCl

Figure 4.2: Ca (II) - SADH (L) SYSTEM (1:1)

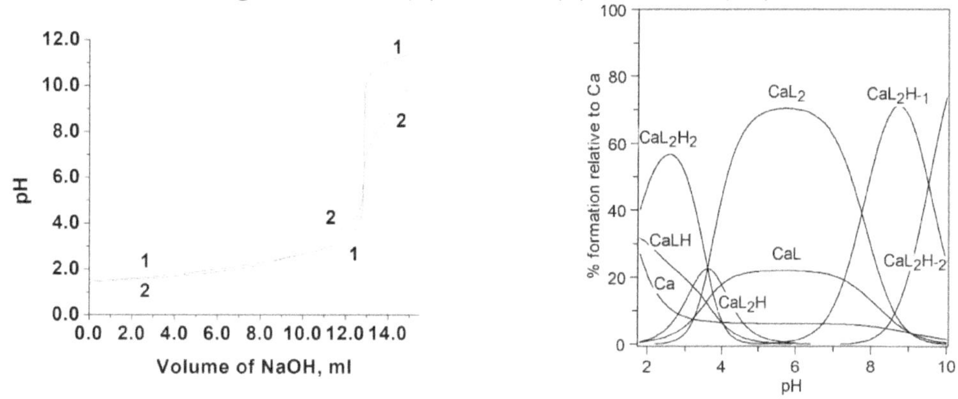

a. 1. Simulated titration curve
2. Experimental titration curve

b. Species distribution diagram

[SADH]= 0.01032 mol dm^{-3} [Ca(II)] = 0.00498 mol dm^{-3}

[HCl] = 0.05344 mol dm^{-3} [NaOH] = 0.2081 mol dm^{-3}

Total Volume= 50.0 cm^3 Temp= 30.0 ± 0.1°C I = 0.1 mol dm^{-3} NaCl

Figure 4.3: Ca (II) - SADH (L) SYSTEM (1:2)

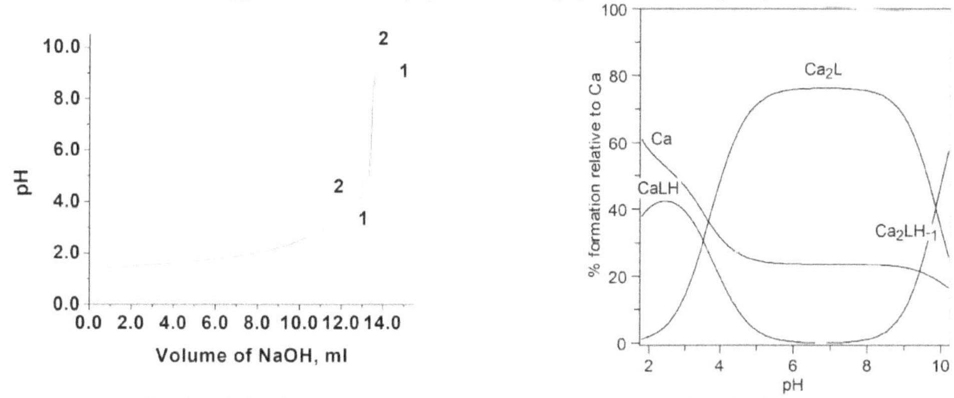

a. 1. Simulated titration curve
2. Experimental titration curve

b. Species distribution diagram

[SADH]= 0.01032 mol dm^{-3} [Ca(II)]= 0.01994 mol dm^{-3}

[HCl] = 0.05591 mol dm^{-3} [NaOH] = 0.2083 mol dm^{-3}

Total Volume= 50.0 cm^3 Temp= 30.0 ± 0.1°C I = 0.1 mol dm^{-3} NaCl

Figure 4.4: Ca (II) - SADH (L) SYSTEM (2:1)

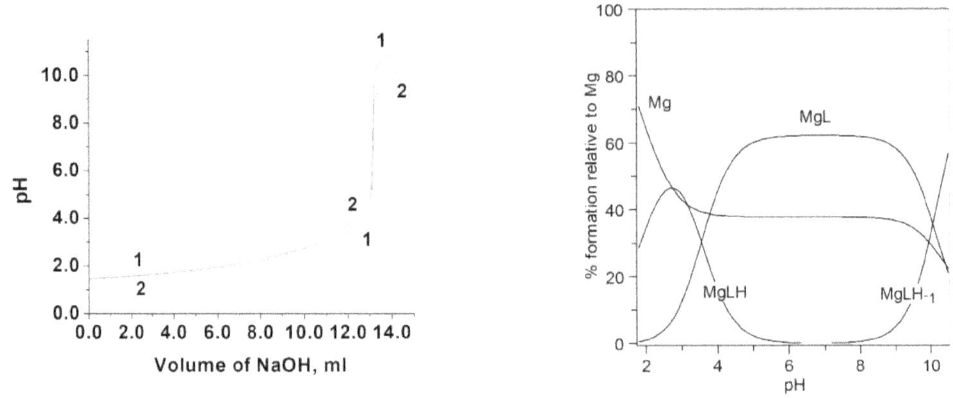

a. 1. Simulated titration curve
2. Experimental titration curve

b. Species distribution diagram

[SADH]= 0.01032 mol dm^{-3} [Mg(II)]= 0.01000 mol dm^{-3}

[HCl] = 0.05469 mol dm^{-3} [NaOH] = 0.2083 mol dm^{-3}

Total Volume= 50.0 cm^3 Temp= 30.0 ± 0.1^{0}C I = 0.1 mol dm^{-3} NaCl

Figure 4.5: Mg (II) - SADH (L) SYSTEM (1:1)

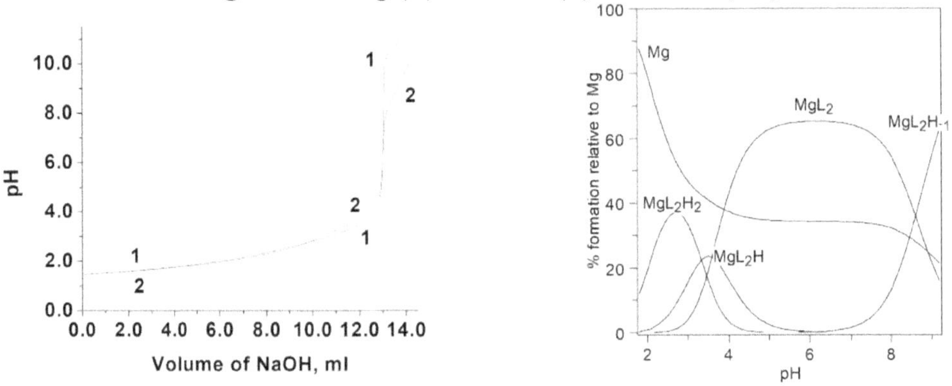

a. 1. Simulated titration curve
2. Experimental titration curve

b. Species distribution diagram

[SADH]= 0.01032 mol dm^{-3} [Mg(II)]= 0.0050 mol dm^{-3}

[HCl] = 0.05418 mol dm^{-3} [NaOH] = 0.2083 mol dm^{-3}

Total Volume= 50.0 cm^3 Temp= 30.0 ± 0.1^{0}C I = 0.1 mol dm^{-3} NaCl

Figure 4.6: Mg (II) - SADH (L) SYSTEM (1:2)

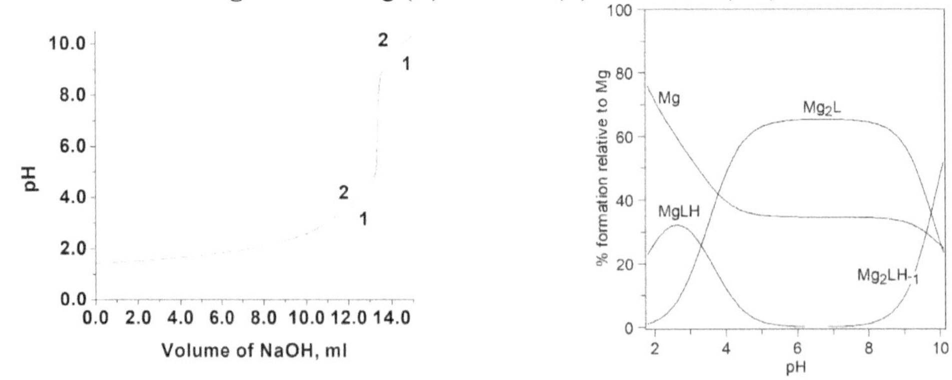

a. 1. Simulated titration curve
2. Experimental titration curve

b. Species distribution diagram

[SADH]= 0.01032 mol dm^{-3} [Mg(II)]= 0.01999 mol dm^{-3}

[HCl] = 0.05571 mol dm^{-3} [NaOH] = 0.2083 mol dm^{-3}

Total Volume= 50.0 cm^3 Temp= 30.0 ± 0.1^{0}C I = 0.1 mol dm^{-3} NaCl

Figure 4.7: Mg (II) - SADH (L) SYSTEM (2:1)

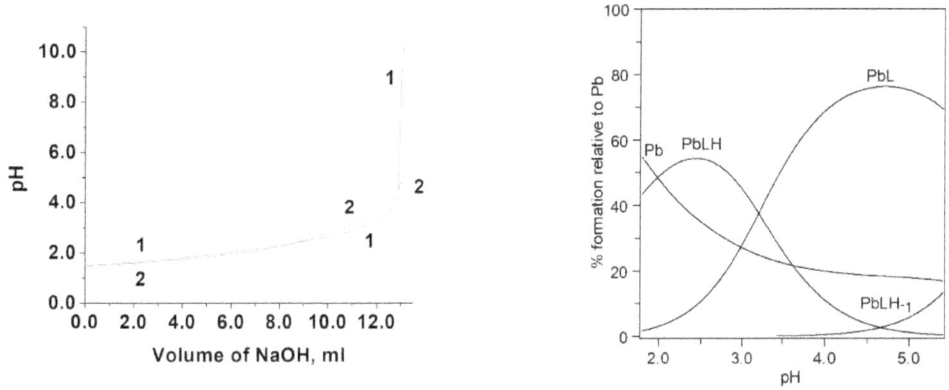

a. 1. Simulated titration curve
2. Experimental titration curve

b. Species distribution diagram

[SADH]= 0.01104 mol dm^{-3} [Pb (II)]= 0.01001 mol dm^{-3}

[HNO_3] = 0.05239 mol dm^{-3} [NaOH] = 0.2016 mol dm^{-3}

Total Volume= 50.0 cm^3 Temp= 30.0 ± 0.1^{0}C I = 0.1 mol $dm^{-3}$$NaNO_3$

Figure 4.8: Pb (II) – SADH (L) SYSTEM (1:1)

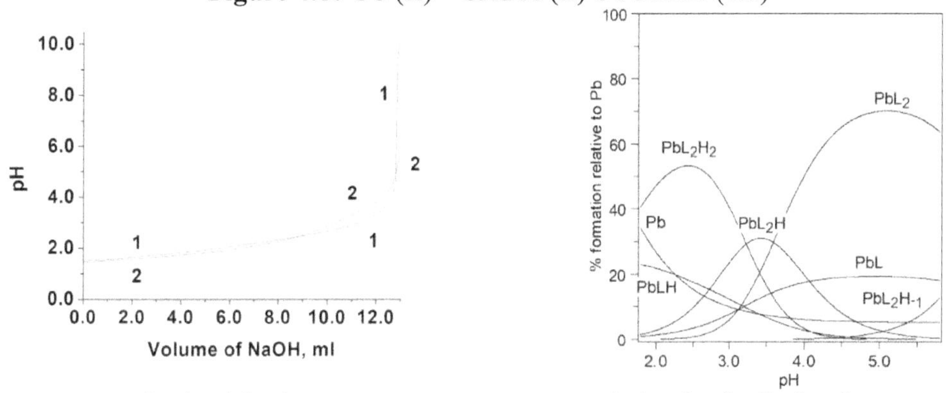

a. 1. Simulated titration curve
2. Experimental titration curve

b. Species distribution diagram

[SADH]= 0.01104 mol dm^{-3} [Pb (II)]= 0.00499 mol dm^{-3}

[HNO_3]= 0.05187 mol dm^{-3} [NaOH] =0.2016 mol dm^{-3}

Total Volume= 50.0 cm^3 Temp= 30.0 ± 0.1^{0}C I = 0.1 mol $dm^{-3}$$NaNO_3$

Figure 4.9: Pb (II) - SADH (L) SYSTEM (1:2)

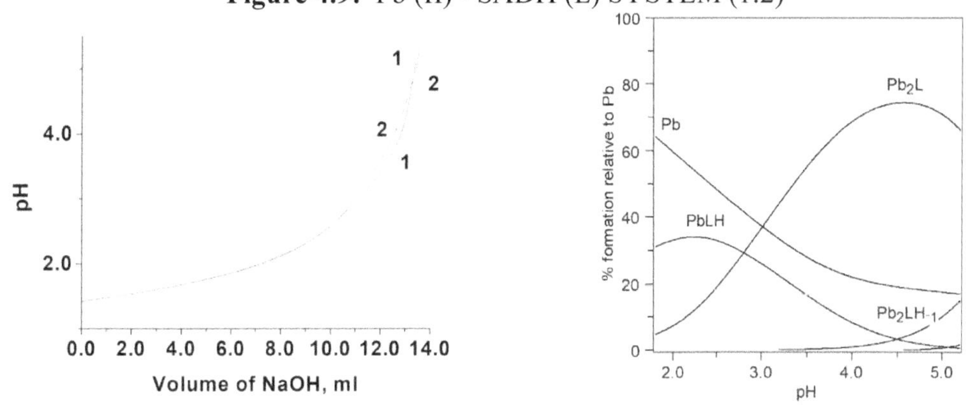

a. 1. Simulated titration curve
2. Experimental titration curve

b. Species distribution diagram

[SADH]= 0.01104 mol dm^{-3} [Pb(II)]= 0.02001 mol dm^{-3}

[HNO_3]= 0.05341 mol dm^{-3} [NaOH] = 0.2016 mol dm^{-3}

Total Volume= 50.0 cm^3 Temp= 30.0 ± 0.1^{0}C I = 0.1 mol $dm^{-3}$$NaNO_3$

Figure 4.10: Pb (II) - SADH (L) SYSTEM (2:1)

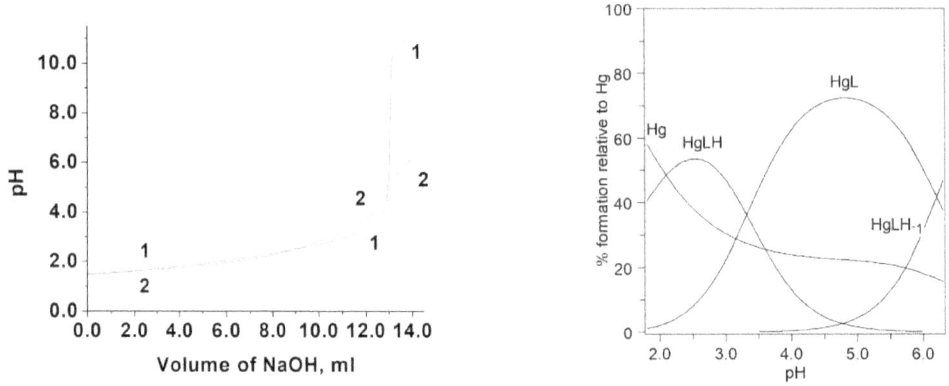

a. 1. Simulated titration curve b. Species distribution diagram
2. Experimental titration curve

[SADH]= 0.01104 mol dm^{-3} [Hg(II)] = 0.01010 mol dm^{-3}
[HCl] = 0.05246 mol dm^{-3} [NaOH] = 0.2016 mol dm^{-3}
Total Volume= 50.0 cm^3 Temp= 30.0 ± 0.1^0C I = 0.1 mol dm^{-3} NaCl

Figure 4.11: Hg (II) - SADH (L) SYSTEM (1:1)

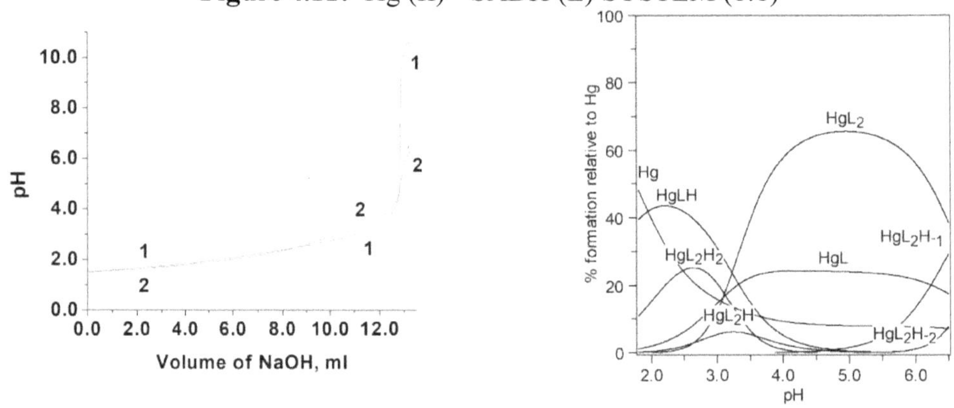

a. 1. Simulated titration curve b. Species distribution diagram
2. Experimental titration curve

[SADH]= 0.01104 mol dm^{-3} [Hg (II)]= 0.00500 mol dm^{-3}
[HCl] = 0.05191 mol dm^{-3} [NaOH] = 0.2016 mol dm^{-3}
Total Volume= 50.0 cm^3 Temp= 30.0 ± 0.1^0C I = 0.1 mol dm^{-3} NaCl

Figure 4.12: Hg (II) - SADH (L) SYSTEM (1:2)

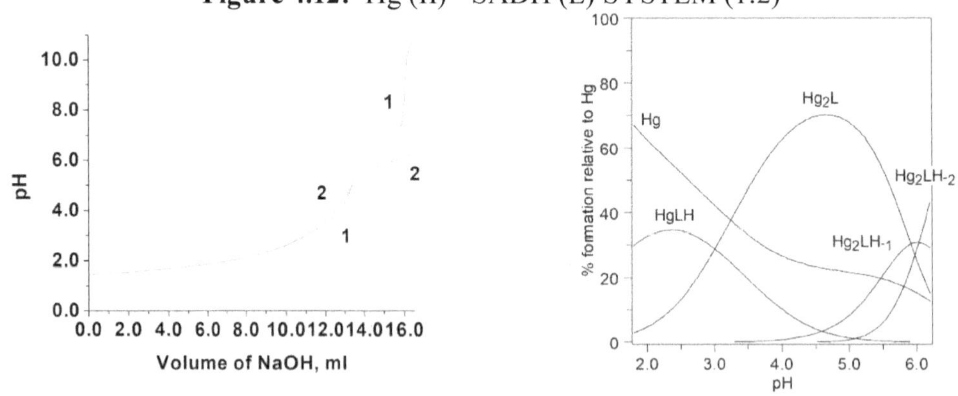

a. 1. Simulated titration curve b. Species distribution diagram
2. Experimental titration curve

[SADH]= 0.01104 mol dm^{-3} [Hg(II)]= 0.02000 mol dm^{-3}
[HCl] = 0.05354 mol dm^{-3} [NaOH] = 0.2016 mol dm^{-3}
Total Volume= 50.0 cm^3 Temp= 30.0 ± 0.1^0C I = 0.1 mol dm^{-3} NaCl

Figure 4.13: Hg (II) - SADH (L) SYSTEM (2:1)

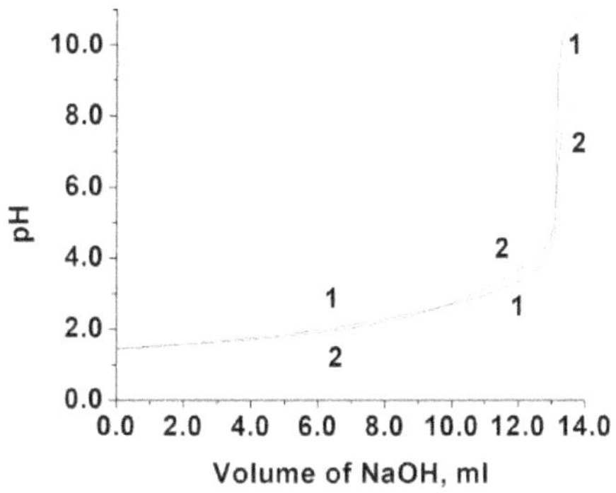

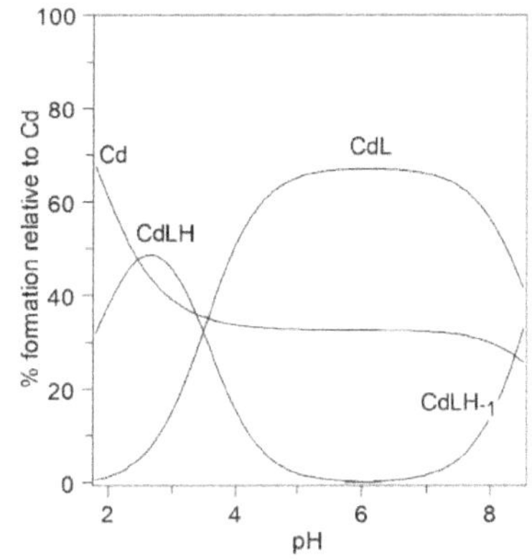

a. 1. Simulated titration curve
2. Experimental titration curve

b. Species distribution diagram

[SADH]= 0.01032 mol dm^{-3}
[HCl] = 0.05492 mol dm^{-3}
[Cd (II)]= 0.01000 mol dm^{-3}
[NaOH] = 0.2083 mol dm^{-3}
Total Volume= 50.0 cm^3 Temp= 30.0 ± 0.1^{0}C I = 0.1 mol dm^{-3} NaCl

Figure 4.14: Cd (II) - SADH (L) SYSTEM (1:1)

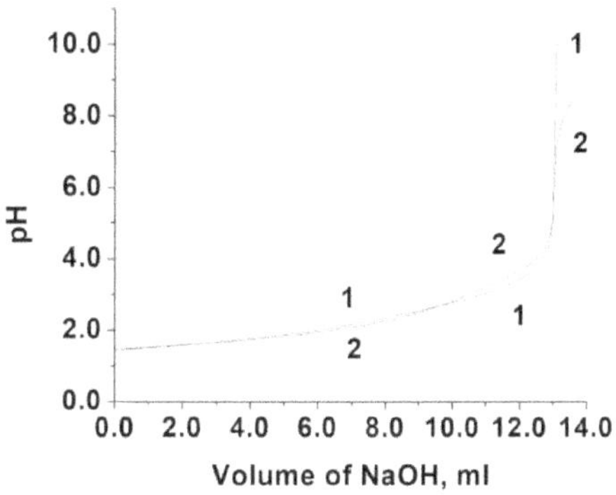

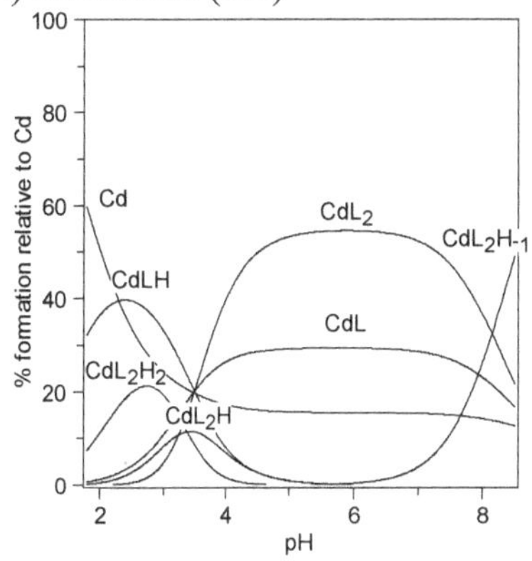

a. 1. Simulated titration curve
2. Experimental titration curve

b. Species distribution diagram

[SADH]= 0.01032 mol dm^{-3}
[HCl] = 0.05430mol dm^{-3}
[Cd (II)]= 0.00504mol dm^{-3}
[NaOH] = 0.2083mol dm^{-3}
Total Volume= 50.0 cm^3 Temp= 30.0 ± 0.1^{0}C I = 0.1 mol dm^{-3} NaCl

Figure 4.15: Cd (II) - SADH (L) SYSTEM (1:2)

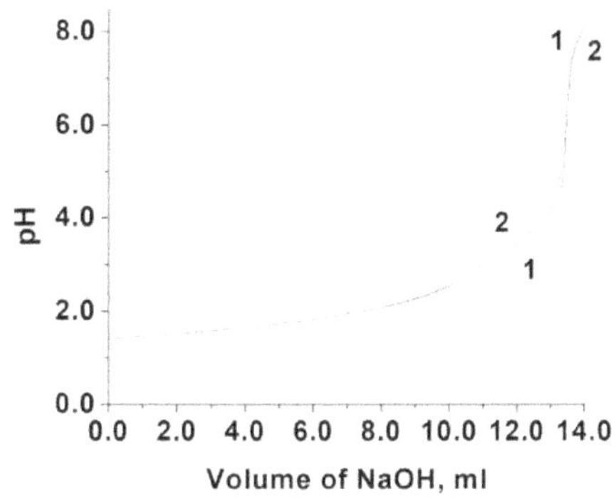

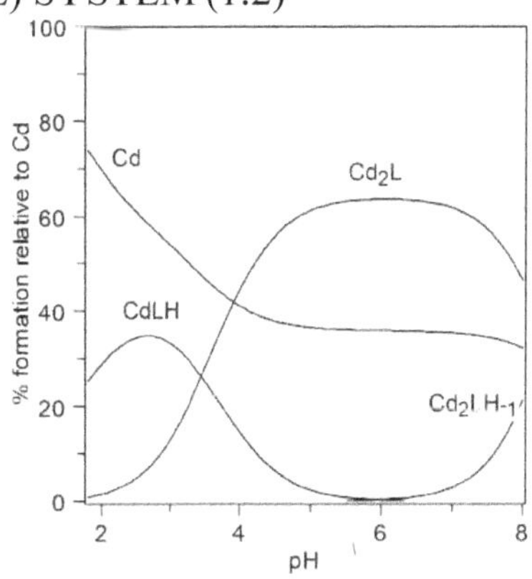

a. 1. Simulated titration curve
2. Experimental titration curve

b. Species distribution diagram

[SADH]= 0.01032 mol dm^{-3}
[HCl] = 0.05617 mol dm^{-3}
[Cd(II)]= 0.02000 mol dm^{-3}
[NaOH] = 0.2083 mol dm^{-3}
Total Volume= 50.0 cm^3 Temp= 30.0 ± 0.1^{0}C I = 0.1 mol dm^{-3} NaCl

Figure 4.16: Cd (II) - SADH (L) SYSTEM (2:1)

The best-fit models obtained for all the M^{2+}-SADH (M^{2+}= Ca^{2+}, Mg^{2+}, Pb^{2+}, Hg^{2+} and Cd^{2+})systems are tabulated in Table 4.1. The table contains the composition and formation constants of all the species converged along with their standard deviations and other statistical parameters used for the selection of best-fit models as discussed in Chapter-2 of the thesis. Inclusion of metal hydroxide species in the models resulted in a final rejection, suggesting their absence or existence at undetectable low concentrations in the pH region of analysis. Only ligand containing deprotonated or hydroxylated species were found to be present in the best-fit models.

Table 4.1: Best fit chemical models of Succinic acid dihydrazide-metal ion systems in aqueous medium at 30.0 ± 0.1^{0}C and ionic strength, I= 0.1mol dm^{-3}
(SD= Standard Deviation in the least significant digit)

Metal ion	Composition (M: L)	Species mlh	Log β_{mlh} (SD)	Statistical parameters
Ca^{2+}	1:1	011	3.58	U/NP = 3.446 X10^{-8}
		012	6.14	NP=55
		01-1	-11.91	χ^2= 43.15
		111	6.87 (4)	R=0.0108
		110	3.31 (4)	Skewness= -0.73
		11-1	-6.42 (11)	Kurtosis= 4.82
	1:2	011	3.58	U/NP =2.925 X10^{-8}
		012	6.14	NP=77
		01-1	-11.91	χ^2= 11.53
		111	6.87	R=0.009
		110	3.31	Skewness= -0.35
		122	13.75(4)	Kurtosis= 4.39
		121	10.17 (7)	
		120	6.58 (8)	
		12-1	-1.17(6)	
		12-2	-10. 69 (8)	
	2:1	011	3.58	U/NP = 1.975 X10^{-7}
		012	6.14	NP=37
		01-1	-11.91	χ^2= 57.86
		111	6.87	R=0.0232
		210	5.16 (6)	Skewness= 1.48
		21-1	-4.69(6)	Kurtosis= 7.66

(Table 4.1: M^{2+} -SADH systems)

Metal ion	**Composition (M: L)**	**Species mlh**	**Log β_{mlh} (SD)**	**Statistical parameters**
Mg^{2+}	1:1	011	3.58	U/NP = $9.913X10^{-8}$
		012	6.14	NP=115
		01-1	-11.91	χ^2= 69.03
		111	6.19 (4)	R=0.0105
		110	2.64 (5)	Skewness= -0.22
		11-1	-7.43 (5)	Kurtosis= 3.55
	1:2	011	3.58	U/NP = $1.925X10^{-8}$
		012	6.14	NP=82
		01-1	-11.91	χ^2= 65.61
		122	12.13 (4)	R=0.0069
		121	8.80 (6)	Skewness= -1.07
		120	5.21 (4)	Kurtosis= 6.81
		12-1	-3.40 (8)	
	2:1	011	3.58	U/NP =$1.782\ X10^{-8}$
		012	6.14	NP=121
		01-1	-11.91	χ^2= 98.86
		111	6.19	R=0.0128
		210	4.60 (4)	Skewness= 1.05
		21-1	-5.16 (7)	Kurtosis= 5.35

Metal ion	**Composition (M: L)**	**Species mlh**	**Log β_{mlh} (SD)**	**Statistical parameters**
Pb^{2+}	1:1	011	3.58	U/NP = $6.237X10^{-8}$
		012	6.14	NP=74
		01-1	-11.91	χ^2= 35.59
		111	6.60 (3)	R=0.0133
		110	3.39 (2)	Skewness= 0.12
		11-1	-2.73 (3)	Kurtosis= 3.51
	1:2	011	3.58	U/NP = $8.097X10^{-8}$
		012	6.14	NP=97
		01-1	-11.91	χ^2= 11.05
		111	6.60	R=0.0142
		110	3.39	Skewness= -0.52
		122	13.61 (5)	Kurtosis= 5.54
		121	10.38 (5)	
		120	6.79 (6)	
		12-1	0.29 (7)	
	2:1	011	3.58	U/NP = $2.485X10^{-7}$
		012	6.14	NP=86
		01-1	-11.91	χ^2= 44.76
		111	6.60	R=0.0204
		210	5.57 (4)	Skewness= 0.35
		21-1	-0.28 (10)	Kurtosis= 2.81
		21-2	-6.45 (10)	

(Table 4.1: M^{2+} -SADH systems)

Metal ion	Composition (M: L)	Species mlh	Log β_{mlh} (SD)	Statistical parameters
Hg^{2+}	1:1	011	3.58	U/NP = $9.970X10^{-8}$
		012	6.14	NP=108
		01-1	-11.91	χ^2= 71.56
		111	6.51 (3)	R=0.0133
		110	3.19 (2)	Skewness= 1.88
		11-1	-3.02 (3)	Kurtosis= 4.53
	1:2	011	3.58	U/NP = $1.421 X10^{-8}$
		012	6.14	NP=72
		01-1	-11.91	χ^2= 31.33
		111	6.51	R=0.0078
		110	3.19	Skewness= -0.32
		122	12.55 (3)	Kurtosis= 4.42
		121	8.97 (9)	
		120	6.33 (2)	
		12-1	-0.29 (4)	
		12-2	-7.37 (3)	
	2:1	011	3.58	U/NP = $3.879 X10^{-8}$
		012	6.14	NP=103
		01-1	-11.91	χ^2= 98.22
		111	6.51	R=0.0256
		210	5.27 (4)	Skewness= 1.75
		21-1	-0.64 (3)	Kurtosis=8.14
		21-2	-6.67 (4)	

Metal ion	Composition (M: L)	Species mlh	Log β_{mlh} (SD)	Statistical parameters
Cd^{2+}	1:1	011	3.58	U/NP = $3.953X10^{-9}$
		012	6.14	NP=77
		01-1	-11.91	χ^2= 77.12
		111	6.28 (1)	R=0.00318
		110	2.80 (1)	Skewness= -0.07
		11-1	-5.80 (1)	Kurtosis= 11.42
	1:2	011	3.58	U/NP = $1.517X10^{-8}$
		012	6.14	NP=86
		01-1	-11.91	χ^2= 16.11
		111	6.28	R=0.0061
		110	2.80	Skewness= -0.41
		122	12.19 (2)	Kurtosis= 3.26
		121	8.83 (5)	
		120	5.59 (2)	
		12-1	-2.55 (4)	
	2:1	011	3.58	U/NP = $5.857X10^{-8}$
		012	6.14	NP=86
		01-1	-11.91	χ^2= 78.0
		111	6.28	R=0.0096
		210	4.54 (2)	Skewness= -0.01
		21-1	-3.80 (4)	Kurtosis= 2.97

M^{2+}- SADH (1:1 concentration ratio) Systems:

There is a wide difference between simulated and experimental titration curves both at lower and higher pH for all the 1:1 M^{2+}-SADH (L) systems as shown in figs. 4.2a, 4.5a. 4,8a, 4.11a and 4.14a respectively for Ca^{2+}, Mg^{2+}, Pb^{2+}, Hg^{2+} and Cd^{2+}. This indicates the presence of other species probably protonated at lower pH and deprotonated or hydroxylated at higher pH in addition to the simple ML type of species. The data were subjected to analysis by the Miniquad-75 program using different models containing chemically plausible species selected on the basis of various protonation forms of the ligand that exist in solution as shown in figure 4.1. The protonation constants of the ligands obtained from the analysis of proton-ligand equilibria (Chapter 3) were considered as known parameters in the evaluation of the binary systems. The best-fit models for metal ion-SADH systems indicate (Table 4.1) the formation of MLH, ML and MLH_{-1} species. The simulated titration curves generated using the obtained formation constants of these species coincided well with the experimental curves, allowing for random experimental errors, indicating the sufficiency of the models selected. The species concentration distribution diagrams for 1:1 (M: L) molar ratio are shown in figures 4.2b, 4.5b, 4.8b, 4.11b and 4.14b for Ca^{2+}, Mg^{2+}, Pb^{2+}, Hg^{2+} and Cd^{2+} respectively. In MLH type of complexes, the metal ion is probably coordinated by one of the hydrazide groups while the other is left protonated and non-bonding. MLH species appear in the solution only below a pH of ~5.0. Its maximum extent of formation varied from45 to 65% for different metal ions around a pH of 2.5. With the increase in pH there is a formation of ML type of species in which the neutral (L) form of the ligand is bonded through one of the hydrazide groups while the other is unprotonated and uncoordinated. On further addition of base,MLH_{-1} type of deprotonated or hydroxylated, species appear in the solution. The extent of formation of MLH_{-1} is 12 to 66% of the total metal for different metal ions in the pH range of study. The acquisition of data at higher pH for some metal ions is limited to appearance of opalescence leading to precipitation. Solid state studies[22-35] of SADH and AADH complexes with Hg^{2+}, Cd^{2+}, Pd^{2+}, Ca^{2+}, Mg^{2+} and several other metal ions using I.R., UV-VIS, ^{1}H NMR, conductivity, magnetic susceptibility, etc. techniques revealed that, these ligands exhibit variousmodes of bonding in different species as shown in Table 4.2.

Table 4.2: Literature reported modes of bonding of dihydrazides and the corresponding plausible species

Mode of bonding	Form of the hydrazide	Nature of the Species	Plausible Species
Bidentate (bonding through carbonyl or enolic oxygen and terminal amino nitrogen of one of the hydrazide groups)	Mono-protonated (LH^+)	Chelating through only one of the two hydrazide groups while the other is left free and protonated	M(LH)
	Neutral (L)	Chelating through only one of the hydrazide groups while the other is left free and unprotonated	M(L)
	Mono-negative, $(LH_{-1})^-$	Deprotonation of the enolic group of the hydrazide moiety that is involved in bonding	$M(LH_{-1})$
	Bi-negative $(LH_{-2})^{2-}$	Deprotonation of both the enolic groups	$M(LH_{-2})$
Tetradentate (bis-bidentate) (bonding through carbonyl or enolic oxygen atoms and terminal amino nitrogen atoms of both the hydrazide groups to two different metal ions-homo metallic or hetero metallic)	Neutral (L)	Both the hydrazide groups are involved in bonding through carbonyl oxygen and amino nitrogen	M_2L
	Mono-negative (L^-)	Both the hydrazide groups are involved in bonding one through carbonyl oxygen and the other through enolic oxygen in addition to amino groups.	M_2LH_{-1}
	Bi-negative (L^{2-})	Both the hydrazide groups are involved in bonding through enolic oxygens and amino nitrogen atoms.	M_2LH_{-2}

The bidentate nature in keto and enol forms leads to the formation of MLH, ML and MLH_{-1} type of species in 1:1 molar mixtures of metal ion and SADH. The probable bonding nature of SADH in these species supported by solid state studies is shown in Fig. 4.17.

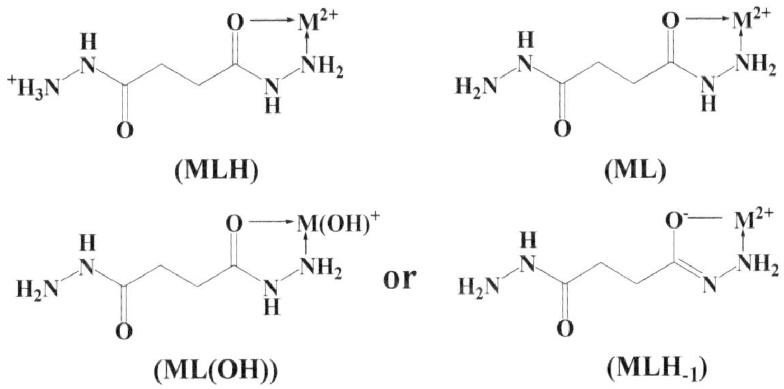

Figure 4.17: Probable bonding nature of SADH in MLH, ML and MLH_{-1} type of species

M^{2+}- SADH (1:2 concentration ratio) Systems:

The experimental titration curves of 1:2 (M: L) concentration composition for all the metal ion-SADH systems exhibited large deviations from simulated titration curves generated assuming the formation of only ML and ML_2 species. This indicates the presence of other species in addition to simple complexes. Keeping in view of the possibility of deprotonation of SADH in enolic form and hydrolysis of metal ions, various chemical models including all the plausible species were tested using the Miniquad-75 program. The best-fit models obtained (Table 4.1) indicate the formation of ML_2H_2, ML_2H, ML_2, ML_2H_{-1} and ML_2H_{-2} species. In each species the metal ion is bonded to two succinic acid dihydrazide molecules. The probable mode of bonding in different types of species can be explained on the basis of the solid state study reports (consolidated in Table 4.2) in the literature. In ML_2H_2 species probably, only one of the hydrazide groups of each of the ligands is involved in bonding with the metal ion, as a bidentate bonding through carbonyl oxygen and terminal nitrogen, while the other is left free and protonated. With the increase in pH the free protonated hydrazide groups of the ligands get deprotonated successively to form ML_2H and ML_2type of species. The formation of ML_2H_{-1} and ML_2H_{-2} type of species may be due to the participation of the mono-deprotonated enolic form (LH_{-1} in Figure 4.1) of one or both of the dihydrazide molecules in complexation or hydroxylation of the species. The probable bonding nature of SADH in some of the species of 1:2 (M: L) molar composition, supported by solid state study reports in the literature are shown in Fig. 4.18.

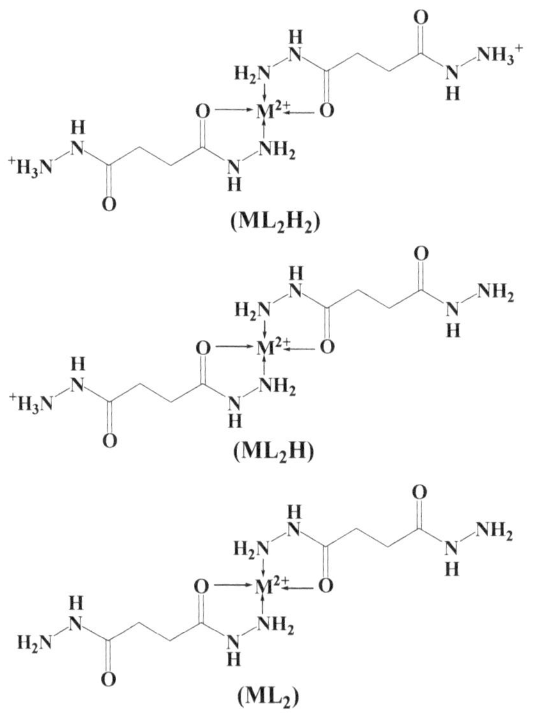

Figure 4.18: Probable bonding nature of SADH in ML_2H_2, ML_2H and ML_2 type of species

The species distribution diagrams indicating the percentage of formation of all the species for 1:2 composition systems are depicted in Figures 4.3b, 4.6b, 4.9b, 4.12b and 4.15b for Ca^{2+}, Mg^{2+}, Pb^{2+}, Hg^{2+} and Cd^{2+} respectively. The maximum extent of formation of various species expressed in percentage of total metal for different metal ions ranges 20-57 % for ML_2H_2, 7.5-31% for ML_2H, 55-71 % for $ML_2$and 12-71% for ML_2H_{-1}. The species ML_2H_{-2} which appears only in Ca^{2+}-SADH (1:2) and Hg^{2+} - SADH systems contribute to an extent of 51- 73% of the total metal.

M^{2+}- SADH (2:1 concentration ratio) Systems:

As succinic acid dihydrazide molecule possesses two coordinating hydrazide units, there is a possibility of formation of binuclear complexes. Therefore, potentiometric titrations were conducted keeping 2:1 metal to ligand concentration ratio for all the metal ions under study. The simulated titration curves obtained assuming the formation of only M_2L deviated from the experimental titration curves in the entire pH region (Figures 4.4a, 4.7a, 4.10a, 4.13a and 4.16a for Ca^{2+}, Mg^{2+}, Pb^{2+}, Hg^{2+} and Cd^{2+}systems respectively) indicating the formation of some other species. The data were subjected to analysis using the Miniquad-75 program and the best- fit models obtained for all the metal ion systems are shown in Table 4.1. The best-fit models obtained indicate the formation of homo binuclear species, M_2L, M_2LH_{-1} and M_2LH_{-2}, where SADH acts as a ditopic ligand and is attached to two metal ions either in neutral or deprotonated enolic form. Although solution phase studies of speciation cannot give the exact structures of species, the probable bonding nature of SADH in binuclear complexes supported by solid state studies(Table 4.2) is shown in Figure 4.19. The ligand acts as a bis-bidentate, coordinating through terminal $-NH_2$ groups and carbonyl or enolic oxygen forming five membered rings on both sides.

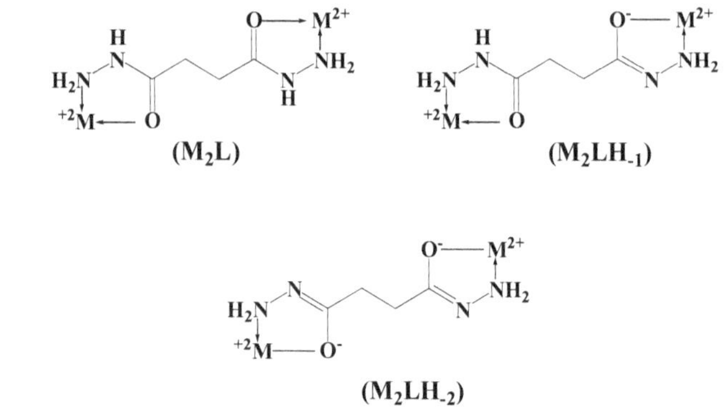

Figure 4.19: Probable bonding nature of SADH in bimetallic complexes.

The coordination of a metal ion at one unit of a ditopic ligand may affect the coordination at the other unit.This leads to the formation of unsymmetrical complexes where the mode of coordination is different at the two structurally identical units of the same ligand. This was observed in the case of M_2LH_{-1} type of species where the two hydrazide groups of the same ligand are involved in bonding differently, one in neutral form and the other in deprotonated enolic form. In the symmetric M_2L type of complexes, as the second metal ion coordinates to a different hydrazide unit of the same ligand which is away from the first unit, it is expected that the formation constant of M_2L must be nearly twice that of ML. For all the metal ions log $\beta_{210}$was found to be less than twice of log β_{110}. This clearly indicates that the bonding at one unit affects the bond strength ofthe other unit. The extent of formation of the symmetric M_2L type of species ranges from 64-76% of total metal for different metal ions in the pH range of study. Beyond this range deprotonation of M_2L takes place leading to the formation of M_2LH_{-1} and M_2LH_{-2} type of species.

4.1.2Adipic Acid Dihydrazide (AADH) - Metal ion systems:

The acquired data for metal ion–adipic acid dihydrazide systems were first subjected to analysis by classical procedures [18, 19] to get the formation constants of simple mono-nuclear complexes,ML andML_2. Simulated titration curves were then generated using computer program SOPHD[48] to see whether these species satisfy the experimental data. Thesimulated titration curves thus obtained were plotted along with the experimental ones to identify the regions of pH where they differ. Titration curves for all the metal ion-AADH systems are shown in Figs. 4.20a to 4.34a. The wide differences between the simulated and experimental curves evince the presence of other major species in addition to simple mono-nuclear complexes.

Different chemical models containing chemically plausible species depending on the nature of the ligand, metal ion and the pH region of difference in the curves were tested using the Miniquad-75 program[20]. The required initial estimates of the formation constants were calculated basing on the formation constants of simple complexes and protonation/ deprotonation constants of the ligand. The best-fit models obtained for all the metal ions and compositions are shown in Table 4.3.

The species converged for 1:1(molar ratio) metal ion-AADH (L) systems were MLH, ML and MLH_{-1} (M= Ca^{2+}, Mg^{2+}, Pb^{2+}, Hg^{2+} and Cd^{2+}). The formation of MLHspecies indicates that one of the hydrazidegroups of AADH is bonded to the metal ion whilethe other is free and protonated. With an increase in the pH of the solution, MLH species loses its proton on the non-bonding side leading to the formation of ML. The formation of MLH_{-1} species may be due to the loss of enolic proton or hydroxylation of the species. The species concentration distribution diagrams generated using HYSS-2009 program[21] are shown in Figs. 4.20b to 4.34b.

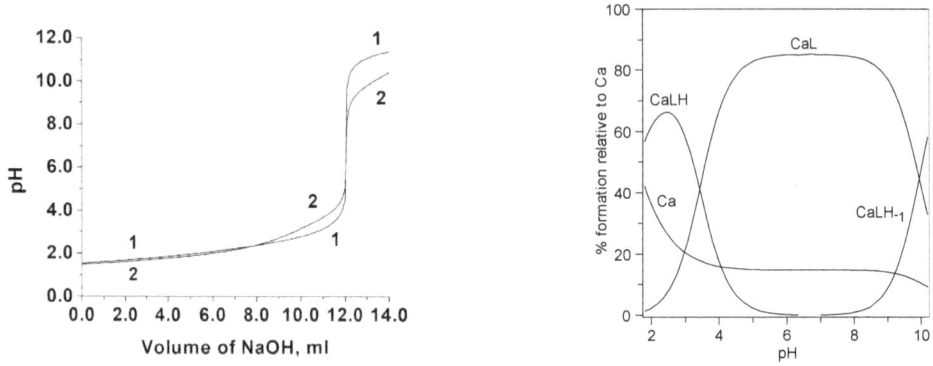

a. 1. Simulated titration curve
2. Experimental titration curve

b. Species distribution diagram

[AADH]= 0.01000 mol dm^{-3}
[HCl] = 0.04731 mol dm^{-3}
Total Volume= 50.0 cm^{3}

[Ca(II)] = 0.0100 mol dm^{-3}
[NaOH] = 0.1960 mol dm^{-3}

Temp= 30.0 ± 0.1^{0}C I = 0.1 mol dm^{-3} NaCl

Figure 4.20: Ca (II) - AADH (L) SYSTEM (1:1)

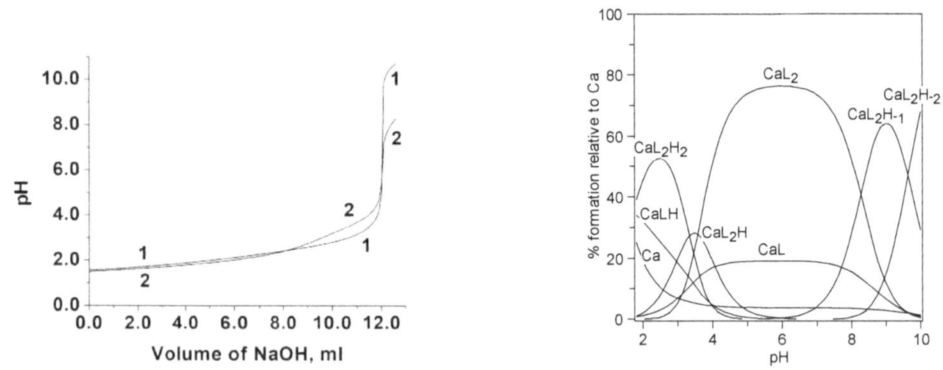

a. 1. Simulated titration curve
2. Experimental titration curve

b. Species distribution diagram

[AADH]= 0.01000 mol dm^{-3}
[HCl] = 0.04715 mol dm^{-3}
Total Volume= 50.0 cm^{3}

[Ca(II)] = 0.00501 mol dm^{-3}
[NaOH] = 0.1960 mol dm^{-3}

Temp= 30.0 ± 0.1^{0}C I = 0.1 mol dm^{-3} NaCl

Figure 4.21: Ca (II) - AADH (L) SYSTEM (1:2)

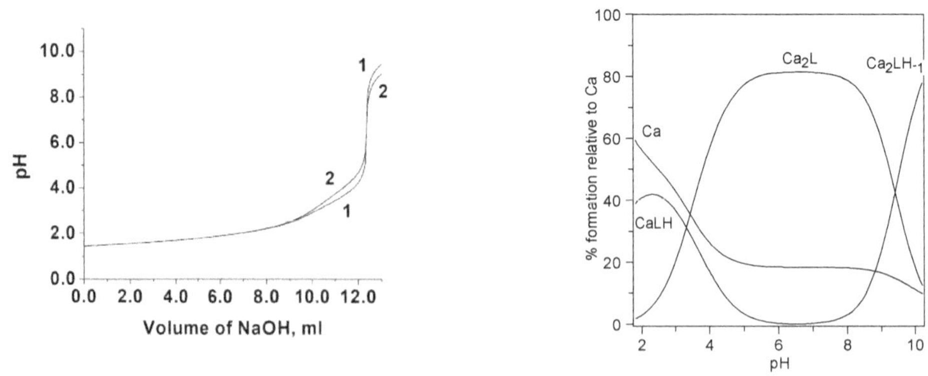

a. 1. Simulated titration curve
2. Experimental titration curve

b. Species distribution diagram

[AADH]= 0.01000 mol dm^{-3}
[HCl] = 0.04843 mol dm^{-3}
Total Volume= 50.0 cm^{3}

[Ca(II)]= 0.01999 mol dm^{-3}
[NaOH] = 0.1960 mol dm^{-3}

Temp= 30.0 ± 0.1^{0}C I = 0.1 mol dm^{-3} NaCl

Figure 4.22: Ca (II) - AADH (L) SYSTEM (2:1)

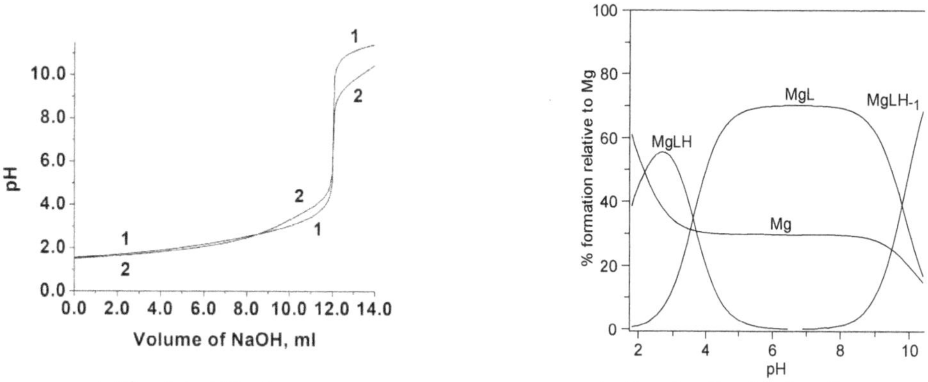

a. 1. Simulated titration curve
2. Experimental titration curve

b. Species distribution diagram

[AADH]= 0.01000 mol dm^{-3} [Mg(II)]= 0.01000 mol dm^{-3}

[HCl] = 0.04720 mol dm^{-3} [NaOH] = 0.1960 mol dm^{-3}

Total Volume= 50.0 cm^3 Temp= 30.0 ± 0.1^{0}C I = 0.1 mol dm^{-3} NaCl

Figure 4.23: Mg (II) - AADH (L) SYSTEM (1:1)

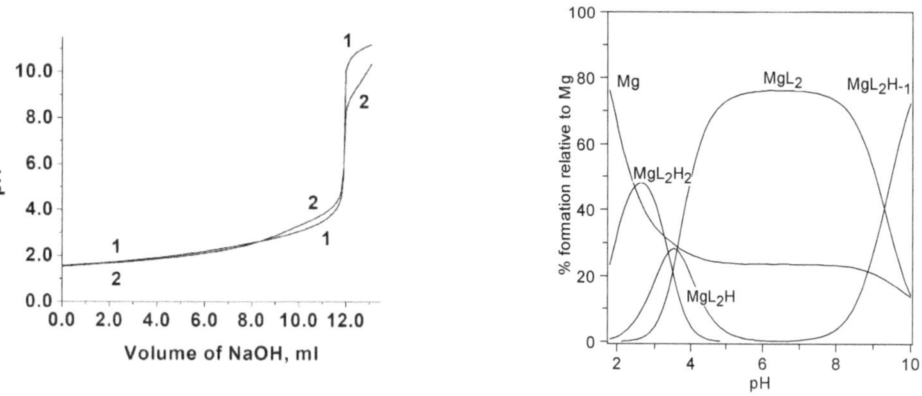

a. 1. Simulated titration curve
2. Experimental titration curve

b. Species distribution diagram

[AADH]= 0.01000 mol dm^{-3} [Mg(II)]= 0.0050 mol dm^{-3}

[HCl] = 0.04669 mol dm^{-3} [NaOH] = 0.1960 mol dm^{-3}

Total Volume= 50.0 cm^3 Temp= 30.0 ± 0.1^{0}C I = 0.1 mol dm^{-3} NaCl

Figure 4.24: Mg (II) - AADH (L) SYSTEM (1:2)

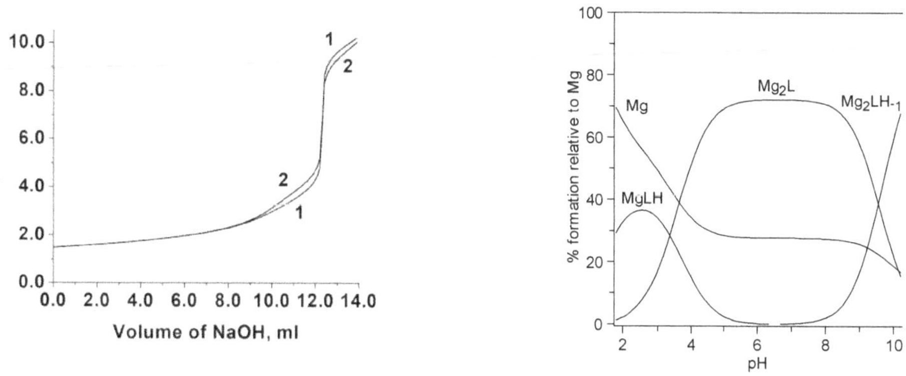

a. 1. Simulated titration curve
2. Experimental titration curve

b. Species distribution diagram

[AADH]= 0.01000 mol dm^{-3} [Mg(II)]= 0.01999 mol dm^{-3}

[HCl] = 0.04822 mol dm^{-3} [NaOH] = 0.1960 mol dm^{-3}

Total Volume= 50.0 cm^3 Temp= 30.0 ± 0.1^{0}C I = 0.1 mol dm^{-3} NaCl

Figure 4.25: Mg (II) - AADH (L) SYSTEM (2:1)

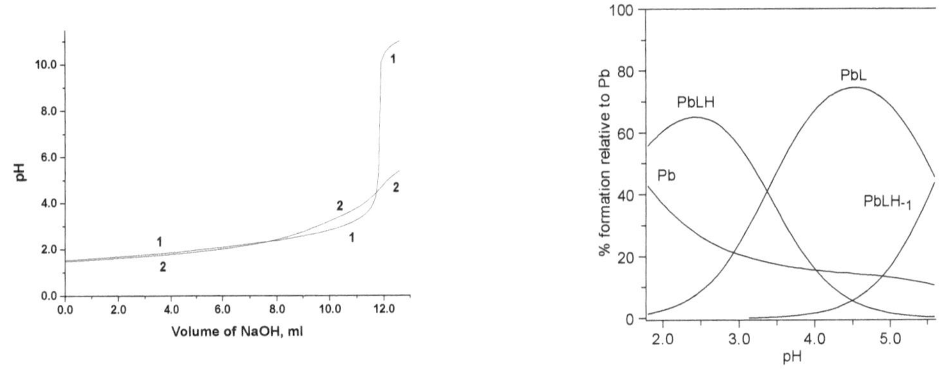

a. 1. Simulated titration curve
2. Experimental titration curve

b. Species distribution diagram

[AADH]= 0.01000 mol dm^{-3} | [Pb (II)]= 0.00998 mol dm^{-3}

$[HNO_3]$ = 0.04762 mol dm^{-3} | [NaOH] = 0.2016 mol dm^{-3}

Total Volume= 50.0 cm^3 | Temp= 30.0 ± 0.1^{0}C | I = 0.1 mol $dm^{-3}NaNO_3$

Figure 4.26: Pb (II) - AADH (L) SYSTEM (1:1)

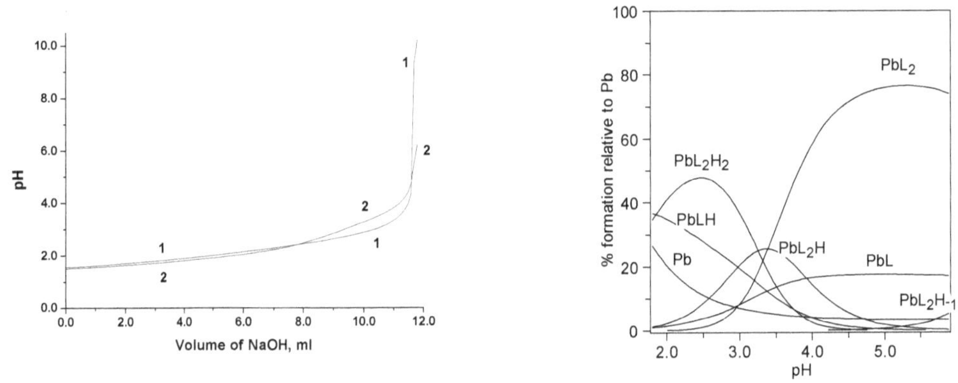

a. 1. Simulated titration curve
2. Experimental titration curve

b. Species distribution diagram

[AADH]= 0.01000 mol dm^{-3} | [Pb (II)]= 0.00501 mol dm^{-3}

$[HNO_3]$ = 0.04711 mol dm^{-3} | [NaOH] = 0.2016 mol dm^{-3}

Total Volume= 50.0 cm^3 | Temp= 30.0 ± 0.1^{0}C | I = 0.1 mol dm^{-3} $NaNO_3$

Figure 4.27: Pb (II) - AADH (L) SYSTEM (1:2)

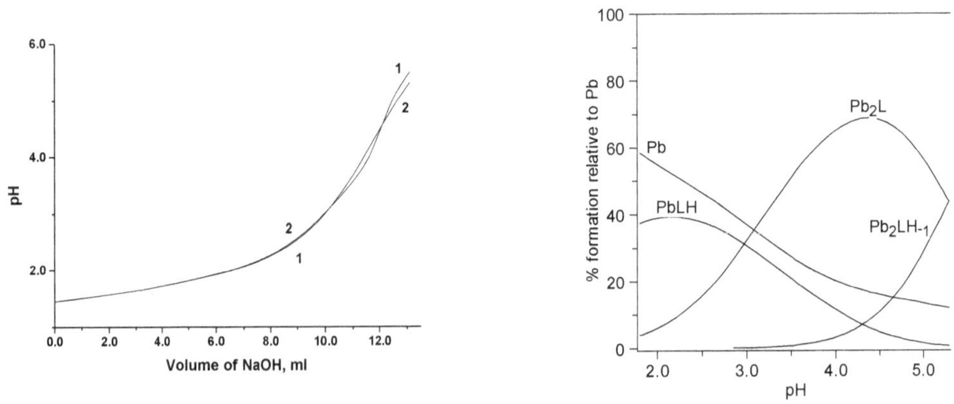

a. 1. Simulated titration curve
2. Experimental titration curve

b. Species distribution diagram

[AADH]= 0.01000 mol dm^{-3} | [Pb(II)]= 0.01999 mol dm^{-3}

$[HNO_3]$ = 0.04864 mol dm^{-3} | [NaOH] = 0.2016 mol dm^{-3}

Total Volume= 50.0 cm^3 | Temp= 30.0 ± 0.1^{0}C | I = 0.1 mol $dm^{-3}NaNO_3$

Figure 4.28: Pb (II) - AADH (L) SYSTEM (2:1)

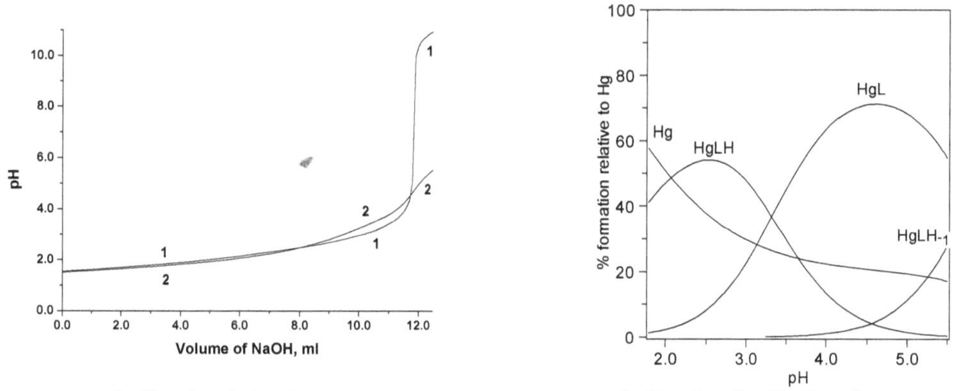

a. 1. Simulated titration curve
2. Experimental titration curve

b. Species distribution diagram

[AADH]= 0.01000 mol dm^{-3}
[HCl] = 0.04768 mol dm^{-3}
[Hg(II)]= 0.00999 mol dm^{-3}
[NaOH] = 0.2016mol dm^{-3}
Total Volume= 50.0 cm^3 Temp= 30.0 ± 0.1°C I = 0.1 mol dm^{-3} NaCl

Figure 4.29: Hg (II) - AADH (L) SYSTEM (1:1)

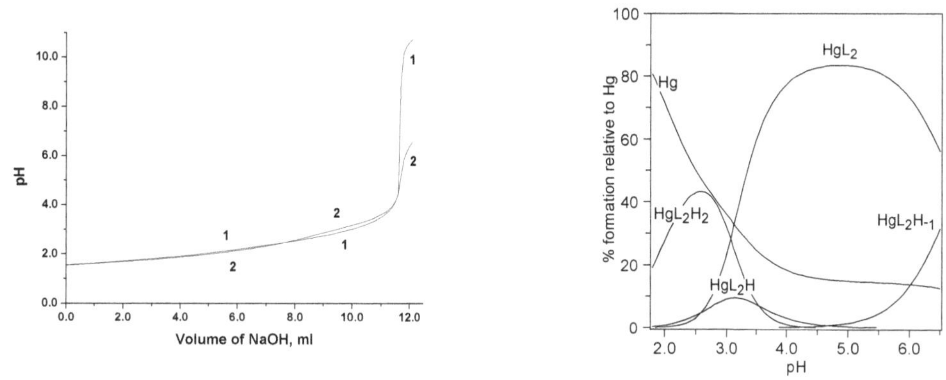

a. 1. Simulated titration curve
2. Experimental titration curve

b. Species distribution diagram

[AADH]= 0.01000 mol dm^{-3}
[HCl] = 0.04714 mol dm^{-3}
[Hg (II)]= 0.00498 mol dm^{-3}
[NaOH] = 0.2016 mol dm^{-3}
Total Volume= 50.0 cm^3 Temp= 30.0 ± 0.1°C I = 0.1 mol dm^{-3} NaCl

Figure 4.30: Hg (II) - AADH (L) SYSTEM (1:2)

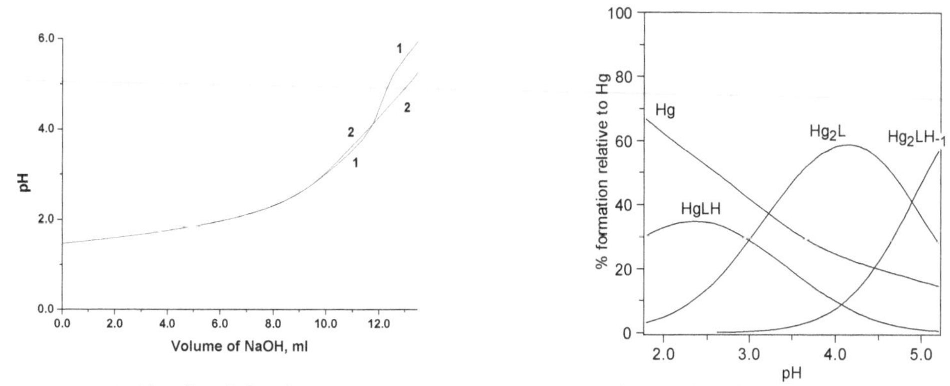

a. 1. Simulated titration curve
2. Experimental titration curve

b. Species distribution diagram

[AADH]= 0.01000 mol dm^{-3}
[HCl] = 0.04877 mol dm^{-3}
[Hg(II)]= 0.02001 mol dm^{-3}
[NaOH] = 0.2016 mol dm^{-3}
Total Volume= 50.0 cm^3 Temp= 30.0 ± 0.1°C I = 0.1 mol dm^{-3} NaCl

Figure 4.31: Hg (II) - AADH (L) SYSTEM (2:1)

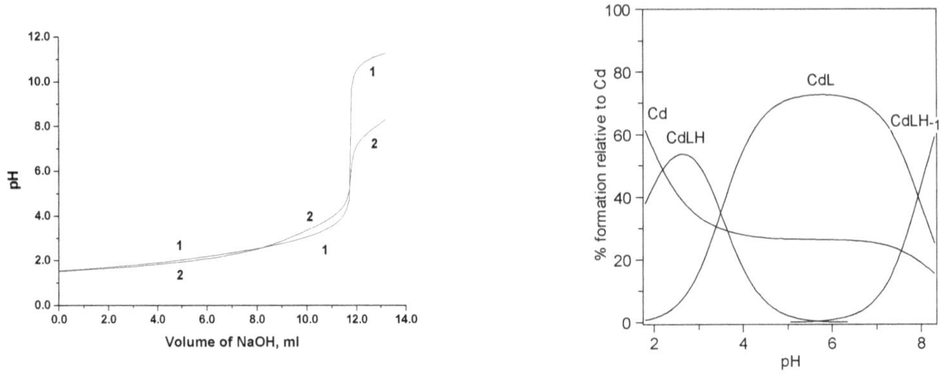

a. 1. Simulated titration curve
2. Experimental titration curve

b. Species distribution diagram

[AADH]= 0.01000 mol dm^{-3} [Cd (II)] = 0.0100 mol dm^{-3}

[HCl] = 0.04743 mol dm^{-3} [NaOH] = 0.2016 mol dm^{-3}

Total Volume= 50.0 cm^{3} Temp= 30.0 ± 0.1^{0}C I = 0.1 mol dm^{-3} NaCl

Figure 4.32: Cd (II) - AADH (L) SYSTEM (1:1)

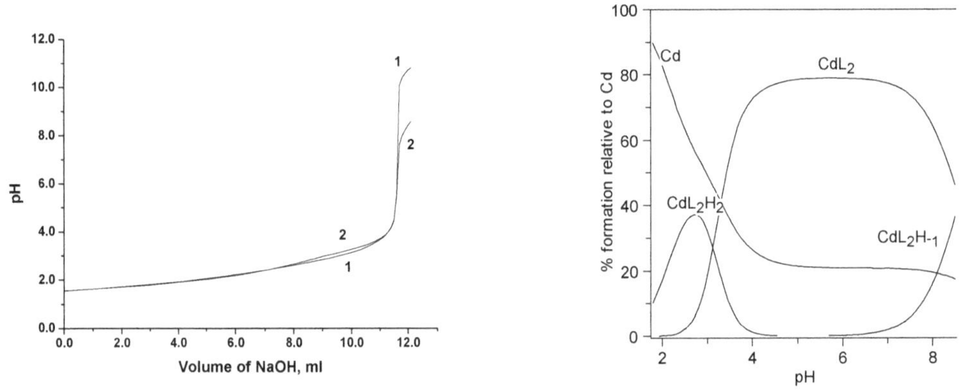

a. 1. Simulated titration curve
2. Experimental titration curve

b. Species distribution diagram

[AADH]= 0.01000 mol dm^{-3} [Cd (II)]= 0.00504mol dm^{-3}

[HCl] = 0.04681mol dm^{-3} [NaOH] = 0.2016 mol dm^{-3}

Total Volume= 50.0 cm^{3} Temp= 30.0 ± 0.1^{0}C I = 0.1 mol dm^{-3} NaCl

Figure 4.33: Cd (II) - AADH (L) SYSTEM (1:2)

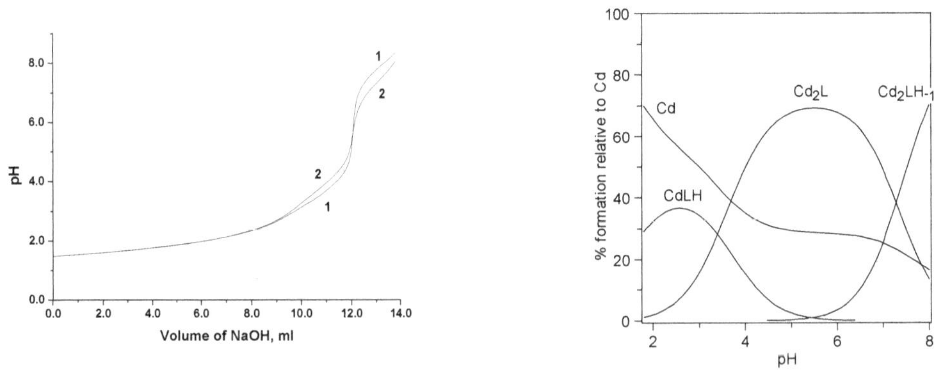

a. 1. Simulated titration curve
2. Experimental titration curve

b. Species distribution diagram

[AADH]= 0. 01000 mol dm^{-3} [Cd(II)]= 0.02000 mol dm^{-3}

[HCl] = 0. 04868 mol dm^{-3} [NaOH] = 0.2016 mol dm^{-3}

Total Volume= 50.0 cm^{3} Temp= 30.0 ± 0.1^{0}C I = 0.1 mol dm^{-3} NaCl

Figure 4.34: Cd (II) - AADH (L) SYSTEM (2:1)

Table 4.3: Best fit chemical models of Adipic acid dihydrazide-metal ion systems in aqueous medium at 30.0 ± 0.1^{0}C and ionic strength, I = 0.1 mol dm^{-3}
(SD= Standard Deviation in the least significant digit)

Metal ion	Composition (M: L)	Species mlh	Log β_{mlh} (SD)	Statistical parameters
Ca^{2+}	1:1	011	3.67	U/NP = 5.081X10^{-7}
		012	6.24	NP=123
		01-1	-12.03	χ^2= 38.96
		111	7.02 (5)	R=0.026
		110	3.59 (6)	Skewness= 0.11
		11-1	-6.36 (12)	Kurtosis= 2.89
	1:2	011	3.67	
		012	6.24	U/NP = 2.032X 10^{-9}
		01-1	-12.03	NP=69
		111	7.02	χ^2= 16.11
		110	3.59	R=0.0028
		122	13.96 (13)	Skewness= 0.02
		121	10.63 (5)	Kurtosis=3.52
		120	7.07 (1)	
		12-1	-1.20 (0.8)	
		12-2	-10.83 (8)	
	2:1	011	3.67	U/NP =5.359 X 10^{-7}
		012	6.24	NP=133
		01-1	-12.03	χ^2= 6.47
		111	7.02	R=0.0389
		210	5.52 (8)	Skewness= -0.76
		21-1	-3.88 (6)	Kurtosis= 3.51

Metal ion	Composition (M: L)	Species mlh	Log β_{mlh} (SD)	Statistical parameters
Mg^{2+}	1:1	011	3.67	U/NP = 5.609X10^{-7}
		012	6.24	NP=123
		01-1	-12.03	χ^2= 67.75
		111	6.52 (6)	R=0.026
		110	2.90 (5)	Skewness= -0.24
		11-1	-6.89 (7)	Kurtosis= 3.11
	1:2	011	3.67	U/NP =4.490 X 10^{-9}
		012	6.24	NP=56
		01-1	-12.03	χ^2= 34.10
		122	12.74 (2)	R=0.0048
		121	9.38 (7)	Skewness= -0.39
		120	5.77 (1)	Kurtosis= 3.53
		12-1	-3.52 (4)	
	2:1	011	3.67	U/NP = 5.301X 10^{-7}
		012	6.24	NP=36
		01-1	-12.03	χ^2= 36.52
		111	6.52	R=0.0441
		210	4.93(7)	Skewness= 0.29
		21-1	-4.62 (10)	Kurtosis= 3.74

(Table 4.3: M^{2+} -AADH systems)

Metal ion	Composition (M: L)	Species mlh	Log β_{mlh} (SD)	Statistical parameters
Pb^{2+}	1:1	011	3.67	U/NP = $3.374X10^{-7}$
		012	6.24	NP=125
		01-1	-12.03	χ^2= 32.02
		111	6.99 (4)	R=0.0204
		110	3.62 (4)	Skewness= 0.88
		11-1	-2.00 (5)	Kurtosis= 3.85
	1:2	011	3.67	
		012	6.24	U/NP = $9.940X10^{-9}$
		01-1	-12.03	NP=59
		111	6.99	χ^2= 27.88
		110	3.62	R=0.0068
		122	13.82 (6)	Skewness= -0.17
		121	10.57 (6)	Kurtosis= 4.40
		120	7.18 (2)	
		12-1	0.13 (5)	
	2:1	011	3.67	U/NP = $3.528X10^{-7}$
		012	6.24	NP=37
		01-1	-12.03	χ^2= 13.76
		111	6.99	R=0.0305
		210	5.84 (5)	Skewness= 0.14
		21-1	0.54 (7)	Kurtosis=3.19

Metal ion	Composition (M: L)	Species mlh	Log β_{mlh} (SD)	Statistical parameters
Hg^{2+}	1:1	011	3.67	U/NP = $1.425 X10^{-8}$
		012	6.24	NP=125
		01-1	-12.03	χ^2= 30.01
		111	6.60 (2)	R=0.0132
		110	3.28 (2)	Skewness= -0.28
		11-1	-2.51 (7)	Kurtosis= 5.38
	1:2	011	3.67	
		012	6.24	U/NP = $8.025X10^{-8}$
		01-1	-12.03	NP=71
		122	12.58(2)	χ^2= 25.69
		121	9.04 (6)	R=0.0055
		120	6.45 (1)	Skewness= -0.29
		12-1	-0.30 (8)	Kurtosis= 4.51
	2:1	011	3.67	U/NP = $4.945X10^{-8}$
		012	6.24	NP=37
		01-1	-12.03	χ^2= 5.11
		111	6.60	R=0.0375
		210	5.38 (7)	Skewness=-0.29
		21-1	0.49 (6)	Kurtosis= 3.16

(Table 4.3: M^{2+} -AADH systems)

Metal ion	Composition (M: L)	Species mlh	Log β_{mlh} (SD)	Statistical parameters
Cd^{2+}	1:1	011	3.67	U/NP = $3.305X10^{-7}$
		012	6.24	NP=121
		01-1	-12.03	χ^2= 62.85
		111	6.52 (4)	R=0.020
		110	3.02 (4)	Skewness= -0.14
		11-1	-4.91 (10)	Kurtosis= 3.23
	1:2	011	3.67	U/NP = $2.809 X 10^{-8}$
		012	6.24	NP=59
		01-1	-12.03	χ^2= 76.24
		122	12.17 (4)	R=0.0117
		120	5.94 (2)	Skewness= -0.36
		12-1	-2.66 (6)	Kurtosis=3.22
	2:1	011	3.67	U/NP =$6.458 X 10^{-7}$
		012	6.24	NP=40
		01-1	-12.03	χ^2= 27.47
		111	6.52	R=0.0425
		210	4.88 (7)	Skewness= -0.40
		21-1	-2.40 (10)	Kurtosis= 3.88

The extent of formation of MLH species varies between 54 to 66% of total metal ion with a maximum around ~2.5 pH. The formation of ML is above 70% of the total metal in all the cases. The formation of MLH_{-1} is around ~65% for Ca^{2+}, Mg^{2+}, Cd^{2+} and around ~30% for Pb^{2+}, Hg^{2+} systems in the pH range of study. In the case of $Pb^{2+}$and Hg^{2+} the study was restricted to a pH of 5.5 due to the appearance of turbidity in the solution.

The best-fit models for 1:2 metal ion to ligand molar concentration ratio for all the metal ion-AADH systems indicate the formation of ML_2H_2, ML_2H, ML_2 and ML_2H_{-1} species. In all these species probably, only one of the hydrazide groups of the ligand is attached to the metal ion. The species distribution diagrams indicate that the extent of formation of ML_2varies from 75 to 85% for different metal ions.

Bimetallic species of the type M_2L andM_2LH_{-1} were found to exist in 2:1 (M: L concentration ratio) solution for all the metal ions under study. In homo-binuclear type of species (M_2L), AADH acts as a ditopic ligand bonding through amino and carbonyl groups on both the sides. These species are predominant in 2:1 systems andrepresent 60 to 80% of the total metal concentration. With an increase in the pH, M_2Lspecies are converted to M_2LH_{-1} by losing an enolic proton. Further deprotonation orhydroxylation could not be observed due to the appearance of turbidity leading to precipitation. Bakir Jeragh et al.[22] in theirstudies on solid state metal complexes of AADH with various metal ions including Hg^{2+} and Cd^{2+},reported the behaviour of the ligand as a neutral bidentate in mononuclear complexes and neutralor binegative tetradentate in binuclear species. In neutral state the ligand bonds throughcarbonyl oxygen and amino group nitrogen of one (bidentate) or both (tetradentate) of thehydrazide moieties. In binegative tetradentate state the ligand bonds through enolic oxygen andamino groups of both the hydrazide moieties. This supports our speciation results ofidentification of mono and binuclear species in protonated, unprotonated and deprotonatedforms in the solution. The probable bonding nature of AADH in some of the observed speciessupported by solid state structural elucidation[8, 22-35] is shown in Fig. 4.35.

The stabilities of the metal complexes of AADH were found to be somewhat higher compared to those of SADH. Similar enhanced stabilities with an increase in the alkyl chain length between the two hydrazide groupswere observed by Suppet al.[37]in the case of Co^{2+} complexes of carbo dihydrazide, succinic acid dihydrazide and adipic acid dihydrazide. Increase in chain length seems to increase the basicity of the coordinating groups leading to an enhancement in the stability of the complexes.

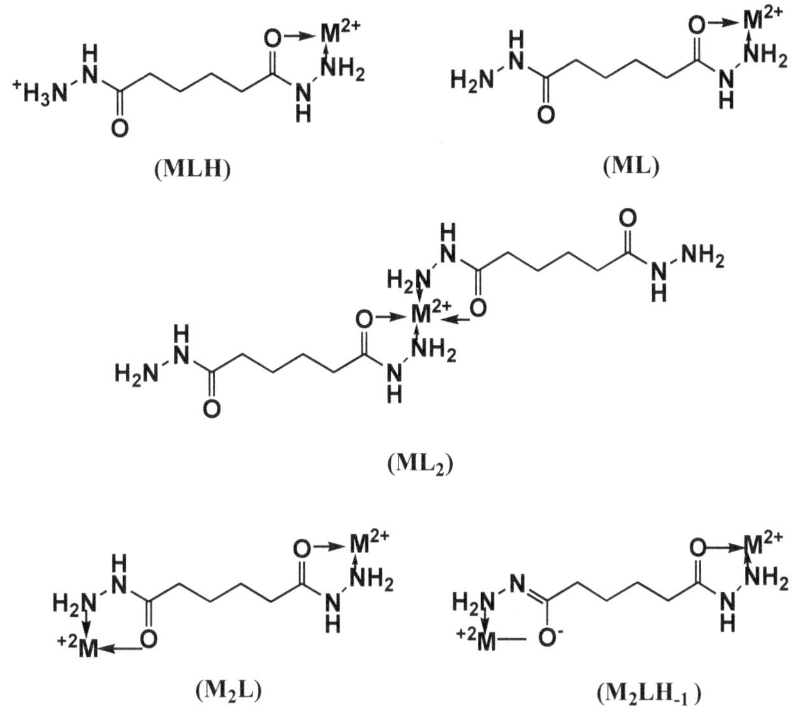

Figure 4.35: Probable bonding modes in some species of metal ion-AADH systems

Formation constants of Ca^{2+} complexes with both SADH and AADHare found to be greater than those of Mg^{2+}. The stability of a complex formedbetween a ligand and a metal ion depends onseveral factors like;

1. Chelating behaviour of the ligand,
2. Type of the bond between a metal ion and a coordinating atom, which may vary from purely electrostatic to nearly covalent,
3. Ionic size and coordination number of the metal ion,
4. Hard & soft acid-base nature of both metal ion and donor atom and
5. Chelate ring size and other geometric factors.

Alkaline earth metal ions, Mg^{2+} and Ca^{2+} are hard acids, not easily polarized, favour oxygen donors and show predominately electrostatic bonding in complexes. Mg^{2+} ion has relatively small size, high charge density and strong affinity for inner sphere water molecules. The relatively higher stability of Ca^{2+} complexes is therefore explicable in terms of smaller hydration energy[52, 53] as the formation of metal-ligand bond requires the breakage of metal ion-solvent bonds. Also neutral oxygen donors prefer large metal ions[57]. Another factor to be considered is the size of the chelate ring[54, 55] relative to the size of the metal ion. Small metal ions favour six membered rings while large ions prefer five membered rings[56]. Therefore, the relative higher stabilities of Ca^{2+}-dihydrazide complexes may be explicable on the basis of the above factors.

In the case of heavy metal ion (Pb^{2+}, Hg^{2+} and Cd^{2+}) –dihydrazide complexes of both SADH and AADH, the relative stabilities were found to be in the order Pb^{2+}>Hg^{2+}> Cd^{2+}. This may be explained on the basis of several factors as follows.

- According to Pearson's HSAB theory, Hg^{2+} and Cd^{2+} are soft Lewis acids while Pb^{2+} belongs to borderline category. On the other hand SADH or AADH provides hard oxygen and borderline -NH_2 donors. Hard acids prefer binding to the hard bases to give ionic complexes, whereas the soft acids prefer binding to soft bases to give covalent complexes. Metal ions of borderline category can behave as either hard or soft acid, depending on solvent, stereochemical and electronic structural factors. Therefore, the HSAB principle accounts well for the decreased affinity of SADH or AADH towards metal ions, from Pb^{2+} to $Hg^{2+}$and Cd^{2+}.
- Another factor to be considered is the size of the chelate ring relative to the size of the metal ion[54, 55]. Ligands that form 5- membered chelate rings are better pre-organized for coordinating with large metal ions[56], while those that form 6- membered chelate rings are better pre-organized for coordinating with

small metal ions. Solid state studies using spectral, thermal and magnetic measurements indicated that each hydrazide group of SADH or AADH acts as a bidentate bonding through terminal -NH_2 group and amide oxygen forming a five membered ring. The ionic sizes of Pb^{2+} (0.118 nm) > Hg^{2+} (0.102 nm) > Cd^{2+} (0.095 nm) which is also the order of the decreasing stabilities of the complexes.

- Oxygen atoms of amide group donors are of great importance in biological reactions. It was shown many times that the use of neutral oxygen donors increases the affinity of ligands towards larger metal ions[57]. This leads to an increase in the stabilities of complexes with large metal ions relative to small ions. A contributing factor to this observation lies in the geometry of chelate rings. Literature reports on infrared spectral studies of SADH and AADH metal complexes[22-33] clearly indicate the involvement of amide oxygen in bonding. The increase in stability of metal complexes from Cd^{2+} to Hg^{2+} to Pb^{2+}, which is also the order of increasing ionic size, is therefore explicable. All the above factors contribute to the observed relative stabilities of the complexes.

4.2 SPECIATION STUDIES OF AMINO ACID- METAL ION BINARY SYSTEMS:

4.2.1 Glycine – Metal Ion Systems:

The amino acid glycine (2-aminoethanoic acid, XH) contains two donor groups (amino and carboxylate groups), that can associate with protons. Therefore, two hydrogen ions candissociate from the fully protonated cations of the amino acid (XH_2^+). Dissociation of these protons occurs stepwise, in well-separated pH regions, and therefore, the amino acid canappear in three different forms in different pH ranges: *viz.* the cationic (XH_2^+),the neutral or zwitter ionic ($XH^\pm$, which is energetically favoured both in solution and solid state) and the most anionic (X^-) forms as discussed in the Section 3.3.1 of Chapter 3.

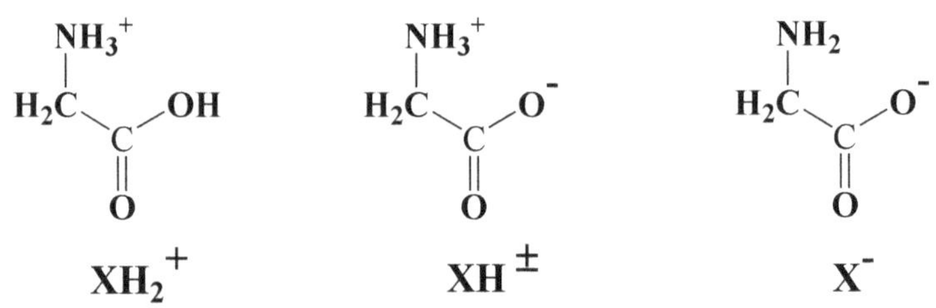

Figure 4.36: Protonated and deprotonated forms of glycine in aqueous solution

Glycine generally acts as a bidentate ligand, yielding mono, bis and tris complexes with most of the metal ions; these complexes contain 5-membered chelate ring formed *via* the coordination of amino-N and carboxylate-O^- donors. With some metal ions, protonated species mayalso be formed, by mono-dentate coordination through the amino or carboxylate group. At high pH the formation of soluble hydroxo complexes is possible, but reliable stability constants are in general not available for these species.

In the literature, there are a number of reports on the stability constants of Ca^{2+}, Mg^{2+}, Pb^{2+}, Hg^{2+} and Cd^{2+} complexes of glycinein aqueous medium. However, most of the reported formation constants in the literature were obtained using classical graphical methods of analysis, ignoring the formation of protonated and hydroxylated species. Protonated and hydroxylated species equilibria normally overlap with those of simple complexes. Hence the stability constants that neglect the formation of protonated species cannot be considered as accurate. The literature survey (Table 4.4) indicated a wide spread in the formation constants of both proton-ligand and metal-ligand complexes.

TABLE 4.4: Some literature reported formation constants of Ca^{2+}, Mg^{2+}, Pb^{2+}, Hg^{2+} and Cd^{2+} complexes of Glycine.

Metal ion	***mlh***	**Formation constants of metal ion-glycine complexes reported in the literature**											
		Ionic Strength, I and Temperature, t^0C											
		0.1M 25^0C	0.1M 25^0C	1.0 M 25^0C	0.1M 30^0C	0.15 M 37^0C	0.1M 25^0C	0.1M 25^0C	0.15 M 37^0C	0.15 M 25^0C	0.1M 25^0C	3.0M 25^0C	0.1M 25^0C
H^+	011	9.60	9.56	9.76	-	-	-	9.62	9.21	9.54	-	-	9.78
	012	11.97	11.92	12.23	-	-	-	11.94	11.52	11.93	-	-	12.13
Mg^{2+}	110	2.23 (30^0C)	2.22	-	1.66		1.90	-	-	-	-	-	3.45
	111	-	-	-	9.98		-	-	-	-	-	-	-
	120	-	-	-	-		-	-		-	-	-	6.46
Ca^{2+}	110	1.35-1.43 (I=0)	1.39 (I=0)		1.12	1.31	-	2.03	1.465	-	-	-	-
	120	-	-	-	-	-	-	4.97	-	-	-	-	-
	111	-	-	-	9.93	-	-	-	-	-	-	-	-
Pb^{2+}	110	5.63	4.36	5.46	4.65	-	-	-	-	4.58	-	4.70	5.53
	120	8.10	7.70	9.32	7.3	-	-	-	-	7.19	-	8.36	9.98
	111	13.33	-	12.60	11.1	-	-	-	-	10.51	-	-	-
	11-1	-2.85	-	-2.77	-	-	-	-	-	-	-	-	-
Cd^{2+}	110	4.28	4.24	-	4.34 $I = 0.5$	-	4.25	-	-	-	4.62	-	4.74
	120	7.72	7.71	-	8.05 $I = 0.5$	-	-	-	-	-	8.33	-	8.60
Hg^{2+}	110	10.3	10.3 I=0.5	-	-	-	4.1	-	-	--	-	-	-
	120	19.2	19.2 I=0.5		-	-	-	-	-		-	-	-
Reference		58	59	60	61	62	63	64	65	66	67	68	99

The use of both activity and concentration scales for hydrogen ion in potentiometric methods may be another reason for the observed inconsistency in the formation constants. The methods used for adjusting the reported equilibrium constants to the required conditions of temperature and ionic strength introduce some uncertainty in the predicted values as experienced by several workers[69-71]. As concentration formation constants are highly dependent on the experimental conditions like ionic strength, temperature, etc., the author has redetermined the formation constants of metal-ligand species of the amino acids of interest under the conditions identical to binary and ternary systems of dihydrazides.

Calvin-Wilson potentiometric titrations[16-19] were conducted for solutions of 1:1 and 1:2 metal to glycine molar concentration ratios in aqueous medium as described in Chapter-2 of the thesis. The upper pH limit of accepting data for analysis was determined by the appearance of opalescence leading to precipitation indicated by a downward drift of the pH-meter dial readings. The acquired data were first analysed using classical methods[18, 19] to obtain the formation constants of simple MX and MX_2 type of complexes for all the metal ion systems under study. Assuming the formation of only these species, simulated titration curves were generated using the program SOPHD[48]. The experimental and simulated titration curves were plotted together to find out the regions where they differ. The experimental and simulated titration curves for metal ion-glycine systems for 1:1 and 1:2 (metal to ligand) molar ratios were depicted in figures 4.37a to 4.46a. The position and extent of deviation give information regarding the nature of missing species for inclusion in the chemical models to be prepared for refinement using the Miniquad-75 program[20].

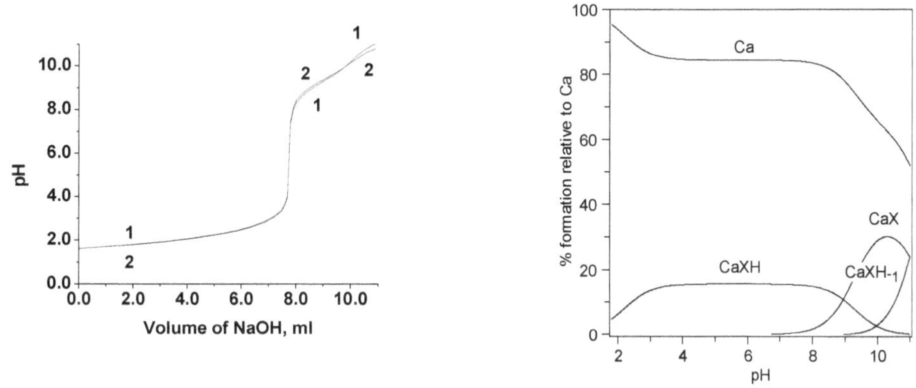

a. (1) Simulated titration curve
(2) Experimental titration curve

b. Species distribution diagram

[Glycine] = 0.0100 mol dm^{-3} [Ca (II)] = 0.00998 mol dm^{-3}

[HCl] = 0.03211 mol dm^{-3} [NaOH] = 0.2066 mol dm^{-3}

Total Volume = 50.0 cm^3 Temp: 30.0 ±0.1°C I = 0.1 mol dm^{-3} NaCl

Figure 4.37: Ca (II) –GLYCINE (XH) SYSTEM (1:1)

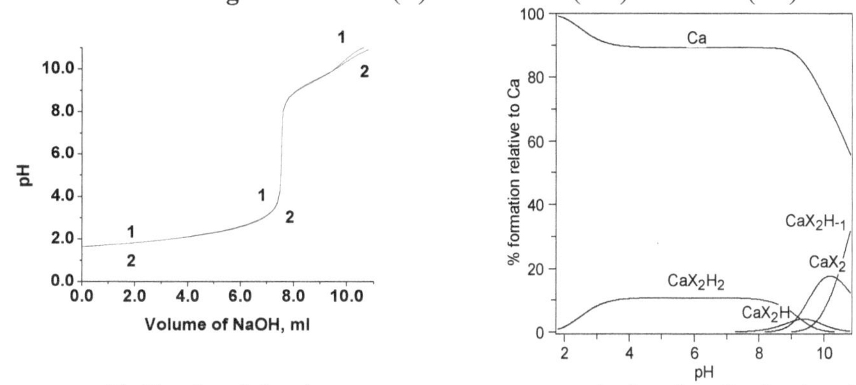

a. (1) Simulated titration curve
(2) Experimental titration curve

b. Species distribution diagram

[Glycine] = 0.0100 mol dm^{-3} [Ca (II)] = 0.00499 mol dm^{-3}

[HCl] = 0.03155 mol dm^{-3} [NaOH] = 0.2066 mol dm^{-3}

Total Volume = 50.0 cm^3 Temp: 30.0 ±0.1°C I = 0.1 mol dm^{-3} NaCl

Figure 4.38: Ca (II) – GLYCINE(XH) SYSTEM (1:2)

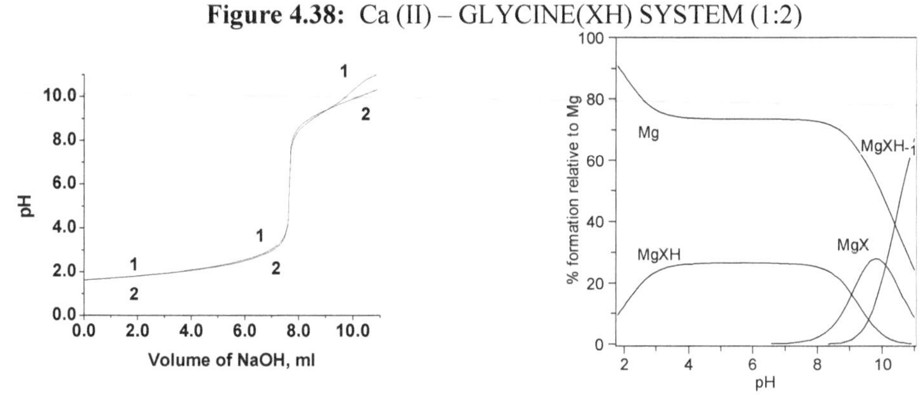

a. (1) Simulated titration curve
(2) Experimental titration curve

b. Species distribution diagram

[Glycine]= 0.0100 mol dm^{-3} [Mg (II)] =0.0100 mol dm^{-3}

[HCl] = 0.03201 mol dm^{-3} [NaOH] = 0.2066 mol dm^{-3}

Total Volume = 50.0 cm^3 Temp: 30.0 ±0.1°C I = 0.1 mol dm^{-3} NaCl

Figure 4.39: Mg (II) – GLYCINE(XH) SYSTEM (1:1)

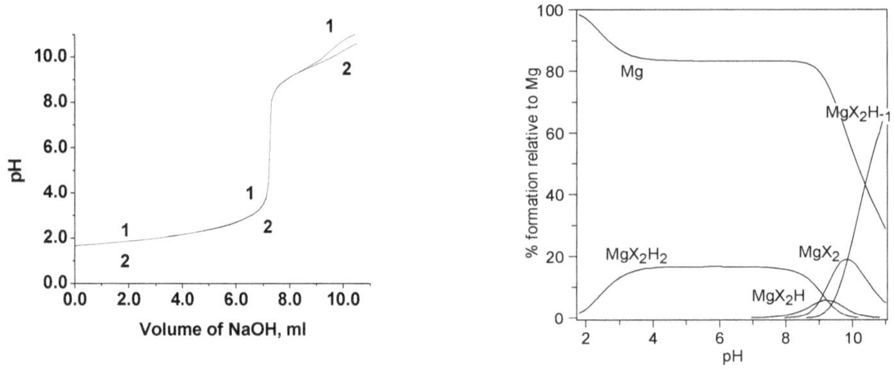

a. (1) Simulated titration curve
(2) Experimental titration curve

b. Species distribution diagram

[Glycine] =0.0100 mol dm^{-3} [Mg(II)] = 0.0050 mol dm^{-3}
[HCl] =0.03150 mol dm^{-3} [NaOH] = 0.2066 mol dm^{-3}
Total Volume = 50.0 cm^3 Temp: 30.0 ±0.1^{0}C I = 0.1 mol dm^{-3} NaCl

Figure 4.40: Mg (II) - GLYCINE(XH) SYSTEM (1:2)

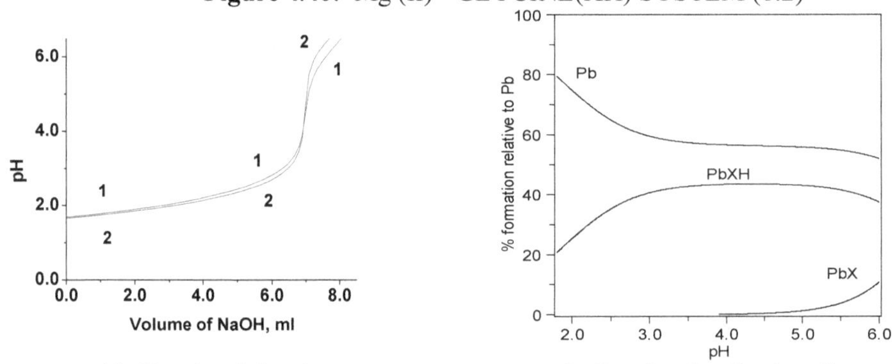

a. (1) Simulated titration curve
(2) Experimental titration curve

b. Species distribution diagram

[Glycine] = 0.0100 mol dm^{-3} [Pb (II)]= 0.00998 mol dm^{-3}
[HNO_3] = 0.03089mol dm^{-3} [NaOH]=0.2053 mol dm^{-3}
Total Volume = 50.0 cm^3 Temp: 30.0 ±0.1^{0}C I = 0.1 mol $dm^{-3}$$NaNO_3$

Figure 4.41: Pb (II) - GLYCINE (XH) SYSTEM (1:1)

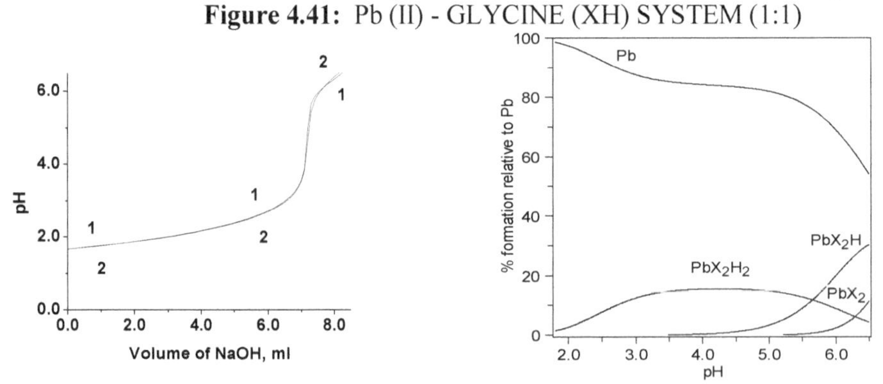

a. (1) Simulated titration curve
(2) Experimental titration curve

b. Species distribution diagram

[Glycine]= 0.0100 mol dm^{-3} [Pb (II)] = 0.00499 mol dm^{-3}
[HNO_3] = 0.03038mol dm^{-3} [NaOH] = 0.2053mol dm^{-3}
Total Volume = 50.0 cm^3 Temp: 30.0 ±0.1^{0}C I = 0.1 mol $dm^{-3}$$NaNO_3$

Figure 4.42: Pb (II) - GLYCINE(XH) SYSTEM (1:2)

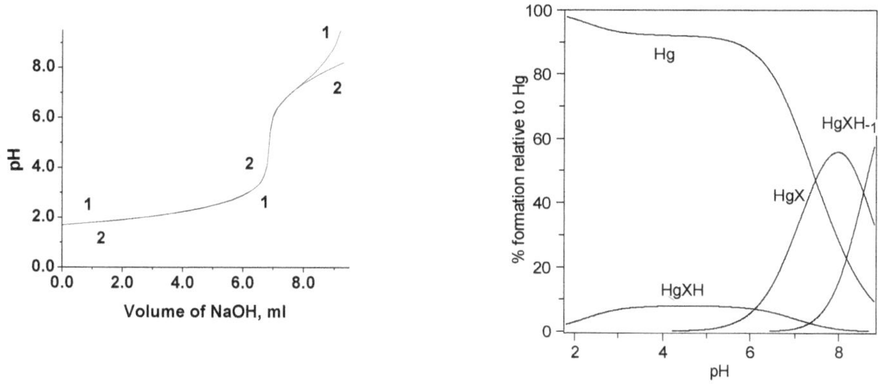

a. (1) Simulated titration curve b. Species distribution diagram
(2) Experimental titration curve

[Glycine] = 0.0100 mol dm^{-3} [Hg (II)]= 0.01004 mol dm^{-3}
[HCl] = 0.03096 mol dm^{-3} [NaOH] = 0.2053mol dm^{-3}
Total Volume = 50.0 cm^3 Temp: 30.0 ±0.1°C I = 0.1 mol dm^{-3} NaCl

Figure 4.43: Hg (II) –GLYCINE (XH) SYSTEM (1:1)

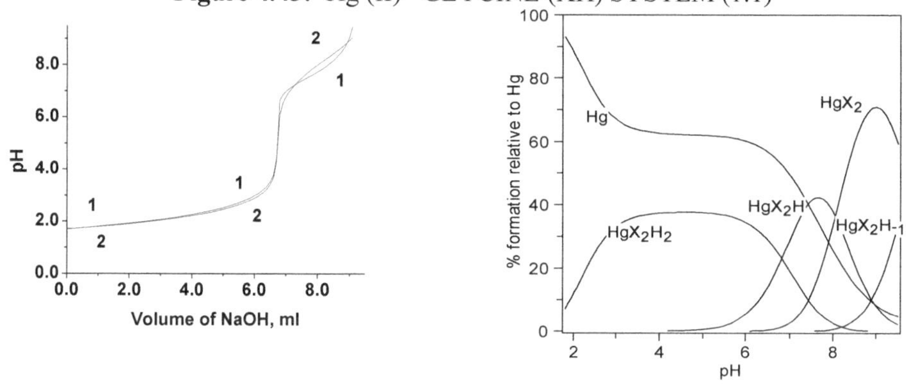

a. (1) Simulated titration curve b. Species distribution diagram
(2) Experimental titration curve

[Glycine] = 0.0100 mol dm^{-3} [Hg (II)] = 0.00501 mol dm^{-3}
[HCl] = 0.03041 mol dm^{-3} [NaOH] = 0.2053 mol dm^{-3}
Total Volume = 50.0 cm^3 Temp:30.0 ± 0.1°C I = 0.1 mol dm^{-3} NaCl

Figure 4.44: Hg (II) – GLYCINE(XH) SYSTEM (1:2)

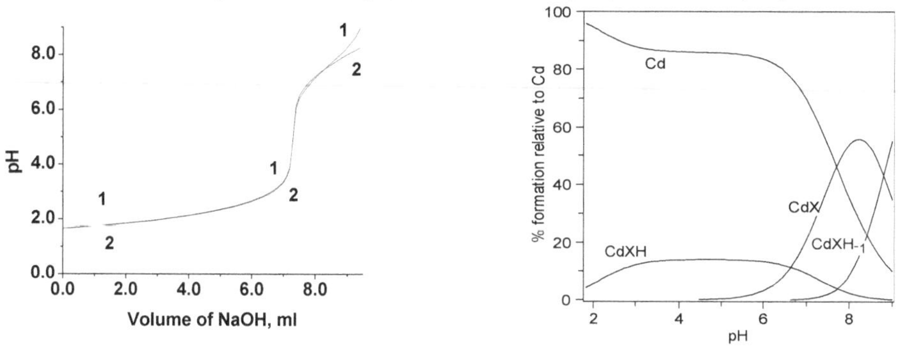

a. (1) Simulated titration curve b. Species distribution diagram
(2) Experimental titration curve

[Glycine]= 0.0100 mol dm^{-3} [Cd (II)]= 0.0100 mol dm^{-3}
[HCl] = 0.03224 mol dm^{-3} [NaOH] = 0.2066 mol dm^{-3}
Total Volume = 50.0 cm^3 Temp: 30.0 ± 0.1°C I = 0.1 mol dm^{-3} NaCl

Figure 4.45: Cd (II) – GLYCINE(XH) SYSTEM (1:1)

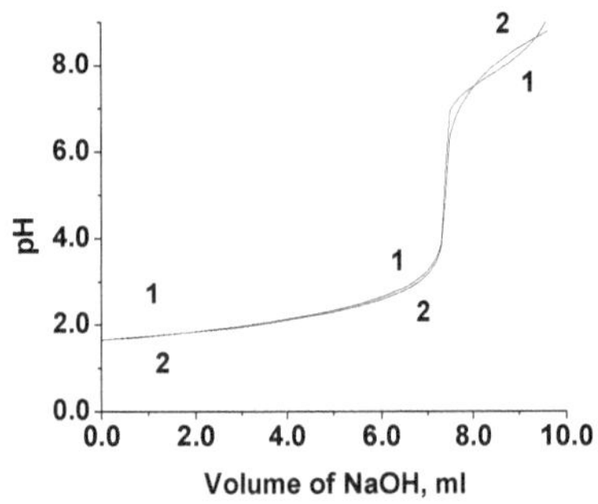

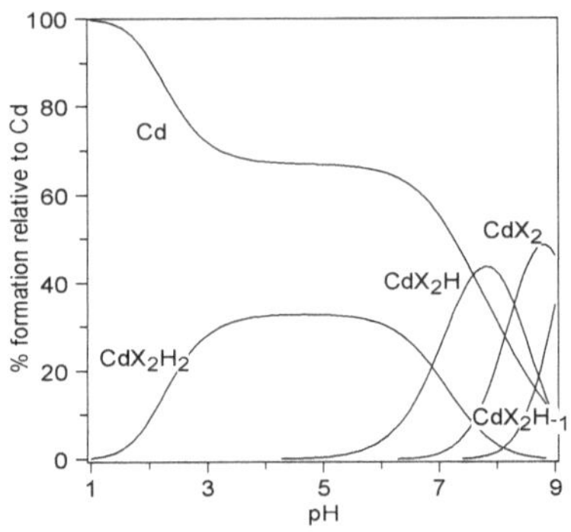

a. (1) Simulated titration curve (2) Experimental titration curve

b. Species distribution diagram

[Glycine]= 0.0100 mol dm^{-3} [Cd (II)]= 0.00499 mol dm^{-3}

[HCl] = 0.03161 mol dm^{-3} [NaOH] = 0.2066 mol dm^{-3}

Total Volume = 50.0 cm^3 Temp: 30.0 ± 0.1°C I = 0.1 mol dm^{-3} NaCl

Figure 4.46: Cd (II) - GLYCINE(XH) SYSTEM (1:2)

The difference between the simulated and experimental titration curves throughout the pH region for all the metal ion-glycine systems suggests the presence of other species. Therefore, various chemical models containing all the plausible species were prepared and submitted for refinement to the Miniquad-75 program[20]. The initial estimates for the protonated species were calculated basing on the formation constants of simple complexes obtained by classical methods and protonation constants of the ligand. As the metal ions are susceptible to hydrolysis, the formation constants of the corresponding hydroxylated species were also included in the models. Initial estimates of the hydrolysis constants were obtained from the literature reports[49-51]. The best-fit models obtained for all the metal ion–amino acid systems together with their standard deviations and the sum of the square of residuals as obtained from the program Miniquad-75 are tabulated in Table 4.5. Inclusion of metal hydroxide species in the models resulted in a final rejection, suggesting their absence or existence at undetectable low concentrations in the pH region of analysis. Only ligand containing hydroxylated species were found to be present in the best-fit models.

Table 4.5: Best-fit models for Glycine- metal ion systems in aqueous mediumat 303.0 K and ionic strength, I=0.1 mol dm^{-3}

Metal ion	Composition	Species, mxh	Log β_{mxh} (SD)	Statistical parameters
Ca^{2+}	(M: X) 1:1	011	9.56	U/NP = 3.687X10^{-8}
		012	11.86	NP=71, χ^2= 77.52
		111	10.90 (7)	R=0.0106
		110	1.96 (4)	Skewness= 0.90
		11-1	-9.03 (3)	Kurtosis= 6.85
	1:2	011	9.56	U/NP = 2.268 X 10^{-8}
		012	11.86	NP=95
		122	22.30 (9)	χ^2= 199.58
		121	13.01 (12)	R=0.0065
		120	3.90 (6)	Skewness= -0.23
		12-1	-6.49 (6)	Kurtosis= 4.96
Mg^{2+}	1:1	011	9.56	U/NP = 1.927 X10^{-8}
		012	11.86	NP= 90, χ^2= 138.24
		111	11.25 (3)	R=0.0057
		110	2.19 (3)	Skewness= -0.05
		11-1	-7.92 (2)	Kurtosis= 4.98
	1:2	011	9.56	U/NP =2.969 X 10^{-9}
		012	11.86	NP=83
		122	22.58 (15)	χ^2= 19.93
		121	13.34 (13)	R=0.0051
		120	4.33 (2)	Skewness= 0.57
		12-1	-5.53 (2)	Kurtosis= 3.81
Pb^{2+}	1:1	011	9.56	U/NP = 7.618 X10^{-9}
		012	11.86	NP=112, χ^2= 134.4
		111	11.70 (1)	R=0.0039, Kurtosis= 2.55
		110	5.16 (9)	Skewness= -0.13
	1:2	011	9.56	U/NP = 9.119 X10^{-9}
		012	11.86	NP=191,.χ^2= 103.7
		122	22.55 (3)	R=0.0060
		121	16.90 (3)	Skewness= -0.19
		120	9.97 (1)	Kurtosis= 4.17
Hg^{2+}	1:1	011	9.56	U/NP = 1.262 X10^{-8}
		012	11.86	NP=88, χ^2= 93.88
		111	10.53 (8)	R=0.0052
		110	4.42 (1)	Skewness= 0.92
		11-1	-4.14 (1)	Kurtosis= 4.26
	1:2	011	9.56	U/NP = 3.933X10^{-8}
		012	11.86	NP=81
		122	23.32 (5)	χ^2= 83.5
		121	16.50 (7)	R=0.009
		120	8.45 (4)	Skewness= -0.08
		12-1	-1.29 (7)	Kurtosis= 3.95
Cd^{2+}	1:1	011	9.56	U/NP = 2.224 X10^{-8}
		012	11.86	NP=79, χ^2= 57.58
		111	10.84 (6)	R=0.0066
		110	4.21 (2)	Skewness= 0.21
		11-1	-4.59 (2)	Kurtosis= 4.58
	1:2	011	9.56	U/NP = 8.218 X 10^{-8}
		012	11.86	NP=78
		122	23.16 (8)	χ^2= 55.30
		121	16.29 (10)	R=0.014
		120	8.00 (7)	Skewness= -0.55
		12-1	-1.12 (9)	Kurtosis= 3.36

The sufficiency of the final model for each system was tested by comparing the experimental titration curve with that of the theoretical curve generated using the formation constants obtained and were found to coincide allowing for random experimental errors. The best-fit models indicate the presence of MXH and MX type of species in 1:1 (M: X) systems and MX_2H_2, MX_2H and MX_2 type of species in 1:2 (M:X) systems. In addition to the protonated and simple species, hydroxylated species were also found in some of the systems. Therefore, it is clearly evident that the metal ions interacted with the ligand, both in the mono-dentate and bidentate forms (Figure 4.47), leading to the formation of various protonated species in addition to simple complexes. The sum of squares of residuals in mass balance equations "U", "χ^2" and "R" are well within the range allowed. The formation constants are in good agreement with the literature values (Table 4.4) allowing for changes in experimental conditions of temperature and ionic strength.

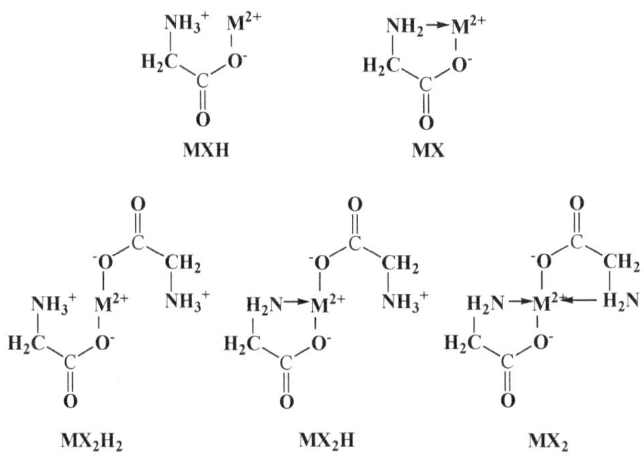

Figure 4.47: Probable bonding in glycine-metal ion complexessupported by the literature reports.

The species distribution diagrams obtained using the program HYSS[21] for all the systems were depicted inFigs. 4.37b to 4.46b. The formation of protonated species varied from 20 to 40% in different metal ion systems. This clearly indicates that the formation of protonated species in solution cannot be ignored like most of the reports in the literature. With the increase in pH the protonated species successively lose protons and form MX and MX_2 type of species. These species are dominating at higher pH and their formation varied from 30 to 70% of the total metal. Further increase in pH leads to the formation of ligand containing hydroxylated species.

The relatively low values of formation constants of Ca^{2+} and Mg^{2+} complexes compared to that of Pb^{2+}, Hg^{2+} and Cd^{2+} may be due to the weak interaction of these ions with glycine.Masunobu Maeda et al.[65], in their study on the complexing ability of Ca^{2+} with amino acids using ^{14}N and ^{17}O nmr, Raman and i.r. spectroscopic techniques reported that amino and carboxylate groups of amino acids have weak interaction with Ca^{2+}. There is no evidence of coordination of Ca^{2+} to the amino acids. The observed bonding may be due to the prevailing electrostatic interactions between the metal ion and -COO^- and -NH_2 groups. Mg^{2+} forms strong electrostatic bonds due to its high charge density relative to Ca^{2+}. Glycine provides hard carboxylate oxygen and borderline nitrogen as bonding centres. According to HSAB theory, Pb^{2+} belongs to borderline category while Hg^{2+} and Cd^{2+} are soft acids. Soft acids prefer to bond with soft bases and hard acids prefer to bond with hard bases. The border line Pb^{2+} can interact with both hard and soft bases. Therefore, it forms stronger bonds with glycine relative to soft Hg^{2+} and Cd^{2+}. This is reflected in the observed order of stabilities Pb^{2+}> Hg^{2+}> Cd^{2+}.

4.2.2 L-Histidine (L-α-amino-β-(4-imidazolyl) propanoic acid)–Metal ion Systems:

Histidine (Fig. 4.48) is an essential basic amino acid and is one of the strongest metal coordinating biological ligands. L-histidine plays an important role in the binding of metal ions by proteins.

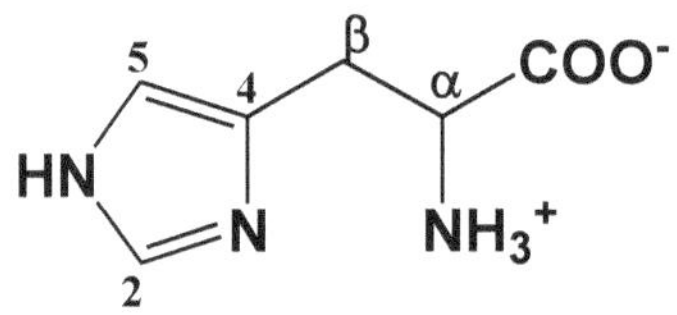

Figure 4.48: L- Histidine (XH)

It has three potential metal-binding sites, namely the carboxylate oxygen, the imidazole imido nitrogen and the α-amino nitrogen. The imidazole nitrogen of histidine residues often provides the primary means by which the metal ions are bound to proteins. Histidine has an exceptional ability to bind metal ions as a mono, bi or tridentate[72-75] ligand. As a monodentate it binds the metal ions through either the carboxylate oxygen or the imidazole imido nitrogen. As a bidentate histidine forms a six membered ring in histamine-like mode,bonding through imidazole nitrogen and α-amino group or a five membered ring analogous to glycine bonding through carboxylate oxygen and α-amino group. Simultaneous coordination may also occur from all the three donor atoms and thus generally it may also show tridentate behaviour forming adjacent six and five membered rings.

The fully protonated histidine cation XH_3^{2+}, has three ionizable hydrogen ions. With the increase in pH the ligand successively loses the carboxylic proton (-COOH) followed by pyridine like imidazole –NH proton and finally protonated α-amino group forming XH_2^+, XH and X^- species respectively as described in Section 3.3 of

Chapter 3 and shown in Figure 4.49. In strong basic solutions > 13 pH, the pyrrole proton may also ionize giving rise to X^{2-} species. The presence of a side chain containing a potential donor atom in addition to glycine-like coordination centre enables histidine to form a variety of protonated and unprotonated complexes with metal ions in different coordination modes.

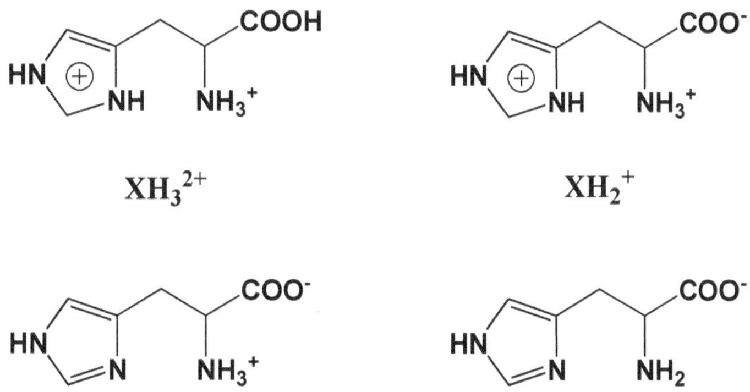

XH (Zwitter ionic form) X^-

Figure 4.49: Protonated and deprotonated species of L-Histidine (XH)

Therefore, it is interesting to study the chemical speciation of L-histidine with both the essential (Mg^{2+} and Ca^{2+}) and the toxic (Pb^{2+}, Hg^{2+} and Cd^{2+}) metal ions in aqueous systems. Only a few reliable literature reports (Table 4.6) were found that too only for Pb^{2+}, Hg^{2+} and Cd^{2+} complexes of L-histidine. The formation of protonated species (in which histidine acts as a monodentate or bidentate) and hydroxylated complexes were seems to be not considered in most of the reports. Classical/ graphical methods of analysis that were used by some investigators approximate the complex systems with several overlapping equilibria to simple systems, assuming the formation of only mono-nuclear complexes with widely separated equilibria. A complete speciation study using modern computational methods is therefore, mandatory to understand the behaviour of such systems in biological fluids.

TABLE 4.6: Some literature reported formation constants of Pb^{2+}, Hg^{2+} and Cd^{2+} complexes of L-Histidine

Metal ion	*mlh*	**Formation constants of Metal ion-L-histidine complexes reported in the literature**					
		Ionic Strength, I and Temperature, t^0C					
		0.1M 25^{0}C	0.1M 25^{0}C	0.1M 25^{0}C	0.1M 25^{0}C	0.1M 25^{0}C	0.15 M 37^{0}C
H^+	011	9.17	9.09	-	9.12	-	-
	012	15.24	15.11	-	15.22	-	-
	013	17.04	16.91	-	16.92	-	-
Pb^{2+}	110	5.95	5.94	-	5.95	-	5.96
	111	-	-	-	-	-	-
	11-1	-	-	-	-		-
	120	10.10	10.11	-	10.11	-	9.806 (*I*=3.0, 25^0)
	121	-	-	-	17.13		
	122	-	-	-	23.39		
Cd^{2+}	110	5.39	6.48 (*I*=3.0)	5.40	-	5.78	-
	120	9.66	11.11 (*I*=3.0)	9.70	-	11.48	-
	121	-	-	-	-	18.53	-
Hg^{2+}	110	-	-	-	-	-	-
	120	-	-	-	-	-	-
	111	12.3	-	-	-		
	112	19.5	-	-			
Reference no.		76	59	77	78	67	68

Thus, the author has taken up a speciation study on L-histidine- metal ion systems in aqueous medium under identical conditions to that of the ternary systems containing dihydrazide, amino acid and metal ion. Keeping in view of the various protonation forms of histidine and its coordination modes, chemical models containing all the plausible species were submitted for analysis to the Miniquad-75 program[20]. The initial estimates of the formation constants for the plausible species were calculated using the formation constants of simple complexes obtained by analysing the data using classical methods[18, 19]. Theoretical titration curves calculated from the values of acid dissociation constants of the ligand and formation constants of the simple complexes obtained from classical methods were plotted together with the experimental curves (Figures 4.50 a to 4.59a) to determine the nature of the missing species.

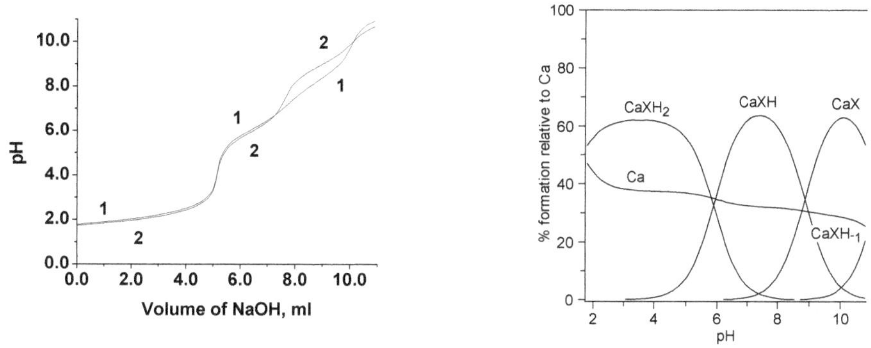

a. (1) Simulated titration curve
(2) Experimental titration curve

b. Species distribution diagram

[Histidine] = 0.0100 mol dm^{-3} [Ca (II)] = 0.00998 mol dm^{-3}
[HCl] = 0.03056 mol dm^{-3} [NaOH] = 0.2030 mol dm^{-3}
Total Volume = 50.0 cm^3 Temp: 30.0 ± 0.1^{0}C I = 0.1 mol dm^{-3} NaCl

Figure 4.50: Ca (II) –HISTIDINE (XH)SYSTEM (1:1)

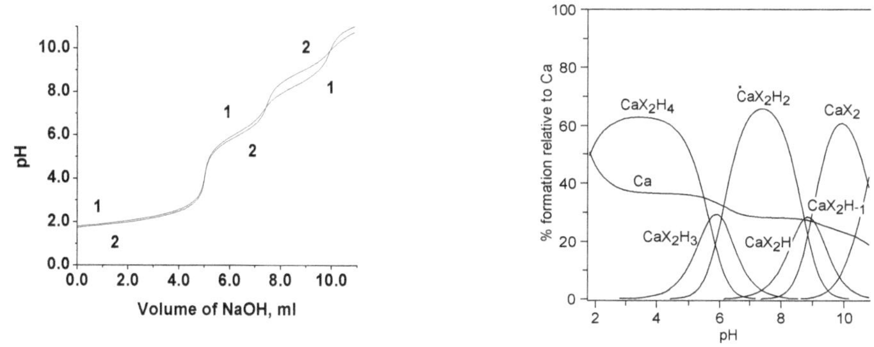

a. (1) Simulated titration curve
(2) Experimental titration curve

b. Species distribution diagram

[Histidine] = 0.0100 mol dm^{-3} [Ca (II)] = 0.00499 mol dm^{-3}
[HCl] = 0.02980 mol dm^{-3} [NaOH] = 0.2030 mol dm^{-3}
Total Volume = 50.0 cm^3 Temp: 30.0 ± 0.1^{0}C I = 0.1 mol dm^{-3} NaCl

Figure 4.51: Ca (II) – HISTIDINE (XH)SYSTEM (1:2)

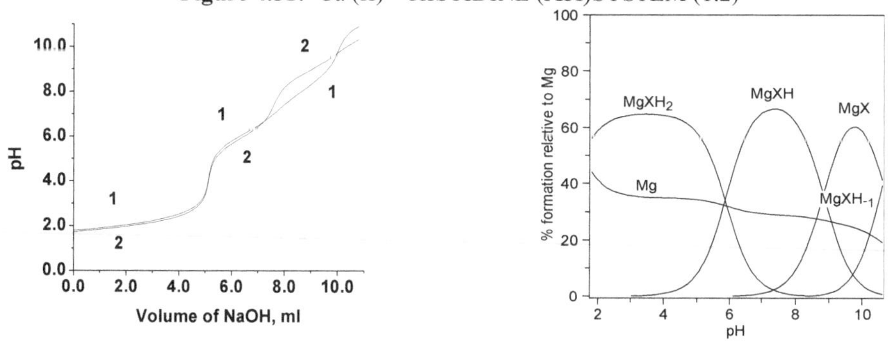

a. (1) Simulated titration curve
(2) Experimental titration curve

b. Species distribution diagram

[Histidine] = 0.0100 mol dm^{-3} [Mg (II)] = 0.0100 mol dm^{-3}
[HCl] = 0.03046 mol dm^{-3} [NaOH] = 0.2030 mol dm^{-3}
Total Volume = 50.0 cm^3 Temp: 30.0 ± 0.1^{0}C I = 0.1 mol dm^{-3} NaCl

Figure 4.52: Mg (II) – HISTIDINE (XH)SYSTEM (1:1)

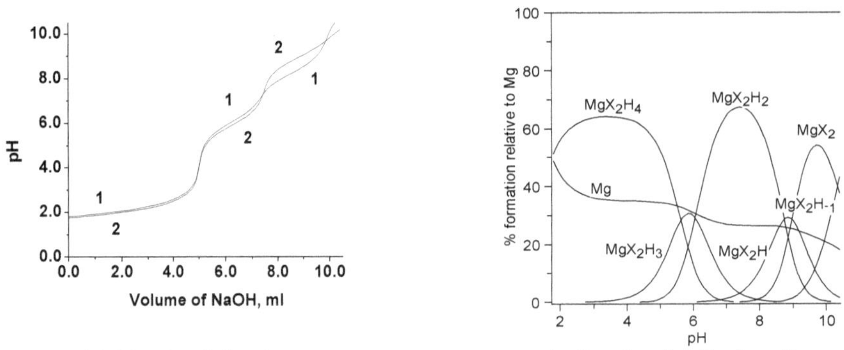

a. (1) Simulated titration curve
(2) Experimental titration curve

b. Species distribution diagram

[Histidine] = 0.0100 mol dm^{-3} [Mg (II)]= 0.0050 mol dm^{-3}
[HCl] = 0.02995 mol dm^{-3} [NaOH] = 0.2030 mol dm^{-3}
Total Volume = 50.0 cm^3 Temp: 30.0 ± 0.1^0C I = 0.1 mol dm^{-3} NaCl

Figure 4.53: Mg (II) - HISTIDINE (XH)SYSTEM (1:2)

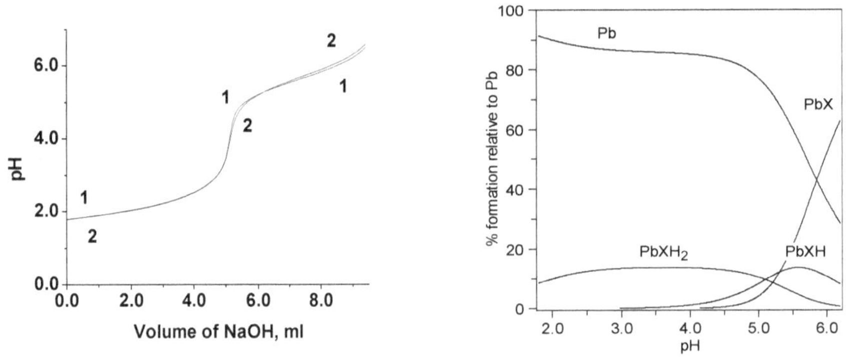

a. (1) Simulated titration curve
(2) Experimental titration curve

b. Species distribution diagram

[Histidine] = 0.0100 mol dm^{-3} [Pb (II)] = 0.01003 mol dm^{-3}
$[HNO_3]$ = 0.03082 mol dm^{-3} [NaOH] = 0.2030 mol dm^{-3}
Total Volume = 50.0 cm^3 Temp: 30.0 ± 0.1^0C I = 0.1 mol dm^{-3} $NaNO_3$

Figure 4.54: Pb (II) - HISTIDINE (XH)SYSTEM (1:1)

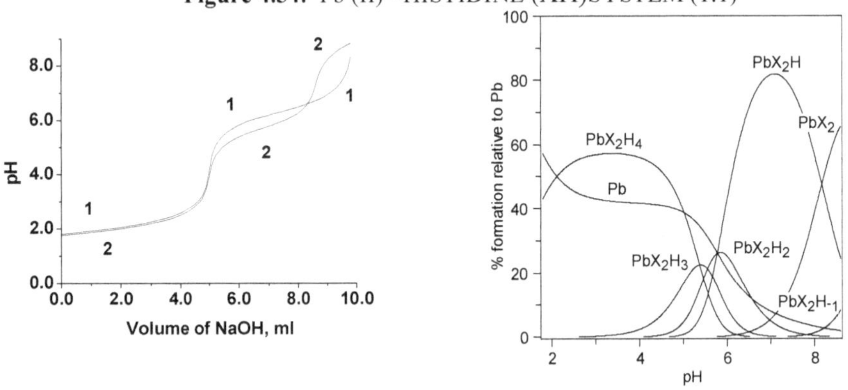

a. (1) Simulated titration curve
(2) Experimental titration curve

b. Species distribution diagram

[Histidine] = 0.0100 mol dm^{-3} [Pb (II)] = 0.00499 mol dm^{-3}
$[HNO_3]$ = 0.02993 mol dm^{-3} [NaOH] = 0.2030 mol dm^{-3}
Total Volume = 50.0 cm^3 Temp: 30.0 ± 0.1^0C I = 0.1 mol dm^{-3} $NaNO_3$

Figure 4.55: Pb (II) - HISTIDINE (XH)SYSTEM (1:2)

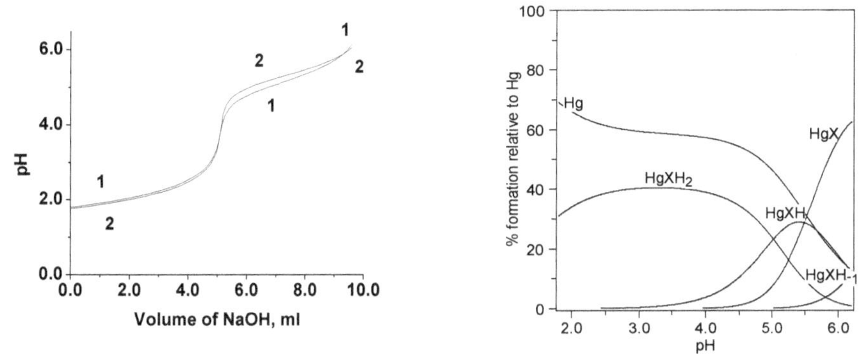

a. (1) Simulated titration curve b. Species distribution diagram
(2) Experimental titration curve

[Histidine] = 0.0100 mol dm^{-3} [Hg (II)] = 0.01006 mol dm^{-3}
[HCl] = 0.04102 mol dm^{-3} [NaOH] = 0.1773mol dm^{-3}
Total Volume = 50.0 cm^3 Temp: 30.0 ± 0.1^{0}C I = 0.1 mol dm^{-3} NaCl

Figure 4.56: Hg (II) –HISTIDINE (XH)SYSTEM (1:1)

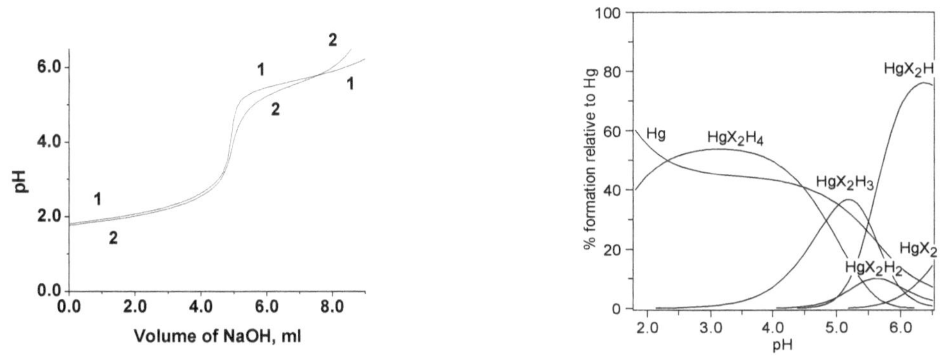

a. (1) Simulated titration curve b. Species distribution diagram
(2) Experimental titration curve

[Histidine] = 0.0100mol dm^{-3} [Hg (II)] = 0.00502 mol dm^{-3}
[HCl] = 0.04069 mol dm^{-3} [NaOH] = 0.1773 mol dm^{-3}
Total Volume = 50.0 cm^3 Temp: 30.0 ± 0.1^{0}C I = 0.1 mol dm^{-3} NaCl

Figure 4.57: Hg (II) – HISTIDINE(XH)SYSTEM (1:2)

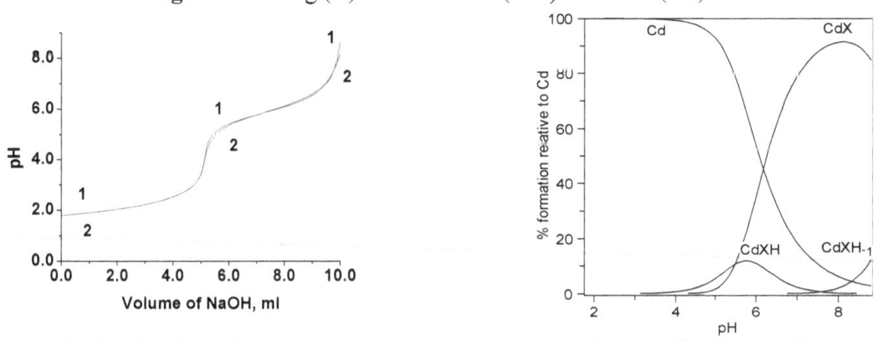

a. (1) Simulated titration curve b. Species distribution diagram
(2) Experimental titration curve

[Histidine] = 0.0100 mol dm^{-3} [Cd (II)] = 0.01003 mol dm^{-3}
[HCl] = 0.03089 mol dm^{-3} [NaOH] = 0.2030 mol dm^{-3}
Total Volume = 50.0 cm^3 Temp: 30.0 ± 0.1^{0}C I = 0.1 mol dm^{-3} NaCl

Figure 4.58: Cd (II) – HISTIDINE (XH)SYSTEM (1:1)

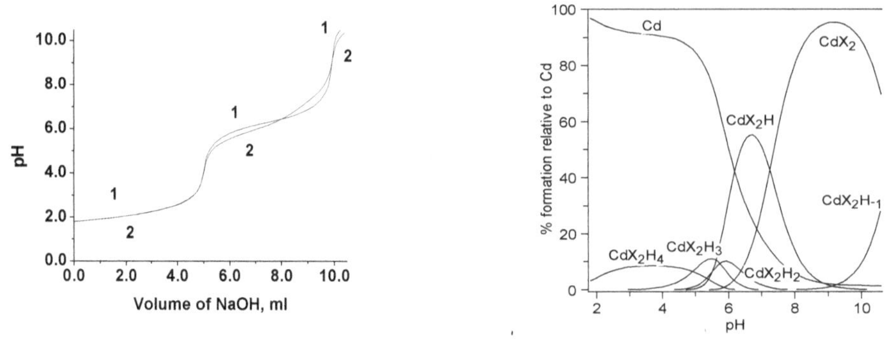

a. (1) Simulated titration curve
(2) Experimental titration curve

b. Species distribution diagram

[Histidine] = 0.0100 mol dm^{-3} [Cd (II)] = 0.00502 mol dm^{-3}
[HCl] = 0.03036 mol dm^{-3} [NaOH] = 0.2030mol dm^{-3}
Total Volume = 50.0 cm^{3} Temp: 30.0 ± 0.1^{0}C I = 0.1 mol dm^{-3} NaCl

Figure 4.59: Cd (II) - HISTIDINE (XH)SYSTEM (1:2)

The wide differences between the experimental and theoretical curves throughout the pH region of study for all the metal ion-histidine systems of compositions 1:1 and 1:2 (M: X) indicate the formation of other species in addition to simple MX and MX_2 type of complexes. The best-fit models obtained after refinement using the Miniquad-75 program along with statistical parametersare included in Table 4.7. The values of formation constants are in good agreement with those reported in the literature (Table 4.6) allowing for changes in the experimental conditions of temperature and ionic strength.

Table 4.7: Best-fit models for L-Histidine- metal ion systems in aqueous mediumat 303.0 K and ionic strength, *I* =0.1 mol dm^{-3}

Metal ion	Composition (M: X)	Species mxh	Log β_{mxh} (SD)	Statistical parameters
Ca^{2+}	1:1	011	8.95	U/NP = 1.841 X10^{-8}
		012	15.02	NP=105
		013	16.74	χ^2= 112.00
		112	17.68 (4)	R=0.0053
		111	11.79 (4)	Skewness= -0.09
		110	2.92 (4)	Kurtosis= 6.56
		11-1	-8.30 (5)	
	1:2	011	8.95	U/NP =3.431 X10^{-8}
		012	15.02	NP=104
		013	16.74	χ^2= 85.79
		124	35.18 (15)	R=0.0078
		123	29.52 (9)	Skewness= -0.39
		122	23.47 (8)	Kurtosis= 7.27
		121	14.73 (9)	
		120	5.79 (8)	
		12-1	-4.99 (9)	

(Table 4.7 contd........)

Mg^{2+}	1:1	011	8.95	U/NP = 7.982 X10^{-9}
		012	15.02	NP=102
		013	16.74	χ^2= 112.67
		112	17.76 (2)	R=0.0035
		111	11.90 (2)	Skewness= 0.27
		110	3.07 (2)	Kurtosis= 5.18
		11-1	-7.55 (3)	
	1:2	011	8.95	U/NP =4.439 X10^{-9}
		012	15.02	NP=111
		013	16.74	χ^2= 70.98
		124	35.24 (8)	R=0.0031
		123	29.61 (12)	Skewness= 0.07
		122	23.56 (9)	Kurtosis= 4.44
		121	14.82 (9)	
		120	5.89 (9)	
		12-1	-4.50 (8)	
Pb^{2+}	1:1	011	8.95	U/NP = 3.090 X10^{-8}
		012	15.02	NP=114
		013	16.74	χ^2= 87.84
		112	16.31 (9)	R=0.007
		111	11.21 (5)	Skewness= 1.50
		110	5.90 (2)	Kurtosis= 5.62
	1:2	011	8.95	
		012	15.02	U/NP =4.264 X10^{-9}
		013	16.74	NP=86
		124	34.96 (2)	χ^2= 111.80
		123	29.59 (5)	R=0.0025
		122	24.04 (3)	Skewness= -0.05
		121	18.27(2)	Kurtosis= 6.18
		120	10.10 (4)	
		12-1	0.60 (4)	
Hg^{2+}	1:1	011	8.95	U/NP = 2.036 X10^{-9}
		012	15.02	NP=211
		013	16.74	χ^2= 445.64
		112	17.11(0.6)	R=0.0013
		111	12.09 (1)	Skewness= -0.76
		110	6.60 (1)	Kurtosis= 5.22
		11-1	-0.32 (1)	
	1:2	011	8.95	U/NP =2.370 X10^{-9}
		012	15.02	NP=271
		013	16.74	χ^2= 36.56
		124	34.86 (1)	R=0.0016
		123	30.02 (1)	Skewness=- 0.10
		122	24.04 (3)	Kurtosis= 5.40
		121	19.02 (1)	
		120	11.80 (1)	
Cd^{2+}	1.1	011	8.95	U/NP = 1.139 X10^{-8}
		012	15.02	NP=105
		013	16.74	χ^2= 118.4
		111	10.88 (4)	R=0.0041
		110	5.38 (1)	Skewness= -0.04
		11-1	-4.26 (1)	Kurtosis= 4.80
	1:2	011	8.95	U/NP = 1.148 X10^{-9}
		012	15.02	NP=103
		013	16.74	χ^2= 44.06
		124	33.13 (7)	R=0.0044
		123	28.22 (7)	Skewness= 0.45
		122	22.48 (10)	Kurtosis= 4.70
		121	16.97 (3)	
		120	9.72 (2)	
		12-1	-1.26 (7)	

The best-fit models obtained indicate the formation of MXH_2, MXH, MX and MXH_{-1} type of species for 1:1 molar (metal ion to histidine) solutions and MX_2H_4, MX_2H_3, MX_2H_2, MX_2H and MX_2 species for 1:2 systems. The species distribution diagrams (Figs. 4.50b to 4.59b) indicate that the species MXH_2 and $M(XH_2)_2$ i.e. MX_2H_4 for different metal ions exist at low pH with a maximum of formation in the pH region of 3.5 to 3.8. This is also the pH region of maximum formation of XH_2^+ species of the histidine by deprotonation of the carboxylic proton of the fully protonated XH_3^+ species. Therefore, the formation of MXH_2 and MX_2H_4 type of species may be due to the involvement of histidine as a mono-dentate bonding through only carboxylate oxygen. Both the amino and imidazole nitrogens are protonated in this pH region, and only the carboxylate group is available to bind the metal ion.The percentages of formation of $M(XH_2)$ and $M(XH_2)_2$ species are relatively high for Ca^{2+} and Mg^{2+} compared to other metal ions. This is expected as Ca^{2+} and Mg^{2+}ions being hard acids prefer bonding with carboxylate oxygen, which is a hard base. Pb^{2+} is of borderline category and Hg^{2+} and Cd^{2+} are soft acids.

With the increase in pH these species lose imidazole –NH or α-NH_3^+ protons to form M(XH) and $M(XH)_2$ type of species. The probable bonding mode in these species may be predicted in different ways as histidine can coordinate in three ways, (a) glycine-like (N-amino and O-carboxyl), or (b) imidazole propionic acid-like (N-imidazole and O-carboxyl) or (c) histamine-like (N-imidazole and N-amino) as shown in Fig. 4.60. Histamine like bonding is not possible for MXH or $M(XH)_2$ type of species as the carboxylate group is already deprotonated and involved in bonding.Therefore, the mode of bonding in MXH and $M(XH)_2$ types of complexes is uncertain. It is also probable that the overall formation constant may have contributions from the possible micro-constants.

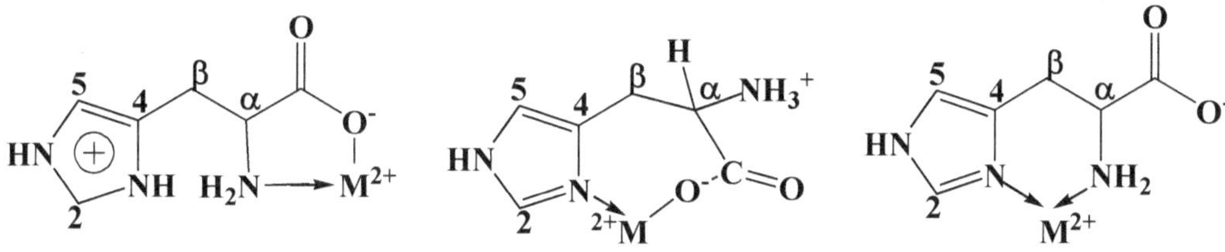

(a) (b) (c)

Figure 4.60: Probable bidentate modes of bonding of histidine

Bonding modes(a) and (c) in which the bonding is either glycine-like or histamine-like (for MX) were proposed by several investigators on the basis of CD[79, 80], ESR[81, 82] and Raman[83] spectral studies on Cu^{2+} complexes of histidine in solid state. Structure (b) in which the coordination is through N-imidazole and O-carboxylate (imidazole propionic acid-like) was supported by some other investigators on the basis of infrared spectral data[83-87] and solution phase studies of histidine-divalent metal ion complexes.

In MX_2H_3(i.e. $M(XH_2)(XH)$) type of species one of the two ligands attached to the metal ion still possesses protonated imidazole and amino groups while the other is deprived of one of them. The step-wise (Table 4.8) protonation constants, $\Delta\log\beta_{111}^{112}$ (column-1), $\Delta\log\beta_{123}^{124}$ (column-3) and $\Delta\log\beta_{122}^{123}$ (column-4) for the formation of MXH_2 from MXH, MX_2H_4 from MX_2H_3 and MX_2H_3 from MX_2H_2 respectively are of the order of the protonation constant (6.07) of the imidazole nitrogen. Further, the species distribution diagrams (Figs. 4.50b to 4.59b) indicate that the pH of the maximum formation of MXH and MX_2H_2type of species is below 7.2. This clearly supports the involvement of the imidazole nitrogen in bonding by deprotonation while the α-amino group is protonated and intact. Therefore, probably, the solution phase studies support the mode of bonding (c) of Fig. 4.60, where histidine acts as a bidentate, bonding through N-imidazole and O-carboxylate (imidazole propionic acid-like) groups.

Table 4.8: Step-wise protonation constants of L-histidine- metal ion complexes

	$\Delta\log\beta$					
Metal ion	(1) $\Delta\log\beta_{111}^{112}$	(2) $\Delta\log\beta_{110}^{111}$	(3) $\Delta\log\beta_{123}^{124}$	(4) $\Delta\log\beta_{122}^{123}$	(5) $\Delta\log\beta_{121}^{122}$	(6) $\Delta\log\beta_{120}^{121}$
	Log β_{112}- Log β_{111}	Log β_{111}- Log β_{110}	Log β_{124}- Log β_{123}	Log β_{123}- Log β_{122}	Log β_{122}- Log β_{121}	Log β_{121}- Log β_{120}
Ca^{2+}	5.89	8.87	5.66	6.05	8.74	8.94
Mg^{2+}	5.86	8.83	5.63	6.05	8.74	8.93
Pb^{2+}	5.10	5.31	5.37	5.55	5.77	8.17
Hg^{2+}	5.02	5.49	4.84	5.98	5.02	7.22
Cd^{2+}	-	5.50	4.91	5.74	5.51	7.25

The species, MXH, MX_2H_2 and MX_2H with increase in pH forfeit α-ammonium protons leading to the formation of MX and MX_2 type of species. Depending on the metal ion, the formation of MX and MX_2 species reach 60 to 92% between 7 and 10 pH. In the case of $Pb^{2+}$and Hg^{2+} systems the analysis was limited to the data points of appearance of opalescence in solution. In some of the systems formation of ligand containing hydroxylated species was observed. The magnitudes of $\Delta\log\beta_{110}^{111}$, $\Delta\log\beta_{121}^{122}$ and $\Delta\log\beta_{120}^{121}$ values (Table 4.8, columns 2, 5 and 6) indicate the involvement of α-amino group in bonding. The higher stabilities (Table 4.9) of these complexes, except for PbX_2, compared to that of glycine indicate the involvement of histidine as a tridentate bonding (Figure 4.61) through carboxylate oxygen, N-imidazole and N-amino groups forming adjacent six and five membered rings.

Table 4.9: Relative stabilities of MX and MX_2 species of L-histidine and Glycine

Metal ion	Log β_{110}		Log β_{120}	
	L-Histidine (from Table 4.7)	Glycine (from Table 4.5)	L-Histidine (from Table 4.7)	Glycine (from Table 4.5)
Ca^{2+}	2.92	1.96	5.79	3.90
Mg^{2+}	3.07	2.19	5.89	4.33
Pb^{2+}	5.90	5.16	10.10	9.97
Hg^{2+}	6.60	4.42	11.80	8.45
Cd^{2+}	5.38	4.21	9.72	8.00

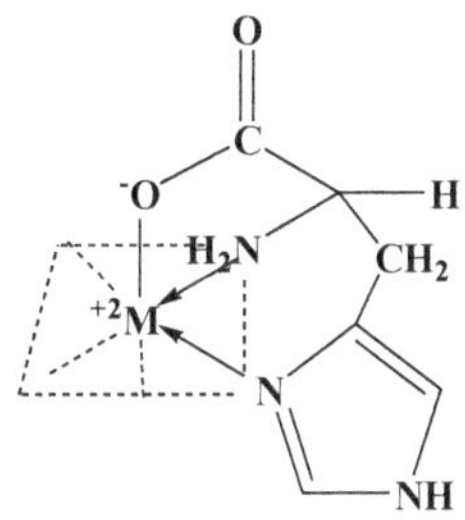

Figure 4.61: Probable bonding mode of L-histidine in MX type of species

This tridentate nature of histidine in MX type of species is supported by CD[79, 80] and ESR[81, 82] spectral studies.

One interesting point about Pb^{2+}- histidine complexes is the formation constant of PbX complex of histidine is relatively high compared to that of glycine (Table 4.9) while that of $PbX_2$is of the same order. The high stability of the PbX complex of histidine compared to that of glycine indicates the tridentate nature of the ligand. All the three donor atoms of histidine are sterically prohibited from simultaneously occupying planar positions about a single metal ion. Therefore, a tetrahedral type of stereochemistry around Pb^{2+}, in which L-histidine occupies three positions, is expected. In the case of PbX_2 complex, histidine may be acting as a bidentate bonding through any two of the three bonding centres as predicted by D.D.Perrin et al.[85] and L.D.Pettit et al.[78] in their study on the complexes of histidine.

Experimental evidences for tetrahedral stereochemistry around Pb^{2+} in amino acid complexes were also shown by Sigel[88] and Kayat et al.[89]. The closeness of the formation constants of the bis complexes of histidine with those of glycine (Table 4.9) clearly illustrates the bidentate[87] behaviour of histidine in PbX_2.

The relative order of stabilities of histidine metal ion complexes was found to be in the order, $Ca^{2+} < Mg^{2+}$ and $Pb^{2+} < Hg^{2+} > Cd^{2+}$, that may be explained as follows,

- Ca^{2+} and Mg^{2+} are classified as hard acids, but there are differences in their acid strength ($Mg^{2+} > Ca^{2+}$). Both the metal ions prefer to bond with hard bases. The bonding nature is mostly electrostatic. Due to the high charge density, Mg^{2+} is expected to form a relatively strong electrostatic bond compared to Ca^{2+} with carboxylate group of amino acid.
- Experimentally Lumb and Martell[90] proved that Mg^{2+} forms relatively strong complexes with carboxylic groups of amino acids compared to Ca^{2+}.
- Histidine in MX type of complexes behaves as a tri-dentate, bonding through carboxylate oxygen (O^-), N-imidazole and N-amino and is therefore a NNO donor. Hg^{2+} and Cd^{2+} are soft acids, while Pb^{2+} is of borderline category. Although nitrogen is classified as a class '**a**'or hard donor atom, it is considered to be more suitable than oxygen for soft acids. Its lower electronegativity (3) as compared to oxygen (3.5) and its neutral character in the studied ligands make it more suitable than oxygen for complexation with softer acids. On the other hand, both oxygen and nitrogen donors bond well with the large Hg^{2+} ion (ionic radius 102 pm) compared to Cd^{2+} (ionic radius 95 pm). This explains the relative stability order, $Pb^{2+} < Hg^{2+} > Cd^{2+}$ for histidine complexes.

The ambidentate nature of the histidine i.e. the ability to coordinate histamine-like, imidazole propionic acid-like and glycine-like modes was therefore, indicated from the results obtained.

4.2.3 L-Aspartic acid (2-Aminobutanedioic acid) – Metal ion Systems:

Aspartic acid is a non-essential aliphatic α-amino acid having an acidic carboxyl group on its side chain. L-Aspartic acid is generally found in proteins, and acts as an excitatory neurotransmitter in the central nervous system.

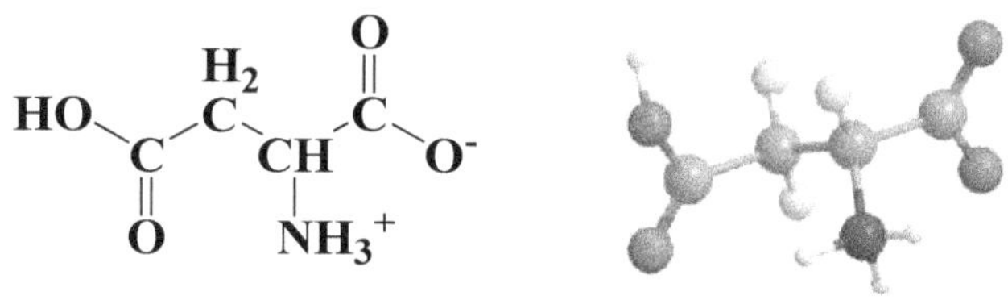

Figure 4.62: L-Aspartic acid (XH_2)

The close proximity of one carboxyl group to another enhances the acidity of the latter. Its acidic side chain adds a negative charge and makes the molecule very hydrophilic. It therefore, enhances the water-solubility of proteins in neutral solution and has been shown to be near the active sites of some enzymes. The charged carboxylate group can form ionic bond with various metal ions and may also have dipole interactions with water, which is an important factor for the solubility of the amino acid in water. Therefore, it is of great interest to study the affinity of aspartic acid towards essential and toxic metal ions.

The order of dissociation of the most protonated (XH_3^+) form of the aspartic acid is first theα-carboxyl group followed by the side chain carboxyl group and finally theammonium group forming,XH_2, XH^- and X^{2-} speciesas described in Section 3.3.3 of Chapter 3 and shown in Figure 4.63. With three ionizable protons aspartic acid is naturally prone to form protonated species in addition to simple complexes. To understand the speciation, one needs reliable formation constants of all the species that exist in solution.

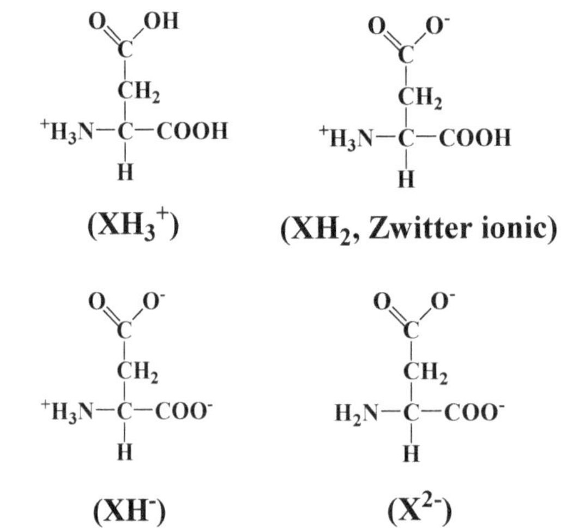

Figure 4.63: Protonated and deprotonated species of L-Aspartic acid (XH_2)

Although stability constants of the complexes of aspartic acid with some metal ions were determined and published using different methods, its complex forming properties cannot be regarded as having been satisfactorily clarified. Some of the reliable formation constants reported in the literature for Ca^{2+}, Mg^{2+}, Pb^{2+} and Cd^{2+} complexes of aspartic acid are included in Table 4.10. No reliable reports were found for Hg^{2+} complexes. The wide spread in the reported formation constants may be due to the use of different experimental conditions, classical methods of analysis and ignoring the possibility of formation of protonated species which may have overlapping equilibria with the simple complexes. Because of the biological importance of aspartic acid, several of the hitherto-reported stability constants have been redetermined at the required temperature and ionic strength. A complete speciation study demands, data acquisition under carefully designed experimental conditions followed by analysis using modern computational methods.

TABLE 4.10: Some literature reported formation constants of Ca^{2+}, Mg^{2+}, Pb^{2+} and Cd^{2+} complexes of L-Aspartic acid

Metal ion	*mlh*	**Formation constants of metal ion- L-Aspartic acid complexes reported in the literature**								
		Ionic Strength, I and Temperature, t^0C								
		0.1M 25^0C	1.0M 25^0C	0.15M 37^0C	0.1M 25^0C	1.0M 30^0C	0.1M 25^0C	0.1 M 25^0C	0.1M 25^0C	0.1M 25^0C
H^+	011	9.63	9.59	9.35	-	-	-	-	-	-
	012	13.33	13.29	12.93	-	-	-	-	-	-
	013	15.26	15.18	14.87	-	-	-	-	-	-
Mg^{2+}	110	2.43	-	-	-	-	2.43	-	-	2.50
Ca^{2+}	110	1.60	-	1.99	-	-	1.60	-	-	1.26
	111	-	-	10.57	-	-	-	-	-	-
Pb^{2+}	110	6.67 (I=3.0)	6.02	-	-	5.88	-	-	-	-
	120	9.40 (I=3.0)	-	-	-	7.38 9.43 (I=3.0)	-	-	-	-
	111	-	11.28	-	-	13.28 (I=3.0)	-	-	-	-
	11-1	-	-3.54	-	-	-	-	-	-	-
Cd^{2+}	110	4.39	-		4.84	-	4.39	4.37	4.5	-
	120	7.55	-	-	8.93	-	-	-	-	-
Reference		59	60	65	67	68	90	91	92	93, 94

The differences and inconsistencies in the reported values of formation constants and the requirement of formation constants under the experimental conditions identical to those of ternary system, prompted the author to perform a complete speciation study on L-aspartic acid-metal ion systems of Ca^{2+}, Mg^{2+}, Pb^{2+}, Hg^{2+} and Cd^{2+}.

Aspartic acid with three potential complex-forming functional groups ($-COO^-$, $-NH_2$ and $-COO^-$ of the side chain) behaves as an ambidentate ligand and can bind the metal ions in different ways.

- As a monodentate bonding through any one of the two carboxylate groups.
- As a bidentate bonding through α-carboxylate oxygen and amino nitrogen forming a five membered ring or through the carboxylate oxygen of the side chain and amino nitrogen forming a six membered ring or through both of the carboxylate oxygens.
- As a tridentate bonding through α-carboxylate oxygen, amino nitrogen and carboxylate oxygen of the side chain.

Calvin-Wilson potentiometric titrations[16-19]were conducted for 1:1 and 1:2 metal to aspartic acid molarconcentration ratios in aqueous medium. The acid dissociation constants of aspartic acid determined in this work (Chapter 3) were used in the calculations of formation constants of aspartic acid-metal ion systems. The acquired data was first analysed using classical methods to obtain the formation constants of simple MX and MX_2 type of complexes for all the metal ion systems under study. Assuming the formation of only these species, simulated titration curves were generated using the program SOPHD[48]. The experimental and simulated titration curves were plotted together to find out the regions where these differ. The position and extent of deviation gives information regarding the nature of missing species for inclusion in the chemical models to be prepared for refinement using the Miniquad-75 program[20].

The experimental and simulated titration curves for aspartic acid -metal ion systems are shown in Figures 4.64a to 4.73a. The difference between the two curves throughout the pH region suggests the presence of other species. Therefore, various chemical models containing all the plausible species, keeping in view of the ambidentate nature of the ligand were prepared and submitted for refinement to the Miniquad-75 program[20]. The initial estimates for the protonated species were calculated basing on the formation constants of simple complexes obtained by classical methods and protonation constants of the ligand.

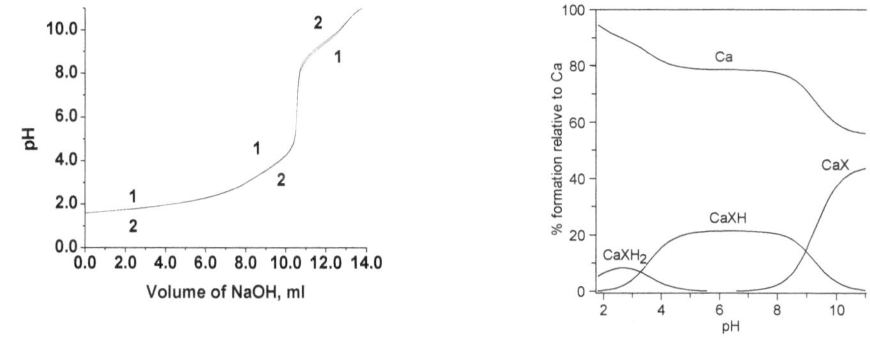

a. (1) Simulated titration curve
(2) Experimental titration curve

b. Species distribution diagram

[Asp] = 0.0100 mol dm^{-3} [Ca (II)]= 0.01179 mol dm^{-3}
[HCl] = 0.03151 mol dm^{-3} [NaOH] = 0.1773 mol dm^{-3}
Total Volume = 50.0 cm^{3} Temp: 30.0 ± 0.1^{0}C I = 0.1 mol dm^{-3} NaCl

Figure 4.64: Ca (II) –ASPARTIC ACID SYSTEM (1:1)

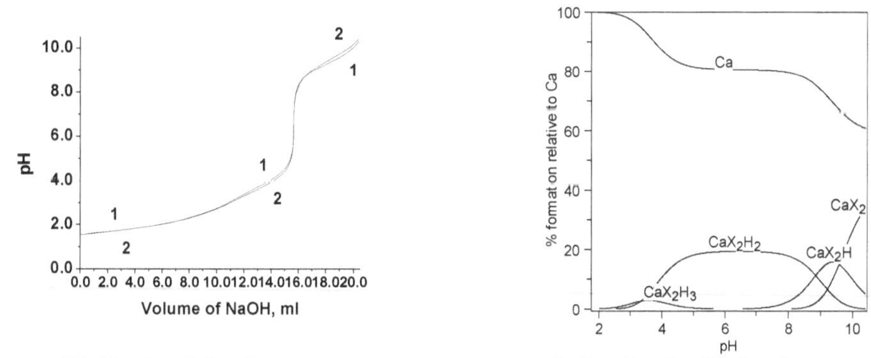

a. (1) Simulated titration curve
(2) Experimental titration curve

b. Species distribution diagram

[Asp] = 0.0200 mol dm^{-3} [Ca (II)] = 0.01179 mol dm^{-3}
[HCl]= 0.04149 mol dm^{-3} [NaOH] = 0.1773 mol dm^{-3}
Total Volume = 50.0 cm^{3} Temp: 30.0 ± 0.1^{0}C I = 0.1 mol dm^{-3} NaCl

Figure 4.65: Ca (II) – ASPARTIC ACID SYSTEM (1:2)

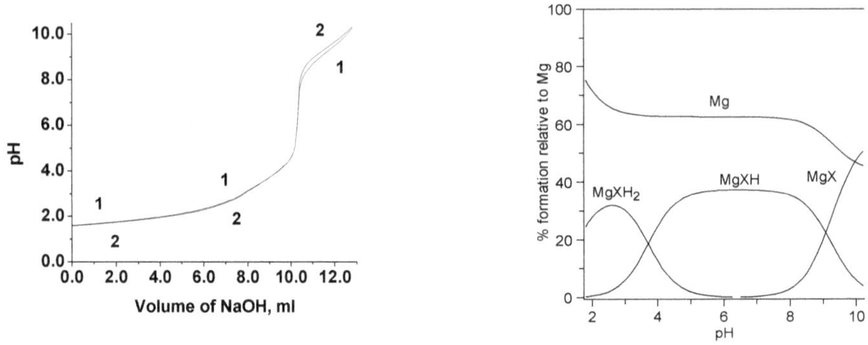

a. (1) Simulated titration curve
(2) Experimental titration curve

b. Species distribution diagram

[Asp] = 0.0100 mol dm^{-3} [Mg (II)]= 0.0100 mol dm^{-3}
[HCl] = 0.03167 mol dm^{-3} [NaOH] = 0.2020 mol dm^{-3}
Total Volume = 50.0 cm^3 Temp: 30.0 ± 0.1^{0}C I = 0.1 mol dm^{-3} NaCl

Figure 4.66: Mg (II) – ASPARTIC ACID SYSTEM (1:1)

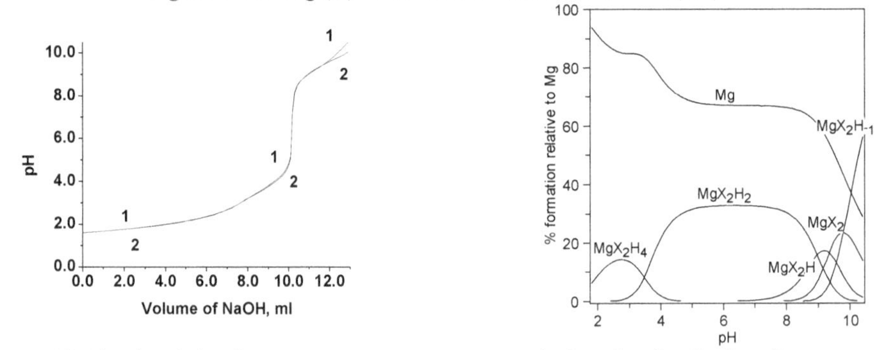

a. (1) Simulated titration curve
(2) Experimental titration curve

b. Species distribution diagram

[Asp] = 0.0100 mol dm^{-3} [Mg(II)] = 0.0050 mol dm^{-3}
[HCl] = 0.03116 mol dm^{-3} [NaOH] = 0.2020 mol dm^{-3}
Total Volume = 50.0 cm^3 Temp: 30.0 ± 0.1^{0}C I = 0.1 mol dm^{-3} NaCl

Figure 4.67: Mg (II) - ASPARTICACID SYSTEM (1:2)

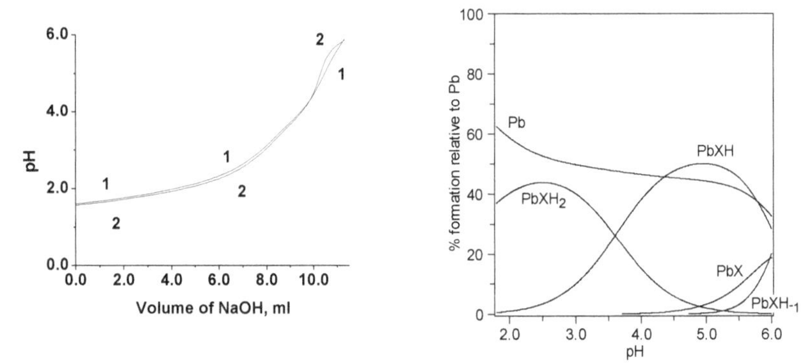

a. (1) Simulated titration curve
(2) Experimental titration curve

b. Species distribution diagram

[Asp] = 0.0100 mol dm^{-3} [Pb (II)] = 0.00998 mol dm^{-3}
[HNO_3] = 0.03169 mol dm^{-3} [NaOH] = 0.2020 mol dm^{-3}
Total Volume = 50.0 cm^3 Temp: 30.0 ± 0.1^{0}C I = 0.1 mol dm^{-3}$NaNO_3$

Figure 4.68: Pb (II) - ASPARTICACID SYSTEM (1:1)

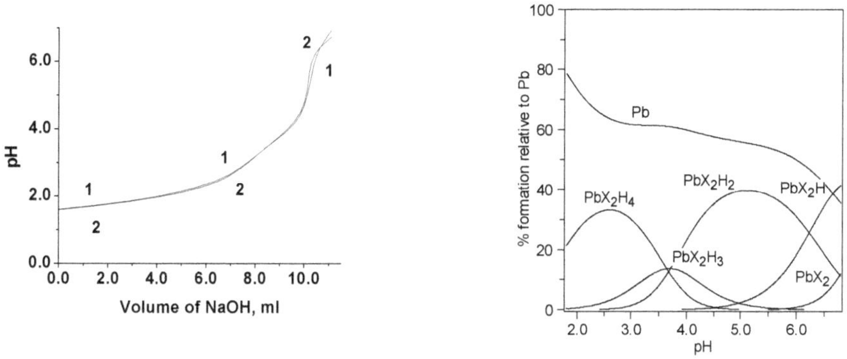

a. (1) Simulated titration curve
(2) Experimental titration curve

b. Species distribution diagram

[Asp]= 0.0100 mol dm^{-3} [Pb (II)] = 0.00499 mol dm^{-3}

[HNO_3] = 0.03115 mol dm^{-3} [NaOH] = 0.2020 mol dm^{-3}

Total Volume = 50.0 cm^3 Temp: 30.0 ± 0.1^{0}C I = 0.1 mol dm^{-3}$NaNO_3$

Figure 4.69: Pb (II) - ASPARTICACID SYSTEM (1:2)

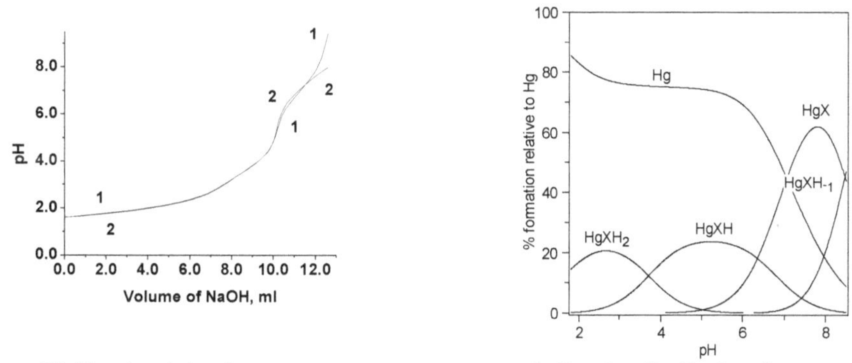

a. (1) Simulated titration curve
(2) Experimental titration curve

b. Species distribution diagram

[Asp] = 0.0100 mol dm^{-3} [Hg (II)]= 0.00995 mol dm^{-3}

[HCl]= 0.03173 mol dm^{-3} [NaOH] = 0.2020mol dm^{-3}

Total Volume = 50.0 cm^3 Temp: 30.0 ± 0.1^{0}C I = 0.1 mol dm^{-3} NaCl

Figure 4.70: Hg (II) –ASPARTIC ACID SYSTEM (1:1)

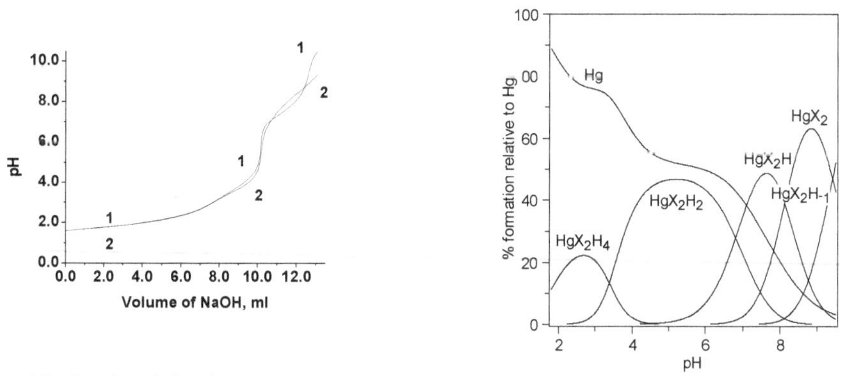

a. (1) Simulated titration curve
(2) Experimental titration curve

b. Species distribution diagram

[Asp] = 0.0100 mol dm^{-3} [Hg (II)]= 0.00498 mol dm^{-3}

[HCl] = 0.03119 mol dm^{-3} [NaOH] = 0.2020 mol dm^{-3}

Total Volume = 50.0 cm^3 Temp: 30.0 ± 0.1^{0}C I = 0.1 mol dm^{-3} NaCl

Figure 4.71: Hg (II) – ASPARTIC ACID SYSTEM (1:2)

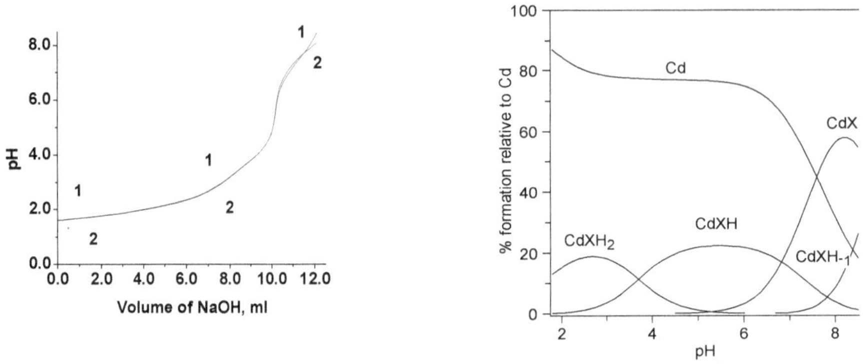

a. (1) Simulated titration curve
(2) Experimental titration curve

b. Species distribution diagram

[Asp] = 0.0100 mol dm^{-3} [Cd (II)] = 0.00993 mol dm^{-3}
[HCl]= 0.03119 mol dm^{-3} [NaOH] = 0.2020 mol dm^{-3}
Total Volume = 50.0 cm^3 Temp: 30.0 ± 0.1^{0}C I = 0.1 mol dm^{-3} NaCl

Figure 4.72: Cd (II) – ASPARTIC ACID SYSTEM (1:1)

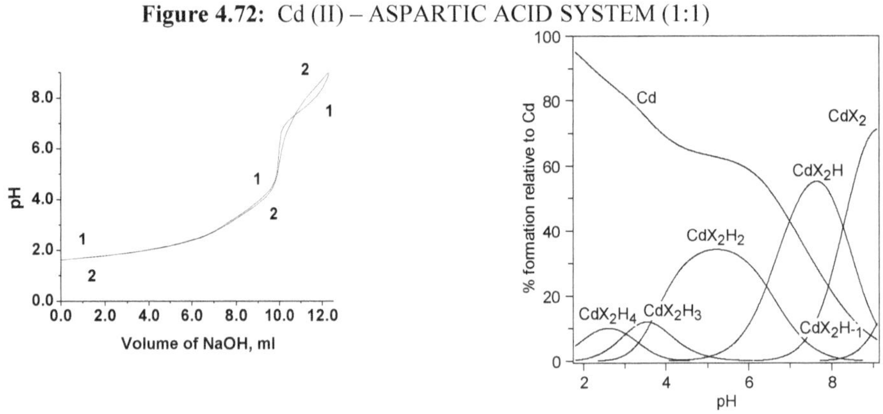

a. (1) Simulated titration curve
(2) Experimental titration curve

b. Species distribution diagram

[Asp] = 0.0100 mol dm^{-3} [Cd (II)] = 0.00497 mol dm^{-3}
[HCl] = 0.03039 mol dm^{-3} [NaOH] = 0.2020 mol dm^{-3}
Total Volume = 50.0 cm^3 Temp: 30.0 ± 0.1^{0}C I = 0.1 mol dm^{-3} NaCl

Figure 4.73: Cd (II) - ASPARTICACID SYSTEM (1:2)

The best-fit models obtained for all metal ion–aspartic acid systems together with their standard deviations and the sum of the square of residuals as obtained from the program Miniquad-75 are tabulated in Table 4.11. The sufficiency of the final model for each system was tested by comparing the experimental titration curve with that of the theoretical curve generated using the formation constants obtained and were found to coincide allowing for the random errors. The formation constants are in good agreement with the literature reported values, allowing for the changes in experimental conditions.

Table 4.11: Best-fit models for L-Aspartic acid- metal ion systems in aqueous medium at 303.0 K and ionic strength, I =0.1 mol dm^{-3}

Metal ion	Composition (M: X)	Species mxh	Log β_{mxh} (SD)	Statistical parameters
Ca^{2+}	1:1	011	9.58	U/NP = 2.804 $X10^{-10}$
		012	13.30	NP=110
		013	15.16	χ^2= 88.13
		112	14.41 (1)	R=0.00059
		111	11.12 (3)	Skewness= -0.18
		110	2.16 (1)	Kurtosis= 6.13
	1:2	011	9.58	U/NP =2.610 $X10^{-9}$
		012	13.30	NP=186
		013	15.16	χ^2= 139.8
		123	26.07 (1)	R=0.0015
		122	22.73 (1)	Skewness= 0.05
		121	13.88 (1)	Kurtosis= 4.08
		120	4.30 (1)	
Mg^{2+}	1:1	011	9.58	U/NP = 5.391 $X10^{-8}$
		012	13.30	NP=96
		013	15.16	χ^2= 72.78
		112	15.27 (6)	R=0.0089
		111	11.56 (9)	Skewness= 0.28
		110	2.48 (6)	Kurtosis= 4.27
	1:2	011	9.58	U/NP =2.405 $X10^{-8}$
		012	13.30	NP=92
		013	15.16	χ^2= 86.77
		124	30.05 (8)	R=0.0073
		122	23.03 (18)	Skewness= 0.46
		121	14.23 (15)	Kurtosis= 6.02
		120	4.88 (10)	
		12-1	-4.91 (6)	
Pb^{2+}	1:1	011	9.58	U/NP = 2.252 $X10^{-8}$
		012	13.30	NP=85
		013	15.16	χ^2= 60.7
		112	15.61 (4)	R=0.006
		111	12.01 (4)	Skewness= -0.31
		110	5.83 (8)	Kurtosis= 4.93
		11-1	-0.14 (4)	
	1:2	011	9.58	U/NP =2.121 $X10^{-8}$
		012	13.30	NP=68
		013	15.16	χ^2=47.61
		124	30.91 (6)	R=0.0067
		123	27.27 (4)	Skewness= -0.05
		122	23.56 (9)	Kurtosis= 3.56
		121	17.33 (10)	
		120	9.99 (9)	
Hg^{2+}	1:1	011	9.58	U/NP = 6.369 $X10^{-8}$
		012	13.30	NP=78
		013	15.16	χ^2= 68.91
		112	14.93 (4)	R=0.0082
		111	11.23 (5)	Skewness= -0.17
		110	4.87 (2)	Kurtosis= 5.22
		11-1	-3.60 (3)	
	1:2	011	9.58	U/NP =3.205 $X10^{-8}$
		012	13.30	NP=97
		013	15.16	χ^2= 55.01
		124	30.48 (7)	R=0.0080
		122	23.71 (13)	Skewness= 0.45
		121	16.90 (9)	Kurtosis= 4.93
		120	8.78 (7)	
		12-1	-0.63 (7)	

(Table 4.11 contd........)

Cd^{2+}	1:1	011	9.58	U/NP = 6.323 X10^{-8}
		012	13.30	NP=89
		013	15.16	χ^2= 90.42
		112	14.87 (6)	R=0.0083
		111	11.17 (3)	Skewness= 0.17
		110	4.34 (3)	Kurtosis=5.04
		11-1	-4.48 (13)	
	1:2	011	9.58	U/NP =4.600 X10^{-9}
		012	13.30	NP=97
		013	15.16	χ^2= 78.13
		124	30.00 (7)	R=0.0030
		123	26.97 (7)	Skewness= -0.00
		122	23.33 (4)	Kurtosis= 7.35
		121	16.90 (3)	
		120	8.62 (2)	
		12-1	-1.27 (5)	

The best-fit models obtained indicate the presence of MXH_2, MXH, MX and MXH_{-1} type of species in 1:1 (M: X) molar ratio systems and MX_2H_4, MX_2H_3, MX_2H_2, MX_2H, MX_2 and MX_2H_{-1} type of species in 1:2 (M: X) systems. Concentration distribution diagrams (Figures 4.64b to 4.73b) were generated using the program HYSS[21]. The diagrams indicate that both the species of type MXH_2 and MX_2H_4 for different metal ions exist only at low pH with a maximum of formation around a pH of 2.8. This is also the pH of maximum formation of the zwitterion form (XH_2) of aspartic acid in which the molecule loses the α-carboxylic proton from the fully protonated form (XH_3^+). Therefore, in MXH_2 and MX_2H_4 type of species aspartic acid may be acting as a monodentate bonding through only α-carboxylate oxygen. The formation of MXH and $M(XH)_2$ reached maxima below a pH of 4.5. This clearly indicates that the protons lost (from XH_3^+) are carboxylic protons and the proton still associated with aspartic acid molecule is α-ammonium proton. This is also confirmed from $\Delta \log \beta_{111}^{112}$, $\Delta \log \beta_{123}^{124}$ and $\Delta \log \beta_{122}^{123}$ values in columns (1), (3) and (4) respectively of Table 4.12, which are less than the protonation constant of the side chain carboxylate group.

Table 4.12: Step-wise protonation constants of L-Aspartic acid- metal ion complexes

Metal ion	Δlog β- Aspartic acid					
	(1) $\Delta \log \beta_{111}^{112}$	(2) $\Delta \log \beta_{110}^{111}$	(3) $\Delta \log \beta_{123}^{124}$	(4) $\Delta \log \beta_{122}^{123}$	(5) $\Delta \log \beta_{121}^{122}$	(6) $\Delta \log \beta_{120}^{121}$
	Log β_{112}- Log β_{111}	Log β_{111}- Log β_{110}	Log β_{124}- Log β_{123}	Log β_{123}- Log β_{122}	Log β_{122}- Log β_{121}	Log β_{121}- Log β_{120}
Ca^{2+}	3.29	8.96	-	3.34	8.85	9.57
Mg^{2+}	3.71	9.08	-	-	8.85	9.35
Pb^{2+}	3.60	6.18	3.64	3.71	6.23	7.34
Hg^{2+}	3.70	6.36	-	-	6.73	8.12
Cd^{2+}	3.70	6.83	3.03	3.64	6.43	8.38

The protonation equilibria of carboxylate groups and α-amino group are widely separated. Formation of MX and MX_2 type of species by deprotonation of α-ammonium group occurs relatively at a higher pH; greater than 7.0 pH for Ca^{2+}, Mg^{2+} and Cd^{2+} systems and greater than 5.0 pH for $Pb^{2+}$and Hg^{2+} systems. The step-wise protonation constants of MX and MX_2 represented by Δlog β values (columns-2, 4 and 5 in table 4.12) are below or close to the protonation constants of α-amino group, indicating the formation of MX and MX_2 type of species by deprotonation of α-ammonium group of aspartic acid.

The relative order of stabilities of the metal ion complexes of L-Aspartic acid was found to be, Mg^{2+}> Ca^{2+} and Pb^{2+}> Hg^{2+}> Cd^{2+}, which may be explained as follows;

- Mg^{2+} is a hard acidaccording to HSAB theory and prefers hard ligands with low polarizability, oxygen being the most preferable coordinating atom followed by nitrogen. Ca^{2+} like Mg^{2+} is also a hard ion and prefers hard oxygen containing ligands as well. Aspartic acid on the other hand provides two hard carboxylate ($-COO^-$) oxygens and one borderline category amino nitrogen for bonding. The higher charge density of smaller Mg^{2+} ion relative to that of Ca^{2+} leads to the formation of stronger electrostatic bonds with negative carboxylates[90].

- Kozlowski et al.[95], in their proton NMR study of the interactions of Calcium and Magnesium with aspartic acid concluded that Mg^{2+} interacts differently with aspartate compared to Ca^{2+}. Although both the metal ions interact with the two carboxylate groups, $Ca^{2+}$was found to exhibit very weak interaction with α-amino group. This preferential binding of Mg^{2+}over Ca^{2+} to amino groups was also supported by Touche and Williams[96] on the basis of thermodynamic data. This distinction could be responsible for the selective binding of Mg^{2+} ions by bio-molecules in the presence of Ca^{2+} ions[97, 98].

- The slight difference between the formation constants obtained for Ca^{2+} complexes of glycine and aspartic acid as shown in Table 4.13, further confirms the bidentate nature of ASP. A feeble interaction with α-amino group(Fig. 4.74) may also be present. In the case of Mg^{2+}, the interaction with α-amino group may be more resulting in an enhanced stability.

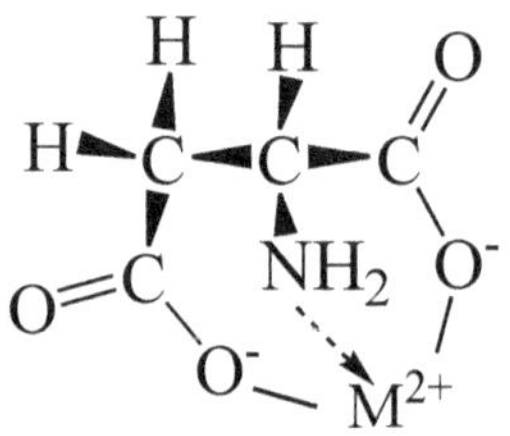

Figure 4.74: Probable nature of bonding in Ca^{2+} and Mg^{2+}complexes of L-Aspartic acid.

Table 4.13: Relative stabilities of MX and MX_2 type of species of L-Aspartic acid and Glycine.

Metal ion	Log β_{110}		Log β_{120}	
	L-Aspartic acid (from Table 4.11)	Glycine (from Table 4.5)	L-Aspartic acid (from Table 4.11)	Glycine (from Table 4.5)
Ca^{2+}	2.16	1.96	4.31	3.90
Mg^{2+}	2.48	2.19	4.88	4.33
Pb^{2+}	5.83	5.16	9.99	9.97
Hg^{2+}	4.87	4.42	8.78	8.45
Cd^{2+}	4.34	4.21	8.62	8.00

- The higher stability of the complex, PbX of aspartic acid, relative to that of glycine (Table 4.13) clearly indicates the tridentate nature of aspartate. A similar observation was made by A.M. Corrie et al.[68] in their study on thermodynamic considerations in coordination of Lead (II)-amino acid complexes. The low valueof the formation constant of PbX_2 generally observed for tridentate ligands was attributed to the tetrahedral stereochemistry around Pb^{2+} which arrests further bonding when three of the four positions are occupied.

- Hg^{2+} and Cd^{2+} are soft Lewis acids and therefore may have weak interaction with carboxylate oxygens of aspartic acid. Therefore a negligible interaction with the carboxylate group of the side chain is expected. It can be seen from Table 4.13 that the stability constants are reasonably close to those listed for the glycinate ion indicating bidentate nature of bonding. It is noteworthy that although the additional carboxylate ion is probably not involved in the metal chelate bonds, it may have an indirect influence on the stability of the chelate ring. The generally greater stability of the aspartate chelates indicates that the inductive effect of the negative carboxylate group lends stability to the structure (i.e., increases basicity of the donor groups toward the metal ion).

4.3: REFERENCES:

1. E. Carpene, G. Andreani and G. Isani, "Metallothionein functions and structural characteristics", *J Trace Elem Med Biol*, 21 (2007) S1, pp 35–39.
2. B. I. Kharisov, P. E. Martinez, V. M. Jimnez-Perez, O. V. Kharissova, B.N. Martinez and N. Perez, Review- "Recent advances on ditopic ligands", *J Coord Chem*, 63(1) (2010) pp.1–25.
3. J. Narayanan, A. Solano-Peralta, V. Manuel, Ugalde-Saldivar, R. Escudero, H. Hopfl, M. Elena and Sosa-Torres, "New dinuclear cobalt(II) octaaza macrocyclic complexes with high oxidation redox potentials: Their crystal structure and unusual magnetic properties", *Inorg. Chim. Acta*, 361(2008) pp.2747–2758.
4. Laszlo Mercs, Antonia Neels and Martin Albrecht, "Probing the potential of *N*-heterocyclic carbenes in molecular electronics: redox-active metal centers interlinked by a rigid ditopic carbene ligand", *Dalton Trans.*, (2008) pp 5570-5576.
5. T. A. Kaden, "Dinuclear metal complexes of bis-macrocycles", *Coord. Chem. Rev*, 190 (1999) pp.371–389.
6. E.K. VandenBeuken and B.L. Feringa, "Bimetallic Catalysis by Late Transition Metal Complexes", *Tetrahedron.*, 54(1998) pp.12985- 13011.
7. H. Steinhagen and G. Helmchen, "Asymmetric Two-Center Catalysis: Learning from Nature", *Angew. Chem. Int. Ed.*, 35(1996) pp.2339-2342.
8. L.D. Tsitsishvili, T.I. Tsutsunava and Yu. Ya. Kharitonov, "Complexes of Cobalt with deprotonated dihydrazides. *koord. khim.*, 8(5) (1982) pp 674-679..
9. EFSA Panel: B. Claudia, C. Laurence, C. Jean-Pierre, E. Karl-Heinz, et al., "Scientific opinion on the safety assessment of the substance adipic acid dihydrazide for use in food contact materials", *EFSA Journal.*, 13(1) (2015) p 3961; CAS No 1071-93-8.
10. M.T. Adrian, R. Xavier, F. Francesc and S. Angels, "The use of dihydrazides as latent curing agents in diglycidyl ether of bisphenol-A coatings", *Prog. Org. Coat.*,74 (2012) pp 59–66.
11. N. VandanaJugran, Ashok Kumar Sharma, N. Jeetendra Singh and Veerma Ram, "Biological activities of hydrazide derivatives in the new millennium", *IJPC.*, 2 (4) (2012) pp 100-109.

12. R. Narang, B.Narasimhan and B. Sharma, "A review on biological activities and chemical synthesis of hydrazide derivatives", *Curr. Med. Chem.*, 19(4) (2012) pp 569-612.
13. B.K. Kaymakçioğlu, E. E. Oruç-Emre ,U. Seda and A. Dimoglo "Synthesis and characterization of novel hydrazide-hydrazones and the study of their structure-antituberculosis activity", *Eur. J. Med. Chem.*, 41(11)(2006) pp 1253-1261.
14. G. Verma, A. Marella, Md. Shaquiquzzaman, M. Akhtar, Md. Rahmat Ali and Md. MumtazAlam, "A review exploring biological activities of hydrazones", *J. Pharm .Bioall. Sci.,* 6(2) (2014) pp 69-80.
15. S. Rollas and Ş. GünizKüçükgüzel, "Review- Biological activities of hydrazone derivatives", *Molecules.,* 12(2007) pp 1910-1939.
16. J. Bjerrum, "Metal ammine formation in aqueous solution: theory of the reversible step reactions", P. Haase and Son, Copenhagen (1941).
17. Calvin, M. and Wilson, K. W, *J. Am. Chem. Soc.* 67 (1945) p 2003.
18. H. M. Irving and H. S. Rossotti, "Methods for Computing Successive Stability Constants from Experimental Formation Curves", *J. Chem. Soc.* (1953) pp 3397–3405.
19. H. M. Irving, H. S. Rossotti, "The Calculation of Formation Curves of Metal Complexes from pH-Titration Curves in Mixed Solvents", *J. Chem. Soc.,* (1954) pp 2904–2910.
20. P. Gans, A. Sabatini and A. Vacca, "An improved computer program for the computation of formation constants from potentiometric data", *Inorg. Chim. Acta.*, 18 (1976) p 237.
21. L. Alderighi, P. Gans, A. Ienco, D.Peters, A. Sabatini and A. Vacca, "Hyperquad simulation and speciation (HySS): A utility program for the investigation of equilibria involving soluble and partially soluble species", *Coord. Chem. Rev.* 184 (1999) pp 311–318.
22. Bakir Jeragh, and Ahmed A. El-Asmy, "Structure and spectroscopic studies of homo- and heterometallic complexes of adipic acid dihydrazide", *Spectrochim. Acta, Part A: Molecular and Biomolecular Spectroscopy*, 125 (2014) pp 25-35.

23. E.B. Miminoshvili, "Metal hydrazide complexes", *J. Struct. Chem.* 50 (2009) pp 168-175.

24. (a) A.A. Adeniyi and K.S. Patel, "Dicarboxylic acid hydrazide complexes of magnesium tetrafluoroborate", *Synth. React. Inorg. Met.-Org. Chem.*, 29(6)(1999) pp1063-1075, (b) A.A. Adeniyi and K.S. Patel, "Dicarboxylic acid hydrazide complexes of manganese(II) tetrafluoroborate.", *ibid*, 23(1993)pp185-198; (c) A.A. Adeniyi and K.S. Patel, "Dicarboxylic acid hydrazide complexes of cadmium(II) tetrafluoroborate", *ibid*, 23 (1993) pp199-211, (d) K.S. Patel and A.A. Adeniyi, "Dicarboxylic acid hydrazide complexes of cobalt(II) tetrafluoroborate", *ibid*, 21 (1991) pp1351-1364 and (e) K.S. Patel and A.A. Adeniyi, "Dicarboxylic acid hydrazide complexes of nickel(II) tetrafluoroborate", *ibid*, 21 (1991) pp1331-1350.

25. Yu. Ya. Kharitonov, L. D. Tsitsishvili, T. I. Tsutsunava, T. M. Chumakova and M. G. Stoppe, "Coordination compounds of some metals with succinic acid dihydrazide", *koord. Khim* .,8 (5) (1982) pp 666-673.

26. L.D. Tsitsishvili, P.V. Gogorishvili and T.I. Tsutsunava, "Complex compounds of transition metals with succinic dihydrazide", *Issledovaniya v OblastiKhimiiKompleksnykhiProstykhSoedineniiNekotorykhPerekhodnykhiRedkikhMetallov*, 2(1974) pp 145-151.

27. R. I. Machkhoshvili, Yu. Ya. Kharitonov and N. N. Vekua, "IR absorption spectra of zinc, cadmium, and strontium complexes with malonic and succinic acid dihydrazides", *RedkikhMetallov* 3 (1978) pp 63-67.

28. R. I. Machkhoshvili, N. N. Vekua, P.V. Gogorishvili, Yu. Ya. Kharitonov and A.E. Shvelashvili, "Complexes of Group II elements (Mg, Ca, Sr, Ba, Zn, and Cd) with dihydrazides of malonic and succinic acids", *koord. Khim.*,3 (3) (1977) pp 332-341

29. R. I. Machkhoshvili, N. N. Vekua, P.V. Gogorishvili, A. E. Shvelashvili, and Yu.Ya. Kharitonov, "Complexes of Group II elements with glutaric and adipic acid dihydrazides", *koord. Khim.*, 3 (1), (1977) pp 22-28.

30. R. I. Machkhoshvili, Yu. Ya. Kharitonov, P. V. Gogorishvili and L. D. Tsitsishvili, "IR-spectroscopic study of complexes of metals with adipic acid dihydrazides", *koord. Khim.,* 3 (3) (1977) pp 402-407.

31. A. Dutta Ahmed and N. Ray Chaudhuri, "Acid hydrazides as ligands- II Metal complexes of dicarboxylic acid (dihydrazides)", *J. Inorg. Nucl. Chemy,* 31 (8) (1969) pp 2545-2456.

32. P.V. Gogorishvili, L.D. Tsitsishvili, M.V. Chrelashvili and R. Perekhodnykh , "Complexes of transition metals with adipic acid dihydrazide", *Metal,* (1970) pp 5-13; CAN 74:82616.

33. P.V. Gogorishvili, L.D. Tsitsishviliand M.V.Chrelashvili, "Complexes of transition metal sulfates with adipic acid dihydrazide", *ibid,* (1970) pp 27-36; CAN 74:60339.

34. R.I. Machkhoshvili, D.A. Gogitidze, R.N. Shchelokov and O.Kh. Shamilishvili, "Scandium, yttrium and lanthanum complexes with hydrazides and isothiocyanato groups",*Zh. Neorg. Khim.*, 33(6) (1988) pp 1408-1414.

35. R.I. Machkhoshvili, D.A. Gogitidze, R.N. Shchelokov and O.Kh. Shamilishvili, "Scandium, yttrium and lanthanum nitrate complexes with hydrazides", *ibid*,33(5) (1988) pp 1139-1143.

36. A.F. Krivis, G. R. Supp and R. L. Doerr,"Polarographic Study of Some Hydrazide Complexes of Cadmium", *Anal. Chem.,* 37 (7) (1965) p 52-54.

37. A.F. Krivis, G. R. Supp and R. L. Doerr, "Stability constants of some dihydrazide complexes of cadmium", *Ibid,* 38 (7) (1966) pp 936-938.

38. G. R. Supp, "Polarographic studies of some mono- and dihydrazide complexes of Zinc", *Anal. Chem.*, 40 (6) (1968) p 981.

39. Babu, A. Ravindra and Rao R. Sambasiva, "Chemometric investigation of complex equilibria in the solution phase- Chemical models for the complexation of nickel(II) with adipic acid dihydrazide and 2-furoic acid hydrazide in water-N,N'-dimcthylformamide and water-dioxane media. Correlation with solvent parameters", *J. Chem. Eng. Data.,* 37(4) (1992) pp 526-531.

40. Babu, A. Ravindra; Krishna, D. Murali; and Rao R. Sambasiva, "Chemometric investigation of complex equilibria in solution phase II: sensitivity of chemical models for the interaction of AADH and FAH with Ni(II) in aqueous medium",*Talanta,* 40(12) (1993) pp 1873-1882.

41. A. RavindraBabu, J.S.V.M. Lingeswara Rao, D. Murali Krishna and R.Sambasiva Rao, "Acid-base equilibria of 2-furoic acid hydrazide and adipic

acid dihydrazide in aqueous-organic media",*Anal. Chim. Acta* , 306 (1995) pp 297-300.

42. S.V.V.S. Rao, J.S.V.M.L. Rao, A.R. Babu, D.M. Krishna and R.S. Rao, "Chemometric Investigation of Complex Equilibria in Solution Phase. Part-V. Correlation of Formation Constants of Manganese (II) or Zinc (II) Complexes of AADH/FAH with Co-solvent Characteristics", *J. Indian Chem. Soc.*, 73 (1) (1996) pp 9-19.
43. G. V. Afanas'eva, T. I. Bychkova, V. G. Shtyrlin, A. R. Shakirova and A. V. Zakharov, "Composition, stability, and structure of Cu(II), Ni(II), and Co(II) complexes with adipic acid dihydrazide in aqueous and aqueous-ethanol solutions", *Russ. J. Gen. Chem.,* 76(5) (2006) pp 757-765.
44. A. Satyanarayana, DunkanaNegussaKenie and P. Shyamala, "Speciation Study on the Interaction of Some Divalent Transition Metal Ions with Succinic acid Dihydrazide in Aqueous Medium", *Acta Chim. Slov.,*60(2013)pp 807–812.
45. DunkanaNegussaKenie, P.Shyamala, A. Satyanarayanaand K.M.M. Krishna Prasad, "Chemical speciation studies on the complexation of ditopic ligands: Interaction of malonic acid dihydrazide with some divalent transition metal ions in aqueous medium", *J. Indian Chem. Soc.*, 91 (2014) pp. 729-737.
46. W. Magdalena, S. P. Ewa, J. Julia, P. Beata, G.S. Joanna and K. Aleksander, "The complexing properties of oxalodihydrazide, acethydrazide and formic hydrazide with Cu(II) in aqueous solution", *Inorg. Chim. Acta.*, 455 (2017) pp 659–665.
47. O.P. Svanidze, A.E. Shvelashvili, T.I.Tsutsunava and L.D. Tsitsishvili, "Complexation of cobalt (II) and nickel (II) in aqueous solution with some cycle-forming amines", *Soobshch.akad.nauk.gruzii.SSR*, 97 (1) (1980) pp 89-92.
48. R. Sambasiva Rao, A. Satyanarayana and P.V. Krishna Rao, "SOPHD- A computer program for the simulation of pH-metric data", *Proc. Summ. Simul. Conf.*, (1984) p 563.
49. D.W. Barnum, "Hydrolysis of cations. Formation constants and standard free energies of formation of hydroxo complexes", Inorg.Chem., 22(1983) pp 2297-2305.

50. Paul L. Brown and Christian Ekberg, " Hydrolysis of metal ions", Publishers: Wiley-VCH Verlag GmbH & Co, Germany, Volume 1 (2016) p 742
51. M.N.V.Prasad, "Heavy Metal Stress in Plants: From Biomolecules to Ecosystems", Second Edition, Springer-Verlag, Berlin, (2004) p 33
52. E.R. Sandra, A.J. Rebecca and Evan R. Williams, "Hydration energies of alkaline earth metal ions, M^{2+} (H_2O) $_n$, n=5-7, M=Mg, Ca, Sr and Ba", *J.Am.Chem Soc.*, 121(38)(1999) pp 888-8906.
53. M. Peschke, Arthur R. Blades and Paul Kebarle, "Hydration Energies and Entropies for Mg^{2+}, Ca^{2+}, Sr^{2+}, and Ba^{2+} from Gas-Phase Ion−Water Molecule Equilibria Determinations", *J.Phys.Chem. A*, 102(48) (1998) pp 9978-9985.
54. R. A. Care and L. A. K. Stavely,"The thermodynamics of the formation of complex ions of EDTA and bivalent cations", *J. Chem. Soc.,* (1956) pp 4571-4579
55. R. D. Hancock and A. E. Martell, "Ligand design for selective complexation of metal ions in aqueous solution", *Chem. Rev.*, 89 (1989) pp 1875-1914.
56. R. D. Hancock, "Chelate ring size and metal ion selection. The basis of selectivity for metal ions in open-chain ligands and macrocycles", *J. Chem. Educ.*, 69(1992) pp 615-620.
57. Laura A. Clapp,Chynthia J. Siddons,Donald G. Van Derveer,Joseph H. Reibenspies,S. Bart Jonesand Robert D. Hancock, "The amide oxygen donor. Metal ion coordinating properties of the ligand nitrilotriacetamide. A thermodynamic and crystallographic study", *Dalton Trans.*, (2006) pp 2001–2007.
58. T. Kiss, I. Sovago and A. Gergely, "Critical survey of stability constants of complexes of Glycine", *Pure Appl.Chem.*, 63(4) (1991) pp. 597-638.
59. A.E. Martell and R.M. Smith, "Critical stability constants", Volume 1: Amino acids (1974) and Volume 5: First Supplement, (1982); Plenum Press, NY and London.
60. Y. Khayat, M. Cromer-Morin and Jean-Pierre Scharff, "Stability constants of lead(II) complexes of glycine, serine, aspartic acid and glycyl-L-leucine", *J.Inorg.Nucl.Chem.* 41(1979) pp. 1496-1498.
61. A. Casale, A. De.Robertis, C. De Stefano, A. Gianguzza, G. Patane , C. Rigano and S. Sammartano, "Thermodynamic parameters for the formation of glycine complexes of Mg(II), Ca(II), Pb(II), MN(II), Co(II), Ni(II), Zn(II) and

Cd(II) at different temperatures and ionic strengths with particular reference to natural fluid conditions, *Thermochim. Acta*, 255(1995) pp.109-141.

62. L. S. Nikolaeva, A. N. Semenov and L. I. Burova, "Mixed ligand complexes of calcium and Magnesium ions with Heparin and Glycine", *Russ. J. inOrg. Chem..,* 56(4) (2011) pp. 644-651.
63. JESS - JOINT EXPERT SPECIATION SYSTEM; by Peter M May, Darren Rowland and Kevin Murray, DATABASE: Last modified April, 2017.
64. Ahmed E. Fazaryb and Ahmed M. Ramadanac, "Stability constants and complex formation equilibria between iron, calcium, and zinc metal ions with vitamin B9 and glycine", *Complex Met*., (2014) p 139.
65. Masunobu Maeda, Kohji Okada, Yoshihiro Tsukamoto, Kazushiro Wakabayashi, and Kaname Ito, "Complex Formation of Calcium(II) with amino acids under physiological Conditions ", *J. Chem.Soc., Dalton Trans.,* (1990) pp. 2337-2339.
66. I. Cukrowski, P. Magampa, and T. Samuel Mkwizu, "Voltammetry as Virtual Potentiometric Sensor in Modelling of a Metal/Ligand System and Refinement of Stability Constants-Part 5-Complexation Studies of Hydrolysis-Prone Lead (II) with Glycine and Sarcosine by Sampled-Direct-Current Polarography Involving Virtual Potential", *Helv. Chim. Acta* , 89 (2006) pp. 2934-2952.
67. Md. M. Shoukry, Md. R.Shehata and Md. M.A. Mohamed, "Binary and ternary Complexes of Cd (II) involving Triethylamine and selected amino acids and DNA units", *Mikrochim. Acta*, 129(1998) pp 107-113.
68. Anna M. Corrie, Murray L. D. Touche, and David R. Williams, "Thermodynamic considerations in co-ordination. Part X1V: Formation constants for Lead(II)-Amino-acid Complexes and their use in Computing the complexing Competition between Lead(II) and *in vivo* essential metal Ions, and in Computer Evaluation of Ligands currently employed as Lead(II) Chelating Therapeuticals", *J.Chem.Soc.* (*Dalton Trans.*), (1973) pp 2561-2565.
69. R.F. Criscent, G.F.Laniak and R.L. Erikson, "Propagation of uncertainty through geochemical code calculations", *Geochim. Cosmochim. Acta*., 60(1996) pp 3551-3568.
70. C. Ekberg and I. Lunden Burro, "Uncertainty analysis for some actinides under groundwater conditions", *J. Stat. Comput. Simul.,* 57(1997) pp 271-284.

71. F.H. Denison and J. Granier-LaPace, "The effect of database parameter uncertainty on uranium (IV) equilibrium calculations", *Geochim. Cosmochim. Acta.,*, 69(2005) pp 2183-2191.
72. R. H. Carlson and L. T. L. Brown, "Infrared and Proton Magnetic Resonance Spectra of Imidazole, α-Alanine, and L-Histidine Complexes in Deuterium Oxide Solution", *Inorg. Chem.* 5(2) (1966) pp.268-277.
73. D. R. Williams, "Thermodynamic considerations in co-ordination. Part X. A potentiometric and calorimetric investigation of copper(II) histidine complexes in solution", *J. Chem. Soc., Dalton Trans.,* Issue 7 (1972) pp. 790-797.
74. R. Leberman and B. R. Rabin, "Metal complexes of Histidine", *Trans. Faraday Soc.,* 55 (1959) 1660.
75. Y. Altun and F. Koseoglu, "Stability of Copper(II), Nickel(II) and Zinc(II) binary and ternary complexes of Histidine, Histamine and Glycine in aqueous solution", *J.Solution Chem.,* 34(2005) pp.213-231.
76. L.D. Pettit, "Critical survey of formation constants of complexes of Histidine, Phenylalanine, Tyrosine, L-Dopa and Tryptophan", *Pure Appl.Chem.*, 56(2) (1984) pp. 247-292.
77. R.J. Sundberg and R. B. Martin, "Interactions of histidine and other imidazole derivatives with transition metal ions in chemical and biological systems", Chem. Rev., 74 (1974) pp.471-517.
78. L. D. Pettit and J. L. M. Swash, "Stereo selectivity in the formation of mononuclear complexes of histidine and some divalent metal ions", *J. Chem. Soc., Dalton. Trans.* (1976) pp 588-594.
79. E. W. Wilson Jr., M.H. Kasperian and R. B. Martin, "Binding of copper (II) to potentially tridentate amino acid ligands", *J. Am. Chem Soc.* 92 (1970)pp.5365-5372.
80. L. Casella and M. Gullotti, "Coordination modes of histidine: 4. Coordination structures in the copper(II)-L-histidine (1:2) system", *J. Inorg. Biochem.* 18(1) (1983) pp.19-31.
81. T. Szabo-Planka, A. Rockenbauer, L. Korecz and D. Nagy, "An electron spin resonance study of coordination modes in the copper(II)–histamine and copper(II)–L-histidine systems in fluid aqueous solution", *Polyhedron* 19 (2000) pp.1123–1131.

82. P. Cocetta, S. Deiana, L. Erre, G. Micera and P. Piu, "Spectroscopic analysis of binary and ternary Copper(II) complexes formed by histidine and glutamic acid", *J. Coord. Chem.*, 12 (1983)pp.213-217.
83. M. Itabashi and K. Itoh," Raman scattering study on coordination structures of Cu(II)-L-Histidine (1:2) in aqueous solutions", *Bull. Chem. Soc. Jpn.* 53 (1980)pp.3131-3137.
84. T. P. A. Kruck and B. Sarkar,"Structure of the Species in the Copper (II)-L-Histidine System", *Can. J. Chem.* 51(1973)pp.3563-3571.
85. D. D. Perrin and V.S. Sharma, "Histidine complexes with some bivalent cations", *J. Chem. Soc.* A (1967) pp.724-728.
86. H. Sigel, R. Griesser and D.B. McCormick, *Arch. Biochem. Biophys.* 134 (1969) 217.
87. P. Deschamps, P.P. Kulkarni, M. Gautam-Basak and B. Sarkar, "The saga of Copper (II)–L-histidine", *Coord. Chem. Rev.,,* 249 (2005) pp.895–909.
88. H. Sigel, "Metal ions in Biological systems, Vol 2 pp 105-111, Marcel Decker, NY (1973);
89. Y. Khayat, M. Cromer-Morin and J.P. Scharff, *C.R.Acad.Sci.*,(Paris) 287(1978) p 265.
90. R.F. Lumb and A.E. Martell, "Metal chelating tendencies of Glutamic and Aspartic acids", *J. Phys. Chem.,* 57 (1953) pp. 690–693.
91. G.R. Lenz andA. E. Martell, "Metal chelates of some sulfur-containing amino acids", *Biochem. J.,*3(6) (I964) pp 745-750.
92. I. Sovago and K. Varnagy, "Cadmium(II) complexes of amino acids and peptides", *Met. Ions Life Sci.*, book, 11(2013) pp 275-302.
93. S. Ali A. Sajadi, "Metal ion-binding properties of L-glutamic acid and L-aspartic acid, a comparative investigation", *Nat. Sci.j.,*2(2) (2010) pp 85-90.
94. S. Ali A. Sajadi and Ali A. Alamolhoda, "The Metal ions absorption and transportation properties of L-Aspartic acid in the Body", *Open Conf Proc J,* 1(2010) pp.207-210.
95. H. Kozlowski, J. Swiatek and Z. Siatecki, "^{1}H NMR studies on interactions of calcium and magnesium with aspartic acid and asparagine", *Acta Biochim. Pol.,*28(1)(1981) pp.1-9.

96. M.L.D. Touch and D.R. Williams, "Formation of ternary complexes containing two dissimilar metal ions and the implication for metal-metal stimulation *in vivo*", *J.Chem.Soc., Dalton,* (1976) pp. 1355-1359.

97. J.J.R. Frausto da Silva and R.J.P. Williams, "The uptake of elements by biological systems", *Struct. Bond.,* 9(1976) pp. 62-121.

98. J.J.R. Frausto da Silva and R.J.P. Williams, "The biological chemistry of the elements: The Inorganic Chemistry of Life", Second Edition, Clarendon Press, Oxford, 2001.

99. L.E. Maley and D.P. Mellor, "The relative stability of internal metal complexes-II: Metal derivatives of 8-hydroxy quinolone 5-sulphonic acid and a series of monocarboxylic mono-α-amino acids including histidine", *CSIRO Australia: Provided by the NASA Astrophysics Data System,* (1949) pp 579-594.

CHAPTER- 5

CHEMICAL MODELLING STUDIES ON THE TERNARY SYSTEMS CONTAINING SUCCINIC or ADIPIC ACID DIHYDRAZIDE, SELECTED AMINO ACID AND A METAL ION

Many reactions of biological importance involve the intermediate formation of mixed-ligand species, in which a metal ion is simultaneously bonded to two or more ligands. Mixed chelation occurs commonly in biological fluids[1] as millions of potential ligands are likely to compete for metal ions *in vivo*. Mixed ligand complexes have a key role in biological chemistry as they possess specific structures[2] and have been implicated in the storage and transport of active substances through membranes. The specificity and selectivity of the vital enzymatic reactions have been attributed to the formation of such a type of ternary species. Further, many biologically active exogenous molecules such as synthetic drugs and natural products possess coordination centres and therefore, are capable of complexing with naturally occurring metal ions, thereby affecting their natural phenomenon and bio-availability. In order to understand the effect of complexation on these biologically important reactions, one must know the actual form of the species formed in the biological fluids. Therefore, the speciation studies, which throw light on the actual form of a particular substance in solution have been, received much attention in recent years. The determination of the nature and extent of formation of the various species in solution requires knowledge of their formation constants.

Dihydrazides are ditopic ligands possessing two coordinating units separated by a carbon-carbon linker. These ligands are prone to form homo or hetero binuclear complexes with metal ions. The interest in binuclear complexes stems from different applications. The presence of two metal ions in the same species separated by some distance not too far, leads to several interesting and important applications including unusual magnetic properties[3]. Depending on the degree of flexibility of the molecule between the two coordination sites there is a possibility of formation of coordination polymers[4] with supramolecular architecture. Binuclear complexes are also interesting as the two metal centres fixed at a certain distance often allow the binding and thus the recognition and/or activation of a substrate molecule. Therefore, they can be used to mimic metalloproteins and to study the structure- reactivity relationships[5]. The metal centres are found to act synergistically in catalysing reactions[6-9]. In the case of dihydrazides the metal- metal separation can be controlled by varying the length of the carbon-carbon link to the two hydrazide groups.

The chemical speciation study of binary succinic and adipic acid dihydrazides with Ca^{2+}, Mg^{2+}, Pb^{2+}, Hg^{2+} and Cd^{2+} (Chpater-4) indicated the formation of a variety of species depending on the metal to ligand concentration ratio in solution. Depending on the composition, MLH_n (n=1, 0,-1), ML_2H_n (n=2, 1, 0,-1, -2) and M_2LH_n (n=0, -1,-2) type of species were observed in which the ligand acts as a bidentate or bis bidentate coordinating through either carbonyl or enolic oxygen and terminal amino group. As the metal ions in both mono and binuclear species have vacant (solvated) positions that can accommodate exogenous ligands, it was interesting to study the formation of ternary species in the presence of amino acids. The formation of ternary species of the bimetallic complexes in solution, leading to supramolecular structure, throws light on such interactions in metalloproteins.

Relatively a few reports on the ternary complexes of dihydrazides were found in the literature. The structures of mixed ligand complexes of oxalic or malonic acid dihydrazide (L) and deprotonated amino acids (glycine, serine, glutamic acid and methionine) with transition metal ions Co^{2+}, Ni^{2+}, and Zn^{2+} were reported by Fridman et al.[10] The complexes are of the type MALX (A^- = deprotonated amino acid,

L=dihydrazide and X= Cl^-, NO_3^-, or $1/2SO_4^{2-}$). The formation constants of these mixed ligand complexes along with those of adipic and succinic acid dihydrazides were also reported using spectrophotometric and pH-metric methods. Mixed ligand complexes of malonic acid dihydrazide (HL) with Co^{2+} were synthesized by Shvelashvili et al.[11] to study the mutual effects of acidic ligands on the coordination capability of cobalt. The complexes were of the type "$CoLXY.2H_2O$", where X, Y = Cl^-, Br^-, NO^{3-}, NCS^-, and SO_4^{2-}. It was observed by infrared spectral studies that the coordination of NCS^- was not affected by the presence of the other ligands. Gobedzhishvili et al.[12] synthesized twenty mixed ligand complexes of malonic, succinic and oxalic acid dihydrazides and pseudo halide groups with Mn^{2+}, Co^{2+}, Ni^{2+}, Cu^{2+}, Zn^{2+} and Cd^{2+}. The prepared complexes were of the type MLX_2 where X= NCS^- or NO_2^-. Dunkana et al., [13] carried out a chemical speciation study of ternary complexes of Cu(II) with Succinic Acid Dihydrazide and some amino acids in aqueous solution. The formation constants of the mixed ligand complexes were determined and the species distribution diagrams were also presented. The relative stabilities of the ternary species were compared with those of binary complexes. Halli et al.[14] synthesized the mixed ligand complexes of the type $[M(L)(X)Cl_2]$ where M= Co^{2+}, Ni^{2+}, Cu^{2+}, Zn^{2+}, Cd^{2+} and Hg^{2+}, L= primary ligand derived from reaction between benzofuran-2-carbohydrazide and 3, 4, 5-trimethoxybenzaldehyde and X = malonyl dihydrazide. The structures of the complexes were proposed in the light of analytical data, IR, UV-Vis, ^1H NMR, DART-MS, ESR spectral and magnetic studies. N.B. Zhorzholiani et al.[15, 16] synthesized mixed ligand complexes of the type $Mn(DM)_2(ClO_4)(NO_3)H_2O$ and $Mn(DS).nX_2.mH_2O$, where DM= Malonic acid dihydrazide and DS= Succinic acid dihydrazide, X=NCS^- or ClO_4^- The X-ray diffraction and other physico-chemical studied indicated that both Malonic and

Succinic acid dihydrazides act as bis bidentate bridging ligands coordinating through the O and the NH_2 groups. K. K. Narang et al.[17] synthesized some mercury (II) chloride, nitrate and thiocyanate complexes of oxalic acid dihydrazide and malonic acid dihydrazide. These complexes were characterized by IR spectral data, X-ray powder diffraction and polarography. Some of the complexes, tested for antifungal and antibacterial activity, were found to be more active than the ligands.

In view of the important factors connected to the formation of mixed ligand complexes in solution, and the paucity of information on speciation of ternary systems of the ditopic ligands, the investigator has taken up a complete speciation study on the interaction of succinic (SADH) and adipic (AADH) acid dihydrazides and amino acids (glycine, L-histidine and L-aspartic acid) with some essential and toxic metal ions (Ca^{2+}, Mg^{2+}, Pb^{2+}, Hg^{2+} and Cd^{2+}) in aqueous phase. These systems can serve as useful models for a better understanding of the naturally occurring phenomenon.

5.1 METHODS OF DATA ACQUISITION AND ANALYSIS FOR TERNARY SYSTEMS:

The potentiometric titrations of solutions containing different mole ratios of metal to primary (L= dihydrazides) and secondary (X=amino acids) ligands (M:L:X= 1:1:1, 1:1:2, 2:1:1 and 2:1:2, where M= Ca(II), Mg(II), Pb(II), Hg(II) and Cd(II)) were carried out with sodium hydroxide as titrant in aqueous medium, under nitrogen, at $30^{o} \pm 0.1^{0}C$ and at a constant ionic strength of 0.1 mol dm^{-3} using the apparatus and procedure described in Chapter -2. The total volume of the solution to be titrated was always 50.0 cm^3. In all the titrations freshly prepared solutions of dihydrazides and amino acids were employed.

In a ternary system containing a metal ion (M) and two ligands, L and X the formation equilibrium of a species can be represented by a general equilibrium (5.1), and the corresponding formation constant of these generalized species is given by the equation (5.2). Charges are omitted for brevity.

$$m.M + l.L + x.X + h.H \rightleftarrows M_m L_l X_x H_h \quad .... (5.1)$$

$$\beta_{mlxh} = \frac{[M_m L_l X_x H_h]}{[M]^m [L]^l [X]^x [H]^h} \quad .... (5.2)$$

Where, m, *l*, x, h are the coefficients of metal (M), primary ligand (L), secondary ligand (X) and proton respectively. The value of 'h' is +*ve* for protonated species and –*ve* for deprotonated or hydroxylated species.

Initially, to ascertain the formation of mixed ligand species, simulated titration data assuming the formation of only binary species of both dihydrazide and amino acid, for a particular metal ion and composition was generated using SOPHD program[18] developed in our laboratory. The formation constants of the binary species of both the ligands were taken from the results of the analysis of binary systems included in Chapter-4. The simulated and experimental titration curves were plotted together to identify the regions of difference. Any difference between the two curves indicates the formation of mixed ligand species. Depending on the position and extent of deviation between simulated and experimental curves and also keeping in view of the nature of the ligands and composition of the system, chemically plausible models were selected for refinement using the Miniquad-75 program[19]. The best-fit models selected on the basis of statistical parameters as discussed in Chapter-2 of the thesis were included at appropriate places.

5.2 CHEMICAL MODELLING STUDIES ON THE INTERACTION OF SUCCINIC ACID DIHYDRAZIDE AND AMINO ACID (GLYCINE/ L-HISTIDINE/ L-ASPARTIC ACID) WITH Ca^{2+}, Mg^{2+}, Pb^{2+}, Hg^{2+} and Cd^{2+} METAL IONS:

5.2.1 SADH- Glycine- Metal Ion Systems:

The experimental and theoretical titration curves of ternary, M^{2+}-succinic acid dihydrazide -glycine systems for molar compositions 1:1:1, 1:1:2, 2:1:1 and 2:1:2 for all the metal ions (M^{2+}=Ca^{2+}, Mg^{2+}, Pb^{2+}, Hg^{2+} and Cd^{2+}) are shown in Figures 5.1a to 5.20a.

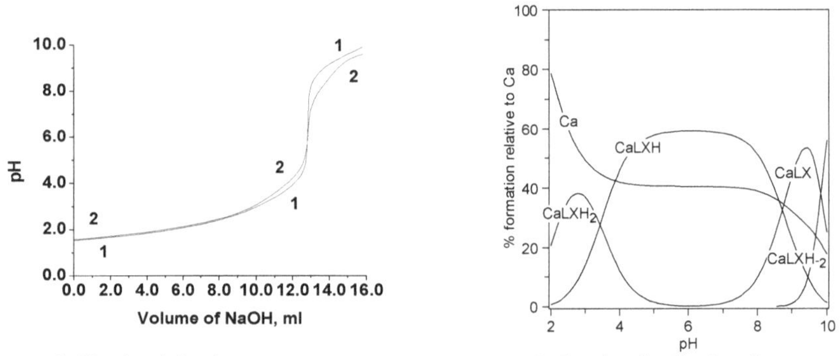

a. 1. Simulated titration curve
2. Experimental titration curve

b. Species distribution diagram

[SADH] = 0.01001 mol dm^{-3} [GLYCINE] = 0.0100 mol dm^{-3} [Ca^{2+}] = 0.00998 mol dm^{-3}
[HCl] = 0.05304 mol dm^{-3} [NaOH] = 0.2066 mol dm^{-3} TOTAL VOLUME= 50.0 cm^3
Temp.: 30.0 ±0.1^{0}C I = 0.1 mol dm^{-3}

Figure 5.1: Ca^{2+}-SADH GLYCINE SYSTEM (1:1:1)

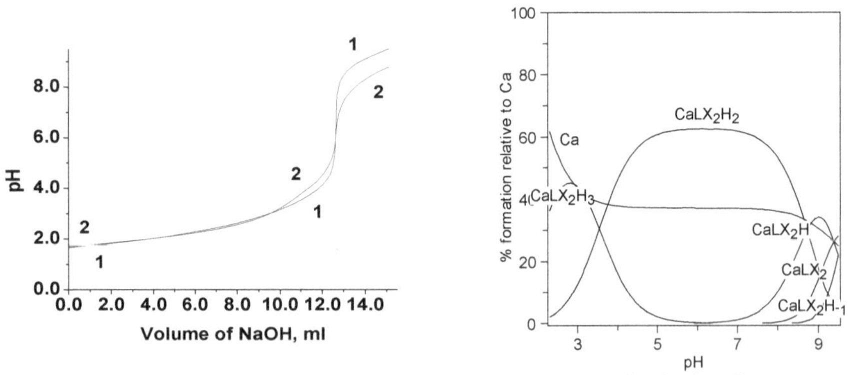

a. 1. Simulated titration curve
2. Experimental titration curve

b. Species distribution diagram

[SADH]= 0.01001 mol dm^{-3} [GLYCINE]= 0.0200 mol dm^{-3} [Ca^{2+}] = 0.00997 moldm^{-3}
[HCl] = 0.05222 mol dm^{-3} [NaOH] = 0.2066 mol dm^{-3} TOTAL VOLUME=50.0 cm^3
Temp.: 30.0 ±0.1^{0}C I = 0.1 mol dm^{-3}

Figure 5.2: Ca^{2+}-SADH-GLYCINE SYSTEM (1:1:2)

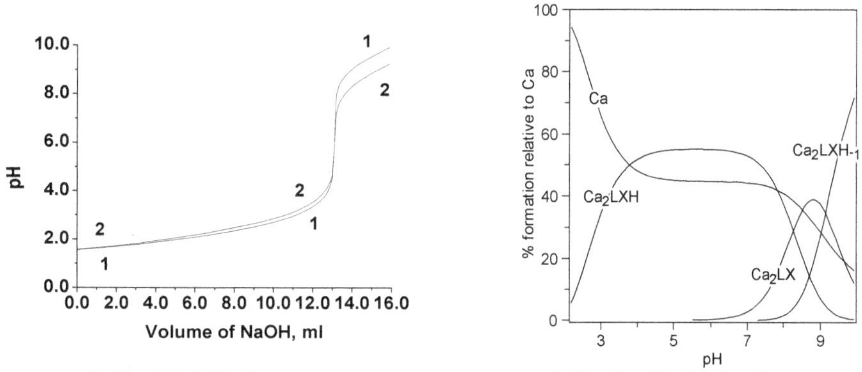

a. 1. Simulated titration curve
2. Experimental titration curve

b. Species distribution diagram

[SADH]= 0.01001 mol dm^{-3} [GLYCINE]= 0.0100 mol dm^{-3} [Ca^{2+}] = 0.01994 mol dm^{-3}
[HCl] = 0.05416 mol dm^{-3} [NaOH] = 0.2066 mol dm^{-3} TOTAL VOLUME=50.0 cm^{3}
Temp.: 30.0 ±0.1^{0}C I = 0.1 mol dm^{-3}

Figure 5.3: Ca^{2+}-SADH-GLYCINE SYSTEM (2:1:1)

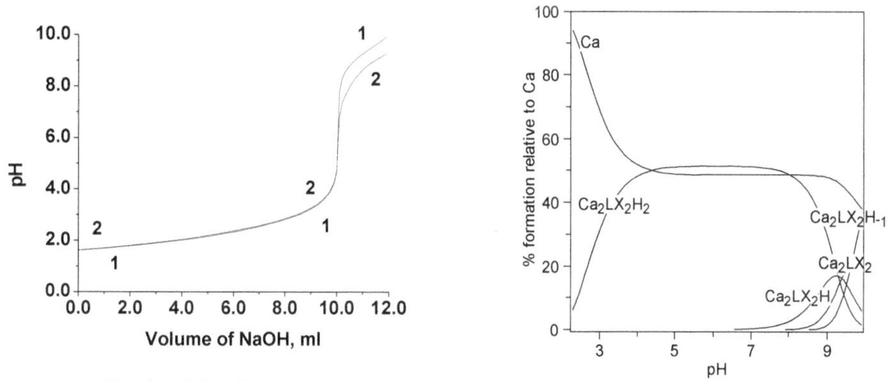

a. 1. Simulated titration curve
2. Experimental titration curve

b. Species distribution diagram

[SADH] = 0.00500 mol dm^{-3} [GLYCINE] = 0.0100 mol dm^{-3} [Ca^{2+}] = 0.00997 mol dm^{-3}
[HCl] = 0.04154 mol dm^{-3} [NaOH] = 0.2066 mol dm^{-3} TOTAL VOLUME= 50.0 cm^{3}
Temp.: 30.0 ±0.1^{0}C I = 0.1 mol dm^{-3}

Figure 5.4: Ca^{2+}-SADH GLYCINE SYSTEM (2:1:2)

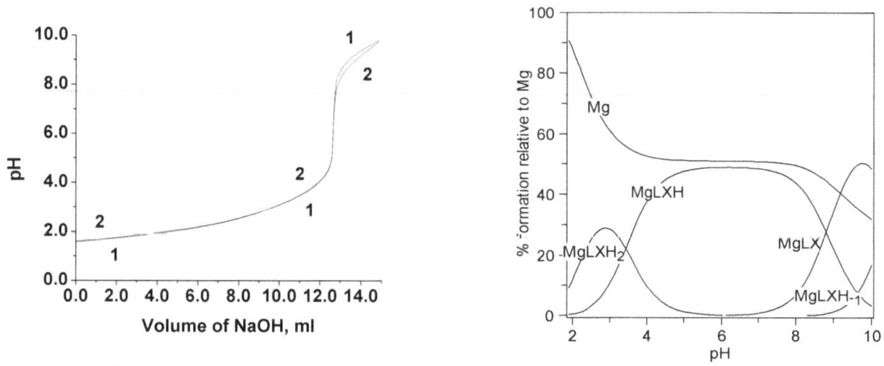

a. 1. Simulated titration curve
2. Experimental titration curve

b. Species distribution diagram

[SADH]= 0.00997 mol dm^{-3} [GLYCINE]= 0.0100 mol dm^{-3} [Mg^{2+}] = 0.0100 mol dm^{-3}
[HCl] = 0.05174 mol dm^{-3} [NaOH] = 0.2040 mol dm^{-3} TOTAL VOLUME=50.0 cm^{3}
Temp.: 30.0 ±0.1^{0}C I = 0.1 mol dm^{-3}

Figure 5.5: Mg^{2+} -SADH-GLYCINE SYSTEM (1:1:1)

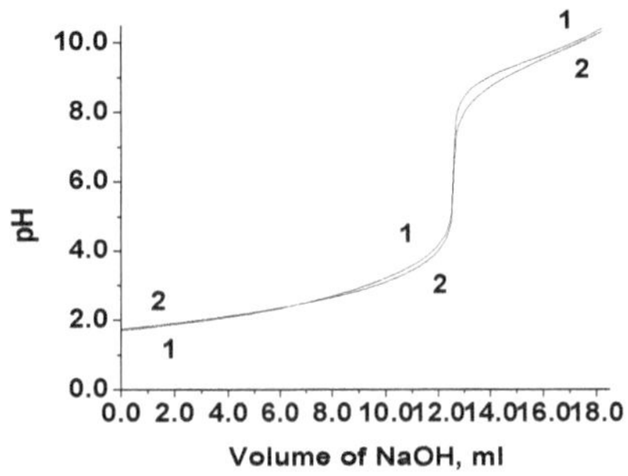

a. 1. Simulated titration curve
2. Experimental titration curve

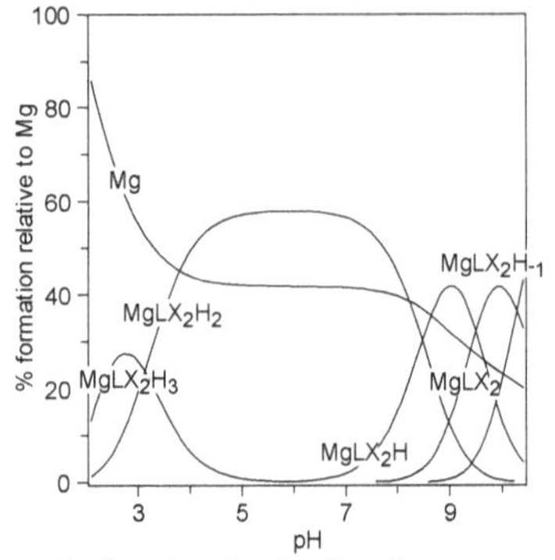

b. Species distribution diagram

[SADH]= 0.00999 mol dm^{-3} [GLYCINE]= 0.0200 mol dm^{-3} [Mg $^{2+}$] = 0.0100 mol dm^{-3}
[HCl] = 0.05137 mol dm^{-3} [NaOH] = 0.2040 mol dm^{-3} TOTAL VOLUME=50.0 cm^3
Temp.: 30.0 ±0.1^{0}C I = 0.1 mol dm^{-3}

Figure 5.6: Mg^{2+}-SADH-GLYCINE SYSTEM (1:1:2)

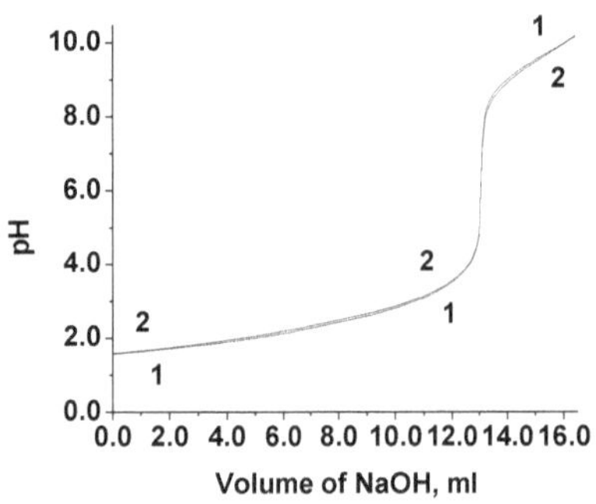

a. 1. Simulated titration curve
2. Experimental titration curve

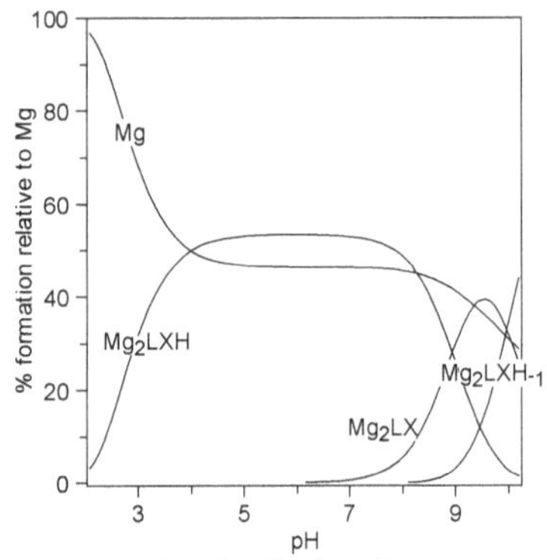

b. Species distribution diagram

[SADH] = 0.00997 mol dm^{-3} [GLYCINE] = 0.0100 mol dm^{-3} [Mg^{2+}] = 0.01999 mol dm^{-3}
[HCl] = 0.05336 mol dm^{-3} [NaOH] = 0.2040 mol dm^{-3} TOTAL VOLUME= 50.0 cm^3
Temp.: 30.0 ±0.1^{0}C I = 0.1 mol dm^{-3}

Figure 5.7: Mg^{2+}-SADH GLYCINE SYSTEM (2:1:1)

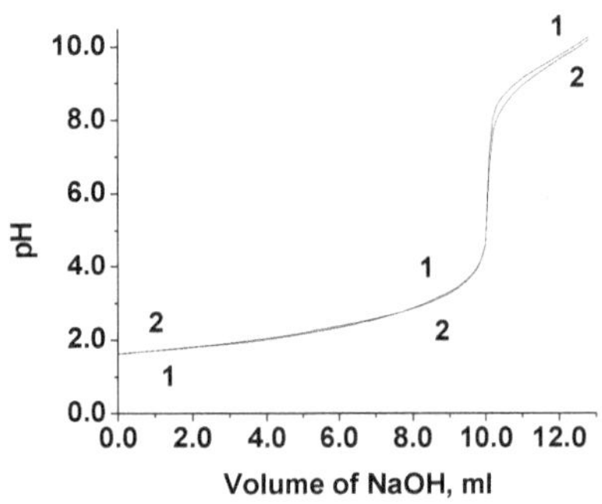

a. 1. Simulated titration curve
2. Experimental titration curve

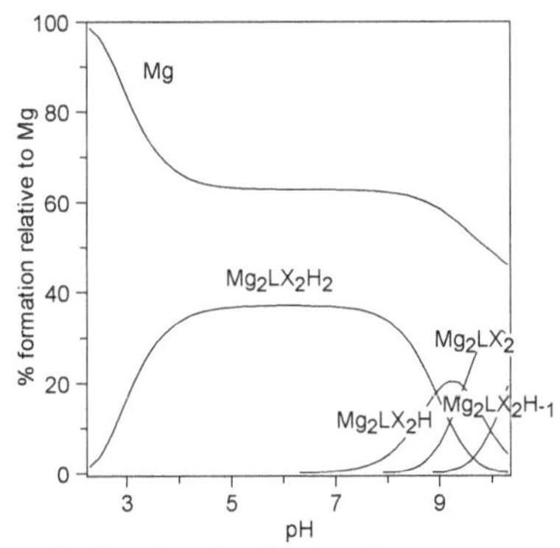

b. Species distribution diagram

[SADH]= 0.00498 mol dm^{-3} [GLYCINE]= 0.0100 mol dm^{-3} [Mg $^{2+}$] = 0.0100 mol dm^{-3}
[HCl] = 0.04115 mol dm^{-3} [NaOH] = 0.2040 mol dm^{-3} TOTAL VOLUME=50.0 cm^3
Temp.: 30.0 ±0.1^{0}C I = 0.1 mol dm^{-3}

Figure 5.8: Mg^{2+}-SADH-GLYCINE SYSTEM (2:1:2)

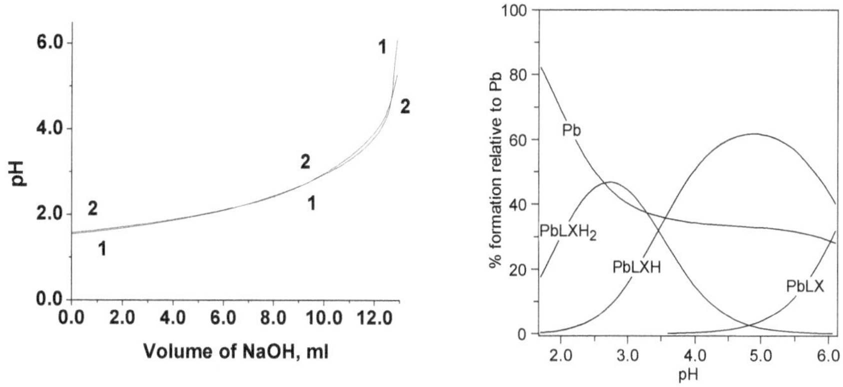

a. 1. Simulated titration curve
2. Experimental titration curve

b. Species distribution diagram

[SADH]= 0.00997 mol dm^{-3} [GLYCINE]= 0.0100 mol dm^{-3} [Pb^{2+}] = 0.00998 mol dm^{-3}
[HNO_3] = 0.05215 mol dm^{-3} [NaOH] = 0.2040 mol dm^{-3} TOTAL VOLUME=50.0 cm^3
Temp.: 30.0 ±0.1°C I = 0.1 mol dm^{-3}

Figure 5.9: Pb^{2+}-SADH-GLYCINE SYSTEM (1:1:1)

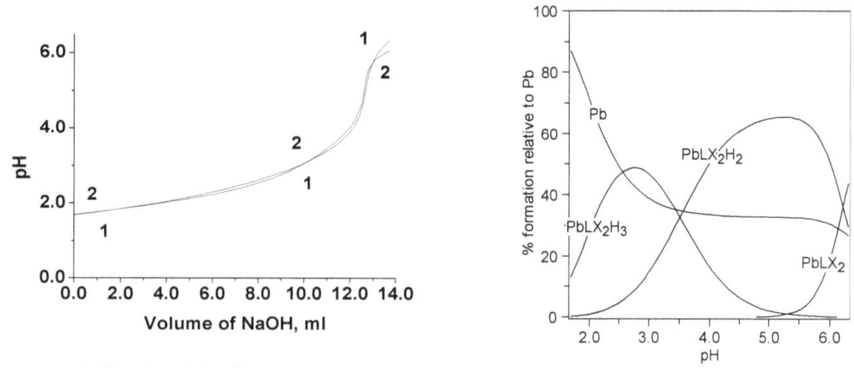

a. 1. Simulated titration curve
2. Experimental titration curve

b. Species distribution diagram

[SADH] = 0.00997 mol dm^{-3} [GLYCINE] =0.0200 mol dm^{-3} [Pb^{2+}] = 0.00998 mol dm^{-3}
[HNO_3] = 0.05175 mol dm^{-3} [NaOH] =0.2040 mol dm^{-3} TOTAL VOLUME= 50.0 cm^3
Temp.: 30.0 ±0.1°C I = 0.1 mol dm^{-3}

Figure 5.10: Pb^{2+}-SADH GLYCINE SYSTEM (1:1:2)

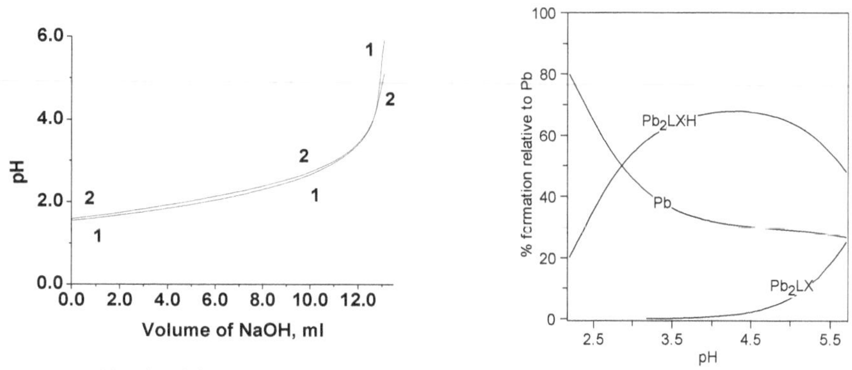

a. 1. Simulated titration curve
2. Experimental titration curve

b. Species distribution diagram

[SADH]= 0.00997 mol dm^{-3} [GLYCINE]= 0.0100 mol dm^{-3} [Pb^{2+}] = 0.01995 mol dm^{-3}
[HNO_3] = 0.05276 mol dm^{-3} [NaOH] = 0.2040 mol dm^{-3} TOTAL VOLUME=50.0 cm^3
Temp.: 30.0 ±0.1°C I = 0.1 mol dm^{-3}

Figure 5.11: Pb^{2+}-SADH-GLYCINE SYSTEM (2:1:1)

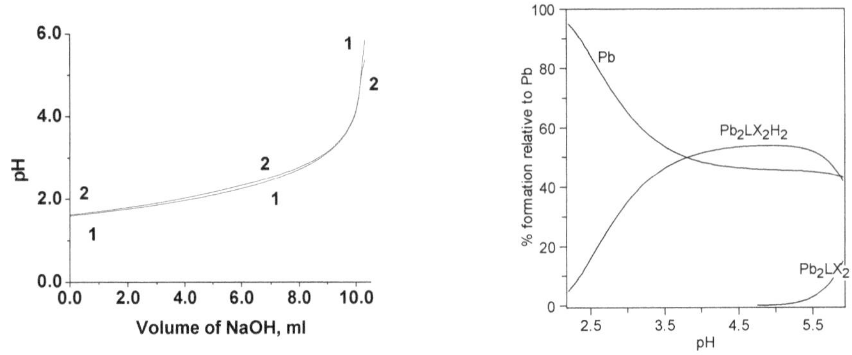

a. 1. Simulated titration curve
2. Experimental titration curve

b. Species distribution diagram

[SADH]= 0.00498 mol dm^{-3} [GLYCINE]= 0.0100 mol dm^{-3} [Pb^{2+}] = 0.00998 mol dm^{-3}
[HNO_3] = 0.04156 mol dm^{-3} [NaOH] = 0.2040 mol dm^{-3} TOTAL VOLUME=50.0 cm^3
Temp.: 30.0 ±0.1^{0}C I = 0.1 mol dm^{-3}

Figure 5.12: Pb^{2+}-SADH-GLYCINE SYSTEM (2:1:2)

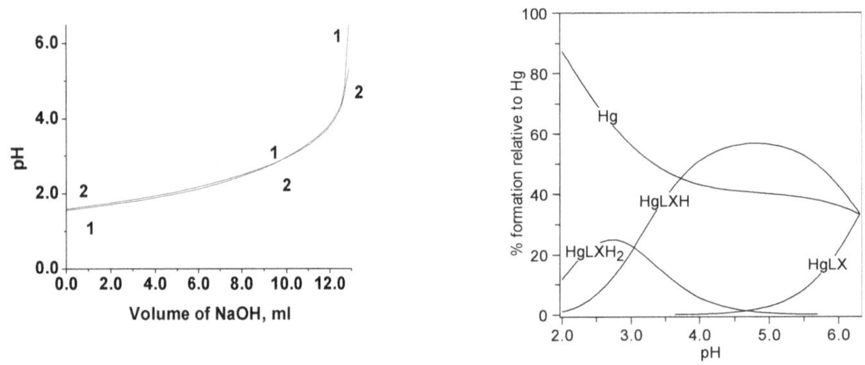

a. 1. Simulated titration curve
2. Experimental titration curve

b. Species distribution diagram

[SADH] = 0.00997 mol dm^{-3} [GLYCINE] = 0.0100 mol dm^{-3} [Hg^{2+}] = 0.00995 mol dm^{-3}
[HCl] = 0.05221 mol dm^{-3} [NaOH] = 0.2040 mol dm^{-3} TOTAL VOLUME= 50.0 cm^3
Temp.: 30.0 ±0.1^{0}C I = 0.1 mol dm^{-3}

Figure 5.13: Hg^{2+}-SADH GLYCINE SYSTEM (1:1:1)

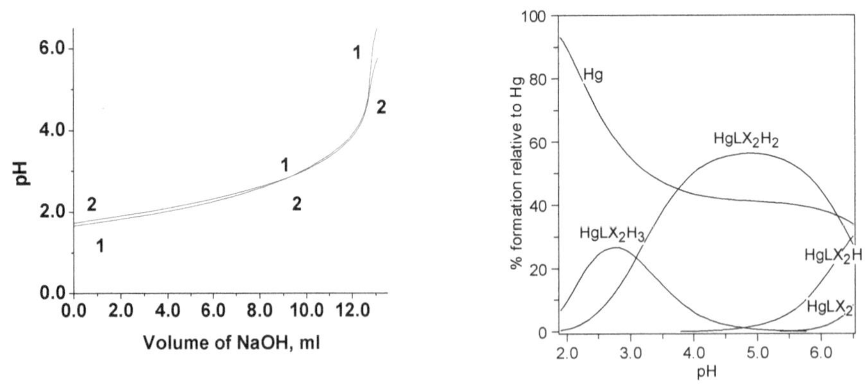

a. 1. Simulated titration curve
2. Experimental titration curve

b. Species distribution diagram

[SADH]= 0.00997 mol dm^{-3} [GLYCINE]= 0.0200 mol dm^{-3} [Hg^{2+}] = 0.00999 mol dm^{-3}
[HCl] = 0.05221 mol dm^{-3} [NaOH] = 0.2040 mol dm^{-3} TOTAL VOLUME=50.0 cm^3
Temp.: 30.0 ±0.1^{0}C I = 0.1 mol dm^{-3}

Figure 5.14: Hg^{2+}-SADH-GLYCINE SYSTEM (1:1:2)

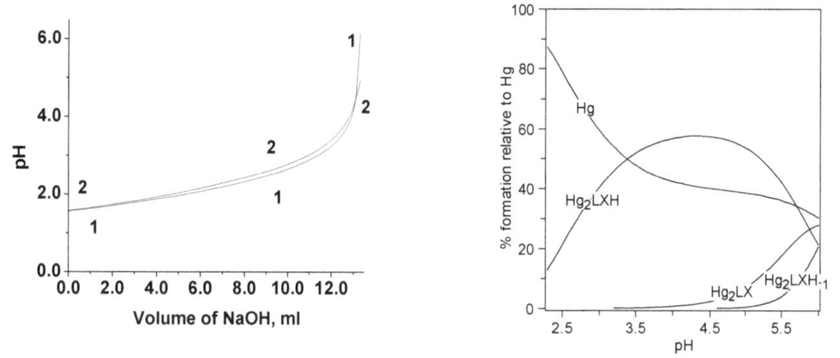

a. 1. Simulated titration curve
2. Experimental titration curve

b. Species distribution diagram

[SADH]= 0.00997 mol dm^{-3}	[GLYCINE]= 0.0100 mol dm^{-3}	[Hg $^{2+}$] = 0.01990 mol dm^{-3}
[HCl] = 0.05390 mol dm^{-3}	[NaOH] = 0.2040 mol dm^{-3}	TOTAL VOLUME=50.0 cm^{3}
Temp.: 30.0 ±0.1^{0}C		I = 0.1 mol dm^{-3}

Figure 5.15: Hg^{2+}-SADH-GLYCINE SYSTEM (2:1:1)

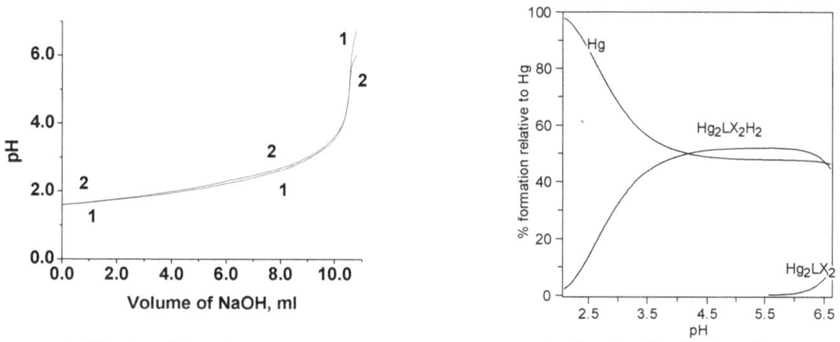

a. 1. Simulated titration curve
2. Experimental titration curve

b. Species distribution diagram

[SADH] = 0.00498 mol dm^{-3}	[GLYCINE] = 0.0100 mol dm^{-3}	[Hg^{2+}] = 0.00995 mol dm^{-3}
[HCl] =0.04306 mol dm^{-3}	[NaOH] = 0.2040 mol dm^{-3}	TOTAL VOLUME= 50.0 cm^{3}
Temp.: 30.0 ±0.1^{0}C		I = 0.1 mol dm^{-3}

Figure 5.16: Hg^{2+}-SADH GLYCINE SYSTEM (2:1:2)

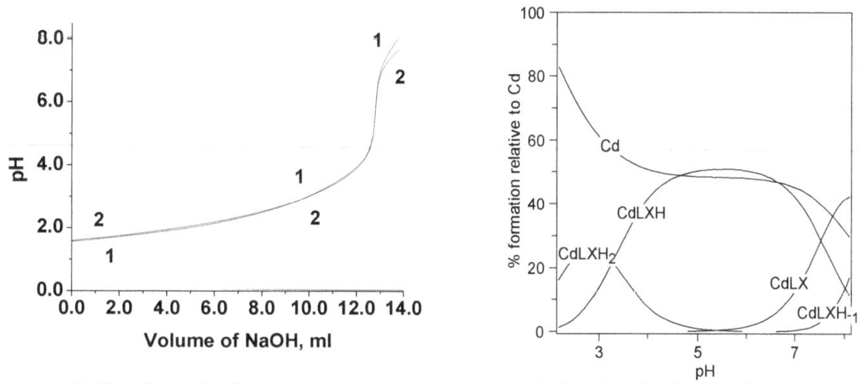

a. 1. Simulated titration curve
2. Experimental titration curve

b. Species distribution diagram

[SADH]= 0.00997 mol dm^{-3}	[GLYCINE]= 0.0100 mol dm^{-3}	[Cd $^{2+}$] = 0.00993 mol dm^{-3}
[HCl] = 0.05217 mol dm^{-3}	[NaOH] =0.2040 mol dm^{-3}	TOTAL VOLUME=50.0 cm^{3}
Temp.: 30.0 ±0.1^{0}C		I = 0.1 mol dm^{-3}

Figure 5.17: Cd^{2+}-SADH-GLYCINE SYSTEM (1:1:1)

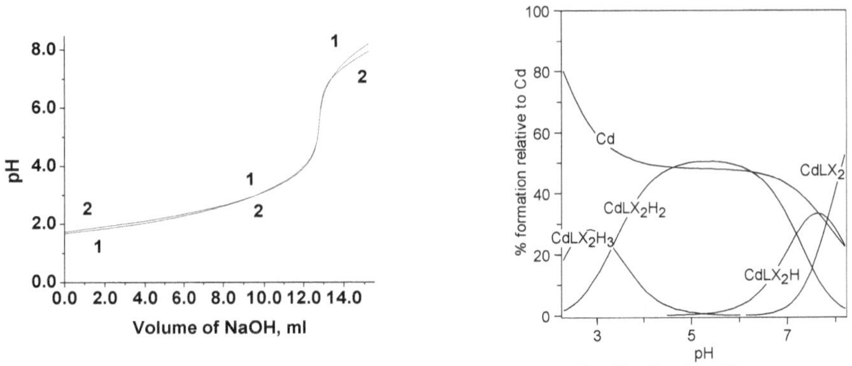

a. 1. Simulated titration curve
2. Experimental titration curve

b. Species distribution diagram

[SADH]= 0.00997 mol dm^{-3} [GLYCINE] = 0.0200 mol dm^{-3} [Cd^{2+}] = 0.00993 mol dm^{-3}
[HCl] = 0.05217 mol dm^{-3} [NaOH] = 0.2040 mol dm^{-3} TOTAL VOLUME=50.0 cm^3
Temp.: 30.0 ±0.1^{0}C I = 0.1 mol dm^{-3}

Figure 5.18: Cd^{2+}-SADH-GLYCINE SYSTEM (1:1:2)

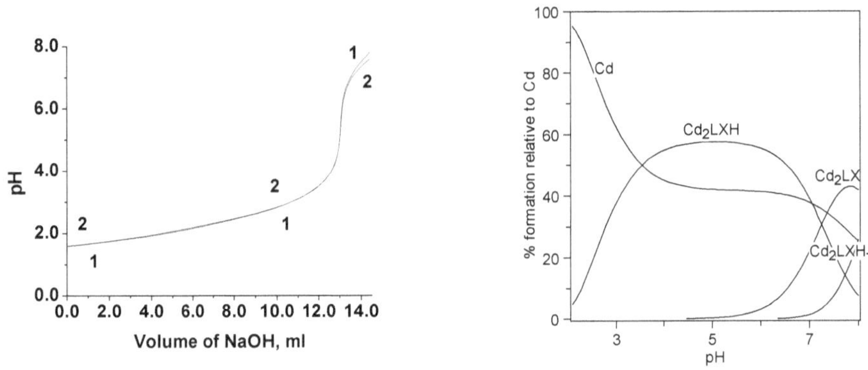

a. 1. Simulated titration curve
2. Experimental titration curve

b. Species distribution diagram

[SADH] = 0.00997 mol dm^{-3} [GLYCINE] = 0.0100 mol dm^{-3} [Cd^{2+}] = 0.02006 mol dm^{-3}
[HCl] = 0.05323 mol dm^{-3} [NaOH] = 0.2040 mol dm^{-3} TOTAL VOLUME= 50.0 cm^3
Temp.: 30.0 ±0.1^{0}C I = 0.1 mol dm^{-3}

Figure 5.19: Cd^{2+}-SADH GLYCINE SYSTEM (2:1:1)

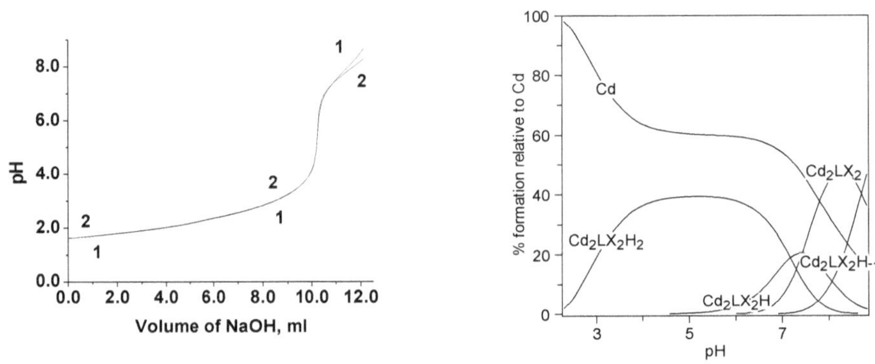

a. 1. Simulated titration curve
2. Experimental titration curve

b. Species distribution diagram

[SADH]= 0.00498 mol dm^{-3} [GLYCINE]= 0.0100 mol dm^{-3} [Cd^{2+}] = 0.01001 mol dm^{-3}
[HCl] = 0.04180 mol dm^{-3} [NaOH] = 0.2040 mol dm^{-3} TOTAL VOLUME=50.0 cm^3
Temp.: 30.0 ±0.1^{0}C I = 0.1 mol dm^{-3}

Figure 5.20: Cd^{2+}-SADH-GLYCINE SYSTEM (2:1:2)

The simulated titration curves were generated using SOPHD program[18], assuming the formation of only binary metal ion-ligand species for both SADH and glycine. The theoretical titration curves were found to differ from those of experimental indicating the formation of mixed ligand species. The experimental data were subjected to analysis using the Miniquad-75 program. The initial estimates of the formation constants for ternary species were calculated from the formation constants of binary species and protonation constants of the ligands. The best-fit models obtained for all the metal ions and compositions are tabulated in Tables 5.1 to 5.5.

Table 5.1 Best fit chemical models of Ca^{2+} -succinic acid dihydrazide-glycine ternary systems in aqueous medium at 303.0 K and ionic strength, I = 0.1 mol dm^{-3}

Metal ion	Composition (M: L: X)	Species mlxh	Log β_{mlxh}	
Ca^{2+}	1:1:1	0101	03.58	U/NP = $5.117X10^{-7}$
		0102	06.14	χ^2= 71.79
		010-1	-11.91	R =0.030
		0011	09.56	Skewness= -0.08
		0012	11.86	Kurtosis= 5.63
		1112	17.93 (7)	Np= 97
		1111	14.51 (6)	pH=2.0-9.9
		1110	05.79 (9)	
		111-2	-13.86 (7)	
	1: 1: 2	0101	03.58	U/NP = $4.127X10^{-8}$
		0102	06.14	χ^2= 52.04
		010-1	-11.91	R =0.0068
		0011	09.56	Skewness= -0.26
		0012	11.86	Kurtosis=6.12
		1123	29.58 (3)	Np=96
		1122	26.04 (8)	pH=2.3-9.5
		1121	17.32 (6)	
		1120	07.93 (5)	
		112-1	-1.68 (4)	
	2: 1: 1	0101	03.58	U/NP = $4.501X10^{-7}$
		0102	06.14	χ^2= 66.08
		010-1	-11.91	R =0.026
		0011	09.56	Skewness= -0.15
		0012	11.86	Kurtosis=4.19
		2111	16.10 (9)	Np=75
		2110	7.83 (11)	pH=2.2-9.9
		211-1	-1.30 (7)	

(Ca^{2+} SADH-glycine system)

Ca^{2+}	2:1 :2	0101	03.58	U/NP = $1.531X10^{-7}$
		0102	06.14	χ^2= 84.07
		010-1	-11.91	R =0.021
		0011	09.56	Skewness=-0.63
		0012	11.86	Kurtosis=4.18
		2122	28.40 (11)	Np=60
		2121	19.11 (16)	pH=2.3-9.9
		2120	9.72 (14)	
		212-1	00.09 (11)	

*Figures in the parentheses are the standard deviations in the least significant digit.

Table 5.2 Best fit chemical models of Mg^{2+} -succinic acid dihydrazide-glycine ternary system in aqueous medium at 303.0 K and ionic strength, I = 0.1 mol dm^{-3}

Metal ion	Composition (M: L: X)	Species mlxh	Log β_{mlxh}	
Mg^{2+}	1:1:1	0101	03.58	U/NP = $6.839X10^{-8}$
		0102	06.14	χ^2= 98.65
		010-1	-11.91	R =0.0091
		0011	09.56	Skewness= -0.81
		0012	11.86	Kurtosis= 4.39
		1112	17.55 (4)	Np=98
		1111	14.13 (4)	pH=1.9-10.0
		1110	05.32 (5)	
		111-1	-5.14 (5)	
	1: 1: 2	0101	03.58	U/NP = $5.318X10^{-8}$
		0102	06.14	χ^2= 105.16
		010-1	-11.91	R =0.0070
		0011	09.56	Skewness= 0.09
		0012	11.86	Kurtosis=6.13
		1123	28.93 (3)	Np=131
		1122	25.80 (2)	pH=2.1-10.4
		1121	17.33 (3)	
		1120	7.83 (2)	
		112-1	-2.45 (2)	
	2: 1: 1	0101	03.58	U/NP = $2.871X10^{-7}$
		0102	06.14	χ^2= 92.33
		010-1	-11.91	R =0.020
		0011	09.56	Skewness= -0.62
		0012	11.86	Kurtosis=5.05
		2111	16.02 (5)	Np=96
		2110	7.08 (9)	pH=2.1-10.2
		211-1	-2.89 (6)	
	2:1 :2	0101	03.58	U/NP = $2.772X10^{-8}$
		0102	06.14	χ^2= 97.30
		010-1	-11.91	R =0.0084
		0011	09.56	Skewness= -1.24
		0012	11.86	Kurtosis= 4.69
		2122	27.70 (4)	Np=74
		2121	18.77 (9)	pH=2.2-10.3
		2120	09.32 (6)	
		212-1	-1.18 (6)	

*Figures in the parentheses are the standard deviations in the least significant digit.

Table 5.3 Best fit chemical models of Pb^{2+}-succinic acid dihydrazide-glycine ternary system in aqueous medium at 303.0 K and ionic strength, I = 0.1 mol dm^{-3}

Metal ion	Composition (M: L: X)	Species mlxh	Log β_{mlxh}	
Pb^{2+}	1:1:1	0101	03.58	U/NP = 2.173X10^{-7}
		0102	06.14	χ^2= 41.01
		010-1	-11.91	R =0.014
		0011	09.56	Skewness= -0.55
		0012	11.86	Kurtosis= 3.29
		1112	18.28 (3)	Np=107
		1111	14.82 (5)	pH=1.7-6.1
		1110	08.62 (8)	
	1: 1: 2	0101	03.58	U/NP = 4.904X10^{-7}
		0102	06.14	χ^2= 42.62
		010-1	-11.91	R =0.015
		0011	09.56	Skewness= -0.76
		0012	11.86	Kurtosis=4.19
		1123	29.80 (4)	Np=133
		1122	26.29 (7)	pH=1.7-6.3
		1120	13.86 (7)	
	2: 1: 1	0101	03.58	U/NP = 2.942X10^{-7}
		0102	06.14	χ^2= 26.88
		010-1	-11.91	R =0.020
		0011	09.56	Skewness= -0.43
		0012	11.86	Kurtosis=2.51
		2111	16.93 (4)	Np=64
		2110	10.95 (11)	pH=2.2 -5.7
	2:1 :2	0101	03.58	U/NP = 7.339X10^{-8}
		0102	06.14	χ^2= 49.22
		010-1	-11.91	R =0.013
		0011	09.56	Skewness= -0.81
		0012	11.86	Kurtosis= 3.64
		2122	28.57(6)	Np=49
		2120	16.32 (7)	pH=2.3-5.9

*Figures in the parentheses are the standard deviations in the least significant digit.

Table 5.4 Best fit chemical models of Hg^{2+} -succinic acid dihydrazide-glycine ternary system in aqueous medium at 303.0 K and ionic strength, I = 0.1 mol dm^{-3}

Metal ion	Composition (M: L: X)	Species mlxh	Log β_{mlxh}	
Hg^{2+}	1:1:1	0101	03.58	U/NP =5.228X10^{-8}
		0102	06.14	χ^2= 48.18
		010-1	-11.91	R =0.0083
		0011	09.56	Skewness= -0.29
		0012	11.86	Kurtosis=3.29
		1112	17.56 (3)	Np=89
		1111	14.52 (2)	pH=2.0-6.3
		1110	08.22 (4)	

(Hg^{2+}- SADH-glycine system)

		0101	03.58	U/NP = $1.082X10^{-7}$
		0102	06.14	χ^2= 48.80
		010-1	-11.91	R =0.0078
		0011	09.56	Skewness= -0.30
	1: 1: 2	0012	11.86	Kurtosis= 2.59
		1123	28.92 (3)	Np=120
		1122	25.83 (2)	pH=1.9-6.5
		1121	19.37 (18)	
		1120	12.31 (7)	
		0101	03.58	U/NP = $1.295X10^{-7}$
		0102	06.14	χ^2= 45.16
		010-1	-11.91	R =0.013
Hg^{2+}	2: 1: 1	0011	09.56	Skewness= 0.05
		0012	11.86	Kurtosis=4.98
		2111	16.36 (3)	Np=76
		2110	10.48 (18)	pH=2.3-6.0
		211-1	04.35 (8)	
		0101	03.58	U/NP = $7.471X10^{-8}$
		0102	06.14	χ^2= 40.80
		010-1	-11.91	R =0.012
	2:1 :2	0011	09.56	Skewness= -0.79
		0012	11.86	Kurtosis= 3.36
		2122	28.44 (6)	Np=65
		2120	14.54 (6)	pH=2.1-6.5

*Figures in the parentheses are the standard deviations in the least significant digit.

Table 5.5 Best fit chemical models of Cd^{2+}-succinic acid dihydrazide-glycine ternary system in aqueous medium at 303.0 K and ionic strength, I = 0.1 mol dm^{-3}

Metal ion	**Composition (M: L: X)**	**Species mlxh**	**Log β_{mlxh}**	
		0101	03.58	U/NP = $7.912X10^{-9}$
		0102	06.14	χ^2= 41.18
		010-1	-11.91	R =0.0036
		0011	09.56	Skewness= -0.20
	1:1:1	0012	11.86	Kurtosis=6.05
		1112	17.49 (1)	Np=71
		1111	14.22 (1)	pH=2.2-8.0
		1110	06.69 (2)	
Cd^{2+}		111-1	-1.81 (3)	
		0101	03.58	U/NP = $1.265X10^{-8}$
		0102	06.14	χ^2= 57.38
		010-1	-11.91	R =0.0033
		0011	09.56	Skewness= -0.23
	1: 1: 2	0012	11.86	Kurtosis=4.23
		1123	28.83 (1)	Np=84
		1122	25.50 (1)	pH=2.3-8.2
		1121	18.31 (2)	
		1120	10.47 (1)	

(Cd^{2+}- SADH-glycine system)

Cd^{2+}	2: 1: 1	0101	03.58	U/NP = $2.676X10^{-7}$
		0102	06.14	χ^2= 87.81
		010-1	-11.91	R =0.018
		0011	09.56	Skewness= -0.95
		0012	11.86	Kurtosis=3.54
		2111	16.24 (5)	Np=86
		2110	8.99 (9)	pH=2.1-8.1
		211-1	0.78 (7)	
	2:1 :2	0101	03.58	U/NP = $4.414X10^{-8}$
		0102	06.14	χ^2= 73.79
		010-1	-11.91	R =0.011
		0011	09.56	Skewness= -0.50
		0012	11.86	Kurtosis= 4.29
		2122	27.83(7)	Np=67
		2121	20.66 (15)	pH=2.3-8.8
		2120	13.23 (6)	
		212-1	4.54 (5)	

*Figures in the parentheses are the standard deviations in the least significant digit.

For 1:1:1 (M:L:X) composition, the species converged for all the metal ion systems are $MLXH_2$, MLXH, MLX, and additionally $MLXH_{-1}$ for Mg^{2+}, Cd^{2+} and $MLXH_{-2}$ for Ca^{2+}. In the $MLXH_2$ type of species succinic acid dihydrazide (L) is present in LH form, i.e. one of the coordinating units of SADH is involved in bonding as a bidentate while the other is non-bonding and protonated. Glycine (XH) is bonded in zwitter ion form as a monodentate bonding through carboxylate oxygen (Figure 5.21) while the α-amino group is protonated and non-bonding.

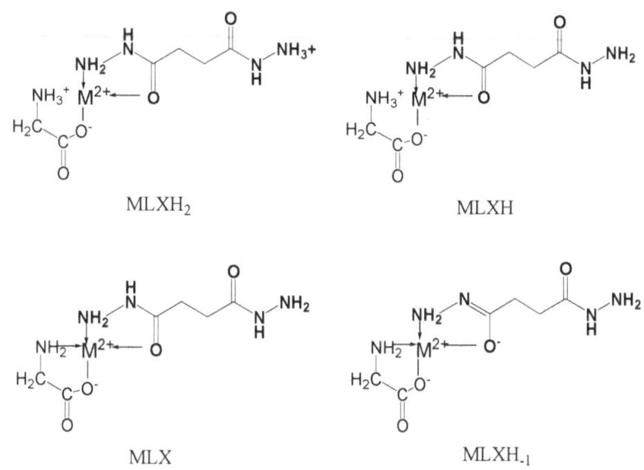

Figure 5.21: Probable mode of bonding in the species of 1:1:1 (M: L: X) composition

This may be ascertained from the stepwise deprotonation of $MLXH_2$ species to form MLXH ($\log \beta_{1112} - \log \beta_{1111}$), which is < 3.58. This value is of the order of the protonation constant of the SADH. Species distribution diagrams (Figures 5.1b, 5.5b, 5.9b, 5.13b and 5.17b for Ca^{2+}, Mg^{2+}, Pb^{2+}, Hg^{2+} and Cd^{2+}systems respectively) indicate that the species $MLXH_2$ reaches a maximum of 25% to 47% , depending on the metal ion with a maximum around a pH of 2.8. Further increase in pH leads to the deprotonation of this species forming successively MLXH and MLX. The deprotonation of MLXH to form MLX is due to the deprotonation of the α-ammonium group on bonding to the metal ion indicated by the step-wise deprotonation constant, "$\log \beta_{1111} - \log \beta_{1110}$" which is less than 9.56, the protonation constant of glycine. A drop of 2 to 3 log units in protonation constant is normally observed on complexation. The formation of species, MLXH ranges from 49 to 62% of the total metal in the pH region 4.7 to 6.2. The deprotonated species $MLXH_{-1}$ and $MLXH_{-2}$ which appear above a pH of 7.0 in the case of Ca^{2+}, Mg^{2+} and Cd^{2+} may be due to the loss of enolic protons or hydroxylation of the MLX type of species. These species were not observed in the case of Pb^{2+} and Hg^{2+} systems as the study was restricted to a pH below 6.5 due to the appearance of turbidity in the solution.

The ternary species converged for 1:1:2 (M:L:X mole ratio) systems, in addition to binary species, were MLX_2H_3, MLX_2H_2, MLX_2H, MLX_2 and MLX_2H_{-1}. The step-wise proton dissociation constants of MLX_2H_3 to form MLX_2H_2 type of species for different metal ions ($\log K_{1122}^{1123} = \log \beta_{1123} - \log \beta_{1122}$) range from 3.09 to 3.54 which are less than the protonation constant of SADH (3.58). This clearly indicates that one of the protons in the MLX_2H_3 type of species is attached to the dihydrazide and the remaining two protons are due to the zwitter ion form of the glycine molecules participating in the bonding as (M.(LH).$(XH)_2$) monodentates bonding through the carboxylate groups. Thus, one of the hydrazide groups of SADH is involved in bonding while the other is free and protonated. Although solution phase studies cannot give the exact structures of the species, the most probable mode of bonding depending on the step-wise protonation constants and pH region of formation of the species is shown in Figure 5.22.

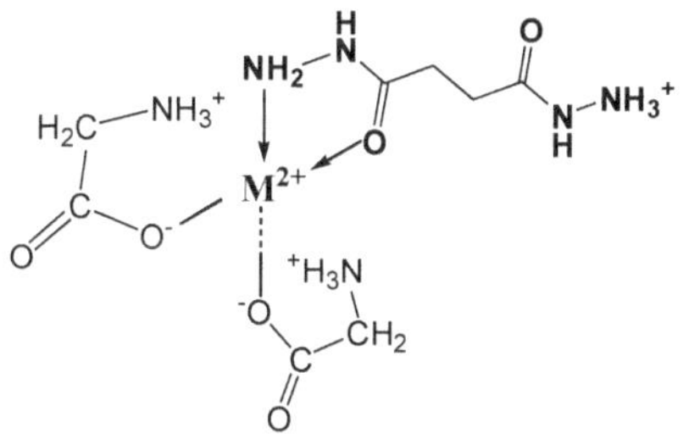

MLX_2H_3[*i.e.* M(LH)$(XH)_2$]

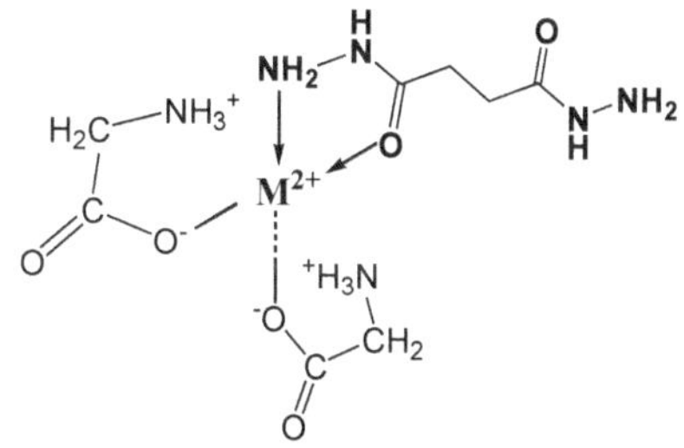

MLX_2H_2[*i.e.* M(L)$(XH)_2$]

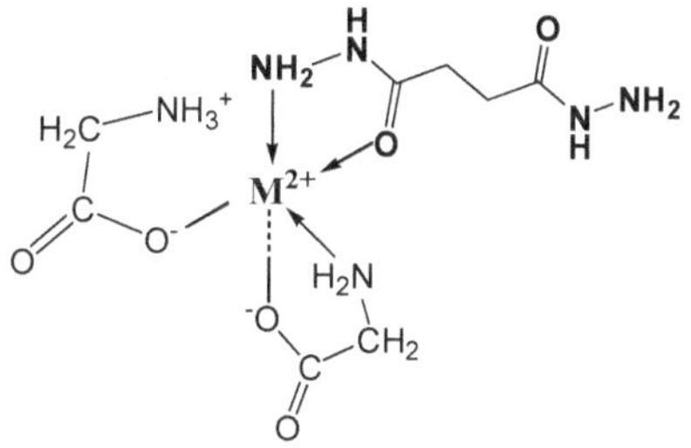

MLX_2H_2[*i.e.* MLX(XH)]

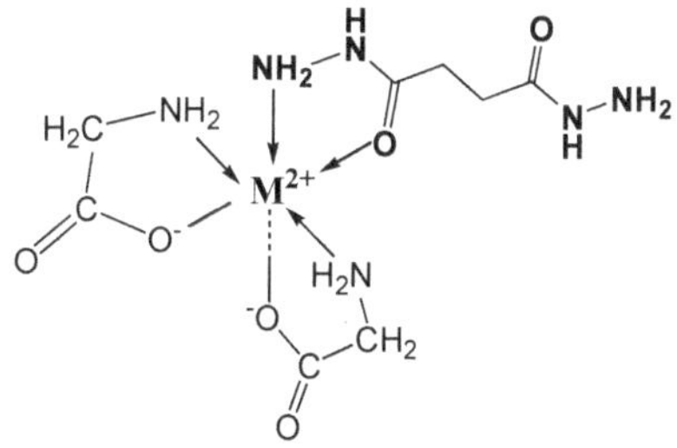

MLX_2

Figure 5.22: Probable mode of bonding in the species of 1:1:2 (M: L: X) composition

With an increase in pH, MLX_2H_3 loses LH proton forming MLX_2H_2 type of species. The maximum extent of formation of MLX_2H_3 type of species ranges from 26 to 49% of the total metal around 2.80 pH. In the MLX_2H_2 type of species, both the protons are attached to α-amino groups of glycine molecules. The step-wise formation constants, $\log K_{1121}^{1122} = \log \beta_{1122} - \log \beta_{1121}$ for the formation of MLX_2H_2 from MLX_2H and $\log K_{1120}^{1121} = \log \beta_{1121} - \log \beta_{1120}$ for the formation of MLX_2H from MLX_2 range from 9.50 to 6.46 indicating the release of α-ammonium proton of glycine on complexation or without any complexation. Solution chemistry cannot ascertain the involvement of α-ammonium groups of both the glycine molecules in bonding as it depends on the coordination number and other factors specific to the metal ion. The formation of MLX_2H_{-1} species at higher pH may be due to hydroxylation or deprotonation of the enolic proton of the dihydrazide. The diagrams (Figures 5.2b, 5.6b. 5.10 b, 5.14 b and 5.18b for Ca^{2+}, Mg^{2+}, Pb^{2+}, Hg^{2+} and Cd^{2+} systems respectively) give the concentration distribution of all these species against pH of the solution.

As succinic acid dihydrazide is a ditopic ligand, Calvin-Wilson titrations were also conducted for compositions in which metal concentration was twice that of dihydrazide i.e. 2:1:1 (M:L:XH), where, M= Ca^{2+}, Mg^{2+}, Pb^{2+}, Hg^{2+} and Cd^{2+}, L= succinic acid dihydrazide and XH is glycine. The simulated titration curves assuming the formation of only simple complexes differed from the experimental curves (Figures 5.3a, 5.7a. 5.11a, 5.15a and 5.19a for Ca^{2+}, Mg^{2+}, Pb^{2+}, Hg^{2+} and Cd^{2+} systems respectively) indicating the formation of other species. The data were subjected to analysis using the Miniquad-75 program and the results were included in Tables 5.1 to 5.5 for different metal ions. The best-fit models obtained indicate, the formation of M_2LXH, M_2LX and M_2LXH_{-1} binuclear mixed ligand species. Succinic acid dihydrazide acts as a bis bidentate bonding to metal ions through carbonyl oxygen and amino nitrogen forming five membered rings, while glycine is bonded to one of the metal ions as a monodentate (in M_2LXH) bonding through carboxylate oxygen and as a bidentate in the M_2LX type of species bonding through both carboxylate oxygen and α-amino nitrogen. The probable bonding nature of the ligands in the species of 2:1:1 molar composition is shown in Figure 5.23.

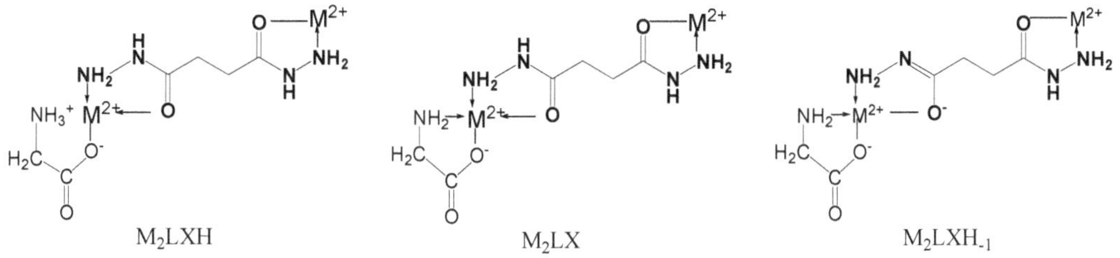

Figure 5.23: Probable nature of bonding in the species of 2:1:1 (M:L:X) composition

The step-wise formation constants $\log K_{2110}^{2111} = \log \beta_{2111} - \log \beta_{2110}$ for the protonation of M_2LX to form M_2LXH lie between 8.94 and 5.88 for Ca^{2+}, Mg^{2+}, Pb^{2+}, Hg^{2+} and Cd^{2+} systems. This clearly indicates that the deprotonation is of the α-ammonium group on complexation to the metal ion. The formation of M_2LXH_{-1} type of species may be due to the deprotonation of the enolic form of the hydrazide group or hydroxylation. The species distribution diagrams ((Figures 5.3b, 5.7b. 5.11b, 5.15b and 5.19b for Ca^{2+}, Mg^{2+}, Pb^{2+}, Hg^{2+} and Cd^{2+} systems respectively) indicate that below 5.9 pH, M_2LXH is the major species, the extent of formation being 53 to 68% depending on the metal ion. Above 5.6 pH the unprotonated and deprotonated species coexist and dominate in solution.

The best-fit models for 2:1:2 (M:L:X) molar composition indicate the formation of four ternary species viz. $M_2LX_2H_2$, M_2LX_2H, M_2LX_2 and $M_2LX_2H_{-1}$. In the symmetric $M_2LX_2H_2$ type of species, succinic acid dihydrazide binds two metal ions on either side as a bis bidentate bonding through carbonyl and terminal amino groups. Two molecules of glycine (XH) also participate in complexation as monodentates bonding through only carboxylate groups. The step-wise formation constants, $\log K_{2121}^{2122} = \log \beta_{2122} - \log \beta_{2121}$ for the formation of $M_2LX_2H_2$ from M_2LX_2H and $\log K_{2120}^{2121} = \log \beta_{2121} - \log \beta_{2120}$ for the formation of M_2LX_2H from M_2LX_2 are

9.29, 9.39 for Ca^{2+}, 8.93, 9.45 for Mg^{2+} and 7.17, 7.43 for Cd^{2+} systems respectively. The closeness of the two values indicates that the amino acid molecules are attached to different metal ions on either side but not to the same metal ion. In the $M_2LX_2H_2$ type of species the α-amino groups of glycine molecules are protonated and non-bonding. With increase in pH this species successively deprotonates to M_2LX_2H and M_2LX_2. Although, solution phase studies cannot ascertain the mode of bonding in various species, most probable bonding mode may be assigned depending on the nature of deprotonation and pH region of existence of the species. Figure 5.24 shows the probable bonding nature in various species that exist in solutions of 2:1:2 (M:L:X) molar composition.

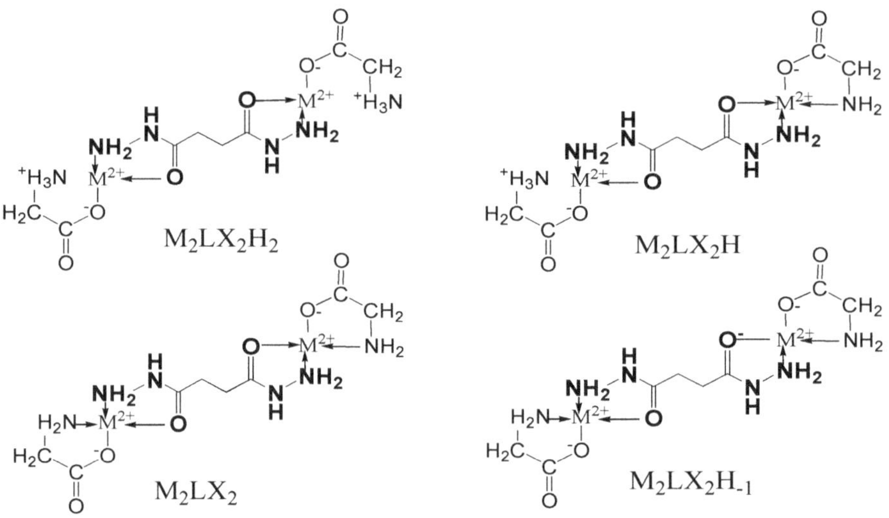

Figure 5.24: Probable boning in the species of 2:1:2 (M;L;X) molar composition

The species distribution diagrams (Figures 5.4b, 5.8b. 5.12b, 5.16b and 5.20b for Ca^{2+}, Mg^{2+}, Pb^{2+}, Hg^{2+} and Cd^{2+} systems respectively) for 2:1:2 composition indicate that $M_2LX_2H_2$ is predominant below 6.1 pH representing 37 to 54 % of total metal depending on the metal ion. Above this pH, M_2LX_2H, M_2LX_2 and $M_2LX_2H_{-1}$ type of species coexist in solution. The formation of $M_2LX_2H_{-1}$ type of species may be due to the deprotonation of the enolic form of SADH or hydroxylation. The formation constants of all the species for all the compositions were found to be in the order Ca^{2+}> $Mg^{2+}$and Pb^{2+}> Hg^{2+} > Cd^{2+}.

5.2.2 SADH- L-histidine- metal ion systems:

Histidine is a basic amino acid, containing weakly basic imidazole group in the side chain. It is one of the essential amino acids and is well known for its biological importance. Its exceptional ability to bind the metal ions is ascribed to the formation of five and /or six membered rings in which the metal ion is attached to different coordinating centres of the molecule. The modes of bonding are through (i) imidazole nitrogen and α-amino group forming a six membered ring or (ii) carboxylate oxygen and α-amino group forming a five membered ring or (iii) carboxylate oxygen and imidazole nitrogen forming a seven membered ring or (iv) imidazole nitrogen, α-amino group and carboxylate oxygen as a tridentate forming adjacent six and five membered rings. A detailed study of the binary systems of metal ion-histidine systems, giving stoichiometry and formation constants of various species formed along with their concentration distribution is included in Section 4.2.2 of Chapter-4 of the thesis. On the other hand, succinic acid dihydrazide is a ditopic ligand and can accommodate two metal ions in different coordination pockets of the same molecule. The details of binary systems of SADH are included in Section 4.1.1 of Chaptet-4. Therefore, it is interesting to study the ternary systems in which both SADH and histidine simultaneously participate in bonding with a metal ion.

Calvin-Wilson potentiometric titrations were conducted for 1:1:1, 1:1:2, 2:1:1 and 2:1:2 (M: L: X) molar compositions, where M= Ca^{2+}, Mg^{2+}, Pb^{2+}, Hg^{2+} and Cd^{2+}, L= SADH and XH_2= L-histidine. To check the presence of ternary species in solution, theoretical titration curves were generated assuming the formation of only binary species for both the ligands using SOPHD program, for comparison with the experimental curves. The simulated and experimental titration curves for all the metal ion systems and compositions are shown in Figures 5.25a to 5.44a. The differences between the experimental and simulated titration curves throughout the pH region indicate the formation of ternary species in addition to binary species. Keeping in view of the coordinating behaviour of SADH and histidine, suitable chemical models containing all the plausible species were prepared for analysis using the Miniquad-75 program.

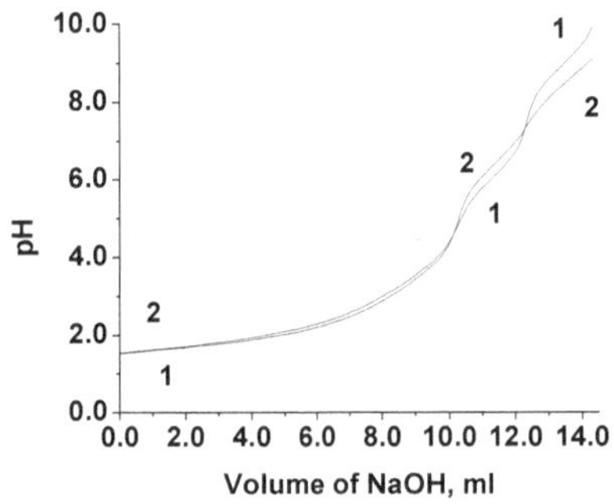

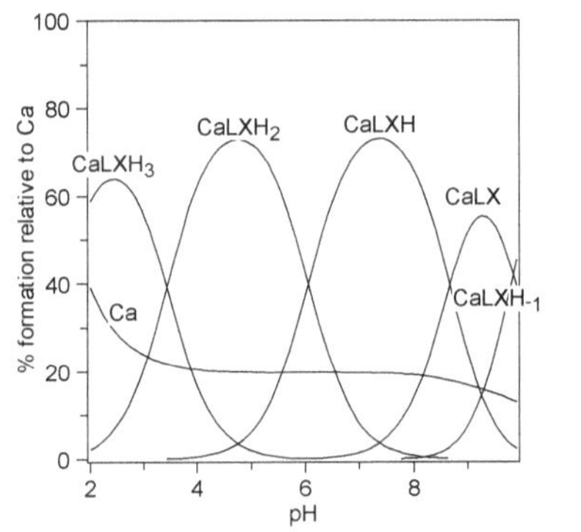

a. 1. Simulated titration curve
2. Experimental titration curve

b. Species distribution diagram

[SADH] = 0.00999 mol dm^{-3} [HISTIDINE] = 0.0100 mol dm^{-3} [Ca^{2+}] = 0.00998 mol dm^{-3}
[HCl] = 0.05876 mol dm^{-3} [NaOH] = 0.2380 mol dm^{-3} TOTAL VOLUME= 50.0 cm^3
Temp.: 30.0 ±0.1^{0}C I = 0.1 mol dm^{-3}

Figure 5.25: Ca^{2+}-SADH-HISTIDINE SYSTEM (1:1:1)

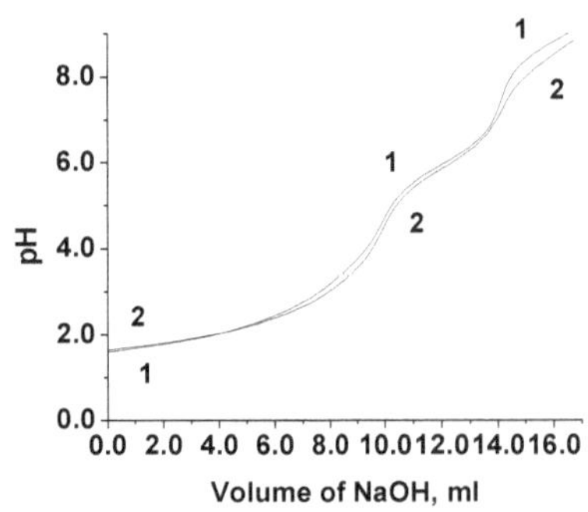

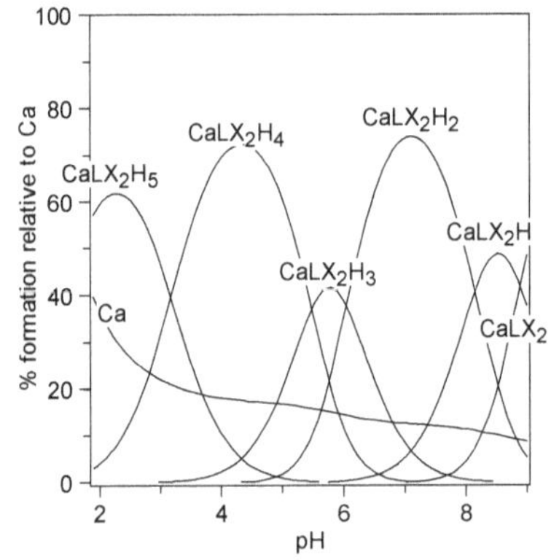

a. 1. Simulated titration curve
2. Experimental titration curve

b. Species distribution diagram

[SADH]= 0.00999 mol dm^{-3} [HISTIDINE] = 0.0200 mol dm^{-3} [Ca^{2+}] = 0.00998 mol dm^{-3}
[HCl] = 0.06728 mol dm^{-3} [NaOH] = 0.2380 mol dm^{-3} TOTAL VOLUME=50.0 cm^3
Temp.: 30.0 ±0.1^{0}C I = 0.1 mol dm^{-3}

Figure 5.26: Ca^{2+}-SADH-HISTIDINE SYSTEM (1:1:2)

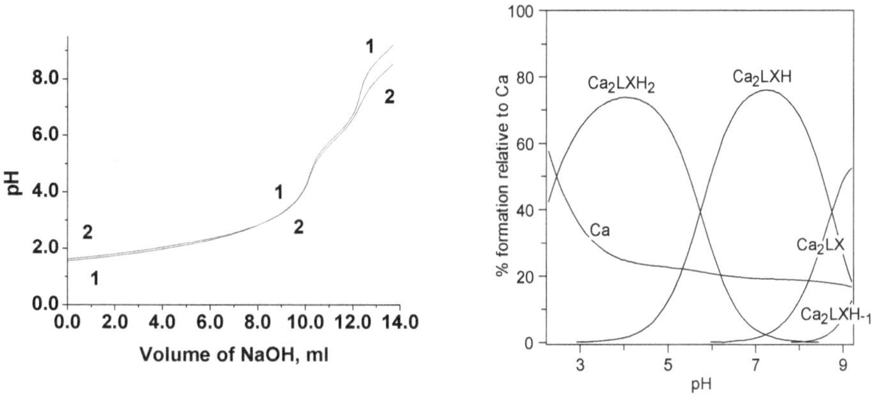

a. 1. Simulated titration curve
2. Experimental titration curve

b. Species distribution diagram

[SADH]= 0.00999 mol dm^{-3}	[HISTIDINE] = 0.0100 mol dm^{-3}	[Ca^{2+}] = 0.01996 mol dm^{-3}
[HCl] = 0.05850 mol dm^{-3}	[NaOH] = 0.2380 mol dm^{-3}	TOTAL VOLUME=50.0 cm^3
Temp.: 30.0 ±0.1^{0}C		I = 0.1 mol dm^{-3}

Figure 5.27: Ca^{2+}-SADH- HISTIDINE SYSTEM (2:1:1)

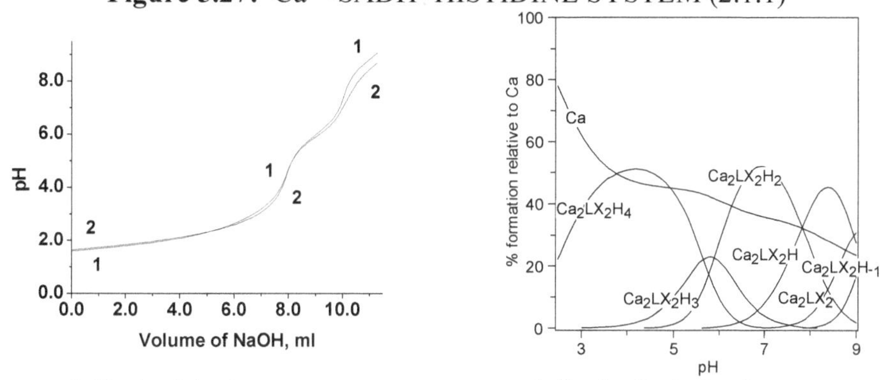

a. 1. Simulated titration curve
2. Experimental titration curve

b. Species distribution diagram

[SADH] = 0.00499 mol dm^{-3}	[HISTIDINE] = 0.0100 mol dm^{-3}	[Ca^{2+}] = 0.00998 mol dm^{-3}
[HCl] = 0.04786 mol dm^{-3}	[NaOH] = 0.2380 mol dm^{-3}	TOTAL VOLUME= 50.0 cm^3
Temp.: 30.0 ±0.1^{0}C		I = 0.1 mol dm^{-3}

Figure 5.28: Ca^{2+}-SADH- HISTIDINE SYSTEM (2:1:2)

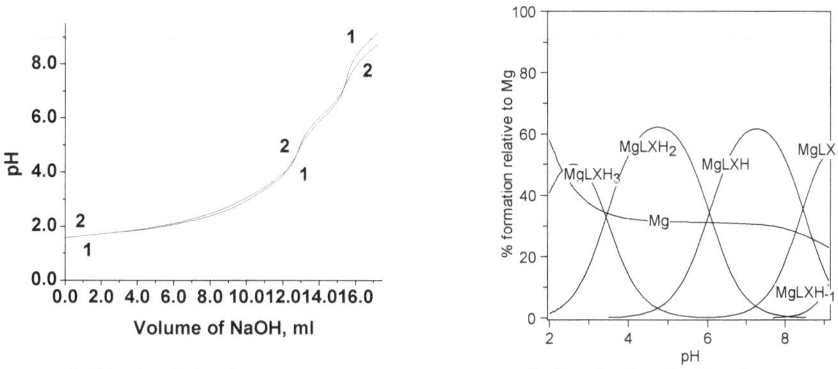

a. 1. Simulated titration curve
2. Experimental titration curve

b. Species distribution diagram

[SADH]= 0.00999 mol dm^{-3}	[HISTIDINE] = 0.0100 mol dm^{-3}	[Mg^{2+}] = 0.0100 mol dm^{-3}
[HCl] = 0.05830 mol dm^{-3}	[NaOH] = 0.1881mol dm^{-3}	TOTAL VOLUME=50.0 cm^3
Temp.: 30.0 ±0.1^{0}C		I = 0.1 mol dm^{-3}

Figure 5.29: Mg^{2+}-SADH- HISTIDINE SYSTEM (1:1:1)

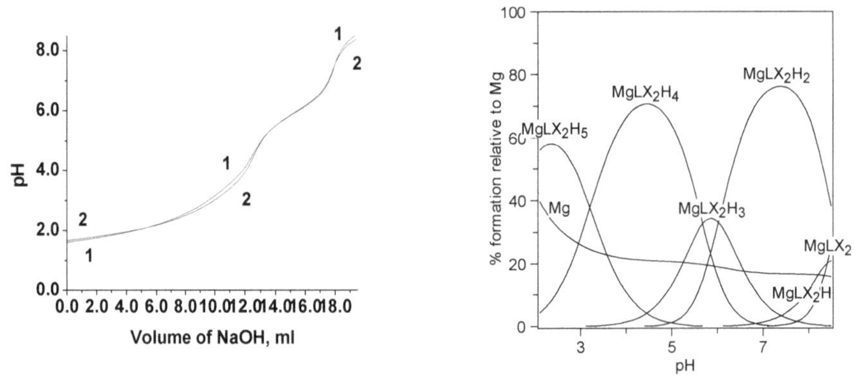

a. 1. Simulated titration curve
2. Experimental titration curve

b. Species distribution diagram

[SADH]= 0.00999 mol dm^{-3} [HISTIDINE] = 0.0200 mol dm^{-3} [Mg^{2+}] = 0.0100 mol dm^{-3}
[HCl] = 0.06746 mol dm^{-3} [NaOH] = 0.1881 mol dm^{-3} TOTAL VOLUME=50.0 cm^3
Temp.: 30.0 ±0.1^{0}C I = 0.1 mol dm^{-3}

Figure 5.30: Mg^{2+}-SADH- HISTIDINE SYSTEM (1:1:2)

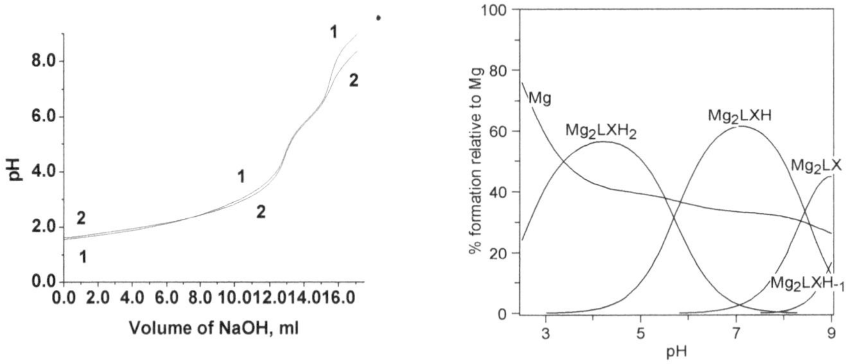

a. 1. Simulated titration curve
2. Experimental titration curve

b. Species distribution diagram

[SADH] = 0.00999 mol dm^{-3} [HISTIDINE] = 0.0100 mol dm^{-3} [Mg^{2+}] = 0.01999 mol dm^{-3}
[HCl] = 0.05852 mol dm^{-3} [NaOH] = 0.1881 mol dm^{-3} TOTAL VOLUME= 50.0 cm^3
Temp.: 30.0 ±0.1^{0}C I = 0.1 mol dm^{-3}

Figure 5.31: Mg^{2+}-SADH- HISTIDINE SYSTEM (2:1:1)

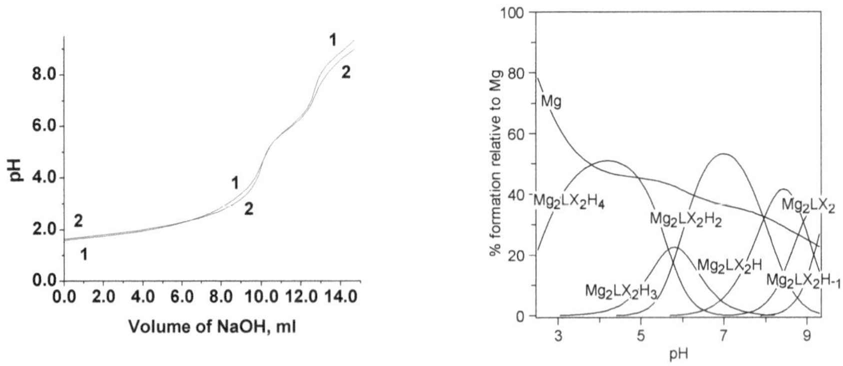

a. 1. Simulated titration curve
2. Experimental titration curve

b. Species distribution diagram

[SADH]= 0.00499 mol dm^{-3} [HISTIDINE] = 0.0100 mol dm^{-3} [Mg^{2+}] = 0.0100 mol dm^{-3}
[HCl] = 0.04779 mol dm^{-3} [NaOH] = 0.1881mol dm^{-3} TOTAL VOLUME= 50.0 cm^3
Temp.: 30.0 ±0.1^{0}C I = 0.1 mol dm^{-3}

Figure 5.32: Mg^{2+}-SADH- HISTIDINE SYSTEM (2:1:2)

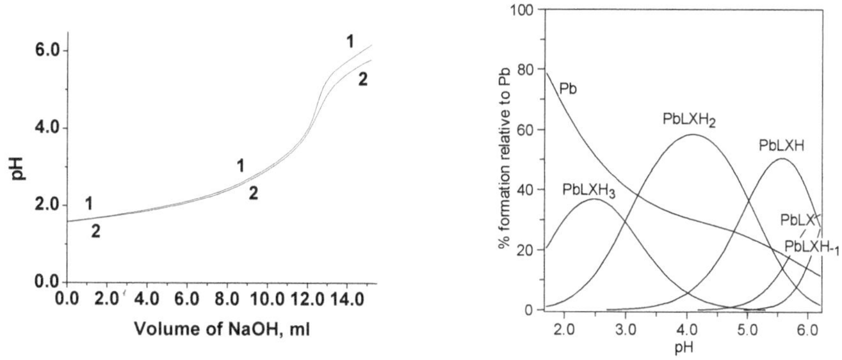

a. 1. Simulated titration curve
2. Experimental titration curve

b. Species distribution diagram

[SADH]= 0.00999 mol dm^{-3} [HISTIDINE] = 0.0100 mol dm^{-3} [Pb $^{2+}$] = 0.01003 mol dm^{-3}
[HNO_3] = 0.05706 mol dm^{-3} [NaOH] = 0.1881mol dm^{-3} TOTAL VOLUME= 50.0 cm^3
Temp.: 30.0 ±0.1^{0}C I = 0.1 mol dm^{-3}

Figure 5.33: Pb^{2+}-SADH- HISTIDINE SYSTEM (1:1:1)

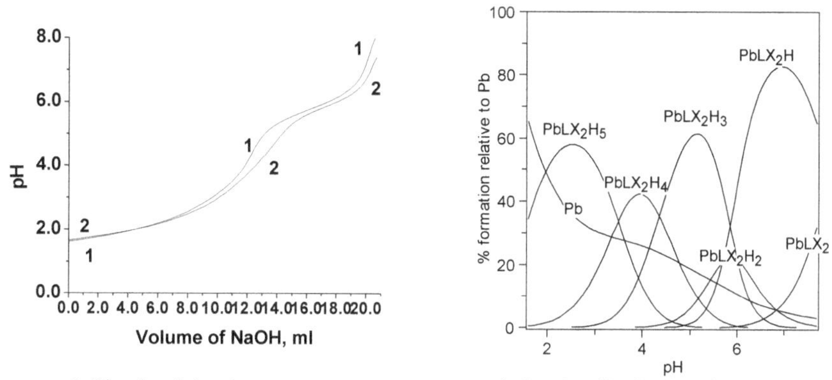

a. 1. Simulated titration curve
2. Experimental titration curve

b. Species distribution diagram

[SADH] = 0.00999 mol dm^{-3} [HISTIDINE] = 0.0200 mol dm^{-3} [Pb^{2+}] = 0.01003 mol dm^{-3}
[HNO_3] = 0.06663 mol dm^{-3} [NaOH] = 0.1881 mol dm^{-3} TOTAL VOLUME= 50.0 cm^3
Temp.: 30.0 ±0.1^{0}C I = 0.1 mol dm^{-3}

Figure 5.34: Pb^{2+}-SADH HISTIDINE SYSTEM (1:1:2)

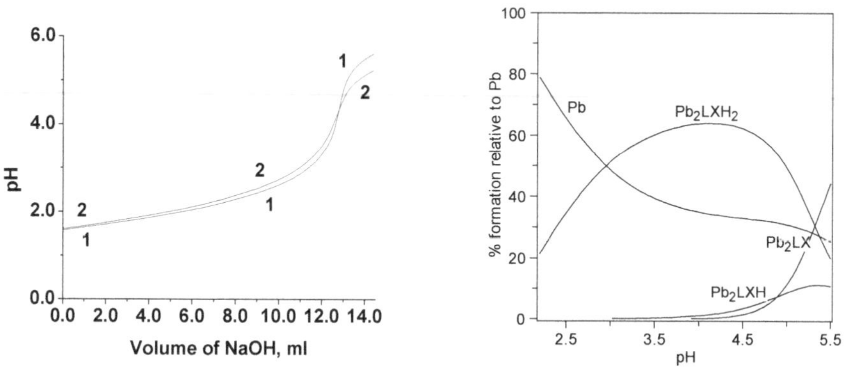

a. 1. Simulated titration curve
2. Experimental titration curve

b. Species distribution diagram

[SADH]= 0.00999 mol dm^{-3} [HISTIDINE] = 0.0100 mol dm^{-3} [Pb $^{2+}$] = 0.02005moldm^{-3}
[HNO_3] = 0.05844 mol dm^{-3} [NaOH] = 0.1881mol dm^{-3} TOTAL VOLUME= 50.0 cm^3
Temp.: 30.0 ±0.1^{0}C I = 0.1 mol dm^{-3}

Figure 5.35: Pb^{2+}-SADH- HISTIDINE SYSTEM (2:1:1)

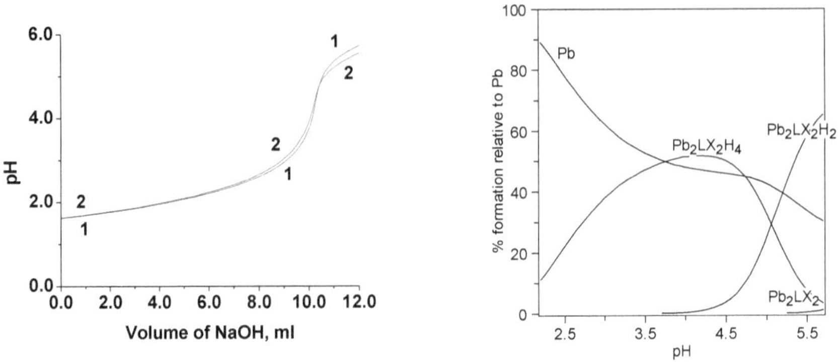

a. 1. Simulated titration curve
2. Experimental titration curve

b. Species distribution diagram

[SADH]= 0.00499 mol dm^{-3} [HISTIDINE] = 0.0100 mol dm^{-3} [Pb^{2+}] = 0.01003 mol dm^{-3}

[HNO_3] = 0.04875 mol dm^{-3} [NaOH] = 0.1881mol dm^{-3} TOTAL VOLUME= 50.0 cm^3

Temp.: 30.0 ±0.1^{0}C I = 0.1 mol dm^{-3}

Figure 5.36: Pb^{2+}-SADH- HISTIDINE SYSTEM (2:1:2)

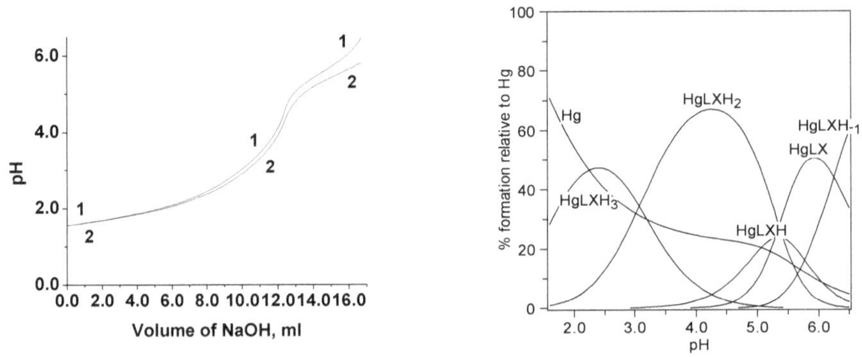

a. 1. Simulated titration curve
2. Experimental titration curve

b. Species distribution diagram

[SADH] = 0.00999 mol dm^{-3} [HISTIDINE] = 0.0100 mol dm^{-3} [Hg^{2+}] = 0.00997 mol dm^{-3}

[HCl] = 0.05932 mol dm^{-3} [NaOH] = 0.1981 mol dm^{-3} TOTAL VOLUME= 50.0 cm^3

Temp.: 30.0 ±0.1^{0}C I = 0.1 mol dm^{-3}

Figure 5.37: Hg^{2+}-SADH-HISTIDINE SYSTEM (1:1:1)

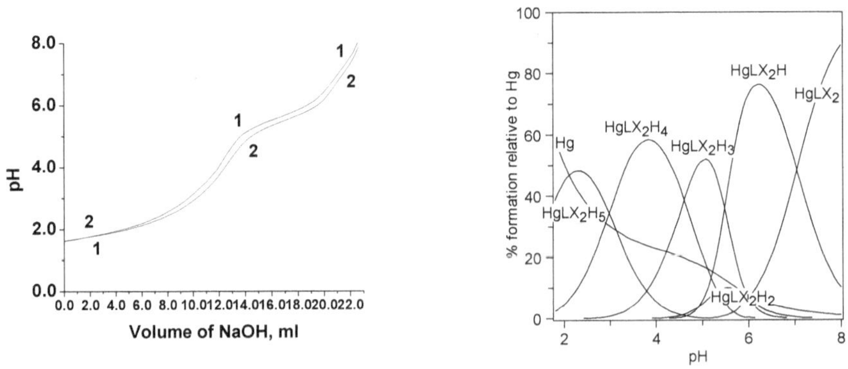

a. 1. Simulated titration curve
2. Experimental titration curve

b. Species distribution diagram

[SADH]= 0.00999 mol dm^{-3} [HISTIDINE] = 0.0200 mol dm^{-3} [Hg^{2+}] = 0.00997 mol dm^{-3}

[HCl] = 0.06710 mol dm^{-3} [NaOH] = 0.1890 mol dm^{-3} TOTAL VOLUME=50.0 cm^3

Temp.: 30.0 ±0.1^{0}C I = 0.1 mol dm^{-3}

Figure 5.38: Hg^{2+}-SADH- HISTIDINE SYSTEM (1:1:2)

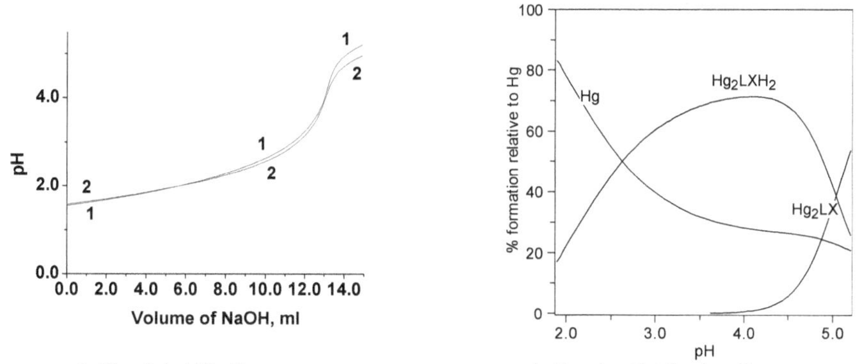

a. 1. Simulated titration curve
2. Experimental titration curve

b. Species distribution diagram

[SADH]= 0.00999 mol dm^{-3} [HISTIDINE] = 0.0100 mol dm^{-3} [Hg^{2+}] = 0.01995 mol dm^{-3}
[HCl] = 0.06017 mol dm^{-3} [NaOH] = 0.1881 mol dm^{-3} TOTAL VOLUME=50.0 cm^3
Temp.: 30.0 ±0.1^{0}C I = 0.1 mol dm^{-3}

Figure 5.39: Hg^{2+}-SADH- HISTIDINE SYSTEM (2:1:1)

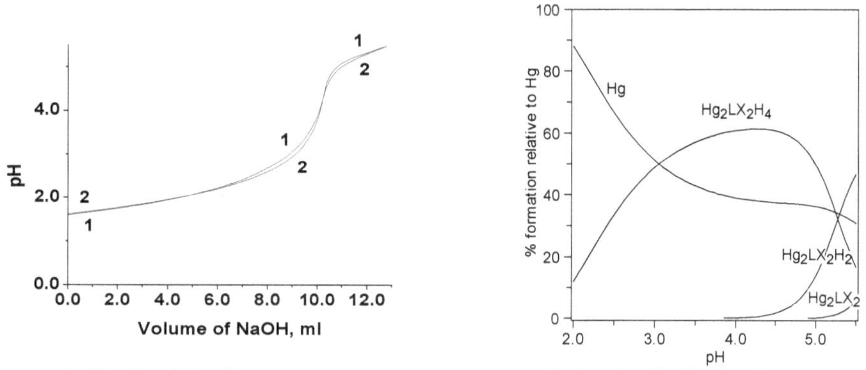

a. 1. Simulated titration curve
2. Experimental titration curve

b. Species distribution diagram

[SADH] = 0.00499 mol dm^{-3} [HISTIDINE] = 0.0100 mol dm^{-3} [Hg^{2+}] = 0.00997 mol dm^{-3}
[HCl] = 0.04882 mol dm^{-3} [NaOH] = 0.1881 mol dm^{-3} TOTAL VOLUME= 50.0 cm^3
Temp.: 30.0 ±0.1^{0}C I = 0.1 mol dm^{-3}

Figure 5.40: Hg^{2+}-SADH-HISTIDINE SYSTEM (2:1:2)

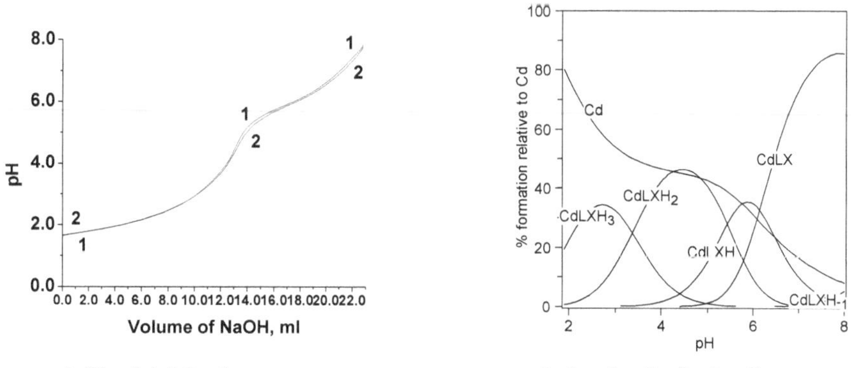

a. 1. Simulated titration curve
2. Experimental titration curve

b. Species distribution diagram

[SADH]= 0.00999 mol dm^{-3} [HISTIDINE] = 0.0100 mol dm^{-3} [Cd^{2+}] = 0.00993 mol dm^{-3}
[HCl] = 0.05951 mol dm^{-3} [NaOH] = 0.1881 mol dm^{-3} TOTAL VOLUME= 50.0 cm^3
Temp.: 30.0 ±0.1^{0}C I = 0.1 mol dm^{-3}

Figure 5.41: Cd^{2+}-SADH- HISTIDINE SYSTEM (1:1:1)

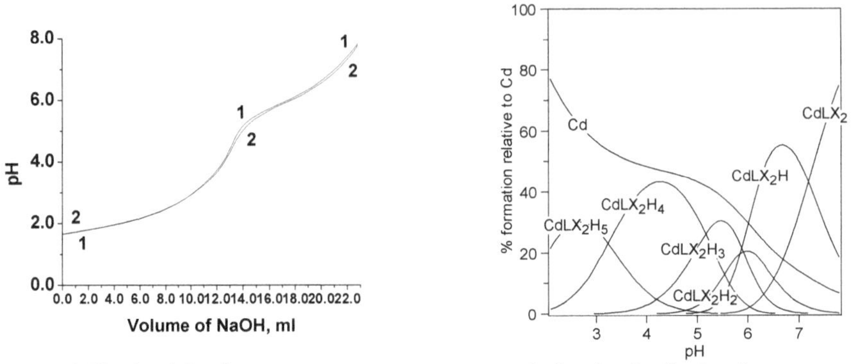

a. 1. Simulated titration curve
2. Experimental titration curve

b. Species distribution diagram

[SADH]= 0.00999 mol dm^{-3} [HISTIDINE] = 0.0200 mol dm^{-3} [Cd $^{2+}$] = 0.00993 mol dm^{-3}
[HCl] = 0.06948 mol dm^{-3} [NaOH] = 0.1881 mol dm^{-3} TOTAL VOLUME=50.0 cm^3
Temp.: 30.0 ±0.1^{0}C I = 0.1 mol dm^{-3}

Figure 5.42: Cd^{2+}-SADH- HISTIDINE SYSTEM (1:1:2)

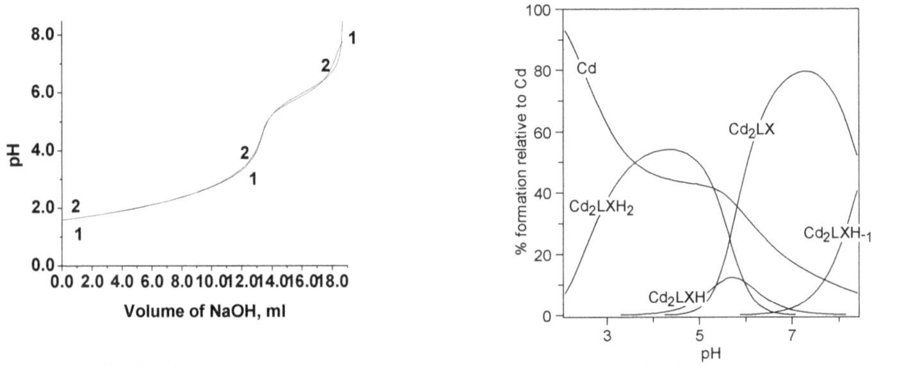

a. 1. Simulated titration curve
2. Experimental titration curve

b. Species distribution diagram

[SADH] = 0.00999 mol dm^{-3} [HISTIDINE] = 0.0100 mol dm^{-3} [Cd^{2+}] = 0.01986 mol dm^{-3}
[HCl] = 0.06035mol dm^{-3} [NaOH] = 0.1881 mol dm^{-3} TOTAL VOLUME= 50.0 cm^3
Temp.: 30.0 ±0.1^{0}C I = 0.1 mol dm^{-3}

Figure 5.43: Cd^{2+}-SADH-HISTIDINE SYSTEM (2:1:1)

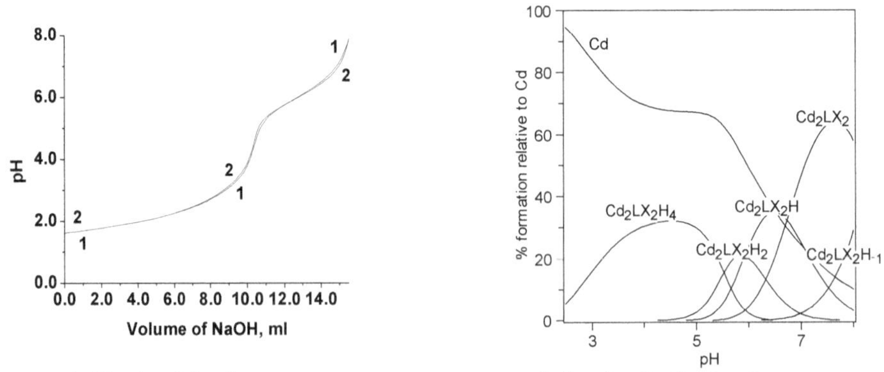

a. 1. Simulated titration curve
2. Experimental titration curve

b. Species distribution diagram

[SADH]= 0.00499 mol dm^{-3} [HISTIDINE] = 0.0100 mol dm^{-3} [Cd $^{2+}$] = 0.00993 moldm^{-3}
[HCl] = 0.04921 mol dm^{-3} [NaOH] = 0.1881mol dm^{-3} TOTAL VOLUME=50.0 cm^3
Temp.: 30.0 ±0.1^{0}C I = 0.1 mol dm^{-3}

Figure 5.44: Cd^{2+}-SADH- HISTIDINE SYSTEM (2:1:2)

The results of the analysis are tabulated in Tables 5.6 to 5.10 for Ca^{2+}, Mg^{2+}, Pb^{2+}, Hg^{2+} and Cd^{2+} systems respectively.

Table 5.6 Best fit chemical models of Ca^{2+}-succinic acid dihydrazide-histidine ternary system in aqueous medium at 303.0 K and ionic strength, I=0.1 mol dm^{-3}

Metal ion	Composition (M: L: X)	Species mlxh	Log β_{mlxh}	
Ca^{2+}	1:1:1	0101	03.58	U/NP = 1.213X10^{-8}
		0102	06.14	χ^2= 82.78
		010-1	-11.91	R =0.0039
		0011	08.95	Skewness= -0.84
		0012	15.02	Kurtosis=8.73
		0013	16.74	Np=79
		1113	24.48 (2)	pH=2.0-9.9
		1112	21.05 (2)	
		1111	14.99 (8)	
		1110	06.32 (6)	
		111-1	-3.52 (5)	
	1: 1: 2	0101	03.58	U/NP = 1.388X10^{-8}
		0102	06.14	χ^2= 99.63
		010-1	-11.91	R =0.0026
		0011	08.95	Skewness= 0.29
		0012	15.02	Kurtosis=5.29
		0013	16.74	Np=107
		1125	41.62 (2)	pH=1.9-9.0
		1124	38.45 (1)	
		1123	32.97 (6)	
		1122	26.92 (6)	
		1121	18.78 (5)	
		1120	9.89 (5)	
	2: 1: 1	0101	03.58	U/NP = 5.342X10^{-8}
		0102	06.14	χ^2= 98.75
		010-1	-11.91	R =0.0082
		0011	08.95	Skewness= -0.74
		0012	15.02	Kurtosis=6.60
		0013	16.74	Np=67
		2112	22.88 (3)	pH=2.3-9.2
		2111	17.16 (10)	
		2110	8.42 (8)	
		211-1	-1.40 (8)	
	2:1 :2	0101	03.58	U/NP = 7.829X10^{-9}
		0102	06.14	χ^2= 101.29
		010-1	-11.91	R =0.0043
		0011	08.95	Skewness=-0.38
		0012	15.02	Kurtosis=7.75
		0013	16.74	Np=59
		2124	39.53 (4)	pH=2.5-9.0
		2123	33.88 (7)	
		2122	27.99 (4)	
		2121	20.17 (5)	
		2120	11.22 (6)	
		212-1	1.95 (8)	

*Figures in the parentheses are the standard deviations in the least significant digit.

Table 5.7 Best fit chemical models of Mg^{2+} -succinic acid dihydrazide-histidine ternary system in aqueous medium at 303.0 K and ionic strength, I=0.1 mol dm^{-3}

Metal ion	Composition (M: L: X)	Species mlxh	Log β_{mlxh}	
Mg^{2+}	1:1:1	0101	03.58	U/NP = $9.578X10^{-9}$
		0102	06.14	χ^2= 97.76
		010-1	-11.91	R =0.0033
		0011	08.95	Skewness=-0.41
		0012	15.02	Kurtosis=5.77
		0013	16.74	Np=93
		1113	23.81 (2)	pH=2.0-9.1
		1112	20.38 (2)	
		1111	14.34 (4)	
		1110	05.89 (3)	
		111-1	-3.90 (4)	
	1: 1: 2	0101	03.58	U/NP = $2.401X10^{-9}$
		0102	06.14	χ^2= 92.47
		010-1	-11.91	R =0.0011
		0011	08.95	Skewness= -0.22
		0012	15.02	Kurtosis=5.49
		0013	16.74	Np=102
		1125	41.32 (1)	pH=2.1-8.4
		1124	38.11 (09)	
		1123	32.42 (3)	
		1122	26.39 (1)	
		1121	17.63 (9)	
		1120	9.21 (3)	
	2: 1: 1	0101	03.58	U/NP = $2.128X10^{-8}$
		0102	06.14	χ^2= 83.71
		010-1	-11.91	R =0.0056
		0011	08.95	Skewness= -0.56
		0012	15.02	Kurtosis=6.80
		0013	16.74	Np=70
		2112	21.81 (2)	pH=2.5-8.9
		2111	16.11 (6)	
		2110	7.67 (9)	
		211-1	-1.76 (9)	
	2:1 :2	0101	03.58	U/NP = $4.660X10^{-9}$
		0102	06.14	χ^2= 107.60
		010-1	-11.91	R =0.0035
		0011	08.95	Skewness= -0.64
		0012	15.02	Kurtosis=8.62
		0013	16.74	Np=60
		2124	39.52 (3)	pH=2.5-9.3
		2123	33.86 (8)	
		2122	27.97(9)	
		2121	20.02 (7)	
		2120	11.11 (7)	
		212-1	01.69 (6)	

*Figures in the parentheses are the standard deviations in the least significant digit.

Table 5.8 Best fit chemical models of Pb^{2+}-succinic acid dihydrazide-histidine ternary system in aqueous medium at 303.0 K and ionic strength, I=0.1 mol dm^{-3}.

Metal ion	Composition (M: L: X)	Species mlxh	Log β_{mlxh}	
Pb^{2+}	1:1:1	0101	03.58	U/NP = $2.111X10^{-8}$
		0102	06.14	χ^2= 91.94
		010-1	-11.91	R =0.0041
		0011	08.95	Skewness= -0.21
		0012	15.02	Kurtosis=3.78
		0013	16.74	Np=145
		1113	23.49 (1)	pH=1.7-6.2
		1112	20.50 (1)	
		1111	15.48 (3)	
		1110	09.34 (5)	
		111-1	03.07 (6)	
	1: 1: 2	0101	03.58	U/NP = $1.608X10^{-8}$
		0102	06.14	χ^2= 72.59
		010-1	-11.91	R =0.0023
		0011	08.95	Skewness= -0.04
		0012	15.02	Kurtosis=4.56
		0013	16.74	Np=184
		1125	41.09 (1)	pH=1.6-8.1
		1124	37.60 (1)	
		1123	33.25 (4)	
		1122	27.25 (4)	
		1121	21.57 (3)	
		1120	13.56 (3)	
	2: 1: 1	0101	03.58	U/NP = $2.677X10^{-8}$
		0102	06.14	χ^2= 79.58
		010-1	-11.91	R =0.0053
		0011	08.95	Skewness= 0.91
		0012	15.02	Kurtosis=5.57
		0013	16.74	Np=86
		2112	22.22 (1)	pH=2.2-5.5
		2111	16.46 (12)	
		2110	11.57 (2)	
	2:1 :2	0101	03.58	U/NP = $2.135X10^{-8}$
		0102	06.14	χ^2= 97.64
		010-1	-11.91	R =0.0057
		0011	08.95	Skewness= -0.71
		0012	15.02	Kurtosis=4.74
		0013	16.74	Np=61
		2124	39.52 (5)	pH=2.2-5.6
		2122	29.40 (6)	
		2120	16.27 (7)	

*Figures in the parentheses are the standard deviations in the least significant digit.

Table 5.9 Best fit chemical models of Hg^{2+} -succinic acid dihydrazide-histidine ternary system in aqueous medium at 303.0 K and ionic strength, I=0.1 mol dm^{-3}

Metal ion	Composition (M: L: X)	Species mlxh	Log β_{mlxh}	
Hg^{2+}	1:1:1	0101	03.58	U/NP = 8.185X10^{-8}
		0102	06.14	χ^2= 54.35
		010-1	-11.91	R =0.0079
		0011	08.95	Skewness= -0.65
		0012	15.02	Kurtosis= 4.28
		0013	16.74	Np=170
		1113	23.90 (3)	pH=1.6-6.5
		1112	20.83 (3)	
		1111	15.41 (8)	
		1110	10.12 (3)	
		111-1	03.87 (4)	
	1: 1: 2	0101	03.58	U/NP = 3.292X10^{-8}
		0102	06.14	χ^2= 64.0
		010-1	-11.91	R =0.0042
		0011	08.95	Skewness= 0.00
		0012	15.02	Kurtosis=4.97
		0013	16.74	Np=202
		1125	40.92 (2)	pH=1.8-8.1
		1124	37.94 (2)	
		1123	33.33 (3)	
		1122	27.29 (7)	
		1121	22.36 (2)	
		1120	15.31 (2)	
	2: 1: 1	0101	03.58	U/NP = 2.249X10^{-7}
		0102	06.14	χ^2= 89.69
		010-1	-11.91	R =0.014
		0011	08.95	Skewness= -0.99
		0012	15.02	Kurtosis=4.61
		0013	16.74	Np=111
		2112	22.64 (5)	pH=1.9-5.2
		2110	12.56 (5)	
	2:1 :2	0101	03.58	U/NP = 1.468X10^{-7}
		0102	06.14	χ^2= 88.85
		010-1	-11.91	R =0.014
		0011	08.95	Skewness= -0.56
		0012	15.02	Kurtosis=5.56
		0013	16.74	Np=80
		2124	40.05 (9)	pH=2.0-5.5
		2122	29.50 (15)	
		2120	17.61 (8)	

*Figures in the parentheses are the standard deviations in the least significant digit.

Table 5.10 Best fit chemical models of Cd^{2+}-succinic acid dihydrazide-histidine ternary system in aqueous medium at 303.0 K and ionic strength, I=0. 1 mol dm^{-3}

Metal ion	Composition (M: L: X)	Species mlxh	Log β_{mlxh}	
Cd^{2+}	1:1:1	0101	03.58	U/NP = $2.363X10^{-8}$
		0102	06.14	χ^2= 47.68
		010-1	-11.91	R =0.0048
		0011	08.95	Skewness=0.69
		0012	15.02	Kurtosis=6.06
		0013	16.74	Np=100
		1113	23.18 (2)	pH=1.9-8.9
		1112	19.81 (3)	
		1111	14.38 (16)	
		1110	08.24 (8)	
		111-1	-0.97 (8)	
	1: 1: 2	0101	03.58	U/NP = $3.677X10^{-9}$
		0102	06.14	χ^2= 62.33
		010-1	-11.91	R =0.0015
		0011	08.95	Skewness= 0.03
		0012	15.02	Kurtosis=4.20
		0013	16.74	Np=146
		1125	39.75 (1)	pH=2.1-7.8
		1124	36.51 (1)	
		1123	31.34 (3)	
		1122	25.43 (1)	
		1121	19.58 (1)	
		1120	12.39 (1)	
	2: 1: 1	0101	03.58	U/NP = $7.267X10^{-8}$
		0102	06.14	χ^2= 70.02
		010-1	-11.91	R =0.0090
		0011	08.95	Skewness= -0.59
		0012	15.02	Kurtosis=4.45
		0013	16.74	Np=109
		2112	21.66 (3)	pH=2.1-8.4
		2111	15.70 (19)	
		2110	10.35 (3)	
		211-1	01.84 (5)	
	2:1 :2	0101	03.58	U/NP = $2.326X10^{-9}$
		0102	06.14	χ^2= 90.79
		010-1	-11.91	R =0.0025
		0011	08.95	Skewness= -0.93
		0012	15.02	Kurtosis=8.78
		0013	16.74	Np=53
		2124	38.50 (4)	pH=2.5-8.0
		2122	27.45 (6)	
		2121	21.53 (2)	
		2120	14.80 (1)	
		212-1	6.50 (4)	

*Figures in the parentheses are the standard deviations in the least significant digit.

The best-fit models obtained gave good statistical fit and were chemically consistent with the titration data without giving any systematic trends in the magnitudes of the residuals. The simulated titration curves generated using all the species in the best-fit models coincided well with the experimental titration curves. The skewness values are close to zero and exhibit slight left or right skewed distribution of errors. The kurtosis values are greater than 3.0 indicating leptokurtic distribution of errors.

The best-fit models for 1:1:1 (M:L:X) composition indicate the formation of $MLXH_3$, $MLXH_2$, MLXH, MLX and $MLXH_{-1}$ type of species. The formation of $MLXH_3$ species covers 34-65% of the total metal depending on the metal ion below a pH of 2.72. The step-wise proton association constants of $MLXH_2$ to from $MLXH_3$ (Table 5.11 (a)) are nearly equal to the protonation constant of SADH (3.58). This clearly indicates that one of the three protons of $MLXH_3$ type of species is attached to SADH molecule. The other two protons belong to histidine in XH_2^+ form, which is participating in coordination as a mono-dentate bonding through only carboxylate oxygen.

Table 5.11: Step-wise protonation constants of MLX type of species of M^{2+}-SADH-histidine systems (from Tables 5.6-5.10)

Metal ion	**(a)** $\log K^{1113}_{1112}$ $(= \log\beta_{1113} - \log\beta_{1112})$	**(b)** $\log K^{1112}_{1111}$ $(= \log\beta_{1112} - \log\beta_{1111})$	**(c)** $\log K^{1111}_{1110}$ $(= \log\beta_{1111} - \log\beta_{1110})$
Ca^{2+}	3.43	6.06	8.67
Mg^{2+}	3.43	6.04	8.45
Pb^{2+}	2.99	5.02	6.14
Hg^{2+}	3.07	5.42	5.29
Cd^{2+}	3.37	5.43	6.14

Histidine (XH) exists in solution as XH_3^{2+}, XH_2^+, XH and X^-. With increase in pH histidine loses first carboxylic proton, followed by proton attached to pyridine-like imidazole-nitrogen of the side chain and finally the α-ammonium proton. In $MLXH_3$ type of species, carboxylate group of histidine is involved in bonding and the other two centres, imidazole nitrogen and α-amine groups are protonated and non-bonding. With increase in pH, $MLXH_3$ loses the proton attached to dihydrazide forming $MLXH_2$ type of species. Probable bonding modes of the ligands in $MLXH_3$ and $MLXH_2$ type of species are shown in Figure 5.45.

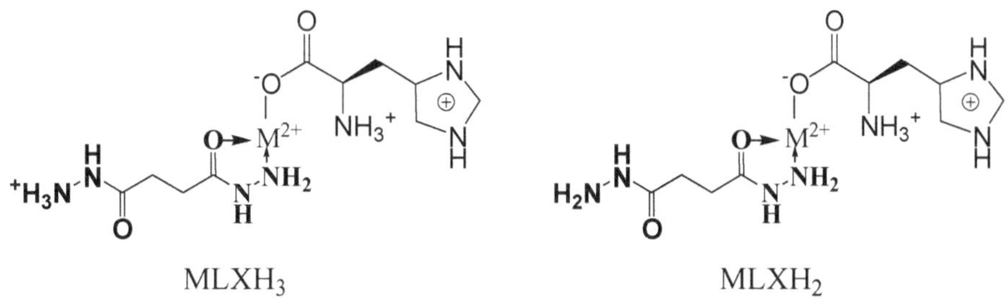

Figure 5.45: Probable bonding scheme in the protonated species of metal ion-SADH- histidine 1:1:1 molar ratio systems.

The successive deprotonation of $MLXH_2$ to form MLXH and MLX type of species involves deprotonation on complexation of either of the imidazole nitrogen or α-ammonium groups. The sequence of bonding cannot be ascertained from the step-wise protonation constants (Table 5.11 columns (b) and (c)) of MLXH to $MLXH_2$ or MLX to MLXH as they are very close to each other. The species distribution diagram for Hg^{2+} (Figure, 5.37b) system (1:1:1) indicate simultaneous formation of MLXH and MLX. The concentration of MLXH is low compared to that of MLX. In the case of Ca^{2+}, Mg^{2+}, Pb^{2+} and Cd^{2+} systems, the maxima of formation of MLXH and MLX fall in the pH ranges 5.3–7.4 and 5.9–9.3 respectively. The formation constants of MLX species of Ca^{2+}, Mg^{2+}, Pb^{2+}, Hg^{2+} and Cd^{2+} for metal ion-SADH-histidine system are high compared to those of metal ion-SADH- glycine system as shown in Table 5.12, indicating the tridentate behaviour of histidine in all these species.

Table 5.12: Relative stabilities of MLX type of species of M^{2+}-SADH- histidine and M^{2+}-SADH- glycine systems (from Tables 5.1-5.10)

Metal ion	Formation constants of MLX species	
	X=Histidine	X= glycine
Ca^{2+}	6.32	5.79
Mg^{2+}	5.89	5.32
Pb^{2+}	9.34	8.62
Hg^{2+}	10.12	8.22
Cd^{2+}	8.24	6.69

The species converged for 1:1:2 (M:L:X) molar ratio systems are, MLX_2H_5, MLX_2H_4, MLX_2H_3, MLX_2H_2, MLX_2H and MLX_2. The step-wise protonation constants of MLX_2H_4 to form MLX_2H_5 type of species range from 2.98 to 3.49 for various metal ions (Tables 6-10), indicating that SADH (L) is present in mono-protonated (LH) form in MLX_2H_5 type of species. This is further supported by its appearance only in lower pH region with a maximum of formation of 30% to 62% below 2.7 pH. The two histidine molecules are bonded to metal ion through carboxylate oxygen atoms as monodentates in XH_2 form. With increase in pH MLX_2H_5 $[M(LH)(XH_2)_2]$ loses the proton attached to dihydrazide forming MLX_2H_4 $[M(L)(XH_2)_2]$ type of species. Histidine in XH_2 form in the complex possesses two protons attached to imidazole nitrogen in the side chain and α-amino group. With increase in pH histidine loses these protons on complexation resulting in the formation of MLX_2H_3, MLX_2H_2, MLX_2H and MLX_2 species. The species distribution diagrams indicating the concentration distribution of these species against pH are depicted in Figures 5.26b, 5.30b, 5.34b, 5.38b and 5.42b for Ca^{2+}, Mg^{2+}, Pb^{2+},

Hg^{2+} and Cd^{2+} systems respectively. The high stabilities of these species relative to ternary species of glycine indicate the tridentate behaviour of at least one of the two histidine molecules attached to the metal ion.

The species converged for 2:1:1 (M:L:X) molar ratio metal ion-SADH-histidine systems are M_2LXH_2, M_2LXH, M_2LX and M_2LXH_{-1}. In all these species succinic acid dihydrazide acts as a ditopic ligand bonding to two metal ions through carbonyl oxygen and terminal $-NH_2$ groups of the two hydrazide moieties. Therefore, two metal ions are bonded to the two coordinating units of SADH in all the complexes and histidine (XH) is bonded to one of the two metal ions as a monodentate or bidentate or tridentate forming different species. In M_2LXH_2 type of species histidine acts as a monodentate (Figure 5.46) bonding through carboxylate group.

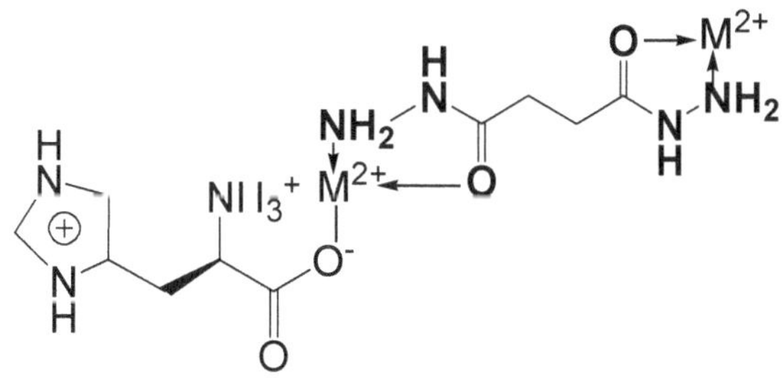

M_2LXH_2

Figure 5.46: Probable nature of bonding of SADH and histidine in M_2LXH_2 type of species in

With increase in pH this species loses the imidazole -NH and α-ammonium protons of the histidine molecule on complexation forming M_2LXH and M_2LX type of species. The species distribution diagrams (Figures 5.35b, 5.39b and 5.43b for Pb^{2+}, Hg^{2+} and Cd^{2+} systems respectively) indicate the simultaneous formation of M_2LXH and M_2LX species. The relative higher stabilities of M_2LX type of species of metal ion-SADH-histidine systems compared to those of metal ion-SADH-glycine systems indicate the involvement of histidine as a tridentate bonding through all the three groups.

The best-fit models obtained for 2:1:2 (M:L:X) metal ion-SADH-histidine systems indicate the formation of (Tables 5.6 to 5.10) $M_2LX_2H_4$, $M_2LX_2H_3$, $M_2LX_2H_2$, M_2LX_2H, M_2LX_2 and $M_2LX_2H_{-1}$ species. All the species are bimetallic complexes in which two metal ions are bonded to different coordinating units of the same SADH molecule. Two molecules of histidine are also most probably coordinated to different metal ions of the binuclear species. The species are modulated to the degree of protonation/ deprotonation of histidine molecules. In the symmetric $M_2LX_2H_4$ type of species (Figure 5.47) both the histidine molecules involve in bonding as monodentates bonding through carboxylate groups. The species distribution diagrams (Figures 5.28b, 5.32b, 5.36b, 5.40b and 5.44b for Ca^{2+}, Mg^{2+}, Pb^{2+}, Hg^{2+} and Cd^{2+} systems respectively) indicate that $M_2LX_2H_4$ type of species are predominant below a pH of 4.56, representing 32 to 61.5 % of the total metal ion

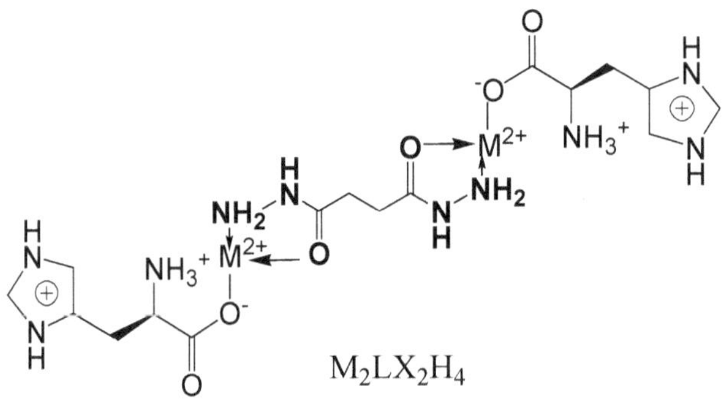

$M_2LX_2H_4$

Figure 5.47: Probable nature of bonding of SADH and histidine in $M_2LX_2H_4$ type of species.

With increase in pH histidine molecules on both sides lose protons forming asymmetric $M_2LX_2H_3$, M_2LX_2H and symmetric $M_2LX_2H_2$, M_2LX_2 type of complexes.

Species distribution diagrams indicate the simultaneous formation of these species making it difficult to predict the order of bonding of imidazole and α- amino nitrogen atoms to the metal ion. The formation of $M_2LX_2H_{-1}$ type of species may be attributed to hydroxylation or deprotonation of the enolic group of dihydrazide. The formation constants of all the species for all the compositions were found to be in the order Ca^{2+}> $Mg^{2+}$and Hg^{2+}> Pb^{2+} > Cd^{2+}.

5.2.3 SADH- L-asparticacid- Metal Ion Systems:

The fully protonated form of L-aspartic acid possesses three dissociable protons. The most acidic of these lies with the α-carboxylic group followed by side chain carboxylic group and α-ammonium group. The molecule exists in solution in different protonated forms, XH_3^+, XH_2, XH^- and X^{2-}. L-aspartic acid with three potential complex-forming functional groups (-COO^-, -NH_2 and –CH_2COO^-) behaves as an ambidentate ligand. On the other hand, succinic acid dihydrazide possesses two coordinating hydrazide units and can act as a bis bidentate coordinating through terminal –NH_2 groups and carbonyl or enolic oxygen atoms forming five membered rings on both sides. Therefore, it is interesting to study the ternary systems containing succinic acid dihydrazide, aspartic acid and metal ions in different compositions.

Calvin-Wilson titrations were conducted for 1:1:1, 1:1:2, 2:1:1 and 2:1:2 (M:L:X) molar concentration ratios, where, M= Ca^{2+}, Mg^{2+}, Pb^{2+}, Hg^{2+} and Cd^{2+}, L= succinic acid dihydrazide and XH_2= L-aspartic acid. Experimental titration curves were compared with simulated titration curves generated assuming the formation of only binary species of both the ligands with metal ions, to confirm the formation of the ternary species. Experimental and simulated titration curves for all the metal ions and compositions are shown in Figures 5.48a to 5.67a.

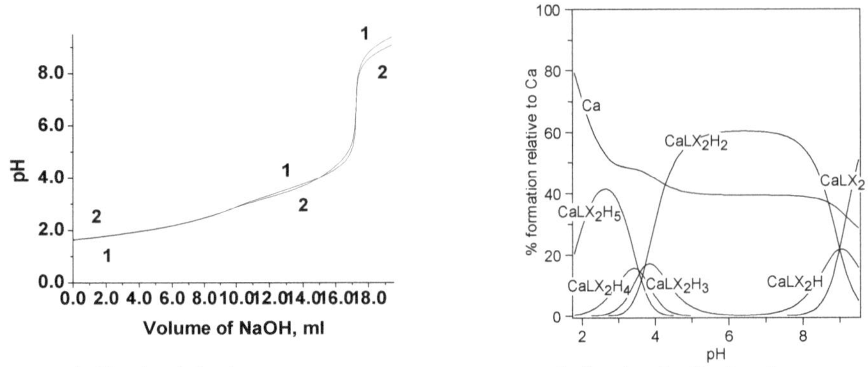

a. 1. Simulated titration curve
2. Experimental titration curve

b. Species distribution diagram

[SADH]= 0.00999 mol dm^{-3} [ASPARTIC ACID] = 0.0200 mol dm^{-3} [Ca^{2+}] = 0.00998 mol dm^{-3}
[HCl] = 0.05083 mol dm^{-3} [NaOH] = 0.2054 mol dm^{-3} TOTAL VOLUME=50.0 cm^3
Temp.: 30.0 ±0.1°C I = 0.1 mol dm^{-3}

Figure 5.49: Ca^{2+}-SADH-ASPARTICACID SYSTEM (1:1:2)

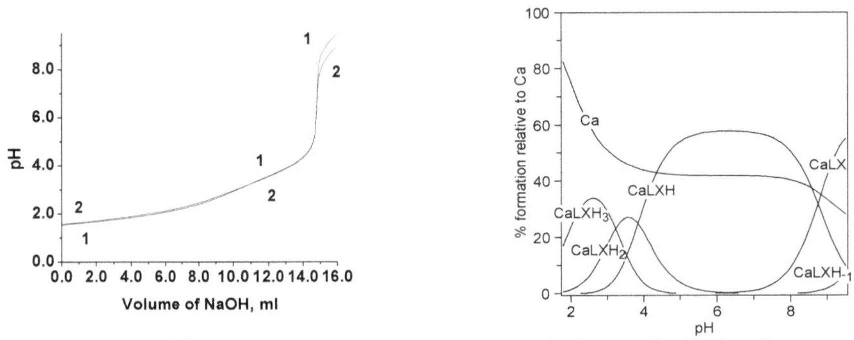

a. 1. Simulated titration curve
2. Experimental titration curve

b. Species distribution diagram

[SADH] = 0.00999 mol dm^{-3} [ASPARTIC ACID] = 0.0100 mol dm^{-3} [Ca^{2+}] = 0.00998 mol dm^{-3}
[HCl] = 0.05083 mol dm^{-3} [NaOH] = 0.2054 mol dm^{-3} TOTAL VOLUME= 50.0 cm^3
Temp.: 30.0 ±0.1°C I = 0.1 mol dm^{-3}

Figure 5.48: Ca^{2+}-SADH-ASPARTICACID SYSTEM (1:1:1)

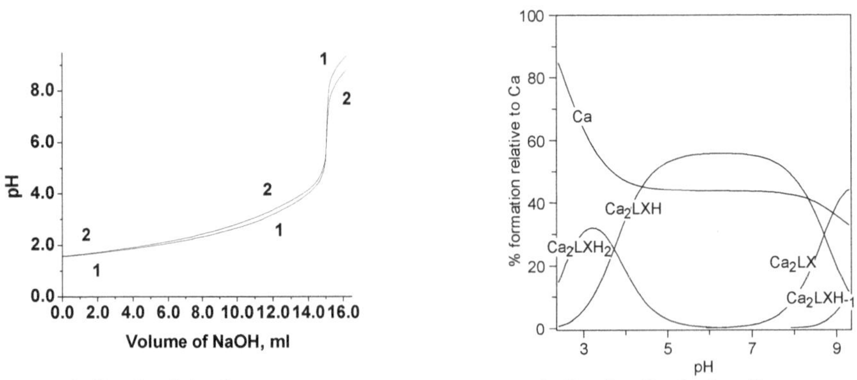

a. 1. Simulated titration curve
2. Experimental titration curve

b. Species distribution diagram

[SADH]= 0.00999 mol dm^{-3} [ASPARTIC ACID] = 0.0100 mol dm^{-3} [Ca^{2+}] = 0.01994 mol dm^{-3}
[HCl] = 0.05195 mol dm^{-3} [NaOH] = 0.2054 mol dm^{-3} TOTAL VOLUME=50.0 cm^3
Temp.: 30.0 ±0.1°C I = 0.1 mol dm^{-3}

Figure 5.50: Ca^{2+}-SADH- ASPARTICACID SYSTEM (2:1:1)

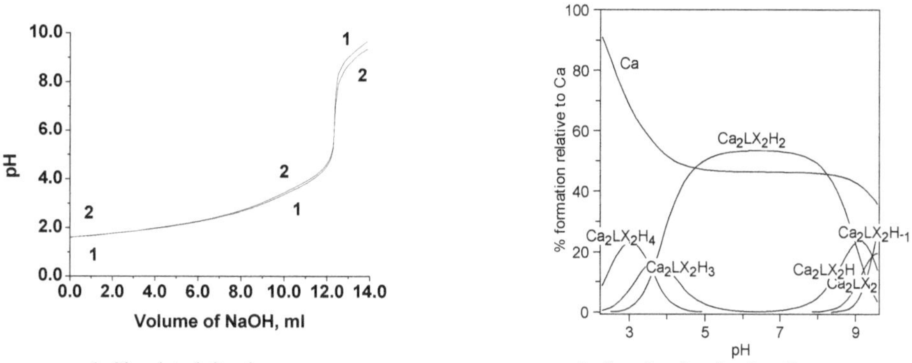

a. 1. Simulated titration curve
2. Experimental titration curve

b. Species distribution diagram

[SADH] = 0.00500 mol dm^{-3} [ASPARTIC ACID] = 0. 0100 mol dm^{-3} [Ca^{2+}] = 0.00997 mol dm^{-3}
[HCl] = 0.04084 mol dm^{-3} [NaOH] = 0.2054 mol dm^{-3} TOTAL VOLUME= 50.0 cm^3
Temp.: 30.0 ±0.1^{0}C I = 0.1 mol dm^{-3}

Figure 5.51: Ca^{2+}-SADH- ASPARTICACID SYSTEM (2:1:2)

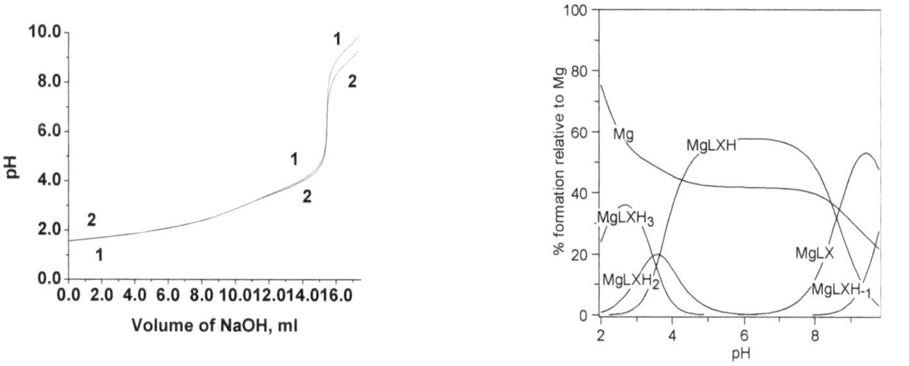

a. 1. Simulated titration curve
2. Experimental titration curve

b. Species distribution diagram

[SADH]= 0.00999 mol dm^{-3} [ASPARTIC ACID] = 0.0100 mol dm^{-3} [Mg^{2+}] = 0.0100 mol dm^{-3}
[HCl] = 0.05060 mol dm^{-3} [NaOH] = 0.1960 mol dm^{-3} TOTAL VOLUME=50.0 cm^3
Temp.: 30.0 ±0.1^{0}C I = 0.1 mol dm^{-3}

Figure 5.52: Mg^{2+}-SADH- ASPARTICACID SYSTEM (1:1:1)

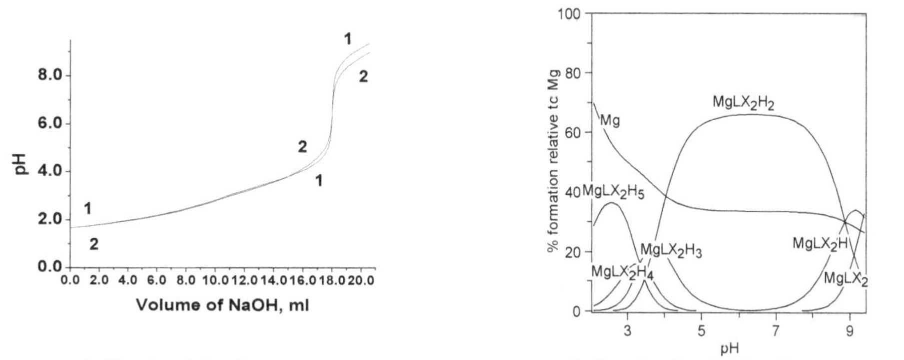

a. 1. Simulated titration curve
2. Experimental titration curve

b. Species distribution diagram

[SADH]= 0.00999 mol dm^{-3} [ASPARTIC ACID] = 0.0200 mol dm^{-3} [Mg^{2+}] = 0.0100 mol dm^{-3}
[HCl] = 0.05060 mol dm^{-3} [NaOH] = 0.1960 mol dm^{-3} TOTAL VOLUME=50.0 cm^3
Temp.: 30.0 ±0.1^{0}C I = 0.1 mol dm^{-3}

Figure 5.53: Mg^{2+}-SADH- ASPARTICACID SYSTEM (1:1:2)

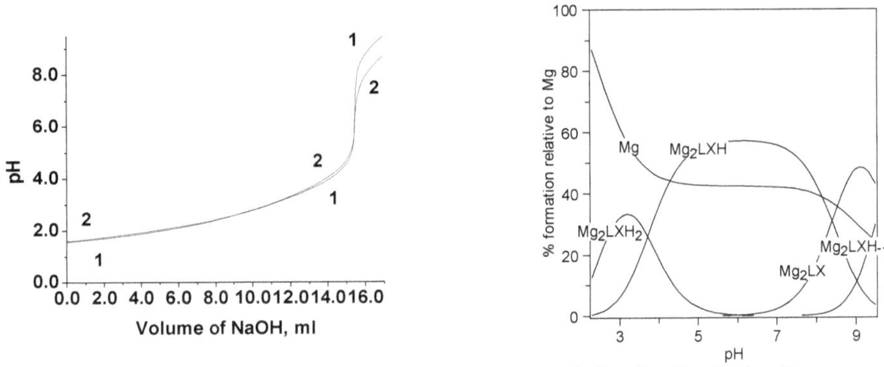

a. 1. Simulated titration curve
2. Experimental titration curve

b. Species distribution diagram

[SADH] = 0.00999 mol dm^{-3} [ASPARTIC ACID] = 0.0100 mol dm^{-3} [Mg^{2+}] = 0.01999 mol dm^{-3}
[HCl] = 0.05064 mol dm^{-3} [NaOH] = 0.1960 mol dm^{-3} TOTAL VOLUME= 50.0 cm^3
Temp.: 30.0 ±0.1^{0}C I = 0.1 mol dm^{-3}

Figure 5.54: Mg^{2+}-SADH- ASPARTICACID SYSTEM (2:1:1)

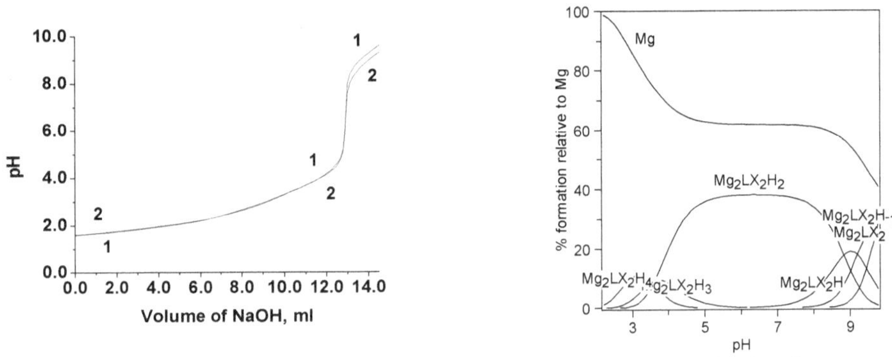

a. 1. Simulated titration curve
2. Experimental titration curve

b. Species distribution diagram

[SADH]= 0.00500 mol dm^{-3} [ASPARTIC ACID] = 0.0100 mol dm^{-3} [Mg^{2+}] = 0.0100 mol dm^{-3}
[HCl] = 0.04061 mol dm^{-3} [NaOH] = 0.1960 mol dm^{-3} TOTAL VOLUME=50.0 cm^3
Temp.: 30.0 ±0.1^{0}C I = 0.1 mol dm^{-3}

Figure 5.55: Mg^{2+}-SADH- ASPARTICACID SYSTEM (2:1:2)

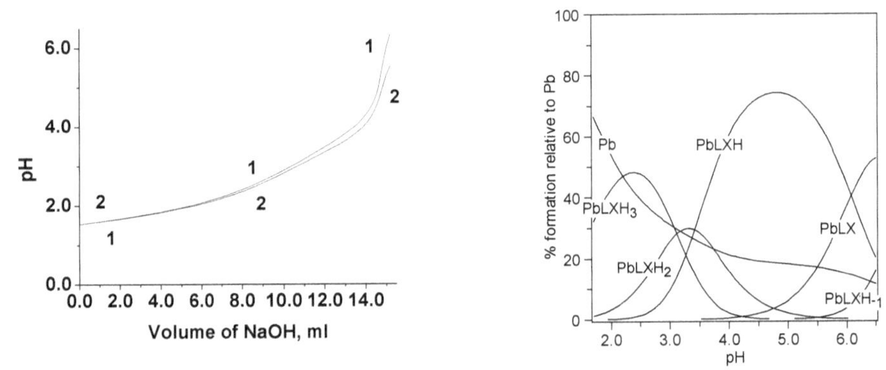

a. 1. Simulated titration curve
2. Experimental titration curve

b. Species distribution diagram

[SADH]= 0.00999 mol dm^{-3} [ASPARTIC ACID] = 0.0100 mol dm^{-3} [Pb^{2+}] = 0.01003 mol dm^{-3}
[HNO_3] = 0.05069 mol dm^{-3} [NaOH] = 0.2054 mol dm^{-3} TOTAL VOLUME=50.0 cm^3
Temp.: 30.0 ±0.1^{0}C I = 0.1 mol dm^{-3}

Figure 5.56: Pb^{2+}-SADH- ASPARTICACID SYSTEM (1:1:1)

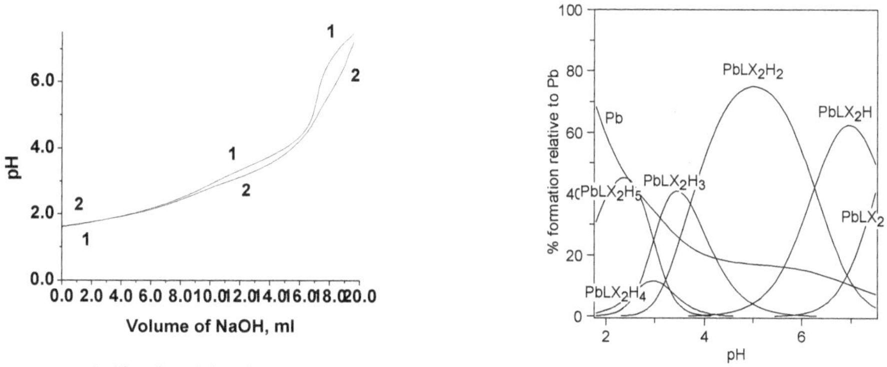

a. 1. Simulated titration curve
2. Experimental titration curve

b. Species distribution diagram

[SADH] = 0.00999 mol dm^{-3} [ASPARTIC ACID] = 0.0200 mol dm^{-3} [Pb^{2+}] = 0.01003 mol dm^{-3}
[HNO_3] = 0.05029 mol dm^{-3} [NaOH] = 0.2054 mol dm^{-3} TOTAL VOLUME= 50.0 cm^3
Temp.: 30.0 ±0.1^{0}C I = 0.1 mol dm^{-3}

Figure 5.57: Pb^{2+}-SADH ASPARTICACID SYSTEM (1:1:2)

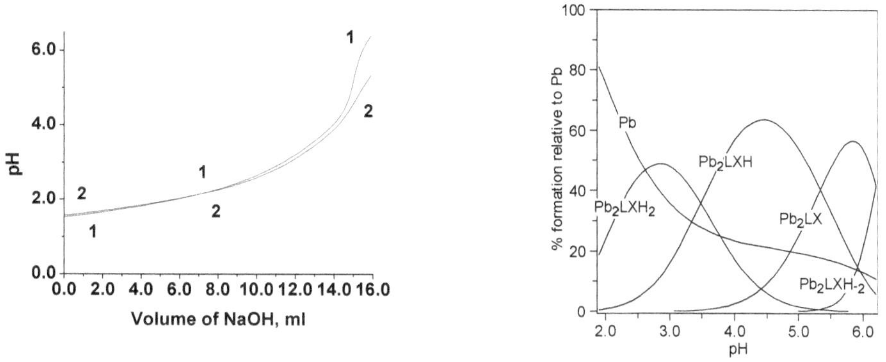

a. 1. Simulated titration curve
2. Experimental titration curve

b. Species distribution diagram

[SADH]= 0.00999 mol dm^{-3} [ASPARTIC ACID] = 0.0100 mol dm^{-3} [Pb $^{2+}$] = 0.02005mol dm^{-3}
[HNO_3] = 0.05167 mol dm^{-3} [NaOH] = 0.2054 mol dm^{-3} TOTAL VOLUME=50.0 cm^3
Temp.: 30.0 ±0.1^{0}C I = 0.1 mol dm^{-3}

Figure 5.58: Pb^{2+}-SADH- ASPARTICACID SYSTEM (2:1:1)

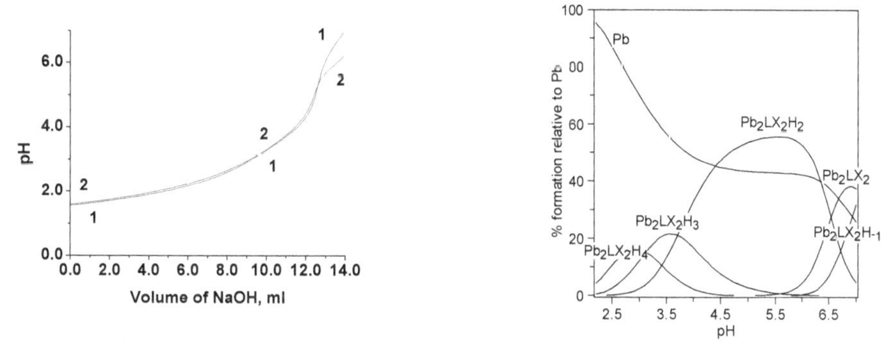

a. 1. Simulated titration curve
2. Experimental titration curve

b. Species distribution diagram

[SADH]= 0.00500 mol dm^{-3} [ASPARTIC ACID] = 0.0100 mol dm^{-3} [Pb $^{2+}$] = 0.01003 mol dm^{-3}
[HNO_3] = 0.04169 mol dm^{-3} [NaOH] = 0.2054 mol dm^{-3} TOTAL VOLUME=50.0 cm^3
Temp.: 30.0 ±0.1^{0}C I = 0.1 mol dm^{-3}

Figure 5.59: Pb^{2+}-SADH- ASPARTICACID SYSTEM (2:1:2)

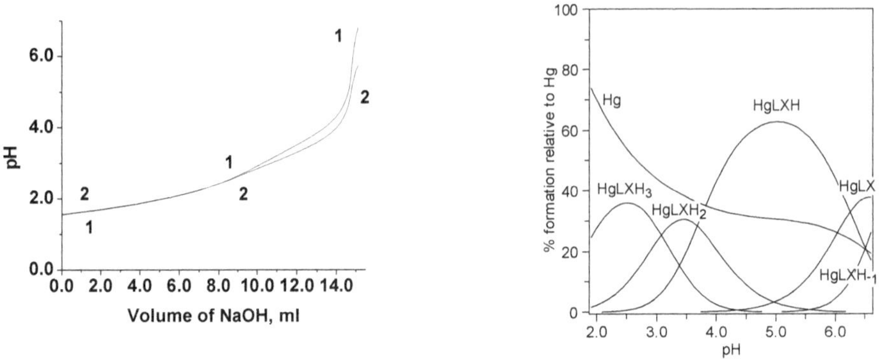

a. 1. Simulated titration curve
2. Experimental titration curve

b. Species distribution diagram

[SADH] = 0.00999 mol dm^{-3} [ASPARTIC ACID] = 0.0100 mol dm^{-3} [Hg^{2+}] = 0.00995 mol dm^{-3}
[HCl] = 0.05075 mol dm^{-3} [NaOH] = 0.2054 mol dm^{-3} TOTAL VOLUME= 50.0 cm^3
Temp.: 30.0 ±0.1^{0}C I = 0.1 mol dm^{-3}

Figure 5.60: Hg^{2+}-SADH-ASPARTICACID SYSTEM (1:1:1)

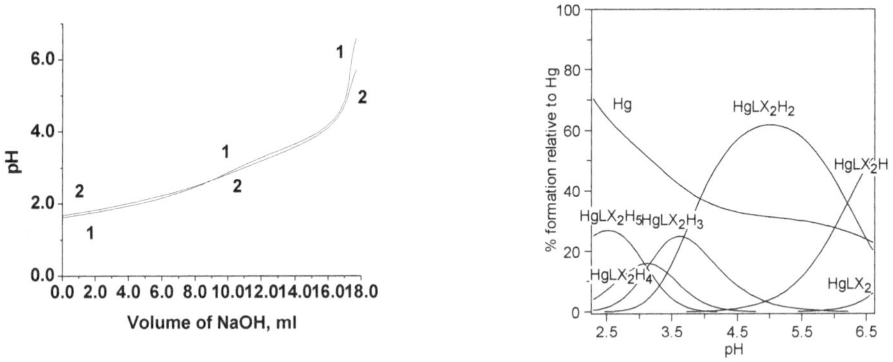

a. 1. Simulated titration curve
2. Experimental titration curve

b. Species distribution diagram

[SADH]= 0.00999 mol dm^{-3} [ASPARTIC ACID] = 0.0200 mol dm^{-3} [Hg^{2+}] = 0.00995moldm^{-3}
[HCl] = 0.05114 mol dm^{-3} [NaOH] = 0.2054 mol dm^{-3} TOTAL VOLUME=50.0 cm^3
Temp.: 30.0 ±0.1^{0}C I = 0.1 mol dm^{-3}

Figure 5.61: Hg^{2+}-SADH- ASPARTICACID SYSTEM (1:1:2)

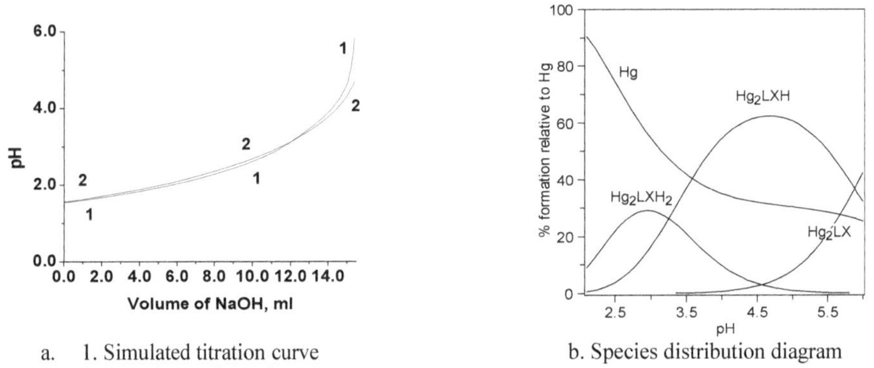

a. 1. Simulated titration curve
2. Experimental titration curve

b. Species distribution diagram

[SADH]= 0.00999 mol dm^{-3} [ASPARTIC ACID] = 0.0100 mol dm^{-3} [Hg^{2+}] = 0.01991 mol dm^{-3}
[HCl] = 0.05298 mol dm^{-3} [NaOH] = 0.2054 mol dm^{-3} TOTAL VOLUME=50.0 cm^3
Temp.: 30.0 ±0.1^{0}C I = 0.1 mol dm^{-3}

Figure 5.62: Hg^{2+}-SADH- ASPARTICACID SYSTEM (2:1:1)

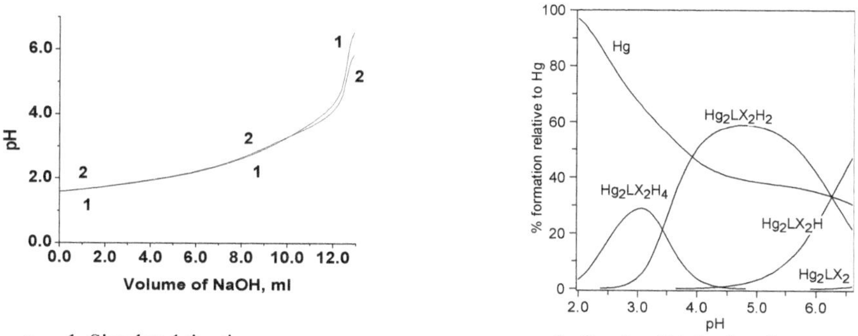

a. 1. Simulated titration curve
2. Experimental titration curve

b. Species distribution diagram

[SADH] = 0.00500 mol dm^{-3} [ASPARTIC ACID] = 0.0100 mol dm^{-3} [Hg^{2+}] = 0.00995 mol dm^{-3}
[HCl] = 0.04175 mol dm^{-3} [NaOH] = 0.2054 mol dm^{-3} TOTAL VOLUME= 50.0 cm^3
Temp.: 30.0 ±0.1°C I = 0.1 mol dm^{-3}

Figure 5.63: Hg^{2+}-SADH- ASPARTICACID SYSTEM (2:1:2)

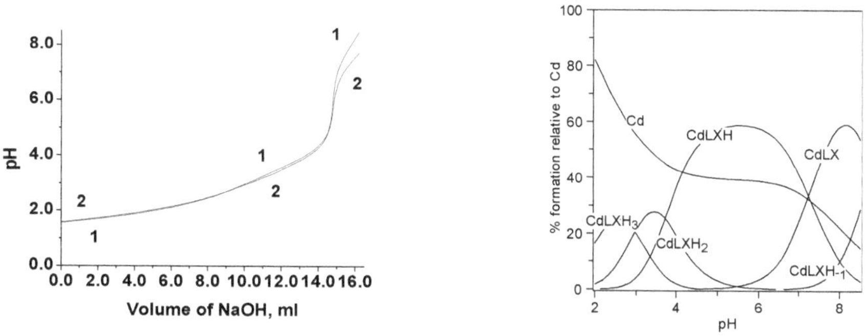

a. 1. Simulated titration curve
2. Experimental titration curve

b. Species distribution diagram

[SADH]= 0.00999 mol dm^{-3} [ASPARTIC ACID] = 0.0100 mol dm^{-3} [Cd^{2+}] = 0.00993 mol dm^{-3}
[HCl] = 0.05075 mol dm^{-3} [NaOH] = 0.2054 mol dm^{-3} TOTAL VOLUME=50.0 cm^3
Temp.: 30.0 ±0.1°C I = 0.1 mol dm^{-3}

Figure 5.64: Cd^{2+}-SADH- ASPARTICACID SYSTEM (1:1:1)

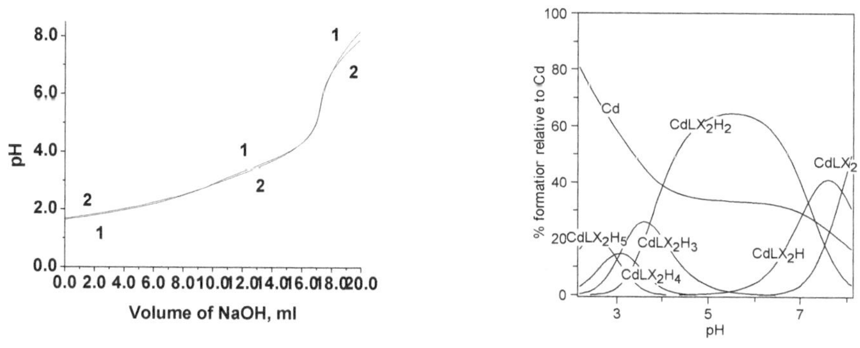

a. 1. Simulated titration curve
2. Experimental titration curve

b. Species distribution diagram

[SADH]= 0.00999 mol dm^{-3} [ASPARTIC ACID] = 0.0200 mol dm^{-3} [Cd^{2+}] = 0.00993 mol dm^{-3}
[HCl] = 0.05075 mol dm^{-3} [NaOH] = 0.2054 mol dm^{-3} TOTAL VOLUME=50.0 cm^3
Temp.: 30.0 ±0.1°C I = 0.1 mol dm^{-3}

Figure 5.65: Cd^{2+}-SADH- ASPARTICACID SYSTEM (1:1:2)

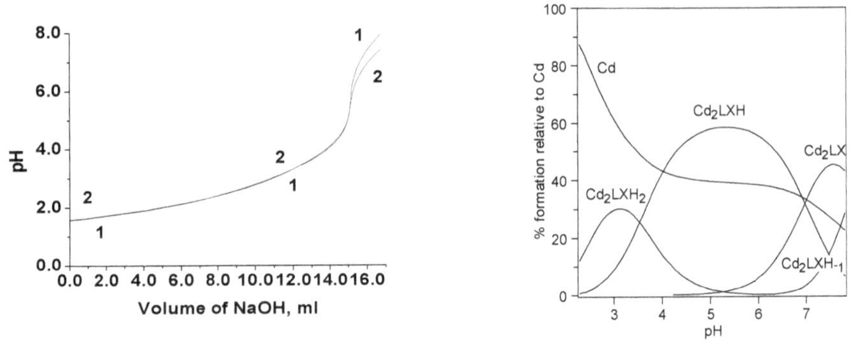

a. 1. Simulated titration curve
2. Experimental titration curve

b. Species distribution diagram

[SADH] = 0.00999 mol dm^{-3} [ASPARTIC ACID] = 0.0100 mol dm^{-3} [Cd^{2+}] = 0.01986 mol dm^{-3}
[HCl] = 0.05218 mol dm^{-3} [NaOH] = 0.2054 mol dm^{-3} TOTAL VOLUME= 50.0 cm^{3}
Temp.: 30.0 ±0.1°C I = 0.1 mol dm^{-3}

Figure 5.66: Cd^{2+}-SADH-ASPARTICACID SYSTEM (2:1:1)

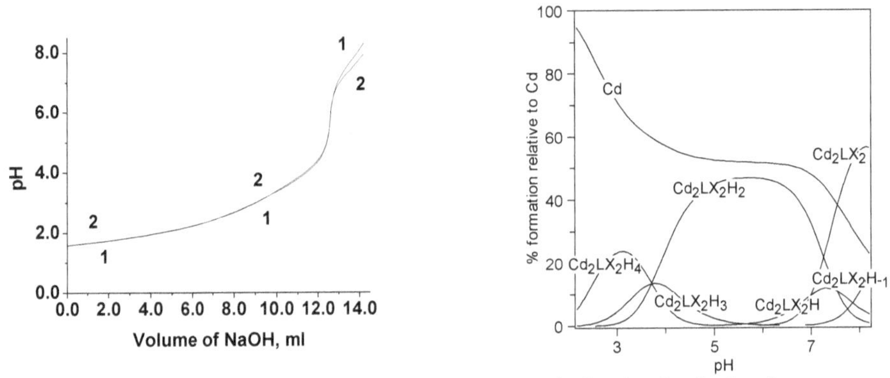

a. 1. Simulated titration curve
2. Experimental titration curve

b. Species distribution diagram

[SADH]= 0.00500 mol dm^{-3} [ASPARTIC ACID] = 0.0100 mol dm^{-3} [Cd^{2+}] = 0.00993 mol dm^{-3}
[HCl] = 0.04175 mol dm^{-3} [NaOH] = 0.2054 mol dm^{-3} TOTAL VOLUME=50.0 cm^{3}
Temp.: 30.0 ±0.1°C I = 0.1 mol dm^{-3}

Figure 5.67: Cd^{2+}-SADH- ASPARTICACID SYSTEM (2:1:2)

The observed differences between simulated and experimental titration curves for all the metal ion systems indicated the formation of ternary species. Various chemically plausible models keeping in view of the bonding behaviour of both aspartic acid and succinic acid dihydrazide were selected for refinement by the Miniquad-75 program. The best-fit models obtained are tabulated in Tables 5.13 to 5.17.

Table 5.13 Best fit chemical models of Ca^{2+}-succinic acid dihydrazide-aspartic acid ternary system in aqueous medium at 303.0 K and ionic strength, I =0.1 mol dm^{-3}

Metal ion	Composition (M: L: X)	Species mlxh	Log β_{mlxh}	
Ca^{2+}	1:1:1	0101	03.58	U/NP = 3.572X10^{-8}
		0102	06.14	χ^2= 93.42
		010-1	-11.91	R =0.0056
		0011	09.58	Skewness= -0.59
		0012	13.30	Kurtosis=5.21
		0013	15.16	Np=124
		1113	21.55 (3)	pH=1.8-9.5
		1112	18.18 (3)	
		1111	14.48 (3)	
		1110	05.74 (4)	
		111-1	-4.63 (11)	
	1: 1: 2	0101	03.58	U/NP = 1.974X10^{-8}
		0102	06.14	χ^2= 95.29
		010-1	-11.91	R =0.0028
		0011	09.58	Skewness= -0.20
		0012	13.30	Kurtosis=6.47
		0013	15.16	Np=135
		1125	36.81 (2)	pH=1.8-9.5
		1124	33.27 (7)	
		1123	29.68 (2)	
		1122	25.96 (8)	
		1121	16.96 (9)	
		1120	07.97 (6)	
	2: 1: 1	0101	03.58	U/NP = 1.188X10^{-8}
		0102	06.14	χ^2= 84.25
		010-1	-11.91	R =0.0037
		0011	09.58	Skewness= -1.27
		0012	13.30	Kurtosis=8.39
		0013	15.16	Np=63
		2112	19.88 (2)	pH=2.4-9.3
		2111	16.16 (2)	
		2110	7.45 (3)	
		211-1	-2.42 (4)	
	2:1 :2	0101	03.58	U/NP = 7.551X10^{-9}
		0102	06.14	χ^2= 96.28
		010-1	-11.91	R =0.0039
		0011	09.58	Skewness= -1.02
		0012	13.30	Kurtosis= 7.07
		0013	15.16	Np=72
		2124	35.79 (4)	pH=2.3-9.6
		2123	32.28 (4)	
		2122	28.56 (5)	
		2121	19.56 (7)	
		2120	10.11 (6)	
		212-1	0.66 (7)	

*Figures in the parentheses are the standard deviations in the least significant digit

Table 5.14 Best fit chemical models of Mg^{2+} -succinic acid dihydrazide-aspartic acid ternary system in aqueous medium at 303.0 K and ionic strength, I =0.1 mol dm^{-3}

Metal ion	Composition (M: L: X)	Species mlxh	Log β_{mlxh}	
Mg^{2+}	1:1:1	0101	03.58	U/NP = $1.248X10^{-8}$
		0102	06.14	χ^2= 56.04
		010-1	-11.91	R =0.0037
		0011	09.58	Skewness= -0.34
		0012	13.30	Kurtosis=4.60
		0013	15.16	Np=105
		1113	21.56 (2)	pH=2.0-9.8
		1112	18.12 (3)	
		1111	14.48 (3)	
		1110	05.87 (3)	
		111-1	-4.17 (2)	
	1: 1: 2	0101	03.58	U/NP = $4.249X10^{-9}$
		0102	06.14	χ^2= 129.82
		010-1	-11.91	R =0.0015
		0011	09.58	Skewness= 0.50
		0012	13.30	Kurtosis=9.84
		0013	15.16	Np=121
		1125	36.68 (1)	pH=2.1-9.4
		1124	33.34 (3)	
		1123	30.00 (2)	
		1122	26.28 (5)	
		1121	17.41 (4)	
		1120	08.03 (5)	
	2: 1: 1	0101	03.58	U/NP = $5.267X10^{-8}$
		0102	06.14	χ^2= 83.21
		010-1	-11.91	R =0.0079
		0011	09.58	Skewness= -0.63
		0012	13.30	Kurtosis=5.04
		0013	15.16	Np=86
		2112	19.95 (3)	pH=2.3-9.5
		2111	16.23 (5)	
		2110	7.84 (5)	
		211-1	-1.82 (3)	
	2:1 :2	0101	03.58	U/NP = $1.227X10^{-8}$
		0102	06.14	χ^2= 120.43
		010-1	-11.91	R =0.0046
		0011	09.58	Skewness= -0.97
		0012	13.30	Kurtosis=5.59
		0013	15.16	Np=74
		2124	34.96 (4)	pH=2.2-9.8
		2123	31.41 (2)	
		2122	27.79(7)	
		2121	18.96 (12)	
		2120	9.76 (7)	
		212-1	0.03 (9)	

*Figures in the parentheses are the standard deviations in the least significant digit.

Table 5.15 Best fit chemical models of Pb^{2+}-succnic acid dihydrazide-aspartic acid ternary system in aqueous medium at 303.0 K and ionic strength, I =0.1 mol dm^{-3}

Metal ion	Composition (M: L: X)	Species mlxh	Log β_{mlxh}	
Pb^{2+}	1:1:1	0101	03.58	U/NP = 5.743X10^{-8}
		0102	06.14	χ^2= 68.91
		010-1	-11.91	R =0.0070
		0011	09.58	Skewness= -0.38
		0012	13.30	Kurtosis=4.64
		0013	15.16	Np=137
		1113	22.25 (3)	pH=1.7-6.5
		1112	19.13 (3)	
		1111	15.71 (2)	
		1110	09.63 (4)	
		111-1	02.61 (8)	
	1: 1: 2	0101	03.58	U/NP = 2.468X10^{-8}
		0102	06.14	χ^2= 85.24
		010-1	-11.91	R =0.0031
		0011	09.58	Skewness= -0.72
		0012	13.30	Kurtosis=6.20
		0013	15.16	Np=135
		1125	37.25 (2)	pH=1.8-7.4
		1124	33.94 (6)	
		1123	31.29 (2)	
		1122	27.57 (2)	
		1121	21.31 (3)	
		1120	13.72 (5)	
	2: 1: 1	0101	03.58	U/NP = 1.732X10^{-7}
		0102	06.14	χ^2= 61.45
		010-1	-11.91	R =0.013
		0011	09.58	Skewness= -0.73
		0012	13.30	Kurtosis=4.93
		0013	15.16	Np=130
		2112	21.07 (4)	pH=1.9-6.2
		2111	17.59 (4)	
		2110	12.25 (5)	
		211-2	-0.15 (4)	
	2:1 :2	0101	03.58	U/NP = 1.118X10^{-8}
		0102	06.14	χ^2= 72.43
		010-1	-11.91	R =0.0046
		0011	09.58	Skewness= -0.60
		0012	13.30	Kurtosis=5.39
		0013	15.16	Np=83
		2124	35.59 (6)	pH=2.2-7.0
		2123	32.47 (4)	
		2122	28.76 (7)	
		2120	15.67 (4)	
		212-1	08.60 (3)	

*Figures in the parentheses are the standard deviations in the least significant digit.

Table 5.16 Best fit chemical models of Hg^{2+}-succinic acid dihydrazide-aspartic acid ternary system in aqueous medium at 303.0 K and ionic strength, I =0.1 mol dm^{-3}

Metal ion	Composition (M: L: X)	Species mlxh	Log β_{mlxh}	
Hg^{2+}	1:1:1	0101	03.58	U/NP = 1.006X10^{-8}
		0102	06.14	χ^2= 86.24
		010-1	-11.91	R =0.0030
		0011	09.58	Skewness=-0.43
		0012	13.30	Kurtosis=7.57
		0013	15.16	Np=102
		1113	21.72 (1)	pH=1.9-6.5
		1112	18.64 (1)	
		1111	14.96 (1)	
		1110	08.71 (6)	
		111-1	01.95 (2)	
	1: 1: 2	0101	03.58	U/NP = 1.848X10^{-9}
		0102	06.14	χ^2= 64.41
		010-1	-11.91	R =0.0010
		0011	09.58	Skewness= 0.03
		0012	13.30	Kurtosis=6.73
		0013	15.16	Np=98
		1125	36.36 (3)	pH=2.3-6.5
		1124	33.28 (1)	
		1123	30.11 (1)	
		1122	26.43 (07)	
		1121	20.23 (2)	
		1120	12.71 (3)	
	2: 1: 1	0101	03.58	U/NP = 9.279X10^{-8}
		0102	06.14	χ^2= 88.60
		010-1	-11.91	R =0.0099
		0011	09.58	Skewness= -0.43
		0012	13.30	Kurtosis=4.01
		0013	15.16	Np=106
		2112	20.12 (4)	pH=2.1-6.0
		2111	16.87 (3)	
		2110	10.99 (4)	
	2:1 :2	0101	03.58	U/NP = 7.677X10^{-9}
		0102	06.14	χ^2= 63.11
		010-1	-11.91	R =0.0031
		0011	09.58	Skewness= 0.42
		0012	13.30	Kurtosis=13.36
		0013	15.16	Np=85
		2124	35.93 (3)	pH=2.0-6.6
		2122	29.07 (2)	
		2121	22.81 (12)	
		2120	14.54 (3)	

*Figures in the parentheses are the standard deviations in the least significant digit.

Table 5.17 Best fit chemical models of Cd^{2+}-succinic acid dihydrazide-aspartic acid ternary system in aqueous medium at 303.0 K and ionic strength, I =0.1 mol dm^{-3}

Metal ion	Composition (M: L: X)	Species mlxh	Log β_{mlxh}	
		0101	03.58	U/NP = 1.532X10^{-8}
		0102	06.14	χ^2= 74.62
		010-1	-11.91	R =0.0041
		0011	09.58	Skewness= -0.23
		0012	13.30	Kurtosis=10.20
	1:1:1	0013	15.16	Np=110
		1113	21.28 (3)	pH=2.0-8.5
		1112	18.30 (2)	
		1111	14.58 (2)	
		1110	07.34 (2)	
		111-1	-01.43 (2)	
		0101	03.58	U/NP = 1.342X10^{-9}
		0102	06.14	χ^2= 47.78
		010-1	-11.91	R =0.00084
		0011	09.58	Skewness= -0.39
		0012	13.30	Kurtosis=5.67
		0013	15.16	Np=107
	1: 1: 2	1125	36.05 (1)	pH=2.2-8.1
		1124	33.10 (1)	
		1123	30.02 (1)	
		1122	26.30 (1)	
		1121	19.13 (1)	
		1120	11.24 (09)	
Cd^{2+}		0101	03.58	U/NP = 1.706X10^{-8}
		0102	06.14	χ^2= 60.63
		010-1	-11.91	R =0.0044
		0011	09.58	Skewness= -0.74
		0012	13.30	Kurtosis=5.14
	2: 1: 1	0013	15.16	Np=76
		2112	19.92 (2)	pH=2.3-7.8
		2111	16.39 (2)	
		2110	09.42 (3)	
		211-1	01.44 (2)	
		0101	03.58	U/NP = 7.464X10^{-9}
		0102	06.14	χ^2= 83.53
		010-1	-11.91	R =0.0035
		0011	09.58	Skewness= -1.46
		0012	13.30	Kurtosis=7.23
	2:1 :2	0013	15.16	Np=68
		2124	35.71 (4)	pH=2.2-8.2
		2123	31.99 (10)	
		2122	28.27 (12)	
		2121	20.74 (22)	
		2120	13.75 (6)	
		212-1	05.02 (8)	

*Figures in the parentheses are the standard deviations in the least significant digit.

The species converged in 1:1:1 (metal ion-SADH-aspartic acid) systems are $MLXH_3$, $MLXH_2$, MLXH, MLX and $MLXH_{-1}$. The step-wise protonation constants for the formation of $MLXH_3$ from $MLXH_2$ for various metal ion systems are shown in Table 5.18(a).

Table 5.18: Step-wise protonation constants of MLX type of species of Metal ion-SADH-aspartic acid systems (from Tables 5.6-5.10)

Metal ion	(a) $\mathrm{Log}\,K^{1113}_{1112}$ $(=\log\beta_{1113}-\log\beta_{1112})$	(b) $\mathrm{Log}\,K^{1112}_{1111}$ $(=\log\beta_{1112}-\log\beta_{1111})$	(c) $\mathrm{Log}\,K^{1111}_{1110}$ $(=\log\beta_{1111}-\log\beta_{1110})$
Ca^{2+}	3.37	3.70	8.74
Mg^{2+}	3.44	3.64	8.61
Pb^{2+}	3.12	3.42	6.08
Hg^{2+}	3.08	3.68	6.25
Cd^{2+}	2.98	3.72	7.24

The $\log K^{1113}_{1112}$ values are of the order of the protonation constant of SADH which is equal to 3.58. Therefore, the species $MLXH_3$ can be represented as $M.(LH).XH_2$, as one of the protons of the species is associated with SADH. Aspartic acid is in XH_2 form in the complex and therefore, acts as a monodentate, bonding through carboxylate oxygen, while side chain carboxylate oxygen and α-ammonium groups are free and protonated. The species distribution diagrams for 1:1:1 systems (Figures 5.48b, 5.52b, 5.56b, 5.60b and 5.67b respectively for Ca^{2+}, Mg^{2+}, Pb^{2+}, Hg^{2+} and Cd^{2+}) indicate 25 to 49 % of formation of $MLXH_3$ type of species below 2.7 pH.

The step-wise deprotonation constants of $MLXH_2$ to form MLXH and MLXH to form MLX type of species (Table 5.17 (b) and (c) respectively) are below the protonation constants of both side chain carboxylate group and α-amine groups of aspartic acid which are 3.72 and 9.58 respectively. Therefore, the sequence of proton dissociation on coordination of the two groups can be ascertained from the step-wise protonation constants. The relatively high stabilities of the MLX type of species of Pb^{2+}-SADH-Aspartic acid system compared to that of Pb^{2+}-SADH-glycine, indicate tridentate behaviour of aspartic acid bonding through carboxylate oxygen, amino nitrogen and side chain carboxylate oxygen. In the case of Ca^{2+}, Mg^{2+}, Hg^{2+} and Cd^{2+} the formation constants of MLX species for M^{2+}-SADH-Aspartic acid and M^{2+}-SADH-glycine are almost same. Hence it can be concluded that in these complexes aspartic acid exhibits bidentate nature bonding through carboxylate oxygen and α-amino nitrogen while the side chain carboxylate oxygen group is deprotonated but may remain non-bonding or weakly bonding.

Table 5.19: Relative stabilities of MLX type of species of M^{2+}-SADH (L)-Aspartic acid (XH_2) and M^{2+}-SADH (L)- Glycine(XH) systems (from Tables 5.1-5.5 and 5.13-5.16)

Metal ion	Formation constants of MLX species	
	M^{2+}-SADH (L)-Aspartic acid (XH_2)	M^{2+}-SADH (L)- Glycine (XH)
Ca^{2+}	5.74	5.79
Mg^{2+}	5.87	5.32
Pb^{2+}	9.63	8.62
Hg^{2+}	8.71	8.22
Cd^{2+}	7.34	6.69

The species converged for 1:1:2 (M:L:X) molar ratio systems are MLX_2H_5, MLX_2H_4, MLX_2H_3, MLX_2H_2, MLX_2H and MLX_2. The first proton dissociation constant of MLX_2H_5 to form MLX_2H_4 (Table 5.20) is less than 3.58 which is the protonation constant of SADH.

Table 5.20: Proton dissociation constants of MLX_2H_5 type of species

Metal ion	$\log K_{1125}^{1124} = \log \beta_{1125} - \log \beta_{1124}$
Ca^{2+}	3.54
Mg^{2+}	3.34
Pb^{2+}	3.31
Hg^{2+}	3.08
Cd^{2+}	2.95

This suggests that one of the hydrazide groups of SADH in MLX_2H_5 type of species is protonated. Therefore in MLX_2H_5 species SADH acts as a bidentate, bonding through carbonyl and $-NH_2$ groups. In MLX_2H_4 species, one of the hydrazide groups of SADH acts as bidentate while the other group remains deprotonated and non-bonding. Aspartic acid molecules act as monodentates bonding through carboxylate groups. With increase in pH aspartic acid molecules lose protons from the side chain carboxylic and α-ammonium groups forming MLX_2H_3, MLX_2H_2, MLX_2H and MLX_2 type of species. The concentration distribution diagrams of these species are shown in Figures 5.49b, 5.53b, 5.57b, 5.61b and 5.65b respectively for Ca^{2+}, Mg^{2+}, Pb^{2+}, Hg^{2+} and Cd^{2+}.

The best-fit models for 2:1:1 (M:L:X) molar ratio systems contain bimetallic species, M_2LXH_2, M_2LXH, M_2LX and M_2LXH_{-1}. In the case of 2:1:2 systems, the species converged are $M_2LX_2H_4$, $M_2LX_2H_2$, $M_2LX_2H_1$, M_2LX_2 and $M_2LX_2H_{-1}$. The corresponding species distribution diagrams are included in Figures 5.50b, 5.54b, 5.58b, 5.62b , 5.66b for 2:1:1 systems and 5.51b, 5.55b, 5.59b, 5.63b , 5.67b for 2:1:2 systems respectively for Ca^{2+}, Mg^{2+}, Pb^{2+}, Hg^{2+} and Cd^{2+}. In all the bimetallic species succinic acid dihydrazide acts as bis bidentate ligand. The bonding centres are carbonyl and terminal $-NH_2$ groups. In both M_2LXH_2 and $M_2LX_2H_4$ type of species aspartic acid acts as monodentate bonding through carboxylate oxygen atoms. The formation of $M_2LX_2H_{-1}$ type of species may be due to the loss of enolic proton of dihydrazide or hydroxylation of the corresponding species.

From the comparison of the stability constants of metal ion-SADH- aspartic acid system with those of metal ion-SADH- glycine system (Table 5.21), it may be proposed that aspartic acid behaves as a tridentate with Pb^{2+} and as a bidentate ligand with the metal ions Ca^{2+}, Mg^{2+}, Hg^{2+} and Cd^{2+}.

Table 5.21: Relative stabilities of M_2LX type of species of M^{2+} -SADH- Aspartic acid and M^{2+}-SADH- Glycine systems (from Tables 5.1-5.5 and 5.13-5.17)

Metal ion	Formation constants of M_2LX species	
	XH_2=Aspartic acid	XH= Glycine
Ca^{2+}	7.45	7.83
Mg^{2+}	7.84	7.08
Pb^{2+}	12.25	10.95
Hg^{2+}	10.99	10.48
Cd^{2+}	9.42	8.99

The formation constants of all the species for all the compositions for M^{2+}-SADH- Aspartic acid systems were found to be in the order $Mg^{2+} > Ca^{2+}$and $Pb^{2+} > Hg^{2+} > Cd^{2+}$.

5.3 CHEMICAL MODELLING STUDIES ON THE INTERACTION OF ADIPIC ACID DIHYDRAZIDE AND AMINO ACID (GLYCINE/ L-HISTIDINE/ L-ASPARTICACID) WITH Ca^{2+}, Mg^{2+}, Pb^{2+}, Hg^{2+} and Cd^{2+} METAL IONS:

5.3.1 AADH- Glycine - Metal Ion Systems:

The experimental and theoretical titration curves of ternary, metal ion adipic acid dihydrazide - glycine systems for compositions 1:1:1, 1:1:2, 2:1:1 and 2:1:2 for all the metal ions under study (Ca^{2+}, Mg^{2+}, Pb^{2+}, Hg^{2+} and Cd^{2+}) are shown in Figures 5.68a to 5.87a.

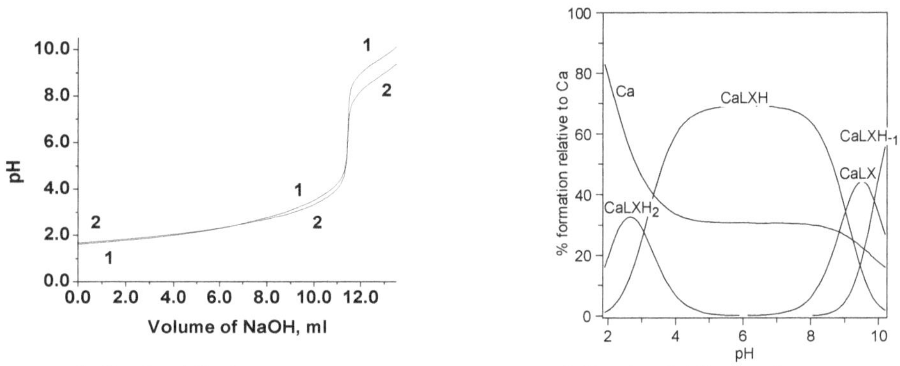

a. 1. Simulated titration curve
2. Experimental titration curve

b. Species distribution diagram

[AADH] = 0.01000 mol dm^{-3} [GLYCINE] = 0.0100 mol dm^{-3} [Ca^{2+}] = 0.00998 mol dm^{-3}
[HCl] = 0.04666 mol dm^{-3} [NaOH] = 0.2040 mol dm^{-3} TOTAL VOLUME= 50.0 cm^3
Temp.: 30.0 ±0.1^{0}C I = 0.1 mol dm^{-3}

Figure 5.68: Ca^{2+}-AADH GLYCINE SYSTEM (1:1:1)

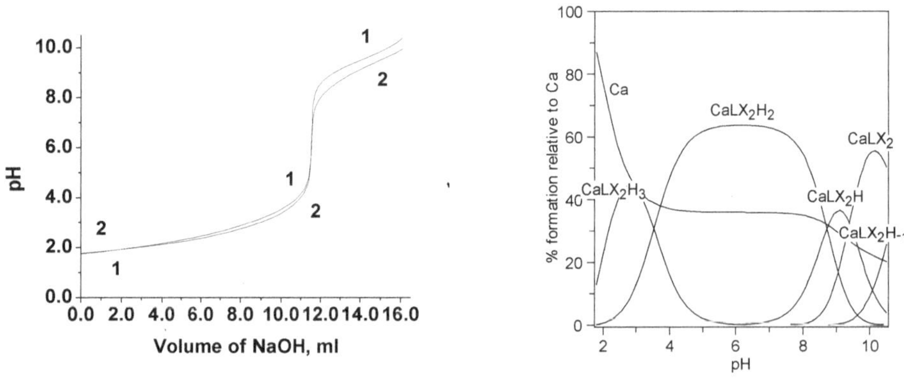

a. 1. Simulated titration curve
2. Experimental titration curve

b. Species distribution diagram

[AADH]= 0.01000 mol dm^{-3} [GLYCINE]= 0.0200 mol dm^{-3} [Ca^{2+}] = 0.00998 mol dm^{-3}
[HCl] = 0.04705 mol dm^{-3} [NaOH] = 0.2040 mol dm^{-3} TOTAL VOLUME=50.0 cm^3
Temp.: 30.0 ±0.1^{0}C I = 0.1 mol dm^{-3}

Figure 5.69: Ca^{2+}-AADH-GLYCINE SYSTEM (1:1:2)

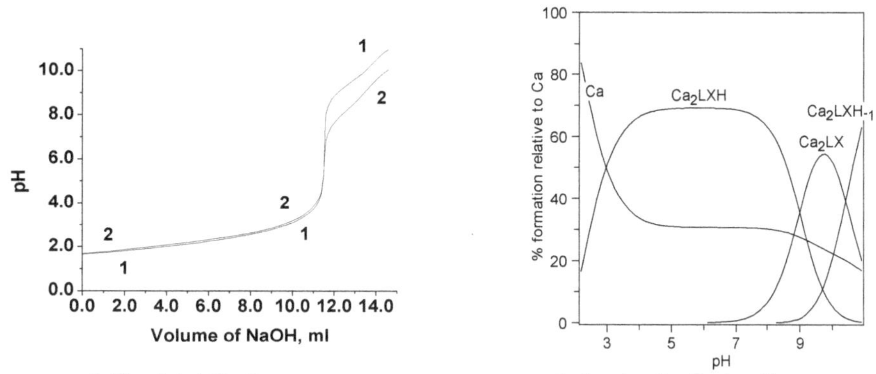

a. 1. Simulated titration curve
2. Experimental titration curve

b. Species distribution diagram

[AADH]= 0.01000 mol dm^{-3} [GLYCINE]= 0.0100 mol dm^{-3} [Ca^{2+}] = 0.01996 mol dm^{-3}
[HCl] = 0.04700 mol dm^{-3} [NaOH] = 0.2040 mol dm^{-3} TOTAL VOLUME=50.0 cm^3
Temp.: 30.0 ±0.1°C I = 0.1 mol dm^{-3}

Figure 5.70: Ca^{2+}-AADH-GLYCINE SYSTEM (2:1:1)

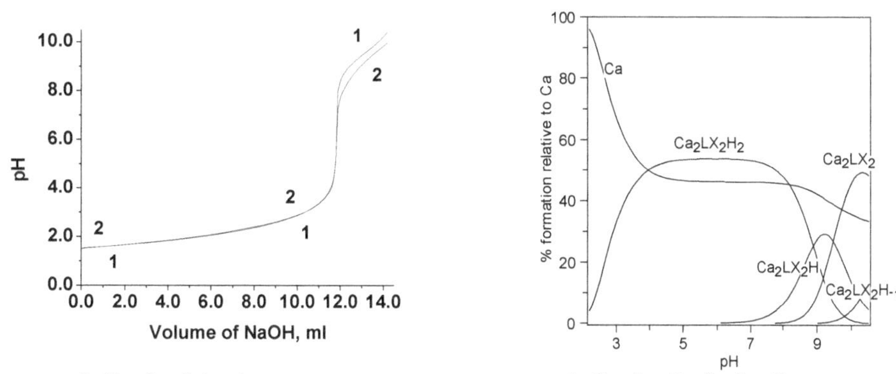

a. 1. Simulated titration curve
2. Experimental titration curve

b. Species distribution diagram

[AADH] = 0.00500 mol dm^{-3} [GLYCINE] = 0.0100 mol dm^{-3} [Ca^{2+}] = 0.00998 mol dm^{-3}
[HCl] = 0.04823 mol dm^{-3} [NaOH] = 0.2040 mol dm^{-3} TOTAL VOLUME= 50.0 cm^3
Temp.: 30.0 ±0.1°C I = 0.1 mol dm^{-3}

Figure 5.71: Ca^{2+}-AADH GLYCINE SYSTEM (2:1:2)

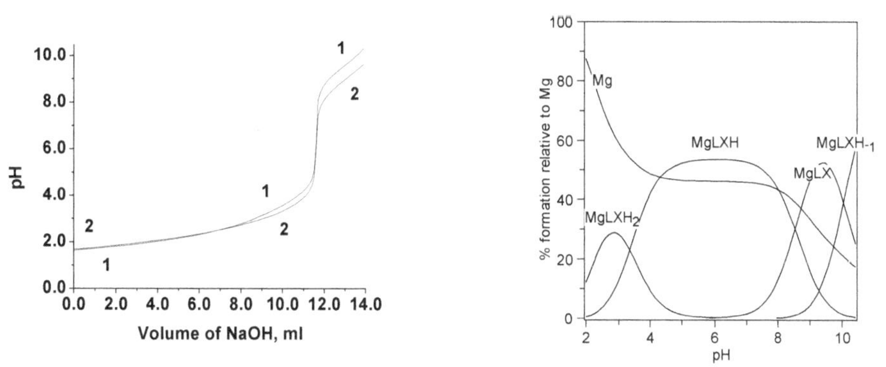

a. 1. Simulated titration curve
2. Experimental titration curve

b. Species distribution diagram

[AADH]= 0.01000 mol dm^{-3} [GLYCINE]= 0.0100 mol dm^{-3} [Mg^{2+}] = 0.0100 mol dm^{-3}
[HCl] = 0.04735 mol dm^{-3} [NaOH] = 0.2040 mol dm^{-3} TOTAL VOLUME=50.0 cm^3
Temp.: 30.0 ±0.1°C I = 0.1 mol dm^{-3}

Figure 5.72: Mg^{2+}-AADH-GLYCINE SYSTEM (1:1:1)

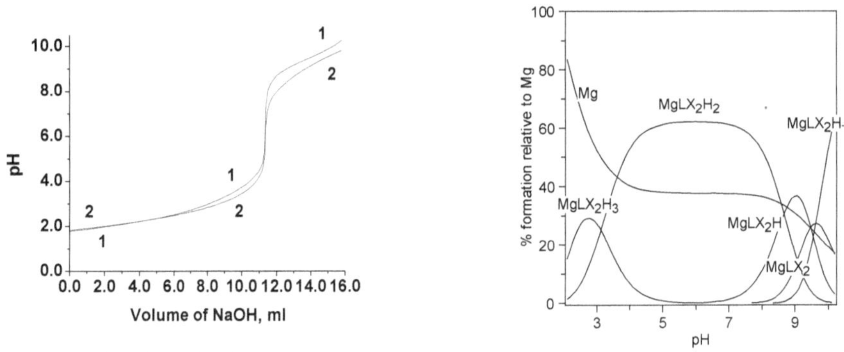

a. 1. Simulated titration curve
2. Experimental titration curve

b. Species distribution diagram

[AADH] = 0.01000 mol dm^{-3}	[GLYCINE]= 0.0200 mol dm^{-3}	[Mg $^{2+}$] = 0.0100 mol dm^{-3}
[HCl] = 0.04637 mol dm^{-3}	[NaOH] = 0.2040 mol dm^{-3}	TOTAL VOLUME=50.0 cm^3
Temp.: 30.0 ±0.1^{0}C		I = 0.1 mol dm^{-3}

Figure 5.73: Mg^{2+}-AADH-GLYCINE SYSTEM (1:1:2)

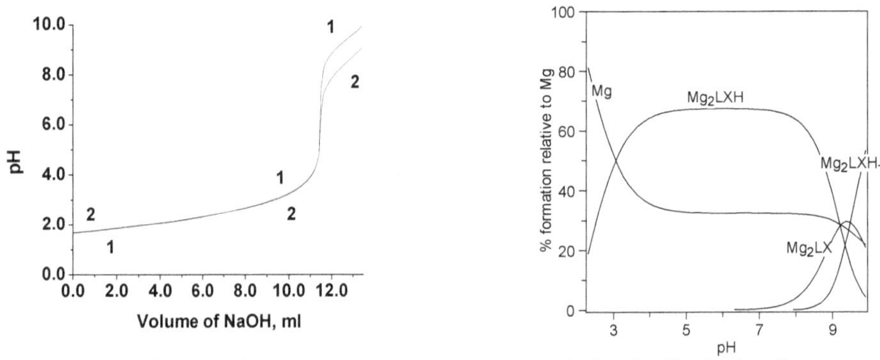

a. 1. Simulated titration curve
2. Experimental titration curve

b. Species distribution diagram

[AADH] = 0.01000 mol dm^{-3}	[GLYCINE] = 0.0100 mol dm^{-3}	[Mg^{2+}] = 0.01999 mol dm^{-3}
[HCl] = 0.04680 mol dm^{-3}	[NaOH] = 0.2040 mol dm^{-3}	TOTAL VOLUME= 50.0 cm^3
Temp.: 30.0 ±0.1^{0}C		I = 0.1 mol dm^{-3}

Figure 5.74: Mg^{2+}-AADH GLYCINE SYSTEM (2:1:1)

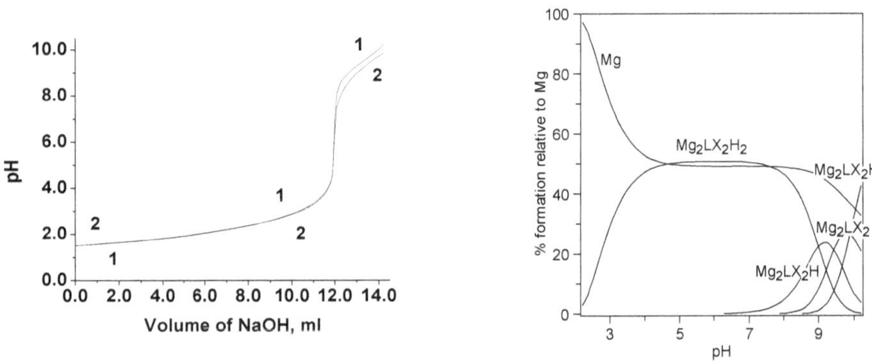

a. 1. Simulated titration curve
2. Experimental titration curve

b. Species distribution diagram

[AADH]= 0.00500 mol dm^{-3}	[GLYCINE]= 0.0100 mol dm^{-3}	[Mg $^{2+}$] = 0.0100moldm^{-3}
[HCl] = 0.04892 mol dm^{-3}	[NaOH] = 0.2040 mol dm^{-3}	TOTAL VOLUME=50.0 cm^3
Temp.: 30.0 ±0.1^{0}C		I = 0.1 mol dm^{-3}

Figure 5.75: Mg^{2+}-AADH-GLYCINE SYSTEM (2:1:2)

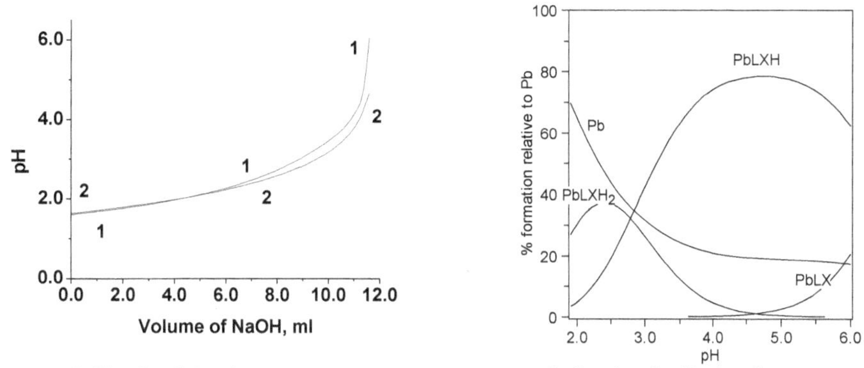

a. 1. Simulated titration curve
2. Experimental titration curve

b. Species distribution diagram

[AADH]= 0.01000 mol dm^{-3} [GLYCINE]= 0.0100 mol dm^{-3} [Pb^{2+}] = 0.00998 mol dm^{-3}
[HNO_3] = 0.04695 mol dm^{-3} [NaOH] = 0.2040 mol dm^{-3} TOTAL VOLUME=50.0 cm^3
Temp.: 30.0 ±0.1^{0}C I = 0.1 mol dm^{-3}

Figure 5.76: Pb^{2+}-AADH-GLYCINE SYSTEM (1:1:1)

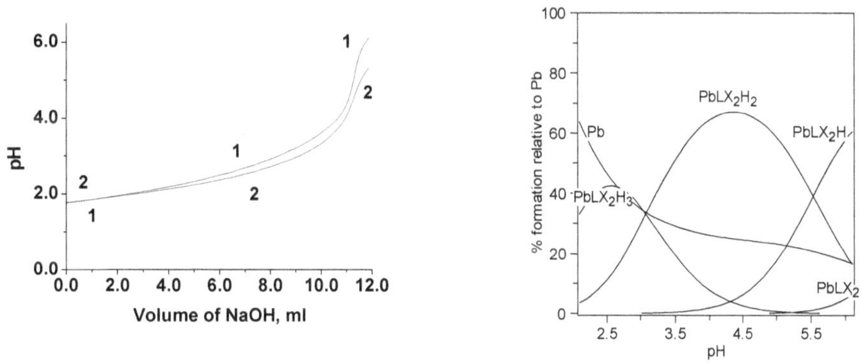

a. 1. Simulated titration curve
2. Experimental titration curve

b. Species distribution diagram

[AADH] = 0.01000 mol dm^{-3} [GLYCINE] = 0.0200 mol dm^{-3} [Pb^{2+}] = 0.00998 mol dm^{-3}
[HNO_3] = 0.04617 mol dm^{-3} [NaOH] = 0.2040 mol dm^{-3} TOTAL VOLUME= 50.0 cm^3
Temp.: 30.0 ±0.1^{0}C I = 0.1 mol dm^{-3}

Figure 5.77: Pb^{2+}-AADH GLYCINE SYSTEM (1:1:2)

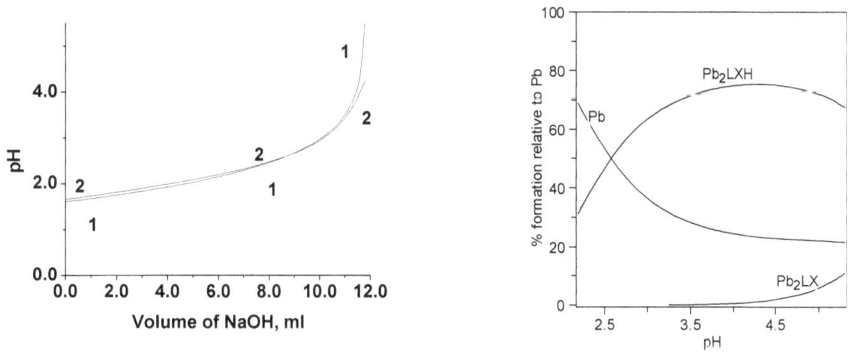

a. 1. Simulated titration curve
2. Experimental titration curve

b. Species distribution diagram

[AADH]= 0.01000 mol dm^{-3} [GLYCINE]= 0.0100 mol dm^{-3} [Pb^{2+}] = 0.01995 mol dm^{-3}
[HNO_3] = 0.04788 mol dm^{-3} [NaOH] = 0.2040 mol dm^{-3} TOTAL VOLUME=50.0 cm^3
Temp.: 30.0 ±0.1^{0}C I = 0.1 mol dm^{-3}

Figure 5.78: Pb^{2+}-AADH-GLYCINE SYSTEM (2:1:1)

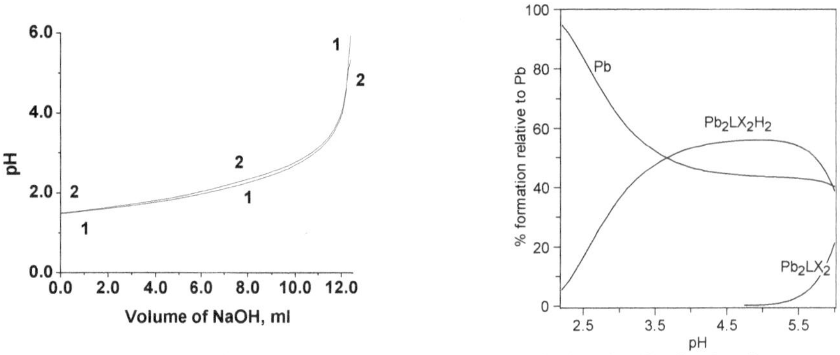

a. 1. Simulated titration curve
2. Experimental titration curve

b. Species distribution diagram

[AADH] = 0.00500 mol dm^{-3} [GLYCINE]= 0.0100 mol dm^{-3} [Pb^{2+}] = 0.00998 mol dm^{-3}
[HNO_3] = 0.05010 mol dm^{-3} [NaOH] = 0.2040 mol dm^{-3} TOTAL VOLUME=50.0 cm^3
Temp.: 30.0 ±0.1^{0}C I = 0.1 mol dm^{-3}

Figure 5.79: Pb^{2+}-AADH-GLYCINE SYSTEM (2:1:2)

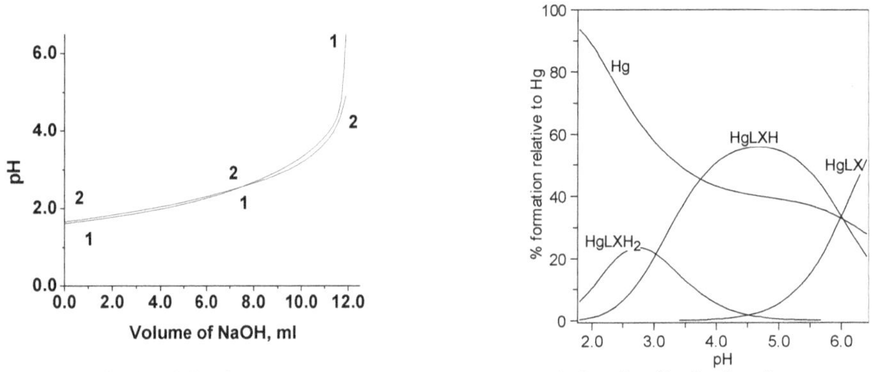

a. 1. Simulated titration curve
2. Experimental titration curve

b. Species distribution diagram

[AADH] = 0.01000 mol dm^{-3} [GLYCINE] = 0.0100 mol dm^{-3} [Hg^{2+}] = 0.00995 mol dm^{-3}
[HCl] = 0.04819 mol dm^{-3} [NaOH] = 0.2040 mol dm^{-3} TOTAL VOLUME= 50.0 cm^3
Temp.: 30.0 ±0.1^{0}C I = 0.1 mol dm^{-3}

Figure 5.80: Hg^{2+}-AADH GLYCINE SYSTEM (1:1:1)

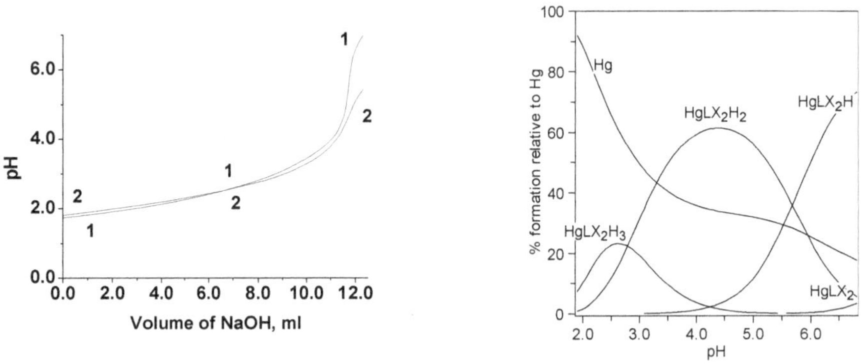

a. 1. Simulated titration curve
2. Experimental titration curve

b. Species distribution diagram

[AADH]= 0.01000 mol dm^{-3} [GLYCINE]= 0.0200 mol dm^{-3} [Hg^{2+}] = 0.00995 mol dm^{-3}
[HCl] = 0.04780 mol dm^{-3} [NaOH] = 0.2040 mol dm^{-3} TOTAL VOLUME=50.0 cm^3
Temp.: 30.0 ±0.1^{0}C I = 0.1 mol dm^{-3}

Figure 5.81: Hg^{2+}-AADH-GLYCINE SYSTEM (1:1:2)

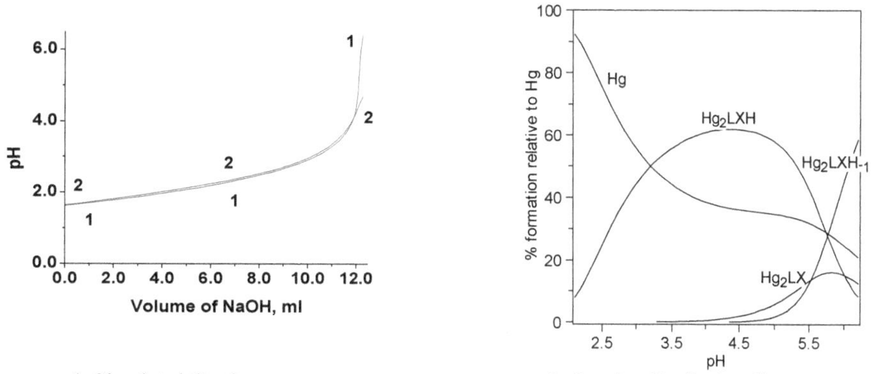

a. 1. Simulated titration curve
2. Experimental titration curve

b. Species distribution diagram

[AADH]= 0.01000 mol dm^{-3} [GLYCINE]= 0.0100 mol dm^{-3} [Hg $^{2+}$] = 0.01990 mol dm^{-3}
[HCl] = 0.04959 mol dm^{-3} [NaOH] = 0.2040 mol dm^{-3} TOTAL VOLUME=50.0 cm^3
Temp.: 30.0 ±0.1^{0}C I = 0.1 mol dm^{-3}

Figure 5.82: Hg^{2+}-AADH-GLYCINE SYSTEM (2:1:1)

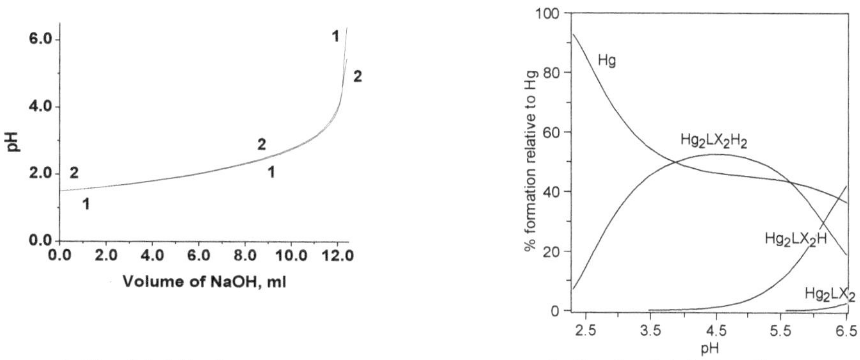

a. 1. Simulated titration curve
2. Experimental titration curve

b. Species distribution diagram

[AADH] = 0.00500 mol dm^{-3} [GLYCINE] = 0.0100 mol dm^{-3} [Hg^{2+}] = 0.00995 mol dm^{-3}
[HCl] = 0.05016 mol dm^{-3} [NaOH] = 0.2040 mol dm^{-3} TOTAL VOLUME= 50.0 cm^3
Temp.: 30.0 ±0.1^{0}C I = 0.1 mol dm^{-3}

Figure 5.83: Hg^{2+}-AADH GLYCINE SYSTEM (2:1:2)

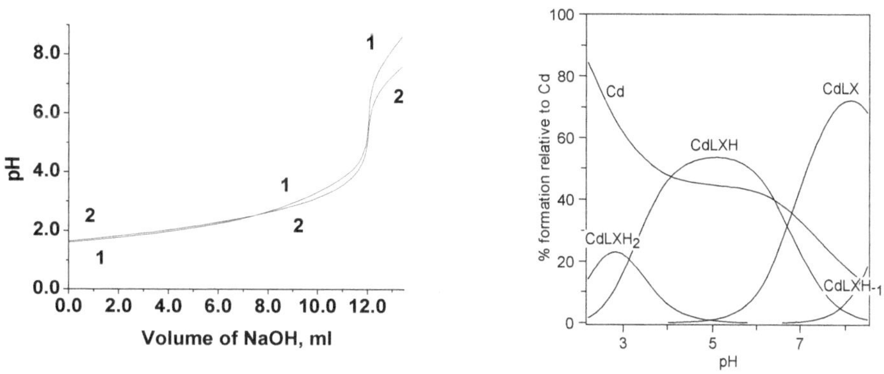

a. 1. Simulated titration curve
2. Experimental titration curve

b. Species distribution diagram

[AADH] = 0.01000 mol dm^{-3} [GLYCINE] = 0.0100 mol dm^{-3} [Cd $^{2+}$] = 0.0100 mol dm^{-3}
[HCl] = 0.04915 mol dm^{-3} [NaOH] = 0.2040 mol dm^{-3} TOTAL VOLUME=50.0 cm^3
Temp.: 30.0 ±0.1^{0}C I = 0.1 mol dm^{-3}

Figure 5.84: Cd^{2+}-AADH-GLYCINE SYSTEM (1:1:1)

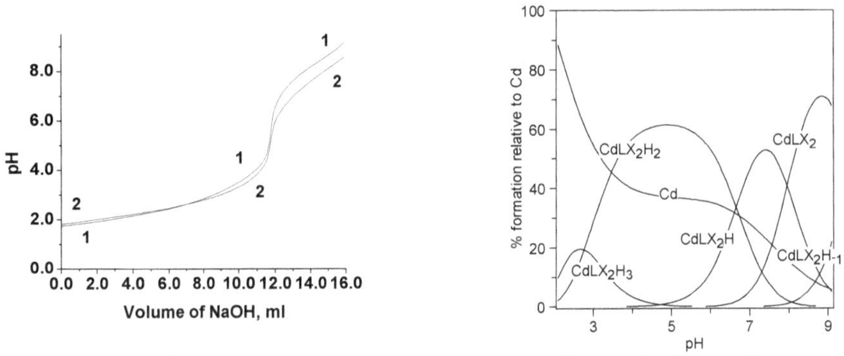

a. 1. Simulated titration curve
2. Experimental titration curve

b. Species distribution diagram

[AADH]= 0.01000 mol dm^{-3} [GLYCINE]= 0.0200 mol dm^{-3} [Cd $^{2+}$] = 0.0100 mol dm^{-3}
[HCl] = 0.04797 mol dm^{-3} [NaOH] = 0.2040 mol dm^{-3} TOTAL VOLUME=50.0 cm^3
Temp.: 30.0 ±0.1^{0}C I = 0.1 mol dm^{-3}

Figure 5.85: Cd^{2+}-AADH-GLYCINE SYSTEM (1:1:2)

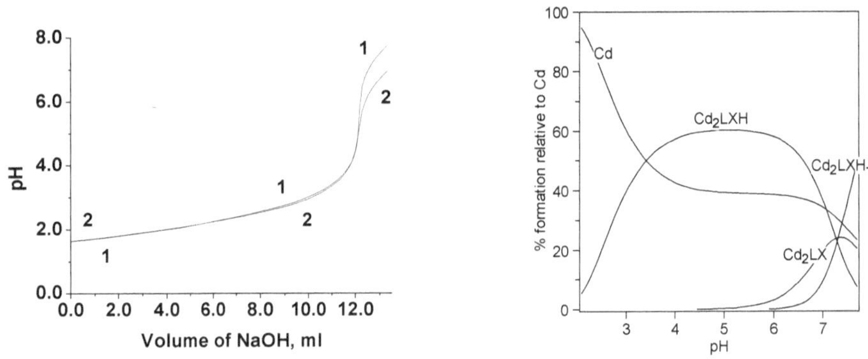

a. 1. Simulated titration curve
2. Experimental titration curve

b. Species distribution diagram

[AADH] = 0.01000 mol dm^{-3} [GLYCINE] = 0.0100 mol dm^{-3} [Cd^{2+}] = 0.0200 mol dm^{-3}
[HCl] = 0.04961 mol dm^{-3} [NaOH] = 0.2040 mol dm^{-3} TOTAL VOLUME= 50.0 cm^3
Temp.: 30.0 ±0.1^{0}C I = 0.1 mol dm^{-3}

Figure 5.86: Cd^{2+}-AADH GLYCINE SYSTEM (2:1:1)

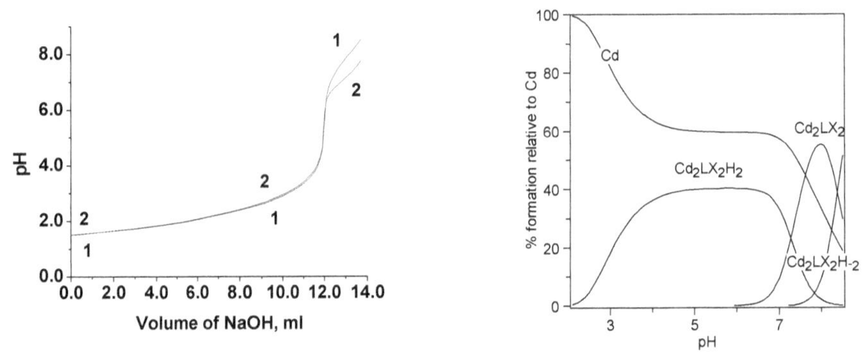

a. 1. Simulated titration curve
2. Experimental titration curve

b. Species distribution diagram

[AADH]= 0.00500 mol dm^{-3} [GLYCINE]= 0.0100 mol dm^{-3} [Cd $^{2+}$] = 0.0100 mol dm^{-3}
[HCl] = 0.04895 mol dm^{-3} [NaOH] = 0.2040 mol dm^{-3} TOTAL VOLUME=50.0 cm^3
Temp.: 30.0 ±0.1^{0}C I = 0.1 mol dm^{-3}

Figure 5.87: Cd^{2+}-AADH-GLYCINE SYSTEM (2:1:2)

A continuous difference between simulated and experimental titration curves indicates the presence of ternary species. The experimental data were analysed using the Miniquad-75 program. The required initial estimates of the mixed ligand species were calculated using the formation constants of the binary systems and protonation constants of the ligand. The best-fit models selected for all the metal ion systems and compositions are tabulated in Tables 5.22 to 5.26.

Table 5.22 Best fit chemical models of Ca^{2+} -adipic acid dihydrazide-glycine ternary system in aqueous medium at 303.0 K and ionic strength, $I = 0.1$ mol dm^{-3}

Metal ion	Composition (M: L: X)	Species mlxh	Log β_{mlxh}	
Ca^{2+}	1:1:1	0101	03.67	U/NP = 2.270X10^{-7}
		0102	06.25	χ^2= 95.17
		010-1	-12.03	R =0.017
		0011	09.56	Skewness=0.03
		0012	11.86	Kurtosis=5.40
		1112	17.99 (6)	Np=106
		1111	14.94 (3)	pH=1.9-10.2
		1110	05.92 (6)	
		111-1	-3.96 (7)	
	1: 1: 2	0101	03.67	U/NP = 4.298X10^{-7}
		0102	06.25	χ^2= 86.91
		010-1	-12.03	R =0.017
		0011	09.56	Skewness= -0.35
		0012	11.86	Kurtosis=3.87
		1123	29.63 (4)	Np=150
		1122	26.10 (5)	pH=1.8-10.5
		1121	17.38 (9)	
		1120	7.99 (6)	
		112-1	-2.80 (9)	
	2: 1: 1	0101	03.67	U/NP = 3.525X10^{-7}
		0102	06.25	χ^2= 55.12
		010-1	-12.03	R = 0.022
		0011	09.56	Skewness= -0.04
		0012	11.86	Kurtosis= 5.84
		2111	16.85 (4)	Np= 95
		2110	7.85 (10)	pH=2.2-10.9
		211-1	-2.55 (9)	
	2:1 :2	0101	03.67	U/NP = 5.214X10^{-8}
		0102	06.25	χ^2= 56.52
		010-1	-12.03	R = 0.012
		0011	09.56	Skewness= -0.56
		0012	11.86	Kurtosis= 4.34
		2122	28.53 (4)	Np= 69
		2121	19.65 (11)	pH=2.2-10.5
		2120	10.18 (8)	
		212-1	-0.86 (9)	

*Figures in the parentheses are the standard deviations in the least significant digit.

Table 5.23 Best fit chemical models of Mg^{2+}-adipic acid dihydrazide-glycine ternary system in aqueous medium at 303.0 K and ionic strength, I = 0.1 mol dm^{-3}

Metal ion	Composition (M: L: X)	Species mlxh	Log β_{mlxh}	
Mg^{2+}	1:1:1	0101	03.67	U/NP = 1.321X10^{-7}
		0102	06.25	χ^2= 84.73
		010-1	-12.03	R =0.014
		0011	09.56	Skewness=0.44
		0012	11.86	Kurtosis=6.92
		1112	17.65 (6)	Np=104
		1111	14.30 (3)	pH=2.0-10.4
		1110	05.76 (4)	
		111-1	-4.28 (4)	
	1: 1: 2	0101	03.67	U/NP = 1.026X10^{-7}
		0102	06.25	χ^2= 92.34
		010-1	-12.03	R =0.0092
		0011	09.56	Skewness= -0.17
		0012	11.86	Kurtosis=4.58
		1123	29.12 (4)	Np=117
		1122	26.01 (2)	pH=2.1-10.2
		1121	17.34 (5)	
		1120	07.87 (3)	
		112-1	-1.75 (4)	
	2: 1: 1	0101	03.67	U/NP = 2.712X10^{-7}
		0102	06.25	χ^2= 73.03
		010-1	-12.03	R =0.020
		0011	09.56	Skewness= 0.22
		0012	11.86	Kurtosis=7.15
		2111	16.74 (4)	Np=78
		2110	07.53 (8)	pH=2.3-9.9
		211-1	-1.96(7)	
	2:1 :2	0101	03.67	U/NP =5.019X10^{-8}
		0102	06.25	χ^2= 75.49
		010-1	-12.03	R =0.011
		0011	09.56	Skewness= -1.06
		0012	11.86	Kurtosis= 4.70
		2122	28.37 (5)	Np=70
		2121	19.37 (11)	pH=2.2-10.2
		2120	9.93 (8)	
		212-1	0.04 (9)	

*Figures in the parentheses are the standard deviations in the least significant digit.

Table 5.24 Best fit chemical models of Pb^{2+}- adipic acid dihydrazide-glycine ternary system in aqueous medium at 303.0 K and ionic strength, I = 0.1 mol dm^{-3}

Metal ion	Composition (M: L: X)	Species mlxh	Log β_{mlxh}	
Pb^{2+}	1:1:1	0102	06.25	χ^2= 46.09
		010-1	-12.03	R =0.019
		0011	09.56	Skewness=0.18
		0012	11.86	Kurtosis=5.13
		1112	18.44 (6)	Np=94
		1111	15.65 (4)	pH=1.9-6.0
		1110	09.17 (6)	

(Pb^{2+}- adipic acid dihydrazide-glycine ternary system)

Pb^{2+}	1: 1: 2	0101	03.67	U/NP = $4.482X10^{-8}$
		0102	06.25	χ^2= 16.12
		010-1	-12.03	R =0.0055
		0011	09.56	Skewness= -0.21
		0012	11.86	Kurtosis=2.98
		1123	29.93 (3)	Np=65
		1122	26.85 (1)	pH=2.1-6.1
		1121	21.32 (7)	
		1120	14.26 (4)	
	2: 1: 1	0101	03.67	U/NP = $2.452X10^{-7}$
		0102	06.25	χ^2= 21.59
		010-1	-12.03	R =0.018
		0011	09.56	Skewness= 0.15
		0012	11.86	Kurtosis=4.28
		2111	17.46 (3)	Np=63
		2110	11.37 (8)	pH=2.2 -5.3
	2:1 :2	0101	03.67	U/NP = $1.641X10^{-7}$
		0102	06.25	χ^2= 37.58
		010-1	-12.03	R =0.020
		0011	09.56	Skewness= -0.76
		0012	11.86	Kurtosis= 2.87
		2122	28.69 (9)	Np=53
		2120	16.43 (10)	pH=2.2-5.9

*Figures in the parentheses are the standard deviations in the least significant digit.

Table 5.25 Best fit chemical models of Hg^{2+}-adipic acid dihydrazide-glycine ternary system in aqueous medium at 303.0 K and ionic strength, I = 0.1 mol dm^{-3}

Metal ion	Composition (M: L: X)	Species mlxh	Log β_{mlxh}	
Hg^{2+}	1:1:1	0101	03.67	U/NP = $2.774X10^{-7}$
		0102	06.25	χ^2= 78.77
		010-1	-12.03	R =0.016
		0011	09.56	Skewness=0.17
		0012	11.86	Kurtosis=7.16
		1112	17.57 (8)	Np=111
		1111	14.54 (4)	pH=1.8-6.4
		1110	08.54 (8)	
	1: 1: 2	0101	03.67	U/NP = $1.641X10^{-7}$
		0102	06.25	χ^2= 61.53
		010-1	-12.03	R =0.0092
		0011	09.56	Skewness= -0.28
		0012	11.86	Kurtosis=3.44
		1123	29.06 (4)	Np=107
		1122	26.27 (3)	pH=1.9-6.8
		1121	20.59 (9)	
		1120	12.46 (6)	
	2: 1: 1	0101	03.67	U/NP = $1.657X10^{-7}$
		0102	06.25	χ^2= 19.23
		010-1	-12.03	R =0.013
		0011	09.56	Skewness= -0.10
		0012	11.86	Kurtosis=3.89
		2111	16.58 (2)	Np=78
		2110	10.57 (13)	pH=2.1-6.2
		211-1	05.04 (5)	

(Hg^{2+}- adipic acid dihydrazide-glycine ternary system)

Hg^{2+}	2:1 :2	0101	03.67	U/NP = 4.042X10^{-8}
		0102	06.25	χ^2= 15.68
		010-1	-12.03	R =0.010
		0011	09.56	Skewness= -0.31
		0012	11.86	Kurtosis=3.08
		2122	28.58(4)	Np=50
		2121	22.43 (21)	pH=2.3-6.5
		2120	14.72 (7)	

*Figures in the parentheses are the standard deviations in the least significant digit.

Table 5.26 Best fit chemical models of Cd^{2+} -adipic acid dihydrazide-glycine ternary system in aqueous medium at 303.0 K and ionic strength, I = 0.1 mol dm^{-3}

Metal ion	Composition (M: L: X)	Species mlxh	Log β_{mlxh}	
Cd^{2+}	1:1:1	0101	03.67	U/NP = 5.130X10^{-8}
		0102	06.25	χ^2= 57.60
		010-1	-12.03	R =0.0097
		0011	09.56	Skewness=0.16
		0012	11.86	Kurtosis=5.35
		1112	17.49 (6)	Np=85
		1111	14.36 (2)	pH=2.2-8.5
		1110	07.64 (3)	
		111-1	-1.43 (4)	
	1: 1: 2	0101	03.67	U/NP = 5.316X10^{-8}
		0102	06.25	χ^2= 98.69
		010-1	-12.03	R =0.0067
		0011	09.56	Skewness= -0.28
		0012	11.86	Kurtosis=4.81
		1123	28.83 (4)	Np=116
		1122	26.06 (1)	pH=2.1-9.1
		1121	19.40 (3)	
		1120	11.44 (2)	
		112-1	01.85 (4)	
	2: 1: 1	0101	03.67	U/NP = 1.537X10^{-7}
		0102	06.25	χ^2= 53.84
		010-1	-12.03	R =0.013
		0011	09.56	Skewness= -0.54
		0012	11.86	Kurtosis=3.80
		2111	16.38 (2)	Np=89
		2110	9.11 (5)	pH=2.1-7.9
		211-1	1.79 (6)	
	2:1 :2	0101	03.67	U/NP = 1.059X10^{-7}
		0102	06.25	χ^2= 78.47
		010-1	-12.03	R =0.015
		0011	09.56	Skewness= 0.34
		0012	11.86	Kurtosis=3.60
		2122	27.85 (10)	Np=81
		2120	13.29 (9)	pH=2.1-8.3
		212-1	-3.47 (10)	

*Figures in the parentheses are the standard deviations in the least significant digit.

The species converged in 1:1:1 (M:L:X) systems include $MLXH_2$, MLXH, MLX and $MLXH_{-1}$. In the $MLXH_2$ type of species adipic acid dihydrazide (L) is present in LH form, i.e. one of the coordinating units of AADH is involved in bonding as a bidentate while the other is non-bonding and protonated. Glycine (XH) is bonded in zwitter ion form as a monodentate bonding through carboxylate oxygen (Figure 5.88) while the α-amino group is protonated and non-bonding.

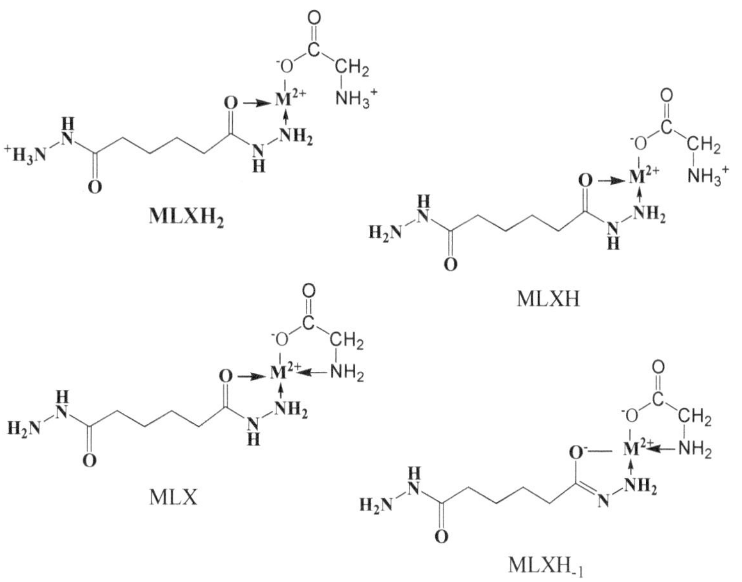

Figure 5.88: Probable bonding modes of the ligands in the species of 1:1:1 (M:L;X) molar composition of M^{2+}- adipic acid dihydrazide-glycine ternary system.

This may be ascertained from the step-wise protonation constants of MLXH type of species to form $MLXH_2$ (i.e. $\log \beta_{1112} - \log \beta_{1111}$) which lie between 2.79 and 3.35 (Table 5.27) and are close to 3.67, the protonation constant of AADH.

Table 5.27: Step-wise protonation constants of MLX type of species of M^{2+}-AADH-glycine systems

Metal ion	$\log \beta_{1112} - \log \beta_{1111}$	$\log \beta_{1111} - \log \beta_{1110}$
Ca^{2+}	3.05	9.02
Mg^{2+}	3.35	8.54
Pb^{2+}	2.79	6.48
Hg^{2+}	3.03	6.00
Cd^{2+}	3.13	6.72

Species distribution diagrams (Figures 5.68b, 5.72b. 5.76b, 5.80b and 5.84b for (Ca^{2+}, Mg^{2+}, Pb^{2+}, Hg^{2+} and Cd^{2+} systems respectively) indicate that the species $MLXH_2$ reaches a maximum of 23% to 38%, depending on the metal ion below a pH of 2.82. Further increase in pH of the solution deprotonates $MLXH_2$ species to MLXH and subsequently to MLX. The deprotonation of MLXH to form MLX is due to the deprotonation of the remaining protonated α-amino group on bonding to the metal ion indicated (Figure 5.88) by the step-wise deprotonation constants, "log β_{1111}– log β_{1110}" (Table 5.27) which are less than 9.56, the protonation constant of glycine. A drop of 2 to 3 log units in protonation constant may be observed on complexation. The formation of $MLXH_{-1}$ type of species which were observed for Ca^{2+}, Mg^{2+} and Cd^{2+} systems may be due to the loss of enolic proton of AADH or hydroxylation of the corresponding species. These species were not observed for Pb^{2+} and Hg^{2+} systems as the upper pH limit of data acquisition and analysis was restricted to the appearance of turbidity in the solution.

The mixed ligand species converged for 1:1:2 (M:L:X) molar ratio of M^{2+}-AADH-glycine systems, in addition to binary species, are MLX_2H_3, MLX_2H_2, MLX_2H, MLX_2 and MLX_2H_{-1}. The step-wise dissociation constant of MLX_2H_3 to form MLX_2H_2 ($\log K_{1122}^{1123} = \log \beta_{1123} - \log \beta_{1122}$) is between 2.77 and 3.53 (Table 5.28) which is less than the protonation constant (3.67) of AADH (L). This clearly indicates that one proton in the MLX_2H_3 type of species is attached to dihydrazide [M.(LH).$(XH)_2$]. Two molecules of glycine in zwitter ion form (XH) are coordinated to the metal ion as monodentates bonding through carboxylate oxygen atoms. Thus, one of the hydrazide groups of AADH is involved in bonding while the other is free and protonated. In the MLX_2H_2 type of species, both the protons are attached to α-amino groups of glycine molecules. The probable bonding modes of the ligands in the species are shown in Figure 5.89.

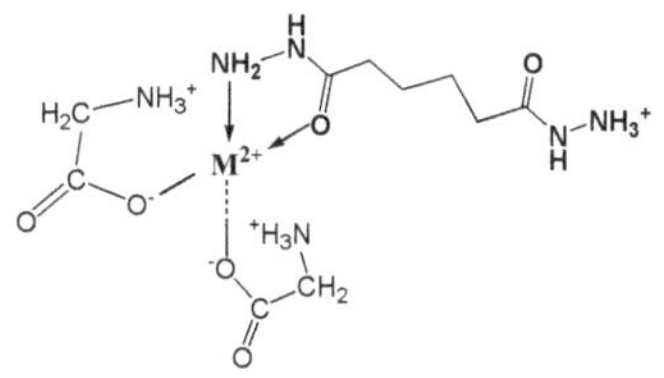

MLX_2H_3[*i.e.* $M(LH)(XH)_2$]

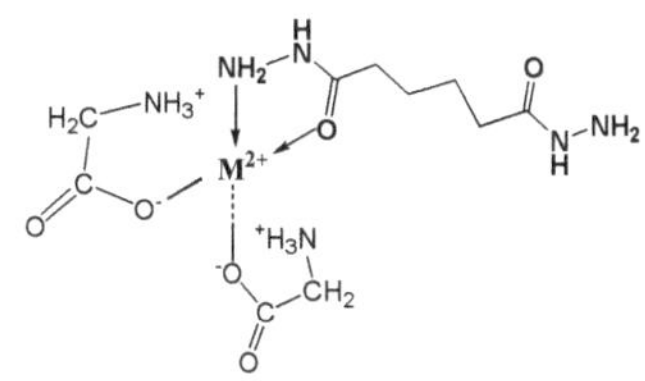

MLX_2H_2[*i.e.* $M(L)(XH)_2$]

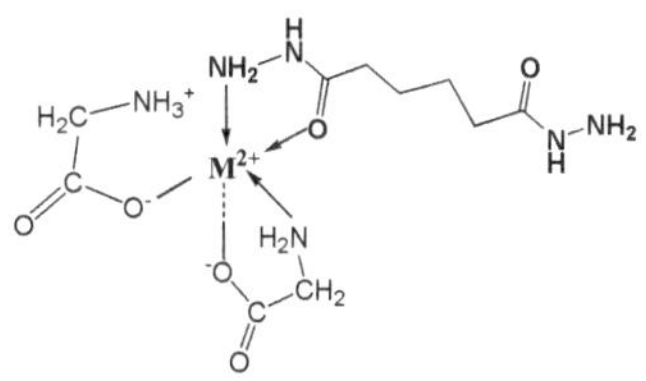

MLX_2H_2[*i.e.* MLX(XH)]

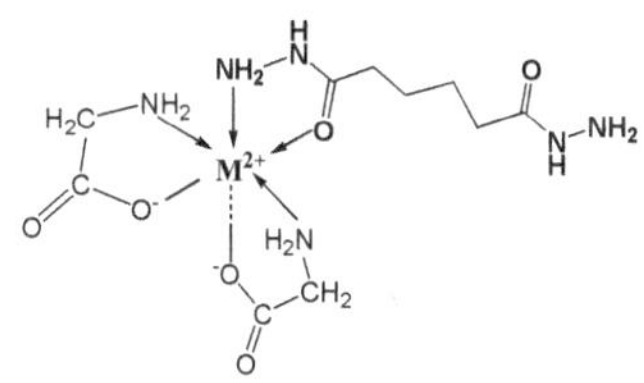

MLX_2

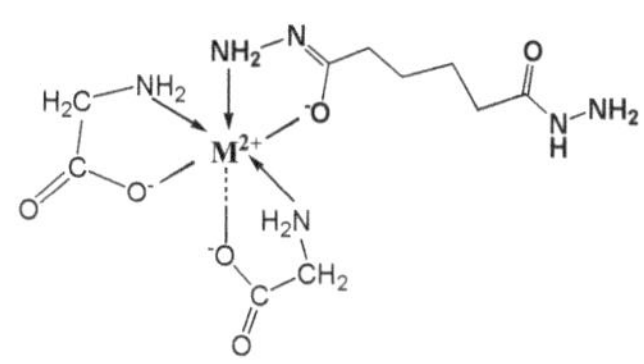

MLX_2H_{-1}

Figure 5.89: Probable bonding modes in the species of 1:1:2 (M:L;X) molar composition of M^{2+}-AADH-Glycine systems.

Table 5.28: Step-wise protonation constants of MLX_2 type of species of Metal ion-AADH-glycine systems

Metal ion	$\log \beta_{1123} - \log \beta_{1122}$	$\log \beta_{1122} - \log \beta_{1121}$	$\log \beta_{1121} - \log \beta_{1120}$
Ca^{2+}	3.53	8.72	9.39
Mg^{2+}	3.11	8.67	9.47
Pb^{2+}	3.08	5.53	7.06
Hg^{2+}	2.79	5.68	8.13
Cd^{2+}	2.77	6.66	7.96

The step-wise formation constants, $\log K_{1121}^{1122} = \log \beta_{1122} - \log \beta_{1121}$ for the formation of MLX_2H_2 from MLX_2H and $\log K_{1120}^{1121} = \log \beta_{1121} - \log \beta_{1120}$ for the formation of MLX_2H from MLX_2 range from 5.53 to 9.47 (Table 5.28) indicating the release of α-ammonium protons of glycine on complexation. The formation of

MLX_2H_{-1} species at higher pH may be due to hydroxylation or deprotonation of the enolic proton of the dihydrazide. The diagrams (Figures 5.69b, 5.73b. 5.77b, 5.81b and 5.85b for Ca^{2+}, Mg^{2+}, Pb^{2+}, Hg^{2+} and Cd^{2+} systems respectively) give the concentration distribution of all these species versus pH of the solution.

As adipic acid dihydrazide is a ditopic ligand, Calvin-Wilson titrations were also conducted for compositions in which metal concentration was twice that of dihydrazide i.e. 2:1:1 (M:L:X), where, M= Ca^{2+}, Mg^{2+}, Pb^{2+}, Hg^{2+} and Cd^{2+}, L= adipic acid dihydrazide and XH is glycine. The simulated titration curves assuming the formation of only simple complexes differed from the experimental curves (Figures 5.70a, 5.74a. 5.78a, 5.82a and 5.86a for Ca^{2+}, Mg^{2+}, Pb^{2+}, Hg^{2+} and Cd^{2+} systems respectively) indicating the formation of other species. The data were subjected to analysis using the Miniquad-75 program and the results are included in Tables 5.22 to 5.26 for different metal ions. The best-fit models obtained indicate, the formation of M_2LXH, M_2LX and M_2LXH_{-1} binuclear mixed ligand species. Adipic acid dihydrazide acts as a bis bidentate ligand, bonding to metal ions through carbonyl oxygen and amino nitrogen forming five membered chelate rings on either side, while glycine is bonded to one of the metal ions as a monodentate (in M_2LXH) bonding through carboxylate oxygen and as a bidentate in the M_2LX type of species bonding through both carboxylate oxygen and α-amino nitrogen. The probable bonding modes of the ligands in the species are shown in Figure 5.90. The step-wise formation constants, $\log K_{2110}^{2111} = \log\beta_{2111} - \log\beta_{2110}$ for the protonation of the M_2LX type of species to form M_2LXH range from 6.01 to 9.21. This clearly indicates that the deprotonation of M_2LXH is due to the loss of α-ammonium proton on complexation to the metal ion.

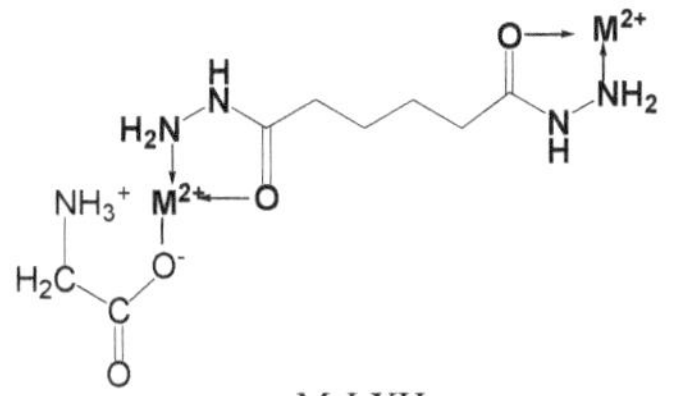

M_2LXH

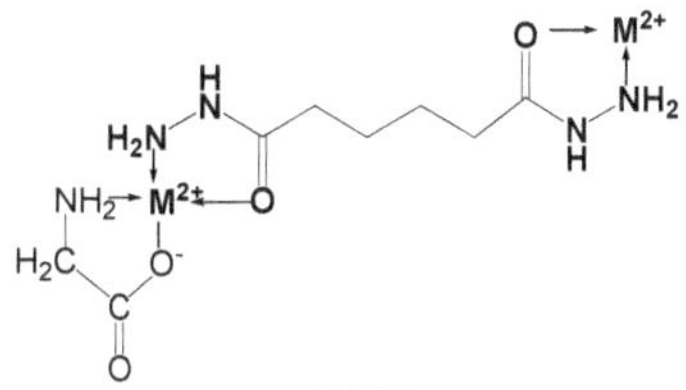

M_2LX

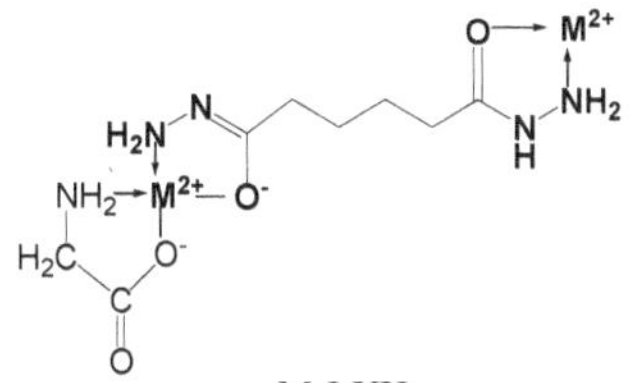

M_2LXH_{-1}

Figure 5.90: Probable bonding modes of ligands in the species of 2:1:1 (M:L:X) molar composition of M^{2+}-AADH-glycine systems

The formation of M_2LXH_{-1} type of species may be due to the deprotonation of one of the enolic groups of the hydrazide or hydroxylation. The species distribution diagrams (Figures 5.70b, 5.74b. 5.78b, 5.82b and 5.86b for Ca^{2+}, Mg^{2+}, Pb^{2+}, Hg^{2+} and Cd^{2+} systems respectively) indicate that below 6.00 pH M_2LXH is the major species, the extent of its formation being 60 to 76% depending on the metal ion. Above 5.97 pH the unprotonated and deprotonated species coexist and dominate in solution.

The species converged for systems of 2:1:2 (M:L:X) molar concentration ratio are $M_2LX_2H_2$, M_2LX_2H, M_2LX_2, $M_2LX_2H_{-1}$ and $M_2LX_2H_{-2}$. In the symmetric $M_2LX_2H_2$ type of species, adipic acid dihydrazide acts as a ditopic ligand binding two metal ions on either side through carboxyl and terminal amino groups. Two molecules of glycine (XH) also participate in complexation as monodentates bonding through carboxylate groups. In the $M_2LX_2H_2$ type of species the α-amino groups of glycine molecules are protonated and non-bonding. With an increase in pH of the solution amino groups participate in bonding by deprotonation leading to the formation of

M_2LX_2H and M_2LX_2 type of species. The species distribution diagrams (Figures 5.71b, 5.75b. 5.79b, 5.83b and 5.87b for Ca^{2+}, Mg^{2+}, Pb^{2+}, Hg^{2+} and Cd^{2+} systems respectively) for 2:1:2 composition indicate that $M_2LX_2H_2$ is predominant below a pH of 5.95 representing ~40 to 57 % of the total metal depending on the metal ion. Above this pH, M_2LX_2H, M_2LX_2, $M_2LX_2H_{-1}$ and $M_2LX_2H_{-2}$ type of species coexist in solution. The formation of $M_2LX_2H_{-1}$ and $M_2LX_2H_{-2}$ type of species may be due to deprotonation of the enolic form of AADH or hydroxylation. The formation constants of all the species for all the compositions were found to be in the order, i.e. $Ca^{2+} > Mg^{2+}$ and $Pb^{2+} > Hg^{2+} > Cd^{2+}$.

5.3.2 AADH- L-histidine- metal ion systems:

L-Histidine (XH) possesses three potential metal-binding sites, namely the carboxylate oxygen, the imidazole imido nitrogen and the α-amino nitrogen. Depending on the pH, histidine can exist in solution as XH_3^{2+}, XH_2^{+}, XH and X^-. On the other hand AADH (L) is a ditopic ligand and can exist in solution as LH_2^{2+}, LH^+ and L. In the presence of a metal ion it may also lose enolic protons, forming L^- and L^{2-} type of species. Thus, in ternary systems containing a metal ion, AADH and histidine there is a chance of formation of a variety of protonated, unprotonated and deprotonated mono and binuclear species.

The simulated and experimental titration curves for all the metal ion systems and compositions are shown in Figures 5.91a to 5.110a. Simulated titration curves were generated assuming the formation of only binary species using the SOPHD program. The observed continuous difference between experimental and simulated titration curves indicates the formation of ternary systems.

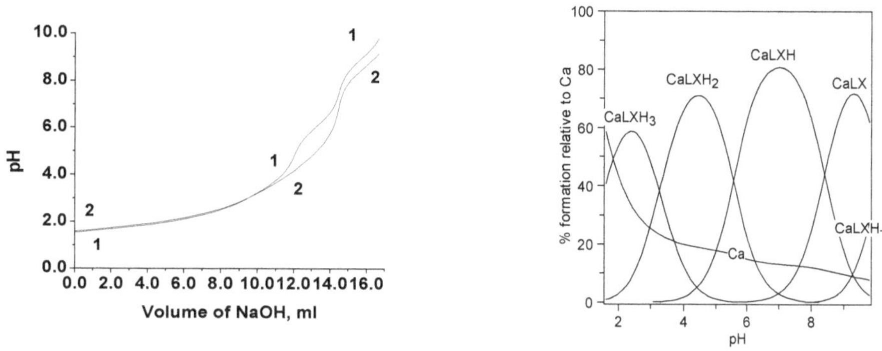

a. 1. Simulated titration curve
2. Experimental titration curve

b. Species distribution diagram

[AADH] = 0.01000 mol dm^{-3} [HISTIDINE] = 0.0100 mol dm^{-3} [Ca^{2+}] = 0.00998 mol dm^{-3}
[HCl] = 0.05880 mol dm^{-3} [NaOH] = 0.2030 mol dm^{-3} TOTAL VOLUME= 50.0 cm^3
Temp.: 30.0 ±0.1^{0}C I = 0.1 mol dm^{-3}

Figure 5.91: Ca^{2+}-AADH-HISTIDINE SYSTEM (1:1:1)

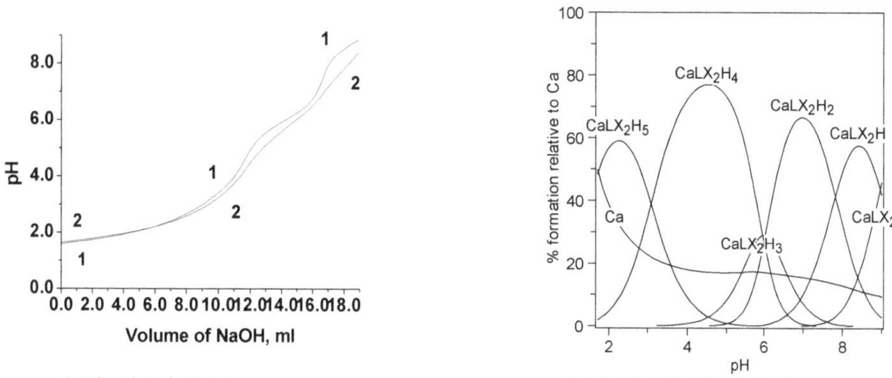

a. 1. Simulated titration curve
2. Experimental titration curve

b. Species distribution diagram

[AADH]= 0.01000 mol dm^{-3} [HISTIDINE]= 0.0200 mol dm^{-3} [Ca^{2+}] = 0.00998 mol dm^{-3}
[HCl] = 0.06755 mol dm^{-3} [NaOH] = 0.2030 mol dm^{-3} TOTAL VOLUME=50.0 cm^3
Temp.: 30.0 ±0.1^{0}C I = 0.1 mol dm^{-3}

Figure 5.92: Ca^{2+}-AADH-HISTIDINE SYSTEM (1:1:2)

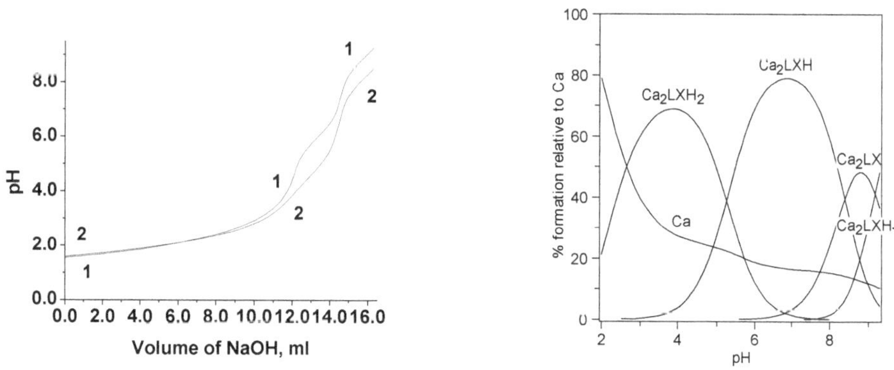

a. 1. Simulated titration curve
2. Experimental titration curve

b. Species distribution diagram

[AADH]= 0.01000 mol dm^{-3} [HISTIDINE]= 0.0100 mol dm^{-3} [Ca^{2+}] = 0.01996 mol dm^{-3}
[HCl] = 0.05913 mol dm^{-3} [NaOH] = 0.2030 mol dm^{-3} TOTAL VOLUME=50.0 cm^3
Temp.: 30.0 ±0.1^{0}C I = 0.1 mol dm^{-3}

Figure 5.93: Ca^{2+}-AADH- HISTIDINE SYSTEM (2:1:1)

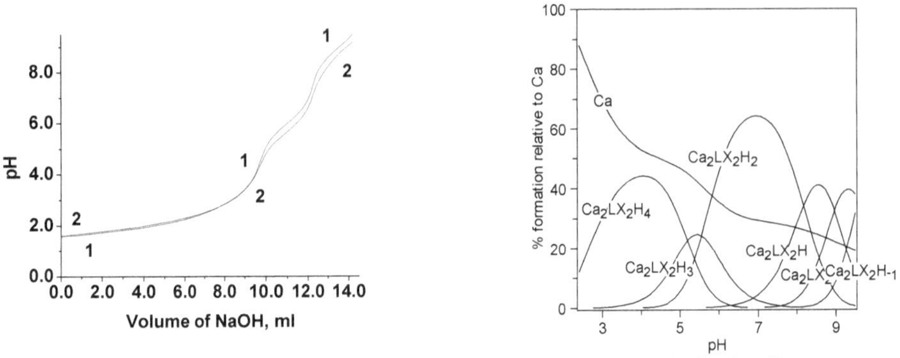

a. 1. Simulated titration curve
2. Experimental titration curve

b. Species distribution diagram

[AADH] = 0.00500 mol dm^{-3}	[HISTIDINE] = 0.0100 mol dm^{-3}	[Ca^{2+}] = 0.00998 mol dm^{-3}
[HCl] = 0.04965 mol dm^{-3}	[NaOH] = 0.2030 mol dm^{-3}	TOTAL VOLUME= 50.0 cm^3
Temp.: 30.0 ±0.1^{0}C		I = 0.1 mol dm^{-3}

Figure 5.94: Ca^{2+}-AADH- HISTIDINE SYSTEM (2:1:2)

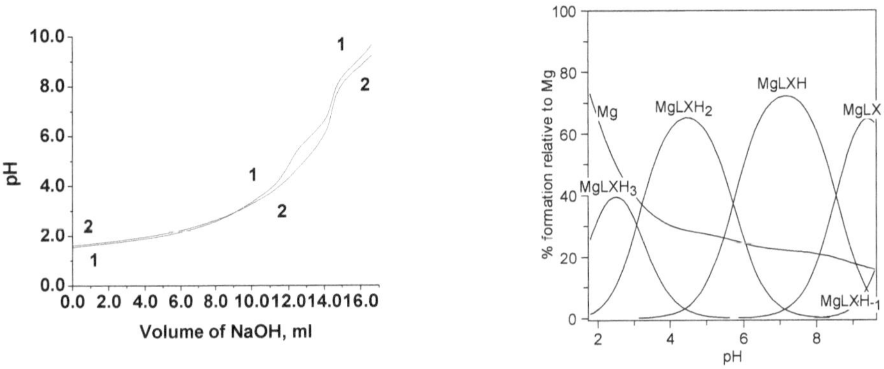

a. 1. Simulated titration curve
2. Experimental titration curve

b. Species distribution diagram

[AADH]= 0.01000 mol dm^{-3}	[HISTIDINE]= 0.0100 mol dm^{-3}	[Mg^{2+}] = 0.0100 mol dm^{-3}
[HCl] = 0.05870 mol dm^{-3}	[NaOH] = 0.2030 mol dm^{-3}	TOTAL VOLUME=50.0 cm^3
Temp.: 30.0 ±0.1^{0}C		I = 0.1 mol dm^{-3}

Figure 5.95: Mg^{2+}-AADH- HISTIDINE SYSTEM (1:1:1)

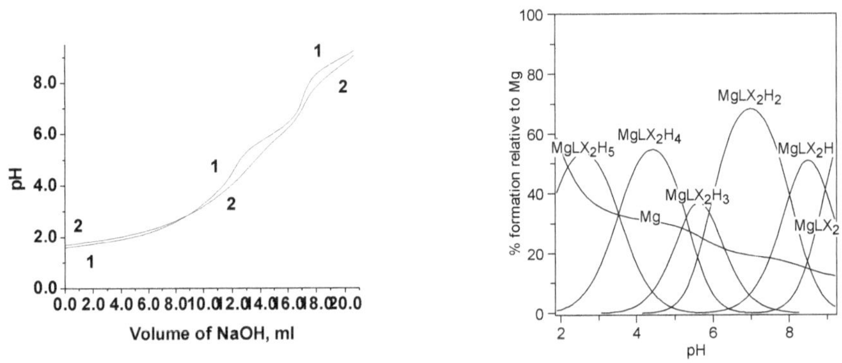

a. 1. Simulated titration curve
2. Experimental titration curve

b. Species distribution diagram

[AADH]= 0.01000 mol dm^{-3}	[HISTIDINE]= 0.0200 mol dm^{-3}	[Mg^{2+}] = 0.0100 mol dm^{-3}
[HCl] = 0.06944 mol dm^{-3}	[NaOH] = 0.2030 mol dm^{-3}	TOTAL VOLUME=50.0 cm^3
Temp.: 30.0 ±0.1^{0}C		I = 0.1 mol dm^{-3}

Figure 5.96: Mg^{2+}-AADH- HISTIDINE SYSTEM (1:1:2)

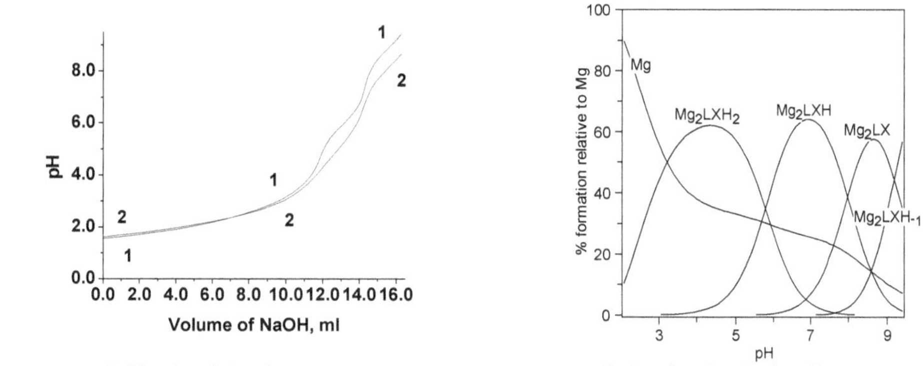

a. 1. Simulated titration curve
2. Experimental titration curve

b. Species distribution diagram

[AADH] = 0.01000 mol dm^{-3}	[HISTIDINE] =0. 0100 mol dm^{-3}	[Mg^{2+}] = 0.01999 mol dm^{-3}
[HCl] = 0.05813 mol dm^{-3}	[NaOH] = 0.2030 mol dm^{-3}	TOTAL VOLUME= 50.0 cm^3
Temp.: 30.0 ±0.1^{0}C		I = 0.1 mol dm^{-3}

Figure 5.97: Mg^{2+}-AADH- HISTIDINE SYSTEM (2:1:1)

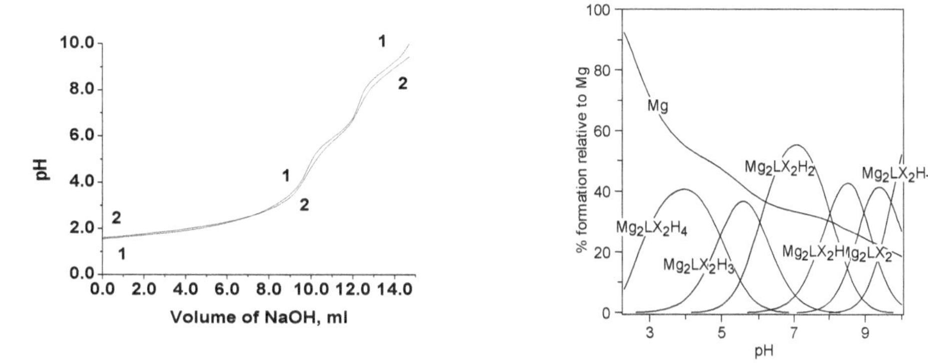

a. 1. Simulated titration curve
2. Experimental titration curve

b. Species distribution diagram

[AADH]= 0.00500 mol dm^{-3}	[HISTIDINE]= 0.0100 mol dm^{-3}	[Mg^{2+}] = 0.0100 mol dm^{-3}
[HCl] = 0.04995 mol dm^{-3}	[NaOH] = 0.2030 mol dm^{-3}	TOTAL VOLUME=50.0 cm^3
Temp.: 30.0 ±0.1^{0}C		I = 0.1 mol dm^{-3}

Figure 5.98: Mg^{2+}-AADH- HISTIDINE SYSTEM (2:1:2)

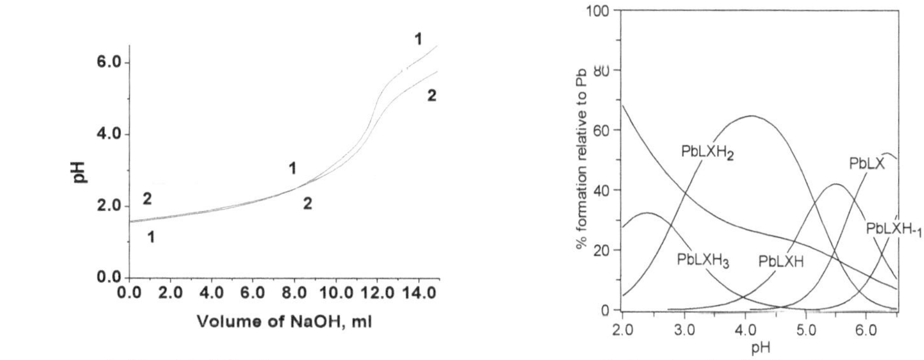

a. 1. Simulated titration curve
2. Experimental titration curve

b. Species distribution diagram

[AADH]= 0.01000 mol dm^{-3}	[HISTIDINE]= 0.0100 mol dm^{-3}	[Pb^{2+}] = 0.01003 mol dm^{-3}
[HNO_3] = 0.05826 mol dm^{-3}	[NaOH] = 0.2030 mol dm^{-3}	TOTAL VOLUME=50.0 cm^3
Temp.: 30.0 ±0.1^{0}C		I = 0.1 mol dm^{-3}

Figure 5.99: Pb^{2+}-AADH- HISTIDINE SYSTEM (1:1:1)

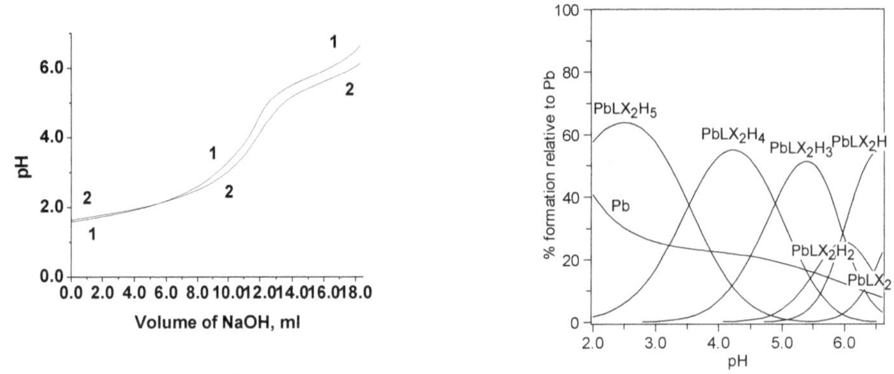

a. 1. Simulated titration curve
2. Experimental titration curve

b. Species distribution diagram

[AADH] = 0.01000 mol dm^{-3} [HISTIDINE] = 0.0200 mol dm^{-3} [Pb^{2+}] = 0.01003 mol dm^{-3}
[HNO_3] = 0.06821mol dm^{-3} [NaOH] = 0.2030 mol dm^{-3} TOTAL VOLUME= 50.0 cm^3
Temp.: 30.0 ±0.1^{0}C I = 0.1 mol dm^{-3}

Figure 5.100: Pb^{2+}-AADH HISTIDINE SYSTEM (1:1:2)

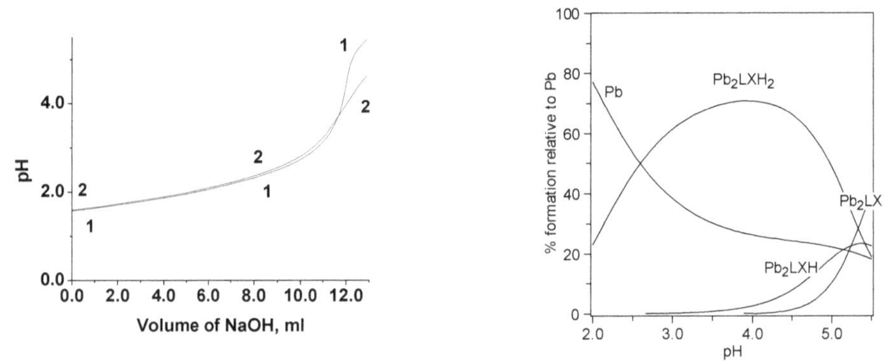

a. 1. Simulated titration curve
2. Experimental titration curve

b. Species distribution diagram

[AADH] = 0.01000 mol dm^{-3} [HISTIDINE] = 0.0100 mol dm^{-3} [Pb^{2+}] = 0.02005 mol dm^{-3}
[HNO_3] = 0.05885 mol dm^{-3} [NaOH] = 0.2030 mol dm^{-3} TOTAL VOLUME=50.0 cm^3
Temp.: 30.0 ±0.1^{0}C I = 0.1 mol dm^{-3}

Figure 5.101: Pb^{2+}-AADH- HISTIDINE SYSTEM (2:1:1)

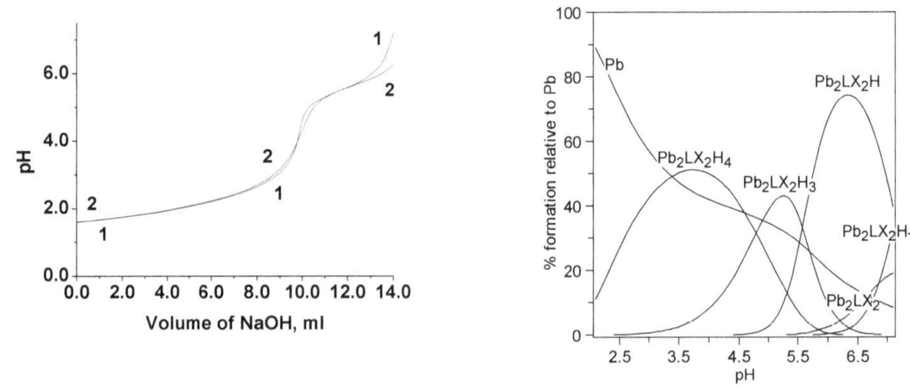

a. 1. Simulated titration curve
2. Experimental titration curve

b. Species distribution diagram

[AADH] = 0.00500 mol dm^{-3} [HISTIDINE] = 0.0100 mol dm^{-3} [Pb^{2+}] = 0.00998 mol dm^{-3}
[HNO_3] = 0.05030 mol dm^{-3} [NaOH] = 0.2030 mol dm^{-3} TOTAL VOLUME=50.0 cm^3
Temp.: 30.0 ±0.1^{0}C I = 0.1 mol dm^{-3}

Figure 5.102: Pb^{2+}-AADH- HISTIDINE SYSTEM (2:1:2)

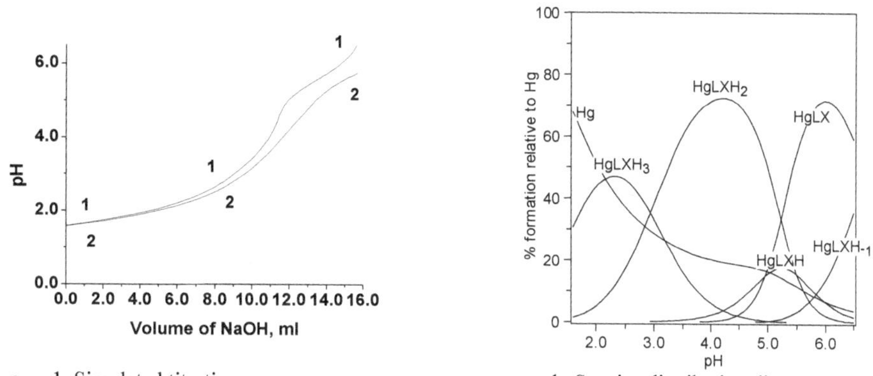

a. 1. Simulated titration curve
2. Experimental titration curve

b. Species distribution diagram

[AADH] = 0.01000 mol dm^{-3} [HISTIDINE] = 0.0100 mol dm^{-3} [Hg^{2+}] = 0.00997 mol dm^{-3}
[HCl] = 0.05674 mol dm^{-3} [NaOH] = 0.2030 mol dm^{-3} TOTAL VOLUME= 50.0 cm^3
Temp.: 30.0 ±0.1^{0}C I = 0.1 mol dm^{-3}

Figure 5.103: Hg^{2+}-AADH-HISTIDINE SYSTEM (1:1:1)

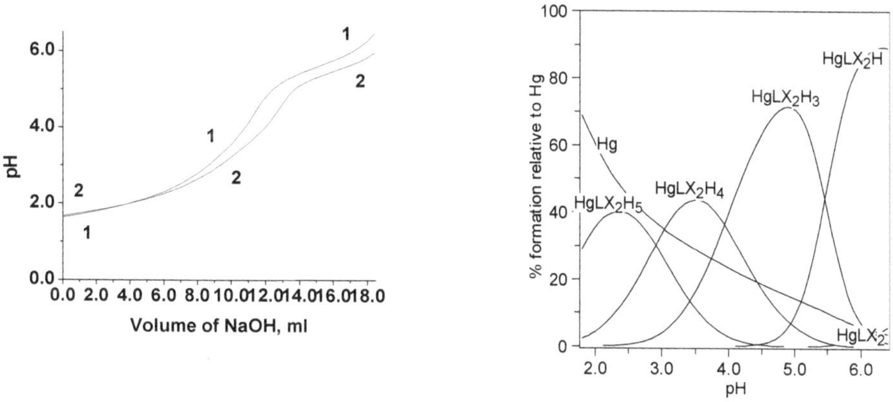

a. 1. Simulated titration curve
2. Experimental titration curve

b. Species distribution diagram

[AADH] = 0.00999 mol dm^{-3} [HISTIDINE] = 0.0200 mol dm^{-3} [Hg^{2+}] = 0.00997 mol dm^{-3}
[HCl] = 0.06589 mol dm^{-3} [NaOH] = 0.1890 mol dm^{-3} TOTAL VOLUME=50.0 cm^3
Temp.: 30.0 ±0.1^{0}C I = 0.1 mol dm^{-3}

Figure 5.104: Hg^{2+}-AADH- HISTIDINE SYSTEM (1:1:2)

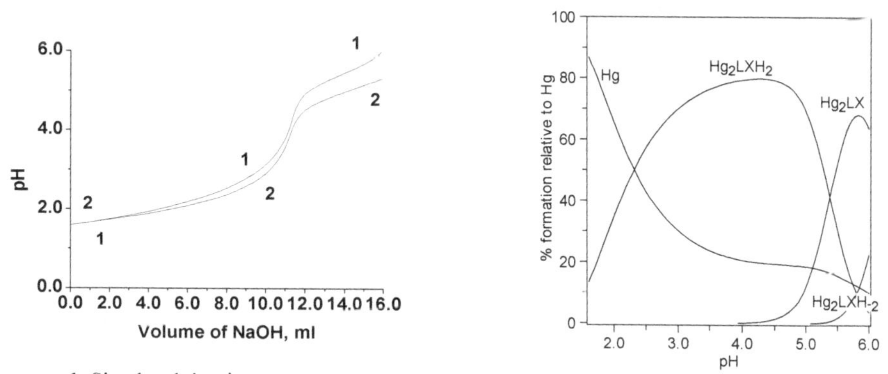

a. 1. Simulated titration curve
2. Experimental titration curve

b. Species distribution diagram

[AADH]= 0.01000 mol dm^{-3} [HISTIDINE] = 0.0100 mol dm^{-3} [Hg^{2+}] = 0.01995 mol dm^{-3}
[HCl] = 0.05660 mol dm^{-3} [NaOH] = 0.2030 mol dm^{-3} TOTAL VOLUME=50.0 cm^3
Temp.: 30.0 ±0.1^{0}C I = 0.1 mol dm^{-3}

Figure 5.105: Hg^{2+}-AADH- HISTIDINE SYSTEM (2:1:1)

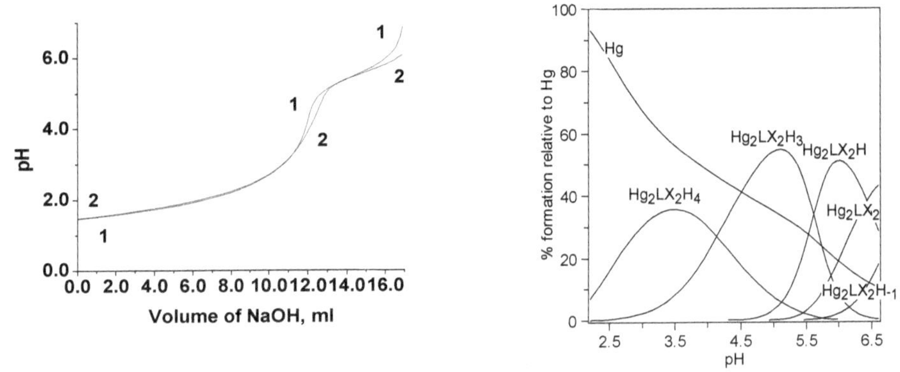

a. 1. Simulated titration curve
2. Experimental titration curve

b. Species distribution diagram

[AADH] = 0.00500 mol dm^{-3} [HISTIDINE] = 0.0100 mol dm^{-3} [Hg^{2+}] = 0.00997 mol dm^{-3}
[HCl] = 0.05933 mol dm^{-3} [NaOH] = 0.2030 mol dm^{-3} TOTAL VOLUME= 50.0 cm^3
Temp.: 30.0 ±0.1°C I = 0.1 mol dm^{-3}

Figure 5.106: Hg^{2+}-AADH-HISTIDINE SYSTEM (2:1:2)

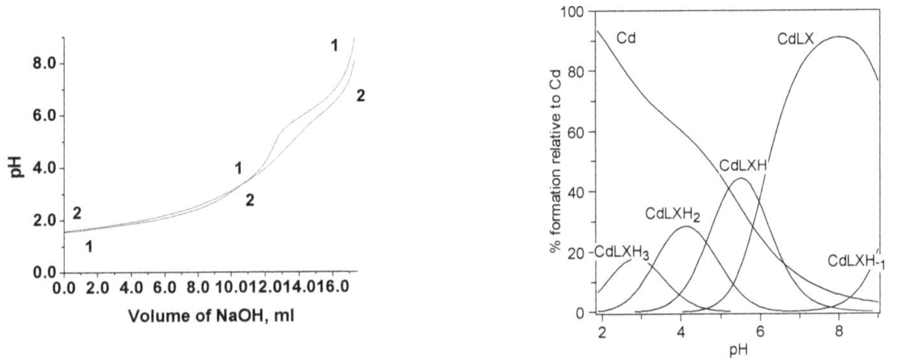

a. 1. Simulated titration curve
2. Experimental titration curve

b. Species distribution diagram

[AADH] = 0.01000 mol dm^{-3} [HISTIDINE] = 0.0100 mol dm^{-3} [Cd^{2+}] = 0.00993 mol dm^{-3}
[HCl] = 0.06071 mol dm^{-3} [NaOH] = 0.2030 mol dm^{-3} TOTAL VOLUME=50.0 cm^3
Temp.: 30.0 ±0.1°C I = 0.1 mol dm^{-3}

Figure 5.107: Cd^{2+}-AADH- HISTIDINE SYSTEM (1:1:1)

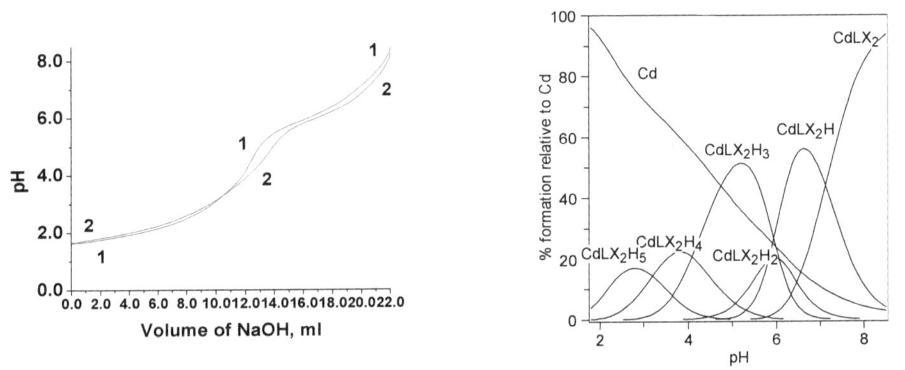

a. 1. Simulated titration curve
2. Experimental titration curve

b. Species distribution diagram

[AADH] = 0.01000 mol dm^{-3} [HISTIDINE = 0.0200 mol dm^{-3} [Cd^{2+}] = 0.00993 mol dm^{-3}
[HCl] = 0.07077 mol dm^{-3} [NaOH] = 0.2030 mol dm^{-3} TOTAL VOLUME=50.0 cm^3
Temp.: 30.0 ±0.1°C I = 0.1 mol dm^{-3}

Figure 5.108: Cd^{2+}-AADH- HISTIDINE SYSTEM (1:1:2)

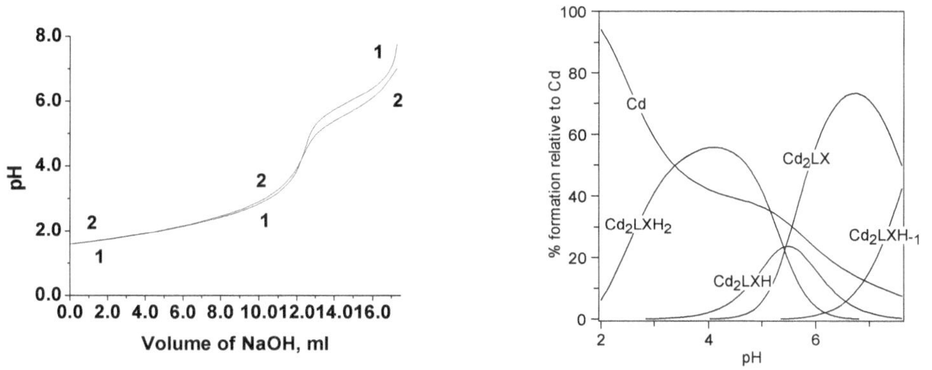

a. 1. Simulated titration curve b. Species distribution diagram
2. Experimental titration curve

[AADH] = 0.01000 mol dm^{-3} [HISTIDINE] = 0.0100 mol dm^{-3} [Cd^{2+}] = 0.01986 mol dm^{-3}
[HCl] = 0.06056 mol dm^{-3} [NaOH] = 0.2030 mol dm^{-3} TOTAL VOLUME= 50.0 cm^3
Temp.: 30.0 ±0.1°C I = 0.1 mol dm^{-3}

Figure 5.109: Cd^{2+}-AADH-HISTIDINE SYSTEM (2:1:1)

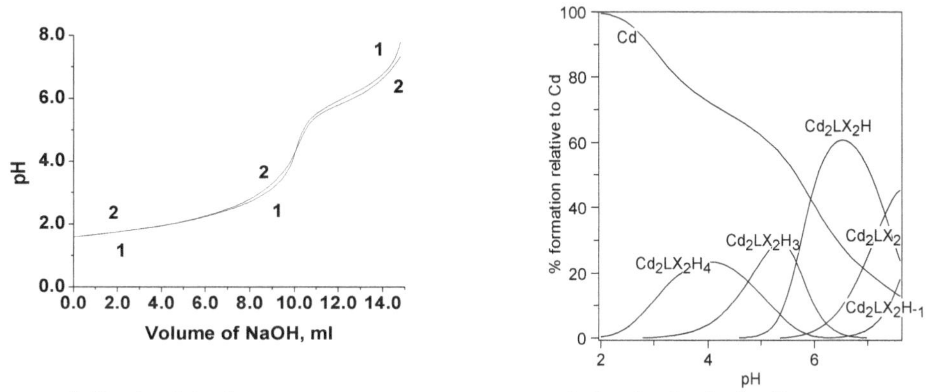

a. 1. Simulated titration curve b. Species distribution diagram
2. Experimental titration curve

[AADH] = 0.00500 mol dm^{-3} [HISTIDINE] = 0.0100 mol dm^{-3} [Cd^{2+}] = 0.00993 mol dm^{-3}
[HCl] = 0.05116 mol dm^{-3} [NaOH] = 0.2030 mol dm^{-3} TOTAL VOLUME=50.0 cm^3
Temp.: 30.0 ±0.1°C I = 0.1 mol dm^{-3}

Figure 5.110: Cd^{2+}-AADH- HISTIDINE SYSTEM (2:1:2)

Keeping in view of the coordination properties of the metal ions and various protonated/ unprotonated/ deprotonated forms of both histidine and AADH, models containing chemically plausible species were generated and analysed by the Miniquad-75 program. The best-fit models obtained for all the metal ion-AADH-histidine along with the statistical parameters are included in Tables 5.29 to 5.33.

Table 5.29 Best fit chemical models of Ca^{2+}-adipic acid dihydrazide-histidine ternary system in aqueous medium at 303.0 K and ionic strength, $I = 0.1$ mol dm^{-3}

Metal ion	Composition (M: L: X)	Species mlxh	Log β_{mlxh}	
Ca^{2+}	1:1:1	0101	03.67	U/NP =9.305X10^{-8}
		0102	06.25	χ^2= 99.62
		010-1	-12.03	R =0.0076
		0011	08.95	Skewness= -0.11
		0012	15.02	Kurtosis= 4.92
		0013	16.74	Np=146
		1113	24.40 (3)	pH=1.6-9.8
		1112	21.14 (4)	
		1111	15.58 (7)	
		1110	07.17 (7)	
		111-1	-2.98 (8)	
	1: 1: 2	0101	03.67	U/NP = 1.600X10^{-7}
		0102	06.25	χ^2= 125.87
		010-1	-12.03	R =0.0079
		0011	08.95	Skewness= -0.40
		0012	15.02	Kurtosis=4.16
		0013	16.74	Np=175
		1125	41.59 (4)	pH=1.7-8.9
		1124	38.50 (4)	
		1123	32.54 (7)	
		1122	26.51 (8)	
		1121	18.69 (7)	
		1120	09.73 (6)	
	2: 1: 1	0101	03.67	U/NP = 6.758X10^{-8}
		0102	06.25	χ^2= 96.04
		010-1	-12.03	R =0.0079
		0011	08.95	Skewness= -0.24
		0012	15.02	Kurtosis= 9.64
		0013	16.74	Np= 98
		2112	22.70 (3)	pH= 2.0-9.3
		2111	17.45 (6)	
		2110	9.06 (6)	
		211-1	-0.12 (7)	
	2:1 :2	0101	08.95	U/NP = 1.575X10^{-8}
		0102	15.02	χ^2= 98.57
		010-1	16.74	R =0.0059
		0011	08.97	Skewness= -0.51
		0012	15.03	Kurtosis= 5.67
		0013	16.76	Np=67
		2124	39.28 (5)	pH=2.4-9.5
		2123	34.08 (14)	
		2122	28.53 (8)	
		2121	20.36 (8)	
		2120	11.40 (8)	
		212-1	01.82 (8)	

*Figures in the parentheses are the standard deviations in the least significant digit.

Table 5.30 Best fit chemical models of Mg^{2+}- adipic acid dihydrazide-histidine ternary system in aqueous medium at 303.0 K and ionic strength, $I = 0.1$ mol dm^{-3}

Metal ion	Composition (M: L: X)	Species mlxh	Log β_{mlxh}	
Mg^{2+}	1:1:1	0101	03.67	U/NP = $3.126X10^{-8}$
		0102	06.25	χ^2= 95.71
		010-1	-12.03	R =0.0053
		0011	08.95	Skewness= -0.30
		0012	15.02	Kurtosis= 5.17
		0013	16.74	Np= 110
		1113	23.63 (5)	pH=1.8-9.6
		1112	20.56 (3)	
		1111	14.84 (7)	
		1110	06.30 (6)	
		111-1	-3.92 (7)	
	1: 1: 2	0101	03.67	U/NP = $4.558X10^{-8}$
		0102	06.25	χ^2= 107.21
		010-1	-12.03	R =0.0044
		0011	08.95	Skewness= -0.02
		0012	15.02	Kurtosis=4.62
		0013	16.74	Np=137
		1125	40.87 (4)	pH=1.9-9.2
		1124	37.34 (4)	
		1123	32.04 (7)	
		1122	26.14 (15)	
		1121	18.13 (9)	
		1120	09.17 (8)	
	2: 1: 1	0101	03.67	U/NP = $1.347X10^{-7}$
		0102	06.25	χ^2= 93.94
		010-1	-12.03	R =0.0119
		0011	08.95	Skewness= -0.53
		0012	15.02	Kurtosis=6.50
		0013	16.74	Np=101
		2112	21.97 (4)	pH=2.1-9.4
		2111	16.19 (7)	
		2110	08.21 (8)	
		211-1	-0.98 (8)	
	2:1 :2	0101	03.67	U/NP = $8.57X10^{-9}$
		0102	06.25	χ^2= 93.04
		010-1	-12.03	R =0.0043
		0011	08.95	Skewness= -0.99
		0012	15.02	Kurtosis=5.69
		0013	16.74	Np=77
		2124	39.17 (4)	pH=2.3-10.0
		2123	34.21 (7)	
		2122	28.17(5)	
		2121	20.14 (6)	
		2120	11.17 (5)	
		212-1	01.46 (4)	

*Figures in the parentheses are the standard deviations in the least significant digit.

Table 5.31 Best fit chemical models of Pb^{2+}-adipic acid dihydrazide-histidine ternary system in aqueous medium at 303.0 K and ionic strength, I = 0.1 mol dm^{-3}

Metal ion	Composition (M: L: X)	Species mlxh	Log β_{mlxh}	
Pb^{2+}	1:1:1	0101	03.67	U/NP = $4.497X10^{-8}$
		0102	06.25	χ^2= 84.54
		010-1	-12.03	R =0.0077
		0011	08.95	Skewness= -1.10
		0012	15.02	Kurtosis=6.14
		0013	16.74	Np=118
		1113	23.51 (5)	pH=2.0-6.5
		1112	20.73 (2)	
		1111	15.58 (4)	
		1110	09.77 (3)	
		111-1	03.07 (4)	
	1: 1: 2	0101	03.67	U/NP = $3.627X10^{-8}$
		0102	06.25	χ^2= 72.98
		010-1	-12.03	R =0.0043
		0011	08.95	Skewness= -0.82
		0012	15.02	Kurtosis=5.07
		0013	16.74	Np=122
		1125	41.51 (4)	pH=2.0-6.6
		1124	37.98 (2)	
		1123	33.09 (4)	
		1122	27.07 (11)	
		1121	21.14 (3)	
		1120	14.14 (9)	
	2: 1: 1	0101	03.67	U/NP = $9.500X10^{-8}$
		0102	06.25	χ^2= 54.15
		010-1	-12.03	R =0.0095
		0011	08.95	Skewness= -0.77
		0012	15.02	Kurtosis=4.04
		0013	16.74	Np=93
		2112	22.78 (3)	pH=2.0-5.4
		2111	17.36 (7)	
		2110	12.11 (4)	
	2:1 :2	0101	03.67	U/NP = $4.187X10^{-8}$
		0102	06.25	χ^2= 37.87
		010-1	-12.03	R =0.0091
		0011	08.95	Skewness= -0.87
		0012	15.02	Kurtosis=5.33
		0013	16.74	Np=92
		2124	39.84 (6)	pH=2.1-7.0
		2123	35.05 (9)	
		2121	23.90 (7)	
		2120	16.48 (6)	
		212-1	9.62 (11)	

*Figures in the parentheses are the standard deviations in the least significant digit.

Table 5.32 Best fit chemical models of Hg^{2+}-adipic acid dihydrazide-histidine ternary system in aqueous medium at 303.0 K and ionic strength, I = 0.1 mol dm^{-3}

Metal ion	Composition (M: L: X)	Species mlxh	Log β_{mlxh}	
Hg^{2+}	1:1:1	0101	03.67	U/NP = 1.100X10^{-7}
		0102	06.25	χ^2= 54.96
		010-1	-12.03	R =0.0091
		0011	08.95	Skewness= -0.30
		0012	15.02	Kurtosis=4.31
		0013	16.74	Np=170
		1113	24.08 (3)	pH=1.6-6.5
		1112	21.15 (3)	
		1111	15.65 (5)	
		1110	10.70 (6)	
		111-1	03.98 (5)	
	1: 1: 2	0101	03.67	U/NP = 2.571X10^{-8}
		0102	06.25	χ^2= 65.28
		010-1	-12.03	R =0.0034
		0011	08.95	Skewness= -0.11
		0012	15.02	Kurtosis= 4.10
		0013	16.74	Np=175
		1125	40.62 (2)	pH=1.8-6.4
		1124	37.71 (1)	
		1123	33.78 (2)	
		1121	22.87 (1)	
		1120	15.28 (2)	
	2: 1: 1	0101	03.67	U/NP = 3.888X10^{-7}
		0102	06.25	χ^2= 88.51
		010-1	-12.03	R =0.016
		0011	08.95	Skewness= -1.34
		0012	15.02	Kurtosis= 7.98
		0013	16.74	Np=188
		2112	23.26 (4)	pH=1.6-6.0
		2110	12.49 (5)	
		211-2	00.04 (4)	
	2:1 :2	0101	03.67	U/NP – 6.832X10^{-9}
		0102	06.25	χ^2= 94.61
		010-1	-12.03	R =0.0040
		0011	08.95	Skewness=-0.80
		0012	15.02	Kurtosis=6.41
		0013	16.74	Np=98
		2124	39.32 (3)	pH=2.2-6.6
		2123	35.18 (3)	
		2121	23.96 (4)	
		2120	17.54 (3)	
		212-1	10.56 (2)	

*Figures in the parentheses are the standard deviations in the least significant digit.

Table 5.33 Best fit chemical models of Cd^{2+}-adipic acid dihydrazide-histidine ternary system in aqueous medium at 303.0 K and ionic strength, $I = 0.1$ mol dm^{-3}

Metal ion	Composition (M: L: X)	Species mlxh	Log β_{mlxh}	
Cd^{2+}	1:1:1	0101	03.67	U/NP = $1.096X10^{-8}$
		0102	06.25	χ^2= 57.11
		010-1	-12.03	R =0.0029
		0011	08.95	Skewness= -0.73
		0012	15.02	Kurtosis= 4.85
		0013	16.74	Np= 90
		1113	22.59 (6)	pH=1.9-9.0
		1112	19.32 (3)	
		1111	14.68 (8)	
		1110	08.71 (8)	
		111-1	-0.86 (8)	
	1: 1: 2	0101	03.67	U/NP = $1.494X10^{-8}$
		0102	06.25	χ^2= 95.98
		010-1	-12.03	R =0.0024
		0011	08.95	Skewness= -0.57
		0012	15.02	Kurtosis=5.09
		0013	16.74	Np=162
		1125	39.16 (3)	pH=1.8-8.5
		1124	35.96 (4)	
		1123	31.88 (6)	
		1122	25.82 (8)	
		1121	20.00 (4)	
		1120	12.88 (3)	
	2: 1: 1	0101	03.67	U/NP = $6.355X10^{-8}$
		0102	06.25	χ^2= 90.59
		010-1	-12.03	R =0.0079
		0011	08.95	Skewness= -0.72
		0012	15.02	Kurtosis=5.13
		0013	16.74	Np=125
		2112	21.86 (3)	pH=2.0-7.5
		2111	16.45 (7)	
		2110	10.99 (3)	
		211-1	03.32 (6)	
	2:1 :2	0101	03.67	U/NP = $6.873X10^{-9}$
		0102	06.25	χ^2= 81.22
		010-1	-12.03	R =0.0032
		0011	08.95	Skewness= -0.15
		0012	15.02	Kurtosis=4.70
		0013	16.74	Np=105
		2124	38.32 (7)	pH=2.0-7.6
		2123	33.57 (6)	
		2121	22.23 (4)	
		2120	14.91 (2)	
		212-1	06.91 (5)	

*Figures in the parentheses are the standard deviations in the least significant digit.

In 1:1:1 (M:L:X) systems, the converged species contain $MLXH_3$, $MLXH_2$, MLXH, MLX and $MLXH_{-1}$ type of species. The step-wise deprotonation constants of $MLXH_3$ species for all the metal ions were calculated (Table 5.34) using the formation constants in the best-fit models. The $\log K^{1113}_{1112}$ values in column (a) of the table are close to the protonation constant of AADH. This indicates that in the $MLXH_3$ type of species AADH is in mono-protonated form. This clearly indicates that one of the hydrazide groups of AADH is involved in bonding while the other is protonated. Histidine in $MLXH_3$ and $MLXH_2$ type of species is present in XH_2 form and therefore may be acting as a monodentate bonding through only carboxylate oxygen.

Table 5.34: Step-wise deprotonation constants of $MLXH_3$ type of species of Metal ion-AADH-histidine systems

Metal ion	**(a)**	**(b)**	**(c)**
	$\log K^{1113}_{1112}$ $(= \log\beta_{1113} - \log\beta_{1112})$	$\log K^{1112}_{1111}$ $(= \log\beta_{1112} - \log\beta_{1111})$	$\log K^{1111}_{1110}$ $(= \log\beta_{1111} - \log\beta_{1110})$
Ca^{2+}	3.26	5.56	8.41
Mg^{2+}	3.07	5.72	8.54
Pb^{2+}	2.78	5.15	5.81
Hg^{2+}	2.93	5.50	4.95
Cd^{2+}	3.27	4.64	5.97

The successive deprotonation of $MLXH_2$ to form MLXH and MLX involve the deprotonation on complexation of either the protonated imidazole nitrogen or α-ammonium groups. The sequence of deprotonation or order of binding of metal ion to imidazole or α-amino nitrogen cannot be predicted in the case of Pb^{2+}, Hg^{2+} and Cd^{2+} as the step-wise deprotonation constants (Table 5.34 (b) and (c)) are very close to each other. The species distribution diagrams (Figures 5.99b, 5.103b and 5.107b) indicate coexisting equilibria of these species. The relatively high stabilities of histidine containing MLX type of species compared to those of glycine containing, indicates tridentate nature of histidine.

The best-fit models for 1:1:2 metal ion-AADH-histidine systems indicate the formation of MLX_2H_5, MLX_2H_4, MLX_2H_3, MLX_2H_2, MLX_2H and MLX_2 type of species in addition to other simple complexes. The differences between the formation constants of MLX_2H_5 and MLX_2H_4 type of species for various metal ion systems range from 2.91 to 3.53. This clearly indicates that one hydrazide group of AADH is involved in bonding as a bidentate while the other is protonated and non-bonding. The different protonated forms of the species are due to histidine, which is acting as a monodentate or bidentate or tridentate. The concentration distribution of various species in 1:1:2 composition against pH are shown in Figures 5.92b, 5.96b, 5.100b, 5.104b and 5.108b for Ca^{2+}, Mg^{2+}, Pb^{2+}, Hg^{2+} and Cd^{2+}systems respectively. The high stabilities of these species relative to ternary species of glycine indicate the tridentate behaviour of at least one of the two histidine molecules attached to the metal ion.

The best-fit models of 2:1:1 and 2:1:2 (M:L:X) compositions (Tables 5.29-5.33) indicate the formation of binuclear species in which AADH acts as a ditopic ligand accommodating two metal ions in different coordination pockets of the same ligand. In 2:1:1 compositions the species converged are M_2LXH_2, M_2LXH, M_2LX, M_2LXH_{-1} and M_2LXH_{-2}. The protonation and deprotonation equilibria are connected to histidine molecule bonded to one of the metal centres of the binuclear species. The formation of the species M_2LXH_{-1} and M_2LXH_{-2} may be due to the deprotonation of the enolic protons of AADH or hydroxylation of the species. In 2:1:2 composition the species converged are $M_2LX_2H_4$, $M_2LX_2H_3$, $M_2LX_2H_2$, M_2LX_2H, M_2LX_2 and $M_2LX_2H_{-1}$. Again the protonated species are due to the histidine molecules which can exist in various protonated forms in the bimetallic species depending on the pH of the solution and mode of bonding. The species distribution diagrams indicate coexisting equilibria of all these species.

5.3.3 AADH- L-Aspartic acid - metal ion systems:

The pH-metric titration curves of metal ion-AADH-Aspartic acid systems for all the metal ions are shown in Figures 5.111a to 5.130 a.

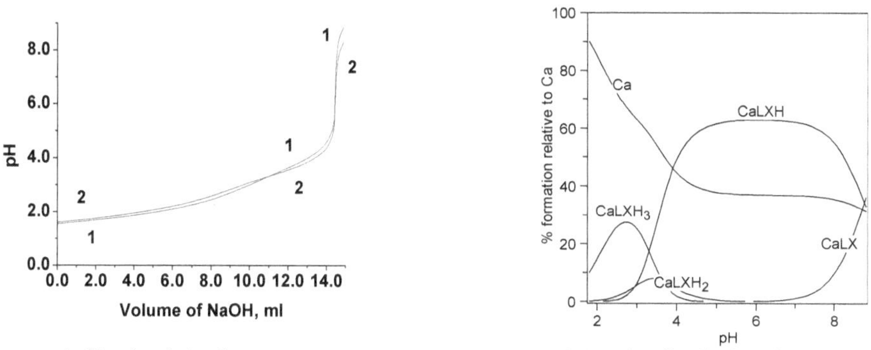

a. 1. Simulated titration curve
2. Experimental titration curve

b. Species distribution diagram

[AADH] = 0.01000 mol dm^{-3} [ASPARTIC ACID] = 0.0100 mol dm^{-3} [Ca^{2+}] = 0.00998 mol dm^{-3}
[HCl] = 0.04931 mol dm^{-3} [NaOH] = 0.2049 mol dm^{-3} TOTAL VOLUME= 50.0 cm^3
Temp.: 30.0 ±0.1^{0}C I = 0.1 mol dm^{-3}

Figure 5.111: Ca^{2+}-AADH-ASPARTICACID SYSTEM (1:1:1)

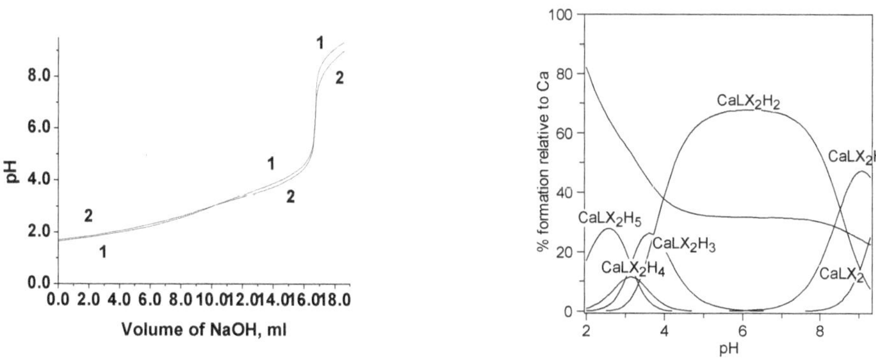

a. 1. Simulated titration curve
2. Experimental titration curve

b. Species distribution diagram

[AADH]= 0.01000 mol dm^{-3} [ASPARTIC ACID] = 0.0200 mol dm^{-3} [Ca^{2+}] = 0.00998 moldm^{-3}
[HCl] = 0.04851 mol dm^{-3} [NaOH] = 0.2049 mol dm^{-3} TOTAL VOLUME=50.0 cm^3
Temp.: 30.0 ±0.1^{0}C I = 0.1 mol dm^{-3}

Figure 5.112: Ca^{2+}-AADH-ASPARTICACID SYSTEM (1:1:2)

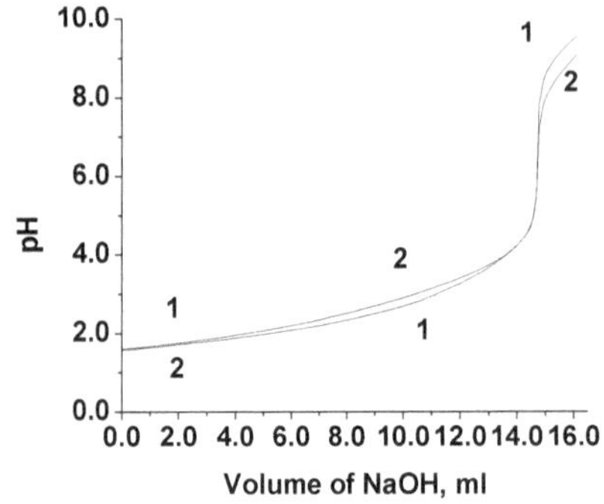

a. 1. Simulated titration curve
2. Experimental titration curve

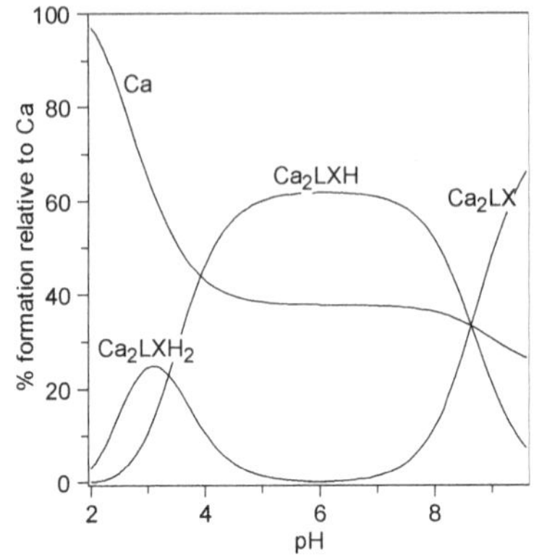

b. Species distribution diagram

[AADH]= 0.01000 mol dm^{-3} [ASPARTIC ACID] = 0.0100 mol dm^{-3} [Ca $^{2+}$] = 0.01996 mol dm^{-3}
[HCl] = 0.05043 mol dm^{-3} [NaOH] = 0.2049 mol dm^{-3} TOTAL VOLUME=50.0 cm^3
Temp.: 30.0 ±0.1^{0}C I = 0.1 mol dm^{-3}

Figure 5.113: Ca^{2+}-AADH- ASPARTICACID SYSTEM (2:1:1)

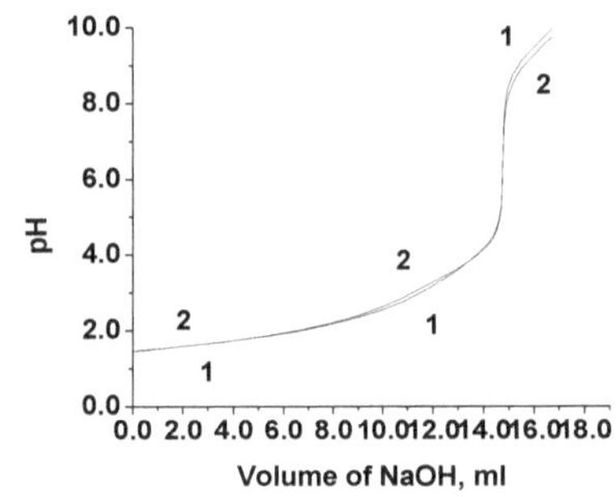

a. 1. Simulated titration curve
2. Experimental titration curve

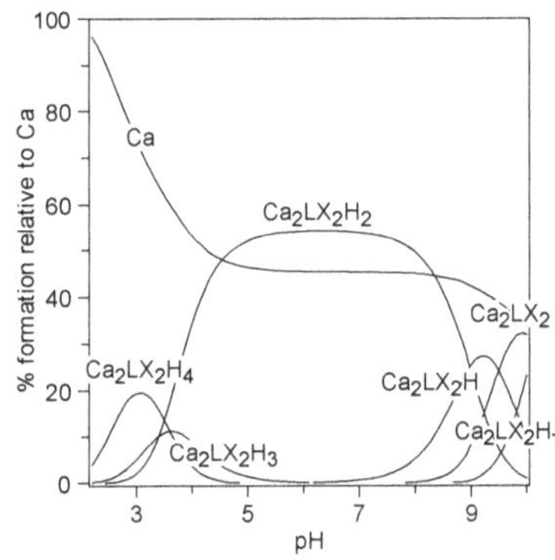

b. Species distribution diagram

[AADH] = 0.00500 mol dm^{-3} [ASPARTIC ACID] = 0.0100 mol dm^{-3} [Ca^{2+}] = 0.00998 mol dm^{-3}
[HCl] = 0.05052 mol dm^{-3} [NaOH] = 0.2049 mol dm^{-3} TOTAL VOLUME= 50.0 cm^3
Temp.: 30.0 ±0.1^{0}C I = 0.1 mol dm^{-3}

Figure 5.114: Ca^{2+}-AADH- ASPARTICACID SYSTEM (2:1:2)

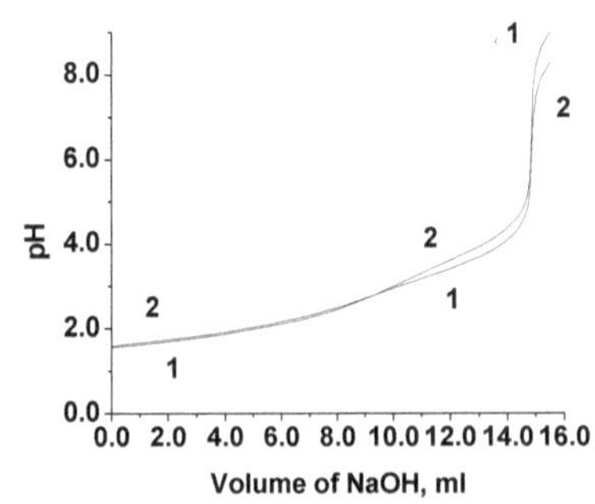

a. 1. Simulated titration curve
2. Experimental titration curve

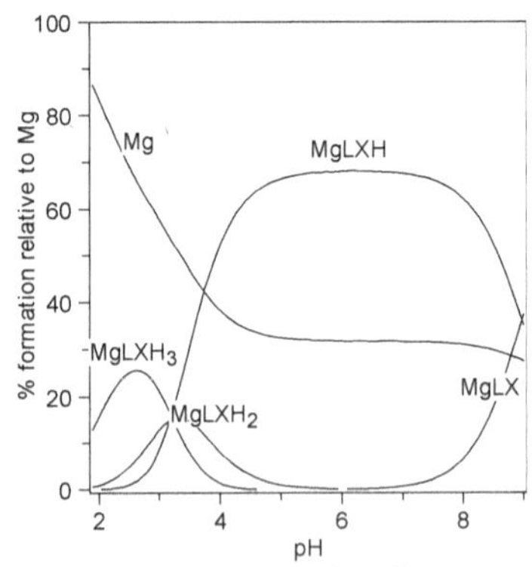

b. Species distribution diagram

[AADH]= 0.01000 mol dm^{-3} [ASPARTIC ACID] = 0.0100 mol dm^{-3} [Mg $^{2+}$] = 0.0100 mol dm^{-3}
[HCl] = 0.05005 mol dm^{-3} [NaOH] = 0.2020 mol dm^{-3} TOTAL VOLUME=50.0 cm^3
Temp.: 30.0 ±0.1^{0}C I = 0.1 mol dm^{-3}

Figure 5.115: Mg^{2+}-AADH- ASPARTICACID SYSTEM (1:1:1)

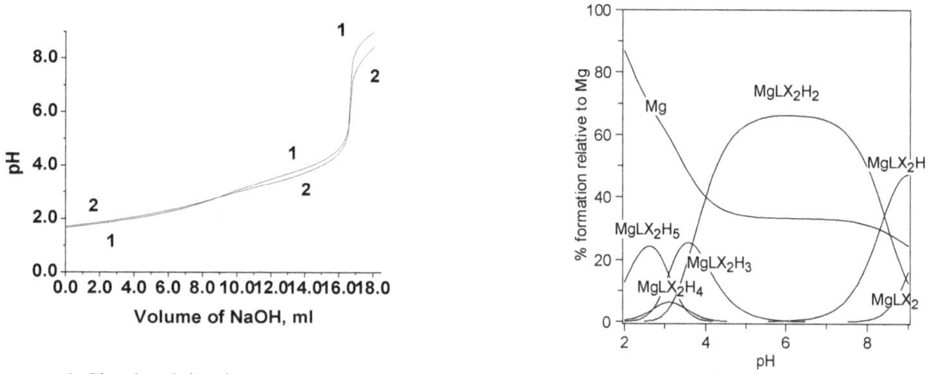

a. 1. Simulated titration curve
2. Experimental titration curve

b. Species distribution diagram

[AADH]= 0.01000 mol dm^{-3} [ASPARTIC ACID] = 0.0200 mol dm^{-3} [Mg^{2+}] = 0.0100 mol dm^{-3}
[HCl] = 0.04898 mol dm^{-3} [NaOH] = 0.2066 mol dm^{-3} TOTAL VOLUME=50.0 cm^3
Temp.: 30.0 ±0.1^{0}C I = 0.1 mol dm^{-3}

Figure 5.116: Mg^{2+}-AADH- ASPARTICACID SYSTEM (1:1:2)

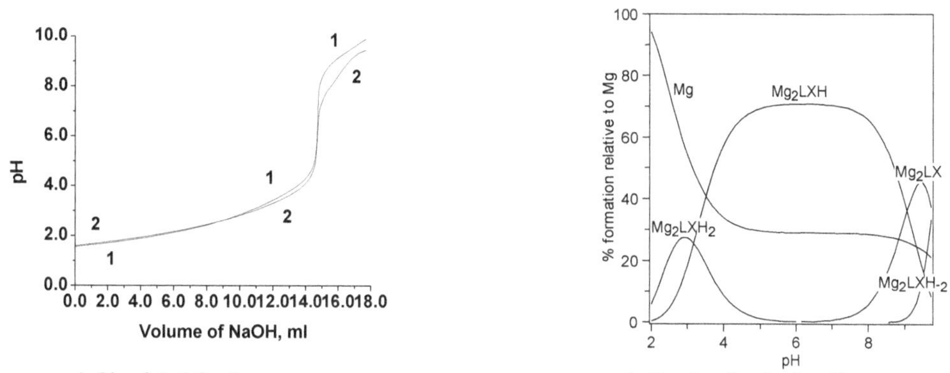

a. 1. Simulated titration curve
2. Experimental titration curve

b. Species distribution diagram

[AADH] = 0.01000 mol dm^{-3} [ASPARTIC ACID] = 0.0100 mol dm^{-3} [Mg^{2+}] = 0.01999 mol dm^{-3}
[HCl] = 0.05081 mol dm^{-3} [NaOH] = 0.2066 mol dm^{-3} TOTAL VOLUME= 50.0 cm^3
Temp.: 30.0 ±0.1^{0}C I = 0.1 mol dm^{-3}

Figure 5.117: Mg^{2+}-AADH- ASPARTICACID SYSTEM (2:1:1)

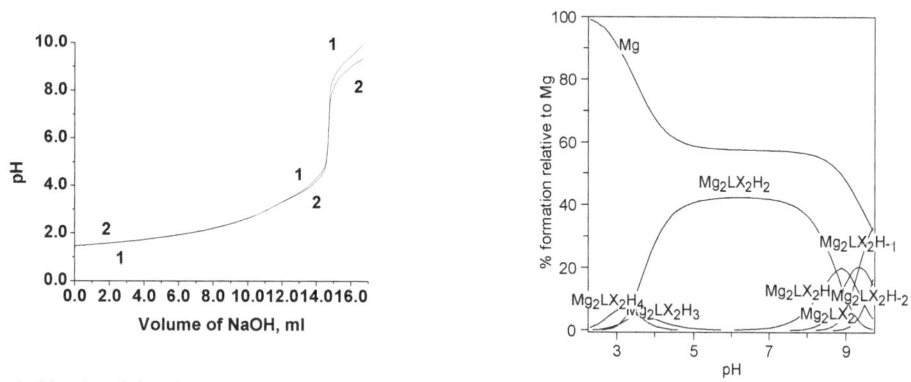

a. 1. Simulated titration curve
2. Experimental titration curve

b. Species distribution diagram

[AADH]= 0.00500 mol dm^{-3} [ASPARTIC ACID] = 0.0100 mol dm^{-3} [Mg^{2+}] = 0.0100 mol dm^{-3}
[HCl] = 0.05080 mol dm^{-3} [NaOH] = 0.2066 mol dm^{-3} TOTAL VOLUME=50.0 cm^3
Temp.: 30.0 ±0.1^{0}C I = 0.1 mol dm^{-3}

Figure 5.118: Mg^{2+}-AADH- ASPARTICACID SYSTEM (2:1:2)

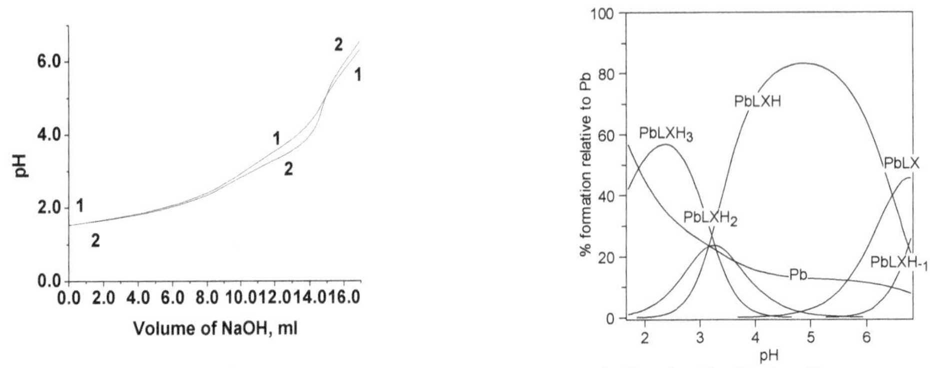

a. 1. Simulated titration curve
2. Experimental titration curve

b. Species distribution diagram

[AADH]= 0.01000 mol dm^{-3} [ASPARTIC ACID] = 0.0100 mol dm^{-3} [Pb^{2+}] = 0.00998 mol dm^{-3}
[HNO_3] = 0.05022 mol dm^{-3} [NaOH] = 0.2049 mol dm^{-3} TOTAL VOLUME=50.0 cm^3
Temp.: 30.0 ±0.1^{0}C I = 0.1 mol dm^{-3}

Figure 5.119: Pb^{2+}-AADH- ASPARTICACID SYSTEM (1:1:1)

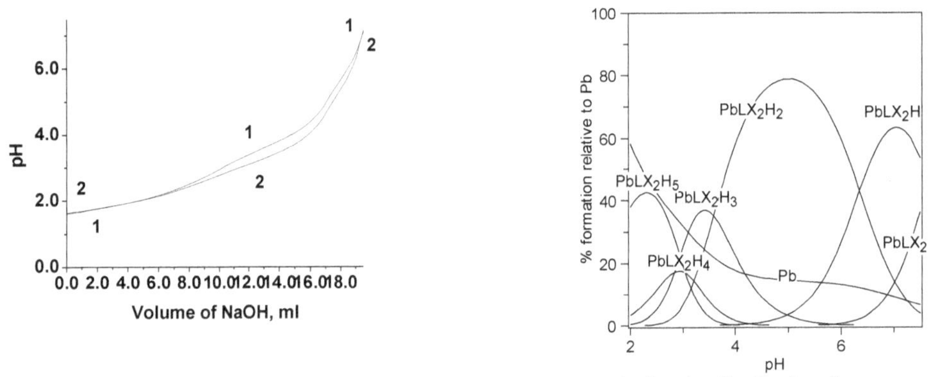

a. 1. Simulated titration curve
2. Experimental titration curve

b. Species distribution diagram

[AADH] = 0.01000 mol dm^{-3} [ASPARTIC ACID] = 0.0200 mol dm^{-3} [Pb^{2+}] = 0.00998 mol dm^{-3}
[HNO_3] = 0.04962 mol dm^{-3} [NaOH] = 0.2049 mol dm^{-3} TOTAL VOLUME= 50.0 cm^3
Temp.: 30.0 ±0.1^{0}C I = 0.1 mol dm^{-3}

Figure 5.120: Pb^{2+}-AADH ASPARTICACID SYSTEM (1:1:2)

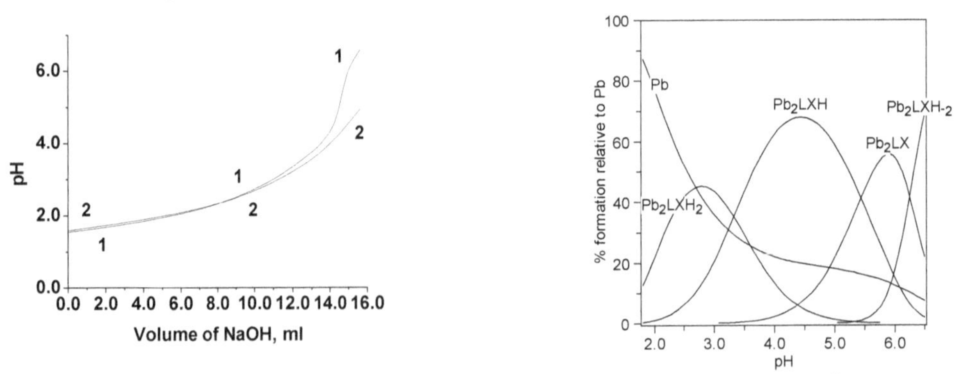

a. 1. Simulated titration curve
2. Experimental titration curve

b. Species distribution diagram

[AADH]= 0.01000 mol dm^{-3} [ASPARTIC ACID] = 0.0100 mol dm^{-3} [Pb^{2+}] = 0.01995 mol dm^{-3}
[HNO_3] = 0.04983 mol dm^{-3} [NaOH] = 0.2049 mol dm^{-3} TOTAL VOLUME=50.0 cm^3
Temp.: 30.0 ±0.1^{0}C I = 0.1 mol dm^{-3}

Figure 5.121: Pb^{2+}-AADH- ASPARTICACID SYSTEM (2:1:1)

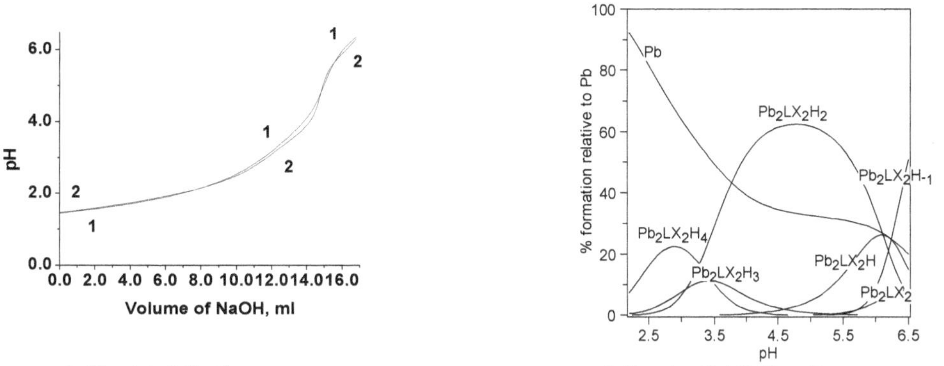

a. 1. Simulated titration curve
2. Experimental titration curve

b. Species distribution diagram

$[AADH] = 0.00500$ mol dm^{-3} [ASPARTIC ACID] = 0.0100 mol dm^{-3} $[Pb^{2+}] = 0.00998$ mol dm^{-3}
$[HNO_3] = 0.05082$ mol dm^{-3} [NaOH] = 0.2049 mol dm^{-3} TOTAL VOLUME=50.0 cm^3
Temp.: 30.0 ±0.1^{0}C $I = 0.1$ mol dm^{-3}

Figure 5.122: Pb^{2+}-AADH- ASPARTICACID SYSTEM (2:1:2)

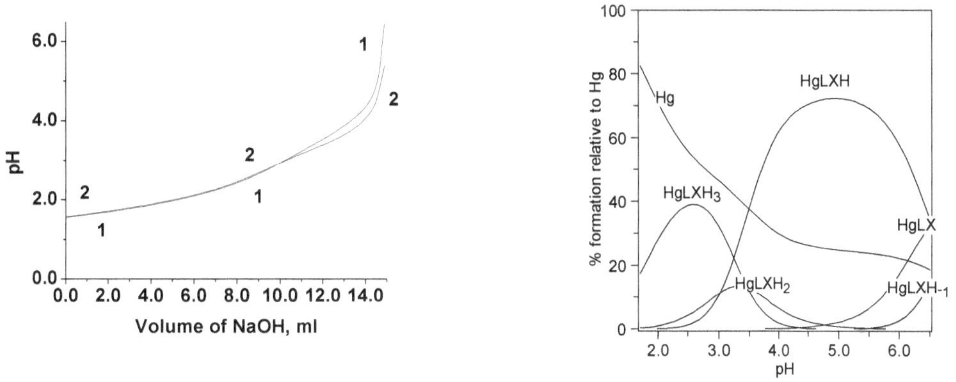

a. 1. Simulated titration curve
2. Experimental titration curve

b. Species distribution diagram

[AADH] = 0.01000 mol dm^{-3} [ASPARTIC ACID] = 0. 0100 mol dm^{-3} $[Hg^{2+}] = 0.00995$ mol dm^{-3}
[HCl] = 0.05044 mol dm^{-3} [NaOH] = 0.2049 mol dm^{-3} TOTAL VOLUME= 50.0 cm^3
Temp.: 30.0 ±0.1^{0}C $I = 0.1$ mol dm^{-3}

Figure 5.123: Hg^{2+}-AADH-ASPARTICACID SYSTEM (1:1:1)

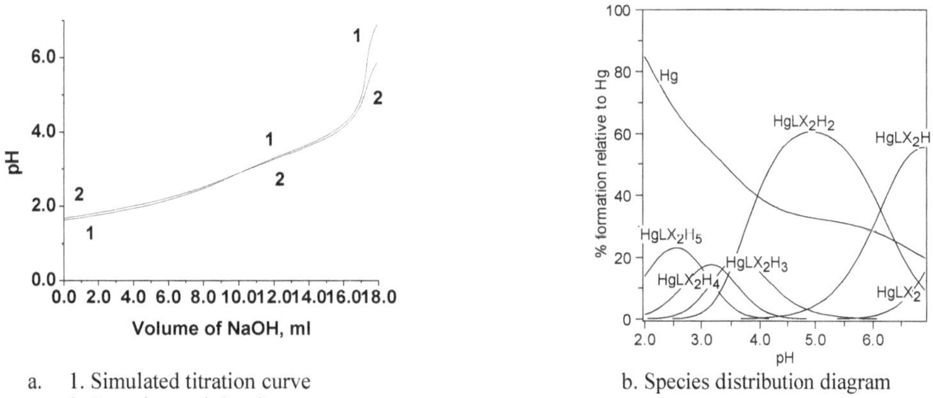

a. 1. Simulated titration curve
2. Experimental titration curve

b. Species distribution diagram

$[AADH] = 0.01000$ mol dm^{-3} [ASPARTIC ACID] = 0.0200 mol dm^{-3} $[Hg^{2+}] = 0.00995$moldm^{-3}
[HCl] = 0.05084 mol dm^{-3} [NaOH] = 0.2049 mol dm^{-3} TOTAL VOLUME=50.0 cm^3
Temp.: 30.0 ±0.1^{0}C $I = 0.1$ mol dm^{-3}

Figure 5.124: Hg^{2+}-AADH- ASPARTICACID SYSTEM (1:1:2)

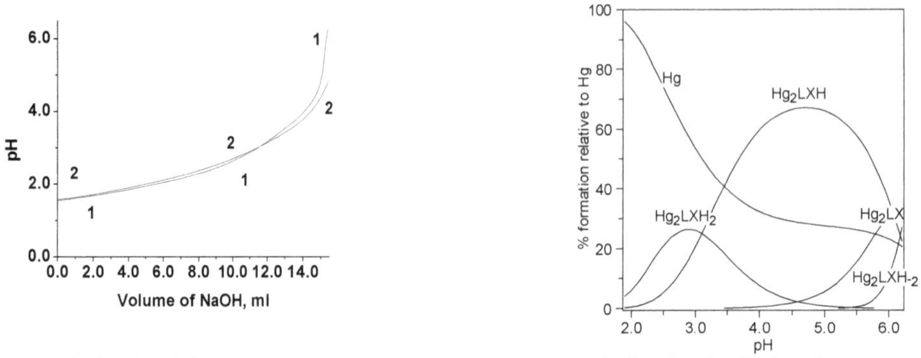

a. 1. Simulated titration curve
2. Experimental titration curve

b. Species distribution diagram

[AADH]= 0.01000 mol dm^{-3} [ASPARTIC ACID] = 0.0100 mol dm^{-3} [Hg^{2+}] = 0.01991 mol dm^{-3}
[HCl] = 0.05228 mol dm^{-3} [NaOH] = 0.2049 mol dm^{-3} TOTAL VOLUME=50.0 cm^3
Temp.: 30.0 ±0.1^{0}C I = 0.1 mol dm^{-3}

Figure 5.125: Hg^{2+}-AADH- ASPARTICACID SYSTEM (2:1:1)

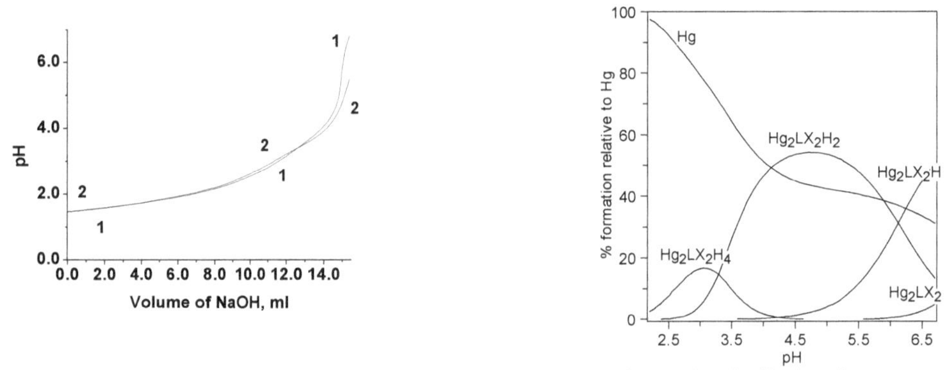

a. 1. Simulated titration curve
2. Experimental titration curve

b. Species distribution diagram

[AADH] = 0.00500 mol dm^{-3} [ASPARTIC ACID] = 0.0100 mol dm^{-3} [Hg^{2+}] = 0.00995 mol dm^{-3}
[HCl] = 0.05124 mol dm^{-3} [NaOH] = 0.2049 mol dm^{-3} TOTAL VOLUME= 50.0 cm^3
Temp.: 30.0 ±0.1^{0}C I = 0.1 mol dm^{-3}

Figure 5.126: Hg^{2+}-AADH-ASPARTICACID SYSTEM (2:1:2)

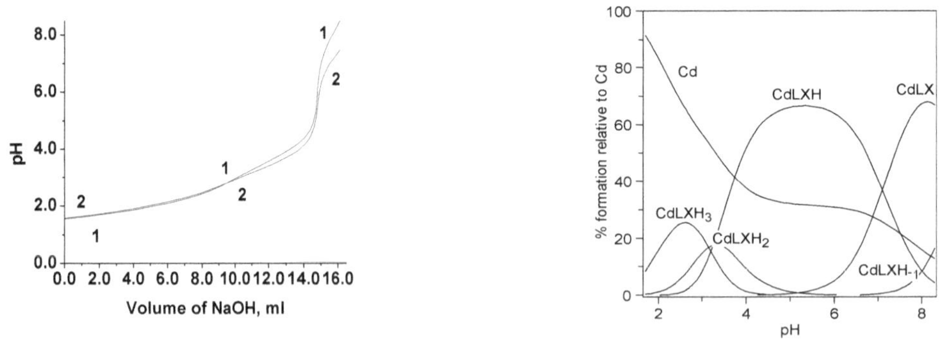

a. 1. Simulated titration curve
2. Experimental titration curve

b. Species distribution diagram

[AADH]= 0.01000 mol dm^{-3} [ASPARTIC ACID] = 0.0100 mol dm^{-3} [Cd^{2+}] = 0.00993 moldm^{-3}
[HCl] = 0.05103 mol dm^{-3} [NaOH] = 0.2066 mol dm^{-3} TOTAL VOLUME=50.0 cm^3
Temp.: 30.0 ±0.1^{0}C I = 0.1 mol dm^{-3}

Figure 5.127: Cd^{2+}-AADH- ASPARTICACID SYSTEM (1:1:1)

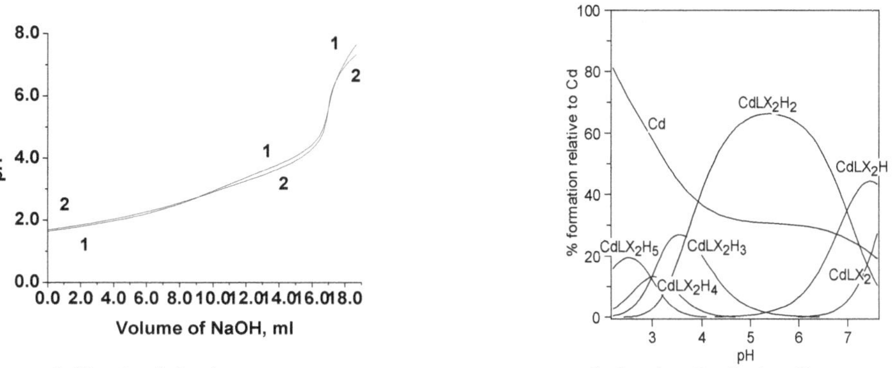

a. 1. Simulated titration curve
2. Experimental titration curve

b. Species distribution diagram

[AADH]= 0.01000 mol dm^{-3} [ASPARTIC ACID] = 0.0200 mol dm^{-3} [Cd^{2+}] = 0.00993 mol dm^{-3}
[HCl] = 0.05021 mol dm^{-3} [NaOH] = 0.2066 mol dm^{-3} TOTAL VOLUME=50.0 cm^3
Temp.: 30.0 ±0.1°C I = 0.1 mol dm^{-3}

Figure 5.128: Cd^{2+}-AADH- ASPARTICACID SYSTEM (1:1:2)

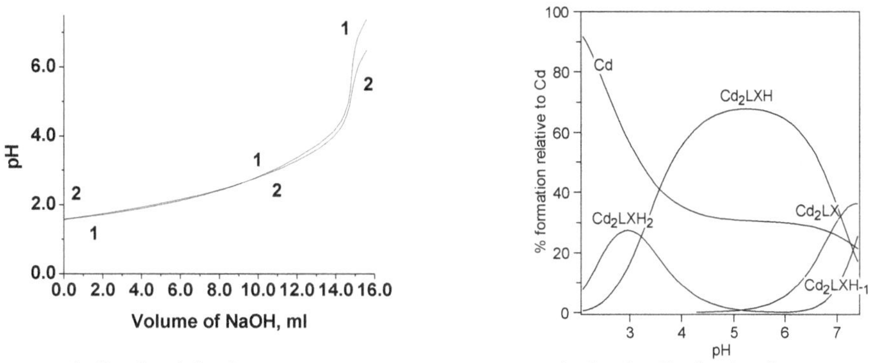

a. 1. Simulated titration curve
2. Experimental titration curve

b. Species distribution diagram

[AADH] = 0.01000 mol dm^{-3} [ASPARTIC ACID] = 0.0100 mol dm^{-3} [Cd^{2+}] = 0.01986 mol dm^{-3}
[HCl] = 0.05125 mol dm^{-3} [NaOH] = 0.2066 mol dm^{-3} TOTAL VOLUME= 50.0 cm^3
Temp.: 30.0 ±0.1°C I = 0.1 mol dm^{-3}

Figure 5.129: Cd^{2+}-AADH-ASPARTICACID SYSTEM (2:1:1)

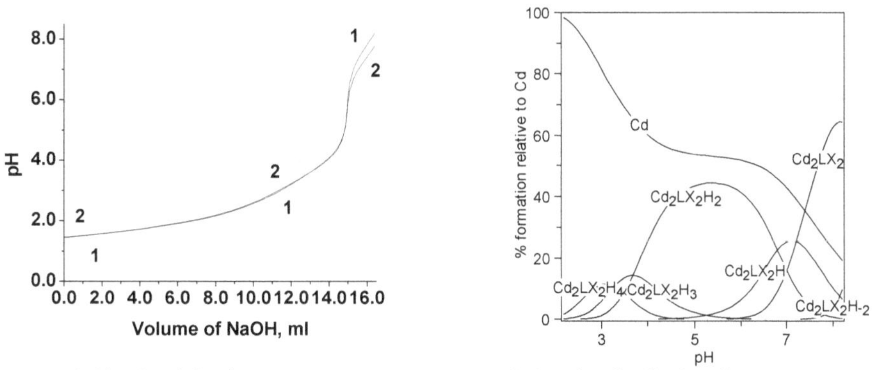

a. 1. Simulated titration curve
2. Experimental titration curve

b. Species distribution diagram

[AADH] = 0.00500 mol dm^{-3} [ASPARTIC ACID] = 0.0100 mol dm^{-3} [Cd^{2+}] = 0.00993 mol dm^{-3}
[HCl] = 0.05184 mol dm^{-3} [NaOH] = 0.2066 mol dm^{-3} TOTAL VOLUME=50.0 cm^3
Temp.: 30.0 ±0.1°C I = 0.1 mol dm^{-3}

Figure 5.130: Cd^{2+}-AADH- ASPARTICACID SYSTEM (2:1:2)

The experimental titration curves for all the metal ion systems of all compositions indicate deviations from simulation curves indicating the formation of ternary species. Aspartic acid (XH_2) possesses three bonding centres, the α-carboxylate, α-amino and side chain carboxylate groups. Depending on the pH of the solution aspartic acid exists in XH_3^+, XH_2, XH^- and X^{2-} forms. Therefore, in ternary systems containing AADH and a metal ion, aspartic acid may exhibit the formation a variety of protonated and deprotonated species depending on its mode of bonding to the metal ion and the pH of the solution. The results of analyses using the Miniquad-75 program are included in Tables 5.35 to 5.39.

The best-fit models obtained for 1:1:1 and 1:1:2 metal ion-AADH-Aspartic acid systems indicate the presence of only mono-nuclear species with different degrees of protonation. The species observed in 1:1:1 (M:L:X) solutions are $MLXH_3$, $MLXH_2$, MLXH, MLX and $MLXH_{-1}$. At double the concentration of aspartic acid i.e., in 1:1:2 composition systems, the species converged are MLX_2H_5, MLX_2H_4, MLX_2H_3, MLX_2H_2, MLX_2H and MLX_2. In both $MLXH_3$ ($M(LH)XH_2$) and MLX_2H_5 ($M(LH)(XH_2)_2$) type of species, one of the protons is associated with dihydrazide molecule and aspartic acid is present in XH_2 form. This can be ascertained from the step-wise deprotonation constants of the two species, which lie between 2.97 and 3.64 and are close to the protonation constant (3.67) of AADH.

In 2:1:1 (M:L:X) systems the species converged include bimetallic species, M_2LXH_2, M_2LXH, M_2LX, M_2LXH_{-1} and M_2LXH_{-2}. The best-fit models obtained for 2:1:2 systems contain $M_2LX_2H_4$, $M_2LX_2H_3$, $M_2LX_2H_2$, M_2LX_2H, M_2LX_2, $M_2LX_2H_{-1}$

and $M_2LX_2H_{-2}$ type of bimetallic species. The corresponding species distribution diagrams are included in Figures 5.114b to 5.130b.

Table 5.35 Best fit chemical models of Ca^{2+}-adipic acid dihydrazide-aspartic acid ternary system in aqueous medium at 303.0 K and ionic strength, $I = 0.1$ mol dm^{-3}

Metal ion	Composition (M: L: X)	Species mlxh	Log β_{mlxh}	
Ca^{2+}	1:1:1	0101	03.67	U/NP = $3.221X10^{-8}$
		0102	06.25	χ^2= 90.22
		010-1	-12.03	R =0.0050
		0011	09.58	Skewness= -1.25
		0012	13.30	Kurtosis=7.15
		0013	15.16	Np=117
		1113	21.28 (3)	pH=1.8-8.8
		1112	17.64 (9)	
		1111	14.68 (2)	
		1110	05.92 (4)	
	1: 1: 2	0101	03.67	U/NP = $9.993X10^{-9}$
		0102	06.25	χ^2= 82.50
		010-1	-12.03	R =0.0021
		0011	09.58	Skewness= -0.63
		0012	13.30	Kurtosis=5.61
		0013	15.16	Np=128
		1125	36.40 (2)	pH=2.0-9.3
		1124	33.12 (4)	
		1123	30.11 (2)	
		1122	26.39 (1)	
		1121	17.87 (2)	
		1120	08.31 (2)	
	2: 1: 1	0101	03.67	U/NP = $8.853X10^{-8}$
		0102	06.25	χ^2= 99.60
		010-1	-12.03	R =0.0089
		0011	09.58	Skewness= -1.65
		0012	13.30	Kurtosis=6.52
		0013	15.16	Np=101
		2112	19.82 (5)	pH=2.0-9.6
		2111	16.46 (3)	
		2110	07.82 (4)	
	2:1 :2	0101	03.67	U/NP = $3.988X10^{-9}$
		0102	06.25	χ^2= 88.53
		010-1	-12.03	R =0.0028
		0011	09.58	Skewness=-1.19
		0012	13.30	Kurtosis=6.40
		0013	15.16	Np=75
		2124	35.62 (4)	pH=2.2-10.0
		2123	32.02 (7)	
		2122	28.61 (3)	
		2121	19.63 (4)	
		2120	10.13 (3)	
		212-1	-0.0087 (6)	

*Figures in the parentheses are the standard deviations in the least significant digit.

Table 5.36. Best fit chemical models of Mg^{2+}-adipic acid dihydrazide-aspartic acid ternary system in aqueous medium at 303.0 K and ionic strength, $I = 0.1$ mol dm^{-3}

Metal ion	Composition (M: L: X)	Species mlxh	Log β_{mlxh}	
Mg^{2+}	1:1:1	0101	03.67	U/NP = 1.276X10^{-8}
		0102	06.25	χ^2= 85.79
		010-1	-12.03	R =0.0035
		0011	09.58	Skewness= -1.27
		0012	13.30	Kurtosis=7.35
		0013	15.16	Np=116
		1113	21.31 (3)	pH=1.9-8.9
		1112	18.09 (3)	
		1111	14.91 (1)	
		1110	05.94 (1)	
	1: 1: 2	0101	03.67	U/NP = 1.205X10^{-8}
		0102	06.25	χ^2= 91.04
		010-1	-12.03	R =0.0023
		0011	09.58	Skewness= -0.43
		0012	13.30	Kurtosis=6.88
		0013	15.16	Np=133
		1125	36.18 (2)	pH=2.0-9.0
		1124	32.70 (9)	
		1123	29.97 (2)	
		1122	26.30 (1)	
		1121	17.88 (2)	
		1120	08.41 (1)	
	2: 1: 1	0101	03.67	U/NP = 5.763X10^{-8}
		0102	06.25	χ^2= 84.80
		010-1	-12.03	R =0.0080
		0011	09.58	Skewness= 0.18
		0012	13.30	Kurtosis=6.31
		0013	15.16	Np=110
		2112	20.16 (5)	pH=2.1-9.7
		2111	16.98 (2)	
		2110	07.93 (3)	
		211-2	-11.52 (2)	
	2:1 :2	0101	03.67	U/NP = 3.413X10^{-9}
		0102	06.25	χ^2= 99.62
		010-1	-12.03	R =0.0028
		0011	09.58	Skewness= -1.40
		0012	13.30	Kurtosis=8.93
		0013	15.16	Np=74
		2124	34.68 (4)	pH=2.3-9.7
		2123	31.09 (6)	
		2122	27.99(3)	
		2121	19.25 (5)	
		2120	10.14 (4)	
		212-1	00.79 (7)	
		212-2	-9.21 (8)	

*Figures in the parentheses are the standard deviations in the least significant digit.

Table 5.37 Best fit chemical models of Pb^{2+} -adipic acid dihydrazide-aspartic acid ternary system in aqueous medium at 303.0 K and ionic strength, $I = 0.1$ mol dm^{-3}

Metal ion	Composition (M: L: X)	Species mlxh	Log β_{mlxh}	
Pb^{2+}	1:1:1	0101	03.67	U/NP = $6.782X10^{-8}$
		0102	06.25	χ^2= 91.26
		010-1	-12.03	R =0.0079
		0011	09.58	Skewness= -0.37
		0012	13.30	Kurtosis=5.39
		0013	15.16	Np=140
		1113	22.65 (3)	pH=1.7-6.8
		1112	19.38 (4)	
		1111	16.22 (3)	
		1110	09.76 (4)	
		111-1	02.71 (7)	
	1: 1: 2	0101	03.67	U/NP = $9.816X10^{-9}$
		0102	06.25	χ^2= 87.40
		010-1	-12.03	R =0.0022
		0011	09.58	Skewness= -0.27
		0012	13.30	Kurtosis=6.77
		0013	15.16	Np=127
		1125	37.35 (2)	pH=2.0-7.5
		1124	34.30 (2)	
		1123	31.46 (2)	
		1122	27.87 (1)	
		1121	21.52 (2)	
		1120	13.85 (4)	
	2: 1: 1	0101	03.67	U/NP = $4.178X10^{-7}$
		0102	06.25	χ^2= 47.29
		010-1	-12.03	R =0.020
		0011	09.58	Skewness= -1.02
		0012	13.30	Kurtosis=5.19
		0013	15.16	Np=158
		2112	21.09 (6)	pH=1.8-6.5
		2111	17.76 (6)	
		2110	12.32 (7)	
		211-2	-0.18 (6)	
	2:1 :2	0101	03.67	U/NP = $1.246X10^{-8}$
		0102	06.25	χ^2= 52.21
		010-1	-12.03	R =0.0052
		0011	09.58	Skewness= -0.95
		0012	13.30	Kurtosis=6.75
		0013	15.16	Np=76
		2124	35.99 (4)	pH=2.2-6.5
		2123	32.53 (6)	
		2122	29.45 (3)	
		2121	23.34 (8)	
		2120	16.57 (4)	
		212-1	10.87 (7)	

*Figures in the parentheses are the standard deviations in the least significant digit.

Table 5.38 Best fit chemical models of Hg^{2+} -adipic acid dihydrazide-aspartic acid ternary system in aqueous medium at 303.0 K and ionic strength, I = 0.1 mol dm^{-3}

Metal ion	Composition (M: L: X)	Species mlxh	Log β_{mlxh}	
Hg^{2+}	1:1:1	0101	03.67	U/NP = $5.907X10^{-8}$
		0102	06.25	χ^2= 84.06
		010-1	-12.03	R =0.0069
		0011	09.58	Skewness= -0.67
		0012	13.30	Kurtosis=6.64
		0013	15.16	Np=124
		1113	21.78 (3)	pH=1.7-6.5
		1112	18.32 (7)	
		1111	15.30 (2)	
		1110	08.77 (8)	
		111-1	01.94 (9)	
	1: 1: 2	0101	03.67	U/NP = $2.031X10^{-8}$
		0102	06.25	χ^2= 88.53
		010-1	-12.03	R =0.0031
		0011	09.58	Skewness= -0.27
		0012	13.30	Kurtosis=8.58
		0013	15.16	Np=144
		1125	36.26 (3)	pH=2.0-6.9
		1124	33.26 (4)	
		1123	29.91 (4)	
		1122	26.35 (2)	
		1121	20.22 (7)	
		1120	12.76 (1)	
	2: 1: 1	0101	03.67	U/NP = $1.271X10^{-7}$
		0102	06.25	χ^2= 45.70
		010-1	-12.03	R =0.010
		0011	09.58	Skewness= -1.10
		0012	13.30	Kurtosis=4.54
		0013	15.16	Np=106
		2112	20.18 (5)	pH=1.9-6.2
		2111	17.08 (3)	
		2110	11.01 (9)	
		211-2	-1.44 (4)	
	2:1 :2	0101	03.67	U/NP = $7.309X10^{-9}$
		0102	06.25	χ^2= 64.05
		010-1	-12.03	R =0.0035
		0011	09.58	Skewness=0.07
		0012	13.30	Kurtosis=8.31
		0013	15.16	Np=73
		2124	35.40 (6)	pH=2.2-6.7
		2122	28.82 (2)	
		2121	22.70 (4)	
		2120	14.99 (3)	

*Figures in the parentheses are the standard deviations in the least significant digit.

Table 5.39 Best fit chemical models of Cd^{2+} -adipic acid dihydrazide-aspartic acid ternary system in aqueous medium at 303.0 K and ionic strength, $I = 0.1$ mol dm^{-3}

Metal ion	Composition (M: L: X)	Species mlxh	Log β_{mlxh}	
Cd^{2+}	1:1:1	0101	03.67	U/NP = 3.201X10^{-8}
		0102	06.25	χ^2= 94.0
		010-1	-12.03	R =0.0051
		0011	09.58	Skewness= -1.24
		0012	13.30	Kurtosis=6.96
		0013	15.16	Np=122
		1113	21.33 (4)	pH=1.7-8.3
		1112	18.18 (4)	
		1111	14.92 (2)	
		1110	07.82 (3)	
		111-1	-01.09 (4)	
	1: 1: 2	0101	03.67	U/NP = 1.715X10^{-9}
		0102	06.25	χ^2= 74.13
		010-1	-12.03	R =0.00094
		0011	09.58	Skewness= -0.29
		0012	13.30	Kurtosis=5.36
		0013	15.16	Np=109
		1125	36.11 (1)	pH=2.2-7.6
		1124	33.14 (1)	
		1123	30.15 (1)	
		1122	26.46 (06)	
		1121	19.48 (1)	
		1120	11.68 (1)	
	2: 1: 1	0101	03.67	U/NP = 4.450X10^{-8}
		0102	06.25	χ^2= 86.80
		010-1	-12.03	R =0.0066
		0011	09.58	Skewness= -1.24
		0012	13.30	Kurtosis=5.71
		0013	15.16	Np=97
		2112	20.11 (3)	pH=2.1-7.4
		2111	16.89 (2)	
		2110	09.82 (7)	
		211-1	02.27 (11)	
	2:1 :2	0101	03.67	U/NP = 3.749X10^{-9}
		0102	06.25	χ^2= 91.01
		010-1	-12.03	R =0.0026
		0011	09.58	Skewness= -1.70
		0012	13.30	Kurtosis=8.04
		0013	15.16	Np=69
		2124	35.18(9)	pH=2.2-8.2
		2123	31.89 (10)	
		2122	28.21 (8)	
		2121	21.40 (8)	
		2120	14.19 (4)	
		212-2	-03.03 (5)	

*Figures in the parentheses are the standard deviations in the least significant digit.

In all the bimetallic species, adipic acid dihydrazide acts as bis bidentate ligand, bonding through carbonyl oxygen and terminal $-NH_2$ groups. In both M_2LXH_2 and $M_2LX_2H_4$ type of species aspartic acid acts as a monodentate bonding through carboxylate oxygen atoms. The nature of bonding in other species cannot be predicted as their equilibria of formation overlap. Formation of $M_2LX_2H_{-1}$ and $M_2LX_2H_{-2}$ type of species may be due to the loss of enolic protons of dihydrazide or hydroxylation of the corresponding species.

In the case of mixed ligand species, the relative stabilities among different metal ion complexes is in general difficult to explain as more than one ligand with different reactive centres and different bonding modes are present in the coordination sphere of a metal ion. However, as dihydrazide (SADH/ AADH) is common in all the ternary systems studied, the relative stabilities among different metal ion species may be explained amino acid –wise, based on the characteristics of the metal ion and the bonding centres.

Relative stabilities among different metal ion complexes of M^{2+}- SADH/ AADH- **Glycine** systems:

The formation constants of all the species for all the compositions of M^{2+}- SADH/ AADH- Glycine systems were found to be in the order $Ca^{2+} > Mg^{2+}$ and $Pb^{2+} > Hg^{2+} > Cd^{2+}$. Several factors affect the relative stabilities of the mixed ligand complexes. Dihydrazide is a hard neutral oxygen and borderline amino nitrogen donor while glycine is a hard carboxylate oxygen and amino nitrogen donor. Both Ca^{2+} and Mg^{2+} are hard acids and prefer to bond with hard bases. The ionic size of Ca^{2+} (100 pm) is greater than that of Mg^{2+} (72 pm). Neutral oxygen donors prefer to bond with large metal ion and five membered chelate ring formations are preferred to that of six membered rings. Mg^{2+}, due to its smaller size and high charge density is heavily hydrated and requires relatively more energy to break solvent bonds prior to the chelation. Small ions prefer the formation of six membered chelate rings. Both dihydrazide and glycine form five membered chelate rings as bidentates. But due to its high charge density Mg^{2+} forms relatively strong electrostatic bond with carboxylate of the glycine. All these factors lead to small enhancement in the stabilities of Ca^{2+} species over to those of Mg^{2+}. On the other hand Pb^{2+} belongs to border line while Hg^{2+} and Cd^{2+} are soft acids. Both dihydrazide and glycine provide hard oxygen and borderline nitrogen donors. Borderline acids accept both hard and soft donors. Therefore, the higher stability of Pb^{2+} species over to those of Hg^{2+} and Cd^{2+} is explicable on the basis of HSAB theory. Large metal ions form sterically stable species with the five membered chelate forming ligands. Both dihydrazide and glycine form five membered chelate rings as bidentates. The ionic sizes are in the order, Pb^{2+} (118 pm) > Hg^{2+} (102 pm) > Cd^{2+} (95 pm) which is also the order of the stabilities.

Relative stabilities among different metal ion complexes of M^{2+}- SADH/ AADH-**Histidine** systems:

The formation constants of the species of M^{2+}-DHZ-histidine systems were found to be in the order, Ca^{2+}> $Mg^{2+}$and Hg^{2+}> Pb^{2+} > Cd^{2+}. Histidine possesses three metal binding centres viz. carboxylate oxygen, the imidazole imido nitrogen and the α-amino nitrogen. It is an ambidentate ligand and has an ability to coordinate histamine-like, imidazole propionic acid-like and glycine-like modes. It may act as a monodentate or bidentate or tri-dentate through one or two or all of the reactive centres. The explanation for the greater stabilities of the Ca^{2+}complexes relative to that of Mg^{2+} is similar to that of the glycine ternary systems. Both $Hg^{2+}$and Cd^{2+} are soft acids, while Pb^{2+} is of borderline category. Soft acids bond well with neutral nitrogen donors compared to hard oxygen donors. Dihydrazide and histidine in combination provide three neutral nitrogen donors, which strongly bind Hg^{2+} relative to borderline Pb^{2+}. The lower stabilities of Pb^{2+} species may also be due to the lower coordination number exhibited by the metal ion. Both oxygen and nitrogen donors bond well with the large Hg^{2+} ion (ionic radius 102 pm) compared to Cd^{2+}. This explains the relative stability order, $Pb^{2+} < Hg^{2+} > Cd^{2+}$ for M^{2+}-DHZ-histidine mixed ligand complexes.

Relative stabilities among different metal ion complexes of M^{2+}- SADH/ AADH- **Aspartic acid** systems:

The formation constants of the species of the M^{2+}-SADH/ AADH- Aspartic acid systems were found to be in the order, $Mg^{2+} \geq Ca^{2+}$and $Pb^{2+} > Hg^{2+} > Cd^{2+}$. Aspartic acid provides two hard carboxylate ($-COO^-$) oxygens and one borderline category amino nitrogen for bonding. The higher charge density of smaller Mg^{2+} ion relative to that of Ca^{2+} leads to the formation of stronger electrostatic bonds with negative carboxylates. Hg^{2+} and Cd^{2+} are soft Lewis acids and therefore may have weak interaction with hard carboxylate oxygens of aspartic acid relative to the border line Pb^{2+}.

5.4 REFERENCES:

1. A. S. Mildvan and M. Cohn, "Kinetic and Magnetic Resonance studies of the pyruvate kinase reaction II: Complexes of enzyme, metal and substrates", *J. Biol. Chem.*, 241 (5) (1966) pp 1178–1193.
2. E. Bouwman, W. L. Driessen, and J. Reedijk, "Model systems for type I copper proteins: Structures of copper coordination compounds with thioether and azole-containing ligands", *Coord. Chem. Rev.*, 104 (1) (1990) pp 143–172.
3. Jayanthi Narayanan, Alejandro Solano-Peralta, Vıctor Manuel Ugalde-Saldivar, Roberto Escudero, Herbert Hopfl and Martha Elena Sosa-Torres, "New dinuclear cobalt (II) octaaza macrocyclic complexes with high oxidation redox potentials : Their crystal structure and unusual magnetic properties", *Inorg. Chim. Acta.*, 361 (2008) pp 2747–2758.
4. Adrian-Mihail Stadler and Jack Harrowfield, "Bis-acyl-/aroyl-hydrazones as multidentate ligands" *Inorg. Chim. Acta.*, 362 (2009) pp 4298–4314.
5. T. A. Kaden, "Dinuclear metal complexes of bis-macocycles", *Coord. Chem. Rev.*, 190 (1999) pp 371–389.
6. E. K. Vanden Beuken, B.L Feringa, "Bimetallic Catalysis by Late Transition Metal Complexes", *Tetrahedron,* 54 (1998) pp 12985-13011.
7. H. B. Jonasse and V. V. Ramanujam, "Binuclear Complexes as Catalysts", *J. Phys. Chem.,* 63 (3) (1959) pp 411-415.
8. C.J.McKenzie and R. Robson, "High turnover catalysis at bimetallic sites of the hydrationof nitriles to carboxamides co-catalysed by acid. Highly specified hydration of acrylonitrile to acrylamide", *J. Chem. Soc., Chem. Commun.,* (1988) pp 112-114.
9. H. Steinhagen, and G. Helmchen, "Asymmetric Two-Center Catalysis: Learning from Nature", *Angew. Chem. Int. Ed.,* 35 (1996) pp 2339-2342.
10. D. Ya. Fridman, O. P. Svanidze, N. V. Dolgashova and P.V. Gogorishvili, " Mixed compounds of cobalt, nickel, and zinc with amino acids and carboxylic acid hydrazides", *Zh. Neorg. Khim.,* 19 (12) (1974) pp 3304-3310.
11. A. E. Shvelashvili, N. E. Zedelashvili and L. Sh. Charelishvili, "Study of IR absorption spectra of mixed coordination compounds of cobalt(II) of CoLXY.nH_2O type", *Zh. Neorg. Khim.,* 29 (4) (1984) pp 1030-1032.

12. K. M. Gobedzhishvili,.; S. Sh. Nagebashvili and G. Ts..Dolidze, "Mixed coordination compounds of some transition metals with dihydrazides and pseudohalide groups", *Nauchnye Trudy - Gruzinskii Politekhnicheskii Institut im. V. I. Lenina,* 11 (1980) pp 12-16.

13. Dunkana Negussa Kenie, A. Satyanarayana and P. Shyamala, "Chemical Speciation Study of Ternary Complexes of Cu(II) with Succinic Acid Dihydrazide and Some Amino Acids in Aqueous Solution", *Chemistry and Materials Research,* 7 (2015) pp 93-102.

14. M. B. Halli, Vijayalaxmi. B. Patil, R. B. Sumathi and K. Mallikarjun, "Synthesis, characterization and biological activity of mixed ligand metal(II) complexes derived from benzofuran-2-carbohydrazide schiff base and malonyldihydrazide", *Der Pharma Chemica,* 4 (6) (2012) pp 2360-2367.

15. N. B. Zhorzholiani, A. E. Shvelashvili, A.N. Sobolev and I. O. Vardosanidze, "Synthesis and X-ray diffraction study of a mixed acido ligand $Mn(DM)_2(ClO_4)(NO_3)H_2O$ type coordinated compound", *Soobshch. Akad. Nauk Gruzinsk SSR,* 123 (3) (1986) pp 541- 544.

16. N. B. Zhorzholiani, A. E. Shvelashvili, A.N. Sobolev , T. O. Vardosanidze and V. I. Sokol, "Synthesis and X-ray analysis of the manganese coordination compounds $Mn(DS).nX_2.mH_2O$ (DS = succinic acid dihydrazide)", *Izv. Akad. Nauk Gruz. SSR, Ser. Khim.*, 13 (2) (1987) pp 102-110.

17. K. K. Narang and Meena Kumari Singh, "Synthesis, characterization, IR spectra and other studies of some mercury(II) chloride, nitrate and thiocyanate complexes of organic acid hydrazides and hydrazones", *Synth. React. Inorg. Met –Org. Chem.*, 17 (1) (1987) pp 57-78.

18. R. Sambasiva Rao, A. Satyanarayana and P.V. Krishna Rao, "A computer program for the simulation of pH-metric data", *Proc. Summ. Simul. Conf.,* (1984) pp 563.

19. P. Gans, A. Sabatini and A. Vacca, "An improved computer program for the computation of formation constants from potentiometric data", *Inorg. Chim. Acta.*, 18 (1976) pp 237-239.

CHAPTER- 6

RELATIVE STABILITY OF TERNARY SPECIES COMPARED TO BINARY

When a metal ion is in contact with more than one ligand, there is a possibility of formation of mixed-ligand complexes in addition to simple mono-nuclear and mono-ligand complexes. In biological fluids that contain several metal ions as well as complexing species, the formation of mixed ligand complexes is generally expected and it is very commonly assumed as the basis for most of the bio-chemical reactions occurring within the coordination sphere of metal ions. A review of literature on mixed ligand complexes in solution revealed that very often these complexes are more stable than the corresponding binary complexes. The relative stability of the ternary complexes compared to binary complexes can be quantitatively expressed in a number of ways; but it can be conveniently characterized by two most common procedures[1, 2].

Procedure 1:

This method of characterization is based on the calculation of the formation constant of the mixed-ligand complex using the dis- proportionate equilibrium,

$$a'.\ ML_a + b'.\ MX_b + c'.\ MY_c + \text{------} \rightleftarrows m'.\ ML_l X_x Y_y \qquad \text{.......}\ (6.1)$$

and the equation,

$$\log \beta_{mix}^{cal} = \frac{l}{a}.\log \beta_{ML_a} + \frac{x}{b}.\log \beta_{MX_b} + \frac{y}{c}.\log \beta_{MY_c} + \ldots\ldots \qquad \ldots\ldots\ (6.2)$$

where, *l*, x, y, ---- are the number of different kinds of ligands attached to the metal ion in the mixed complex and a, b, c --- are the number of ligands in the corresponding simple complexes with the same metal to ligand ratio and a', b', c', m' are coefficients. The calculated value of the formation constant is then compared with the experimentally determined one by calculating $\Delta \log\beta$ also known as log X given by,

$$\log X = \Delta \log\beta = \log\beta_{mix}^{exp} - \log\beta_{mix}^{cal} \qquad \text{.................. (6.3)}$$

The sign and the magnitude of $\Delta \log\beta$ provide a measure of the enhanced or diminished stability of the mixed ligand complex. Considering the formation of a ternary species MAB, in which a metal ion is simultaneously bonded to ligands "A" and "B", the disproportionate constant, X is defined by,

$$MA_2 + MB_2 \overset{X}{\rightleftarrows} 2MAB \qquad \text{........................ (6.4)}$$

i.e X is given by, $$X = \frac{[MAB]^2}{[MA_2].[MB_2]} \qquad \text{........................(6.5)}$$

Substituting the values of, $[MA_2] = \beta_{MA_2}^{M}.[M].[A]^2$ and $[MB_2] = \beta_{MB_2}^{M}.[M].[B]^2$ in

the above equation, then, $$X = \frac{[MAB]^2}{\beta_{MA_2}^{M}.\beta_{MB_2}^{M}.[M]^2.[A]^2.[B]^2} = \frac{(\beta_{MAB}^{M})^2}{\beta_{MA_2}^{M}.\beta_{MB_2}^{M}}$$ and

$$\log X = 2.\log\beta_{MAB}^{M} \quad (\log\beta_{MA_2}^{M} + \log\beta_{MB_2}^{M}) \text{ .... (6.6)}$$

The value of log X can be calculated if the values of $\log\beta_{MA_2}^{M}$ and $\log\beta_{MB_2}^{M}$ are known. Statistically, the value expected [3] for X is 4 i.e. log X = 0.6. Therefore, if we consider only statistical parameters the formation of MAB should be up to 50%, while binary parent complexes are to be formed to an extent of 25% each.

Procedure 2 :

The second approach relates the stability of the mixed-ligand complex to the binary complexes according to the equations 6.7 to 6.12.

$$M + A \rightleftharpoons MA \qquad K^{M}_{MA} = \frac{[MA]}{[M].[A]} \quad \ldots\ldots\ldots\ldots\ldots\ldots(6.7)$$

$$M + B \rightleftharpoons MB \qquad K^{M}_{MB} = \frac{[MB]}{[M].[B]} \quad \ldots\ldots\ldots\ldots\ldots\ldots(6.8)$$

$$MA + B \rightleftharpoons MAB \qquad K^{MA}_{MAB} = \frac{[MAB]}{[MA].[B]} \quad \ldots\ldots\ldots\ldots\ldots\ldots(6.9)$$

$$MB + A \rightleftharpoons MAB \qquad K^{MA}_{MAB} = \frac{[MAB]}{[MB].[A]} \quad \ldots\ldots\ldots\ldots\ldots\ldots(6.10)$$

$$\Delta \log K = K^{MA}_{MAB} - K^{M}_{MB} \quad \ldots\ldots\ldots\ldots\ldots\ldots (6.11)$$

$$= K^{MB}_{MAB} - K^{M}_{MA} \quad \ldots\ldots\ldots\ldots\ldots\ldots(6.12)$$

or

$$\Delta \log K = \log \beta_{MAB} - (\log \beta_{MA} + \log \beta_{MB}) \ldots\ldots\ldots\ldots (6.13)$$

or generalizing for any mixed-ligand complex MA_aB_b

$$\Delta \log K = \log \beta_{MA_aB_b} - (\log \beta_{MA_a} + \log \beta_{MB_b}) \ldots\ldots\ldots\ldots (6.14)$$

The value of Δ log K should be negative as the ligand A or B coordinates more easily to the free metal ion in comparison with the simple complex. This is normally observed in simple binary systems where log K_1, is always greater than log K_2. On the contrary, in the case of mixed ligand complexes Δ log K is *+ve* for certain combinations of ligands. This parameter has been considered to be a better measure of the tendency towards mixed-ligand complex formation than severely criticized log X[4, 5].

In Δ log K formulation, the stabilities of reactions between ligand "B" and aqua metal ion and ligand "B" and MA are compared. Since more coordination positions are available on the aquo metal ion in comparison with 'MA' the first reaction is statistically more probable compared to the second one, leading to *–ve* values of Δ log K. In the case where A and B are bidentate ligands, there are, twelve edges of the regular octahedron available for the first entering ligand, but only five for the second i.e., the statistical factor is 5/12 and accordingly[6], $\Delta\log K_{oh} = -0.4$. For a planar complex the statistical factor is 1/4 i.e. $\Delta \log K_{pl} = -0.6$. For distorted octahedron like Cu^{2+} (aq) the value of $\Delta\log K$ lies[7] between -0.9 to -0.3. If the experimental value is greater than the statistical value, the formation of mixed ligand complex is favoured. However, lower values compared to statistical, do not preclude the formation of ternary species. Electrostatic factors cancel in $\Delta\log K$ formulation, if any one of the ligands possesses zero charge. In the log X expression electrostatic factors cancel only when the charges of the two ligands are equal.

6.1 FACTORS AFFECTING THE STABILITY OF MIXED LIGAND COMPLEXES:

In ternary complexes, a metal ion is bound to two different ligands at different stages and there are numerous factors which contribute towards the stability of the mixed ligand complexes [1, 8]. The most important factor is the intra-molecular or inter-ligand interaction between the non-coordinating groups of the two ligands[9, 10]. However, the factors influencing the formation and stability of mixed ligand complexes may be classified into (1) statistical effect (2) ligand effect and (3) interaction between ligands.

6.1.1 Statistical Effect

Consider a mixed ligand system containing a metal ion, M and two ligands L and X. When equal concentrations of M, L and X are present, the following equilibria may exist in solution

$$\left.\begin{array}{l} M + L \rightleftharpoons ML \\ ML + X \rightleftharpoons MLX \\ ML + L \rightleftharpoons ML_2 \\ M + 2L \rightleftharpoons ML_2 \\ M + L + X \rightleftharpoons MLX \\ M + X \rightleftharpoons MX \\ MX + L \rightleftharpoons MXL \\ MX + X \rightleftharpoons MX_2 \\ M + 2X \rightleftharpoons MX_2 \end{array}\right\} \quad \ldots\ldots\ldots\ldots (6.15)$$

The ternary complexes MLX and MXL are identical for labile species in solution. According to Watters et.al.[11, 12] the formation of a mixed complex MLX is statistically more favoured than the formation of ML_2 or MX_2, when equal concentrations of M, L and X are present in solution. The statistical probability was calculated on the basis of, "the number of ways the mixed ligand complexes can be formed relative to the simple complexes". The treatment of Bjerrum[13] for calculating the statistical factor for the formation of ML_n complexes is also applicable to mixed ligand complexes.

V.S Sharma and J.Schubert[14] generalized this concept of expressing the statistical probability (which is proportional to the number of ways a mixed ligand complex $ML_lX_xY_y$.......... can be formed) by means of the equation.

$$S = \frac{n!}{l!.x!.y!} \quad \ldots\ldots\ldots\ldots (6.16)$$

Where `n' is the total number of ligands attached to the metal ion in the mixed complex. The statistical factor 'S' which is independent of the nature of the ligand explains to some extent the stabilization of the mixed ligand complex relative to binary complexes. However, it cannot explain the high *+ve* values of Δlog K observed in some cases, for example in the mixed ligand complexes of amines and amino acids or carboxylic acids.

6.1.2 Ligand Effect

The effect of a ligand may be further classified into (i) electrostatic, (ii) basicity, (iii) "Hard" and "Soft" acid -base nature, (iv) Chelate effect and (v) Redox potential.

(i) Electrostatic effect:

According to Kida[15], the electrostatic effect is of decisive importance in the formation of mixed-ligand complexes. He developed a simple theory to explain the higher stability of mixed-ligand complexes compared to their parent binary complexes. The formation energy of the mixed-ligand complex may be obtained by assuming +e', -e' and -e" as the electric point charges of the metal ion, M and ligands L and X respectively, where the metal ion M is at the centre of a square plane formed by the ligand L and X, the latter being at a distance 'r' from the metal ion M, in a mixed-ligand complex ML_2X_2. The formation energy of the mixed-ligand complex, therefore, exceeds the mean value of the formation energies of the corresponding parent binary complexes ML_4 and MX_4 by

$$\sqrt{2/r}\ .\ (e' - e'')^2 \geq 0. \qquad \text{..... (6.17)}$$

In other words, the formation of mixed-ligand complex from its parent complexes takes place readily.

This treatment of Kida was a very approximate one and Marcus and Eliazer[16] considerably improved it by introducing polarization effects in the calculation. This was done by means of point dipoles assumed at the centre of the sphere. The electrostatic energies E_{MLX} for mixed-ligand complex and E_{ML} and E_{MX} for simple parent complexes were calculated. The energy terms account for ion-ion, ion-dipole and dipole-dipole interactions. Comparison of these energies gives an expression, $\Delta E = E_{mixed} - E_{average\ binary}$, which contains both stabilizing and destabilizing terms. Thus, the important feature of this treatment is that this model can explain the increase and decrease of the stability of the mixed-ligand complex in comparison with the statistically calculated value. However, this method has only a limited applicability due to the complexity of charge distribution in amino acid molecules leading to the lack of correct values of polarizability.

Studies of the mixed-ligand complexes in non-aqueous solvents are sparse. Beck and Gaizer[17] suggested that the stabilization of the mixed-ligand complexes in aqueous medium is due to the dipole-dipole interaction of the asymmetric polar mixed complex with the polar solvent molecules. In non-polar solvents the mixed-ligand complexes are less stable due to the lack of such interactions[18]. The neutral mixed–ligand complex formed by the neutralization of charges on the central metal ion and ligands is more stable than the one whose formation does not involve neutralization of charges. The formation of such neutral mixed-ligand complexes is entropy favoured by the release of the oriented solvent molecules. The stabilization of mixed complexes is also affected by the variations in ionic strength[19]. If the binary and ternary complexes carry equal charges, the stability of the ternary complexes increases with ionic strength[20].

(ii) Basicity of the ligands:

The fact that "the stability of a binary complex increases[21] with the basicity of the ligand", may also be extended to the formation of mixed ligand complexes. The linear dependence of $\Delta \log K$ or $\Delta \log \beta$ on ligand basicity is markedly affected by the presence of aromatic rings due to the influence of π-electron density on the ligand basicity[22].

(iii) Hard and Soft Acid-Base nature:

Pearson[23] classified metal ions and ligands as hard and soft acids and bases depending upon the bonding behaviour. "Hard" acids are associated with small size and high oxidation state, whereas "soft" acid behaviour is characterized by a low or zero oxidation state, large size and easily distorted outer electrons. "Hard" bases are difficultly polarisable and form bonds with high ionic character, whereas soft bases are easily polarisable and tend to form largely covalent bonds. Hard acids prefer to associate with hard bases and soft acids prefer to associate with soft bases. The application of the HSAB concept to the formation of mixed ligand complexes was well demonstrated by Greisser and Sigel [7].

(iv) Chelate effect:

The kinetic and thermodynamic stabilities of the chelates are always higher than those of non-chelate complexes. The chelate effect is found to be essentially an entropy effect from a gain in translational entropy, associated with ring closure. The stability of the chelates decreases monotonically as the ring size increases, the maximum stability being with five membered chelates in the ease of transition metal ions. It is also found that the stability of chelates increases with an increase in the number of chelate rings. Sigel[6] observed that in the case of ternary complexes, species containing five and six membered rings are more favourable than those containing rings of equal size. He also demonstrated that the mixed-ligand complexes containing two six membered rings are somewhat more stable than the corresponding complexes with two five membered rings.

(v) Redox potential:

The overall stability of the mixed-ligand complex was found to increase with "increase in the redox potential of the central ion and decrease in the potential of the ligand" if the metal-ligand bond is predominantly covalent in character. If the bond is ionic, the stability increases with an increase in the ligand potential[24].

6.1.3 Interaction between ligands

The presence of different ligands in the same coordination sphere of metal ions, may lead to a direct interaction which results in higher stabilities of mixed-ligand complexes, such interactions may bring about a distinct structural quality of complexes. The selectivity and specificity achieved by nature in biological systems is certainly due to the formation of such higher order mixed-ligand complexes. The interaction may result in the Schiff base formation within the coordination sphere of the metal ion. This leads to a ligand of higher denticity and therefore higher stability[25-27].

Hydrogen bond formation is also possible between the ligands, especially in biological systems where ligands like proteins and nucleic acids participate in complex formation[28-30]. This type of bonding stabilizes the ternary complex relative to that of binary systems.

6.2. RELATIVE STABILITIES OF TERNARY SPECIES OF METAL ION-DIHYDRAZIDE-AMINO ACID SYSTEMS:

6.2.1 Relative stabilities of MLX type of ternary species compared to binary:

The values of Δlog K for the formation of MLX type of species are incorporated in Table 6.1 for all the systems under investigation. The Δlog K values are either very nearer to or on the *+ve* side of the statistically expected values, indicating the tendency towards the formation of MLX species. As both the ligands may be charged depending on the pH, the electrostatic factors should also be considered, to understand the relative stabilities of the ternary species. If we consider the two equations,

$$\begin{aligned} M^{2+} + X^- &\rightleftarrows MX^+ \quad \text{and} \\ ML^{2+} + X^- &\rightleftarrows MLX^+ \end{aligned} \qquad \ldots\ldots\ldots\ldots\ldots\ldots(6.18)$$

where, L is dihydrazide and X^- is the deprotonated form of the amino acid, as one of the ligands i.e. dihydrazide (L) is neutral, electrostatic factors are same in both the cases and therefore cancel each other in Δlog K. On the other hand, as the charges of the two ligands are not equal the electrostatic factors may have some contribution in log X formulation. The negative Δlog K values however do not preclude the formation of ternary species.

Table 6.1: ΔLog K values for the formation of **MLX** type of species

M^{2+}- SADH-GLYCINE SYSTEMS

Metal ion	$\log\beta_{1100}$ (A)	$\log\beta_{1010}$ (B)	C = A+B	$\log\beta_{1110}$ (D)	Δlog K = D-C
Ca^{2+}	3.31	1.96	5.27	5.79	0.52
Mg^{2+}	2.64	2.19	4.83	5.32	0.49
Pb^{2+}	3.39	5.16	8.55	8.62	0.07
Hg^{2+}	3.19	4.42	7.61	8.22	0.61
Cd^{2+}	2.80	4.21	7.01	6.69	-0.32

M^{2+}-SADH-HISTIDINE SYSTEMS

Metal ion	$\log\beta_{1100}$ (A)	$\log\beta_{1010}$ (B)	C = A+B	$\log\beta_{1110}$ (D)	Δlog K = D-C
Ca^{2+}	3.31	2.92	6.23	6.32	0.09
Mg^{2+}	2.64	3.07	5.71	5.89	0.18
Pb^{2+}	3.39	5.90	9.29	9.34	0.05
Hg^{2+}	3.19	6.60	9.79	10.12	0.33
Cd^{2+}	2.80	5.38	8.18	8.24	0.06

M^{2+}- SADH-ASPARTIC ACID SYSTEMS

Metal ion	$\log\beta_{1100}$ (A)	$\log\beta_{1010}$ (B)	C = A+B	$\log\beta_{1110}$ (D)	Δlog K = D-C
Ca^{2+}	3.31	2.16	5.47	5.74	0.27
Mg^{2+}	2.64	2.48	5.12	5.87	0.75
Pb^{2+}	3.39	5.83	9.22	9.63	0.41
Hg^{2+}	3.19	4.87	8.06	8.71	0.65
Cd^{2+}	2.80	4.34	7.14	7.34	0.20

M^{2+}-AADH-GLYCINE SYSTEMS

Metal ion	$\log\beta_{1100}$ (A)	$\log\beta_{1010}$ (B)	C = A+B	$\log\beta_{1110}$ (D)	Δlog K = D-C
Ca^{2+}	3.59	1.96	5.55	5.92	0.37
Mg^{2+}	2.90	2.19	5.09	5.76	0.67
Pb^{2+}	3.62	5.16	8.78	9.17	0.39
Hg^{2+}	3.28	4.42	7.70	8.54	0.84
Cd^{2+}	3.02	4.21	7.23	7.64	0.41

M^{2+}-AADH- HISTIDINE SYSTEMS

Metal ion	$\log\beta_{1100}$ (A)	$\log\beta_{1010}$ (B)	C = A+B	$\log\beta_{1110}$ (D)	$\Delta\log K$ = D-C
Ca^{2+}	3.59	2.92	6.51	7.17	0.66
Mg^{2+}	2.90	3.07	5.97	6.30	0.33
Pb^{2+}	3.62	5.90	9.52	9.77	0.25
Hg^{2+}	3.28	6.60	9.88	10.70	0.82
Cd^{2+}	3.02	5.38	8.40	8.71	0.31

M^{2+}-AADH-ASPARTIC ACID SYSTEMS

Metal ion	$\log\beta_{1100}$ (A)	$\log\beta_{1010}$ (B)	C = A+B	$\log\beta_{1110}$ (D)	$\Delta\log K$ = D-C
Ca^{2+}	3.59	2.16	5.75	5.92	0.17
Mg^{2+}	2.90	2.48	5.38	5.94	0.56
Pb^{2+}	3.62	5.83	9.45	9.76	0.31
Hg^{2+}	3.28	4.87	8.15	8.77	0.62
Cd^{2+}	3.02	4.34	7.36	7.82	0.46

6.2.2 Relative stabilities of M_2LX type of ternary species compared to binary:

In the case of M_2LX type of ternary species, the primary ligand dihydrazide acts as a neutral ditopic ligand forming a binuclear complex with the two metal ions. The secondary ligand may coordinate with any of the two metal ions already bonded to dihydrazide.

$$M^{2+} + X^- \rightleftarrows MX^+ \quad \text{and}$$
$$M^{2+}L\,M^{2+} + X^- \rightleftarrows M^{2+}L\,MX^+ \quad \ldots\ldots\ldots\ldots (6.19)$$

X = Glycine or Histidine

$$M^{2+} + X^{2-} \rightleftarrows MX \quad \text{and}$$
$$M^{2+}L\,M^{2+} + X^{2-} \rightleftarrows M^{2+}L\,MX \quad \ldots\ldots\ldots\ldots (6.20)$$

X= Aspartic acid as a tridentate

The secondary ligand is a mono negative (glycine or histidine) or binegative (aspartic acid) ion. As one of the ligands i.e. dihydrazide (L) is neutral, electrostatic factors are same in both the equilibria and therefore cancel each other in $\Delta\log K$.

Table 6.2: ΔLog K values for the formation of $\mathbf{M_2LX}$ species

M^{2+} -SADH-GLYCINE SYSTEMS

Metal ion	$Log\beta_{2100}$ (A)	$log\beta_{1010}$ (B)	C = A+B	$log\beta_{2110}$ (D)	Δlog K = D-C
Ca^{2+}	5.16	1.96	7.12	7.83	0.71
Mg^{2+}	4.60	2.19	6.79	7.08	0.29
Pb^{2+}	5.57	5.16	10.73	10.95	0.22
Hg^{2+}	5.27	4.42	9.69	10.48	0.79
Cd^{2+}	4.54	4.21	8.75	8.99	0.24

M^{2+}-SADH-HISTIDINE SYSTEMS

Metal ion	$Log\beta_{2100}$ (A)	$log\beta_{1010}$ (B)	C = A+B	$log\beta_{2110}$ (D)	Δlog K = D-C
Ca^{2+}	5.16	2.92	8.08	8.42	0.34
Mg^{2+}	4.60	3.07	7.67	7.67	0.00
Pb^{2+}	5.57	5.90	11.47	11.57	0.10
Hg^{2+}	5.27	6.60	11.87	12.56	0.69
Cd^{2+}	4.54	5.38	9.92	10.35	0.43

M^{2+}-SADH-ASPARTIC ACID SYSTEMS

Metal ion	$Log\beta_{2100}$ (A)	$log\beta_{1010}$ (B)	C = A+B	$log\beta_{2110}$ (D)	Δlog K = D-C
Ca^{2+}	5.16	2.16	7.32	7.45	0.13
Mg^{2+}	4.60	2.48	7.08	7.84	0.76
Pb^{2+}	5.57	5.83	11.4	12.25	0.85
Hg^{2+}	5.27	4.87	10.14	10.99	0.85
Cd^{2+}	4.54	4.34	8.88	9.42	0.54

M^{2+}-AADH-GLYCINE SYSTEMS

Metal ion	$Log\beta_{2100}$ (A)	$log\beta_{1010}$ (B)	C = A+B	$log\beta_{2110}$ (D)	Δlog K = D-C
Ca^{2+}	5.52	1.96	7.48	7.85	0.37
Mg^{2+}	4.93	2.19	7.12	7.53	0.41
Pb^{2+}	5.84	5.16	11.00	11.37	0.37
Hg^{2+}	5.38	4.42	9.80	10.57	0.77
Cd^{2+}	4.88	4.21	9.09	9.11	0.02

M^{2+}-AADH-HISTIDINE SYSTEMS

Metal ion	$Log\beta_{2100}$ (A)	$log\beta_{1010}$ (B)	C = A+B	$log\beta_{2110}$ (D)	Δlog K = D-C
Ca^{2+}	5.52	2.92	8.44	9.06	0.62
Mg^{2+}	4.93	3.07	8.00	8.21	0.21
Pb^{2+}	5.84	5.90	11.74	12.11	0.37
Hg^{2+}	5.38	6.60	11.98	12.49	0.51
Cd^{2+}	4.88	5.38	10.26	10.99	0.73

M^{2+}-AADH-ASPARTIC ACID SYSTEMS

Metal ion	$Log\beta_{2100}$ (A)	$log\beta_{1010}$ (B)	C = A+B	$log\beta_{2110}$ (D)	Δlog K = D-C
Ca^{2+}	5.52	2.16	7.68	7.82	0.14
Mg^{2+}	4.93	2.48	7.41	7.93	0.52
Pb^{2+}	5.84	5.83	11.67	12.32	0.65
Hg^{2+}	5.38	4.87	10.25	11.01	0.76
Cd^{2+}	4.88	4.34	9.22	9.82	0.60

6.2.3 Relative stabilities of M_2LX_2 type of ternary species compared to binary:

In M_2LX_2 type of species two amino acid molecules are added to binuclear complex of the dihydrazide. As the two molecules are added to metal ions in different coordination pockets of the ligand, there is no steric hindrance to the bonding of amino acid molecules. The complex formation equilibria for Δlog K formulation may be represented as,

$2M^{2+} + 2X^{-} \rightleftarrows 2MX^{+}$ and

$M^{2+}L\,M^{2+} + 2X^{-} \rightleftarrows {}^{+}XMLMX^{+}$ .... (6.21)

X= Glycine or Histidine

$2M^{2+} + 2X^{2-} \rightleftarrows 2MX$ and

$M^{2+}L\,M^{2+} + 2X^{2-} \rightleftarrows XMLMX$ .... (6.22)

X= Aspartic acid as a tridentate

As secondary ligands are added to a species in which primary ligand is neutral, electrostatic factors do not affect the Δlog K values. In most of the cases, Δlog K values for the formation of M_2LX_2 species are on the positive side of the statistically (Table 6.3) expected values indicating the preference for the formation of ternary species.

Table 6.3: Δlog K values for the formation of $\mathbf{M_2LX_2}$ species

METAL ION -SADH-GLYCINE SYSTEMS

Metal ion	Logβ_{2100} (A)	2 x logβ_{1010} (B)	C = A+B	logβ_{2120} (D)	ΔlogK= D-C
Ca^{2+}	5.16	3.92	9.08	9.72	0.64
Mg^{2+}	4.60	4.38	8.98	9.32	0.34
Pb^{2+}	5.57	10.32	15.89	16.32	0.43
Hg^{2+}	5.27	8.84	14.11	14.54	0.43
Cd^{2+}	4.54	8.42	12.96	13.23	0.27

METAL ION -SADH-HISTIDINE SYSTEMS

Metal ion	Logβ_{2100} (A)	2 x logβ_{1010} (B)	C = A+B	logβ_{2120} (D)	ΔlogK= D-C
Ca^{2+}	5.16	5.84	11.00	11.22	0.22
Mg^{2+}	4.60	6.14	10.74	11.11	0.37
Pb^{2+}	5.57	11.80	17.37	16.27	-1.10
Hg^{2+}	5.27	13.20	18.47	17.61	-0.86
Cd^{2+}	4.54	10.76	15.30	14.80	-0.50

METAL ION -SADH-ASPARTIC ACID SYSTEMS

Metal ion	Logβ_{2100} (A)	2 x logβ_{1010} (B)	C = A+B	logβ_{2120} (D)	ΔlogK= D-C
Ca^{2+}	5.16	4.32	9.48	10.11	0.63
Mg^{2+}	4.60	4.96	9.56	9.76	0.20
Pb^{2+}	5.57	11.66	17.23	15.67	-1.56
Hg^{2+}	5.27	9.74	15.01	14.54	-0.47
Cd^{2+}	4.54	8.68	13.22	13.75	0.53

METAL ION -AADH-GLYCINE SYSTEMS

Metal ion	Logβ_{2100} (A)	2 x logβ_{1010} (B)	C = A+B	logβ_{2120} (D)	Δlog K= D-C
Ca^{2+}	5.52	3.92	9.44	10.18	0.74
Mg^{2+}	4.93	4.38	9.31	9.93	0.62
Pb^{2+}	5.84	10.32	16.16	16.43	0.27
Hg^{2+}	5.38	8.84	14.22	14.72	0.50
Cd^{2+}	4.88	8.42	13.30	13.29	-0.01

METAL ION -AADH-HISTIDINE SYSTEMS

Metal ion	Logβ_{2100} (A)	2 x logβ_{1010} (B)	C = A+B	logβ_{2120} (D)	ΔlogK= D-C
Ca^{2+}	5.52	5.84	11.36	11.40	0.04
Mg^{2+}	4.93	6.14	11.07	11.17	0.10
Pb^{2+}	5.84	11.80	17.64	16.48	-1.16
Hg^{2+}	5.38	13.20	18.58	17.54	-1.04
Cd^{2+}	4.88	10.76	15.64	14.91	-0.73

METAL ION -AADH-ASPARTIC ACID SYSTEMS

Metal ion	$Log\beta_{2100}$ (A)	2 x $log\beta_{1010}$ (B)	C = A+B	$log\beta_{2120}$ (D)	ΔlogK= D-C
Ca^{2+}	5.52	4.32	9.84	10.13	0.29
Mg^{2+}	4.93	4.96	9.89	10.14	0.25
Pb^{2+}	5.84	11.66	17.50	16.57	-0.93
Hg^{2+}	5.38	9.74	15.12	14.99	-0.13
Cd^{2+}	4.88	8.68	13.56	14.19	0.63

6.2.4 Relative stabilities of MLX_2 type of ternary species compared to binary:

In the case of MLX_2 type of species metal ion is attached to one of the coordination pockets of dihydrazide. Two molecules of amino acid in anionic form interact with the metal ion to form the ternary species. The relevant equilibria may be represented as,

$$M^{2+} + 2X^- \rightleftarrows MX_2 \quad \text{and}$$
$$ML^{2+} + 2X^- \rightleftarrows MLX_2 \quad \ldots\ldots\ldots\ldots\ldots (6.23)$$

As dihydrazide is in neutral form the addition of amino acid does not affect the ΔlogK formulation. The entropy factors due to charge neutralization favour both the equilibria to the same extent. The Δ logK, values in most of the cases, are on the positive side of the statistically allowed values indicating the stabilization of ternary species.

Table 6.4: Δlog K values for the formation of MLX_2 type of species

METAL ION -SADH-GLYCINE SYSTEMS

Metal ion	$log\beta_{1100}$ (A)	$log\beta_{1020}$ (B)	C = A+B	$log\beta_{1120}$ (D)	Δlog K= D-C
Ca^{2+}	3.31	3.90	7.21	7.93	0.72
Mg^{2+}	2.64	4.33	6.97	7.83	0.86
Pb^{2+}	3.39	9.97	13.36	13.86	0.50
Hg^{2+}	3.19	8.45	11.64	12.31	0.67
Cd^{2+}	2.80	8.00	10.80	10.47	-0.33

METAL ION -SADH-HISTIDINE SYSTEMS

Metal ion	$\log\beta_{1100}$ (A)	$\log\beta_{1020}$ (B)	C = A+B	$\log\beta_{1120}$ (D)	Δlog K= D-C
Ca^{2+}	3.31	5.79	9.10	9.89	0.79
Mg^{2+}	2.64	5.89	8.53	9.21	0.68
Pb^{2+}	3.39	10.10	13.49	13.56	0.07
Hg^{2+}	3.19	11.80	14.99	15.31	0.32
Cd^{2+}	2.80	9.72	12.52	12.39	-0.13

METAL ION -SADH-ASPARTIC ACID SYSTEMS

Metal ion	$\log\beta_{1100}$ (A)	$\log\beta_{1020}$ (B)	C = A+B	$\log\beta_{1120}$ (D)	Δlog K= D-C
Ca^{2+}	3.31	4.30	7.61	7.97	0.36
Mg^{2+}	2.64	4.88	7.52	8.03	0.51
Pb^{2+}	3.39	9.99	13.38	13.72	0.34
Hg^{2+}	3.19	8.78	11.97	12.71	0.74
Cd^{2+}	2.80	8.62	11.42	11.24	-0.18

METAL ION -AADH-GLYCINE SYSTEMS

Metal ion	$\log\beta_{1100}$ (A)	$\log\beta_{1020}$ (B)	C = A+B	$\log\beta_{1120}$ (D)	Δlog K= D-C
Ca^{2+}	3.59	3.90	7.49	7.99	0.50
Mg^{2+}	2.90	4.33	7.23	7.87	0.64
Pb^{2+}	3.62	9.97	13.59	14.26	0.67
Hg^{2+}	3.28	8.45	11.73	12.46	0.73
Cd^{2+}	3.02	8.00	11.02	11.44	0.42

METAL ION -AADH-HISTIDINE SYSTEMS

Metal ion	$\log\beta_{1100}$ (A)	$\log\beta_{1020}$ (B)	C = A+B	$\log\beta_{1120}$ (D)	Δlog K= D-C
Ca^{2+}	3.59	5.79	9.38	9.73	0.35
Mg^{2+}	2.90	5.89	8.79	9.17	0.38
Pb^{2+}	3.62	10.10	13.72	14.14	0.42
Hg^{2+}	3.28	11.80	15.08	15.28	0.20
Cd^{2+}	3.02	9.72	12.74	12.88	0.14

METAL ION -AADH-ASPARTIC ACID SYSTEMS

Metal ion	$\log\beta_{1100}$ (A)	$\log\beta_{1020}$ (B)	C = A+B	$\log\beta_{1120}$ (D)	Δlog K= D-C
Ca^{2+}	3.59	4.30	7.89	8.31	0.42
Mg^{2+}	2.90	4.88	7.78	8.41	0.63
Pb^{2+}	3.62	9.99	13.61	13.85	0.24
Hg^{2+}	3.28	8.78	12.06	12.76	0.70
Cd^{2+}	3.02	8.62	11.64	11.68	0.04

6.2.5 ΔLog K values for the formation of protonated ternary Species:

The Δ log K values obtained for the formation of protonated species of some representative systems are shown in Tables 6.5-6.13. The neutral form of SADH (L) or AADH (L) and zwitter ionic form of the amino acid are involved in bonding resulting in the cancellation of electrostatic factors in Δ log K formulations. Most of the Δlog K values are on the positive side of the statistically expected values indicating the greater stability of ternary species relative to that of binary. However, the negative values of Δ log K do not preclude the formation of ternary species.

Table 6.5: ΔLog K values for the formation of **MLXH** species

METAL ION-SADH-GLYCINE SYSTEMS

Metal ion	$\log\beta_{1100}$ (A)	$\log\beta_{1011}$ (B)	C = A+B	$\log\beta_{1111}$ (D)	Δlog K = D-C
Ca^{2+}	3.31	10.90	14.21	14.51	0.30
Mg^{2+}	2.64	11.25	13.89	14.13	0.24
Pb^{2+}	3.39	11.70	15.09	14.82	-0.27
Hg^{2+}	3.19	10.53	13.72	14.52	0.80
Cd^{2+}	2.80	10.84	13.64	14.22	0.58

METAL ION-SADH-HISTIDINE SYSTEMS

Metal ion	$\log\beta_{1100}$ (A)	$\log\beta_{1011}$ (B)	C = A+B	$\log\beta_{1111}$ (D)	Δlog K = D-C
Ca^{2+}	3.31	11.79	15.10	14.99	-0.11
Mg^{2+}	2.64	11.90	14.54	14.34	-0.20
Pb^{2+}	3.39	11.21	14.6	15.48	0.88
Hg^{2+}	3.19	12.09	15.28	15.41	0.13
Cd^{2+}	2.80	10.88	13.68	14.38	0.70

METAL ION-SADH-ASPARTIC ACID SYSTEMS

Metal ion	$\log\beta_{1100}$ (A)	$\log\beta_{1011}$ (B)	C = A+B	$\log\beta_{1111}$ (D)	Δlog K = D-C
Ca^{2+}	3.31	11.12	14.43	14.48	0.05
Mg^{2+}	2.64	11.56	14.20	14.48	0.28
Pb^{2+}	3.39	12.01	15.4	15.71	0.31
Hg^{2+}	3.19	11.23	14.42	14.96	0.54
Cd^{2+}	2.80	11.17	13.97	14.58	0.61

METAL ION-AADH-GLYCINE SYSTEMS

Metal ion	$\log\beta_{1100}$ (A)	$\log\beta_{1011}$ (B)	C = A+B	$\log\beta_{1111}$ (D)	Δlog K = D-C
Ca^{2+}	3.59	10.90	14.49	14.94	0.45
Mg^{2+}	2.90	11.25	14.15	14.30	0.15
Pb^{2+}	3.62	11.70	15.32	15.65	0.33
Hg^{2+}	3.28	10.53	13.81	14.54	0.73
Cd^{2+}	3.02	10.84	13.86	14.36	0.50

METAL ION-AADH-HISTIDINE SYSTEMS

Metal ion	$\log\beta_{1100}$ (A)	$\log\beta_{1011}$ (B)	C = A+B	$\log\beta_{1111}$ (D)	Δlog K = D-C
Ca^{2+}	3.59	11.79	15.38	15.58	0.20
Mg^{2+}	2.90	11.90	14.80	14.84	0.04
Pb^{2+}	3.62	11.21	14.83	15.58	0.75
Hg^{2+}	3.28	12.09	15.37	15.65	0.28
Cd^{2+}	3.02	10.88	13.90	14.68	0.78

METAL ION-AADH-ASPARTIC ACID SYSTEMS

Metal ion	$\log\beta_{1100}$ (A)	$\log\beta_{1011}$ (B)	C = A+B	$\log\beta_{1111}$ (D)	Δlog K = D-C
Ca^{2+}	3.59	11.12	14.71	14.68	-0.03
Mg^{2+}	2.90	11.56	14.46	14.91	0.45
Pb^{2+}	3.62	12.01	15.63	16.22	0.59
Hg^{2+}	3.28	11.23	14.51	15.30	0.79
Cd^{2+}	3.02	11.17	14.19	14.92	0.73

Table 6.6: ΔLog K values for the formation of **$MLXH_2$** species

METAL ION-SADH-GLYCINE SYSTEMS

Metal ion	$\log\beta_{1101}$ (A)	$\log\beta_{1011}$ (B)	C = A+B	$\log\beta_{1112}$ (D)	Δlog K = D-C
Ca^{2+}	6.87	10.90	17.77	17.93	0.16
Mg^{2+}	6.19	11.25	17.44	17.55	0.11
Pb^{2+}	6.60	11.70	18.30	18.28	-0.02
Hg^{2+}	6.51	10.53	17.04	17.56	0.52
Cd^{2+}	6.28	10.84	17.12	17.49	0.37

METAL ION-SADH-HISTIDINE SYSTEMS

Metal ion	$\log\beta_{1100}$ (A)	$\log\beta_{1012}$ (B)	C = A+B	$\log\beta_{1112}$ (D)	Δlog K = D-C
Ca^{2+}	3.31	17.68	20.99	21.05	0.06
Mg^{2+}	2.64	17.76	20.40	20.38	-0.02
Pb^{2+}	3.39	16.31	19.70	20.50	0.80
Hg^{2+}	3.19	17.11	20.30	20.83	0.53

METAL ION-SADH-ASPARTIC ACID SYSTEMS

Metal ion	$\log\beta_{1100}$ (A)	$\log\beta_{1012}$ (B)	C = A+B	$\log\beta_{1112}$ (D)	Δlog K = D-C
Ca^{2+}	3.31	14.41	17.72	18.18	0.46
Mg^{2+}	2.64	15.27	17.91	18.12	0.21
Pb^{2+}	3.39	15.61	19.0	19.13	0.13
Hg^{2+}	3.19	14.93	18.12	18.64	0.52
Cd^{2+}	2.80	14.87	17.67	18.30	0.63

METAL ION-AADH-GLYCINE SYSTEMS

Metal ion	$\log\beta_{1101}$ (A)	$\log\beta_{1011}$ (B)	C = A+B	$\log\beta_{1112}$ (D)	Δlog K = D-C
Ca^{2+}	7.02	10.90	17.92	17.99	0.07
Mg^{2+}	6.52	11.25	17.77	17.65	-0.12
Pb^{2+}	6.99	11.70	18.69	18.44	-0.25
Hg^{2+}	6.60	10.53	17.13	17.57	0.44
Cd^{2+}	6.52	10.84	17.36	17.49	0.13

METAL ION-AADH-HISTIDINE SYSTEMS

Metal ion	$\log\beta_{1100}$ (A)	$\log\beta_{1012}$ (B)	C = A+B	$\log\beta_{1112}$ (D)	Δlog K = D-C
Ca^{2+}	3.59	17.68	21.27	21.14	-0.13
Mg^{2+}	2.90	17.76	20.66	20.56	-0.10
Pb^{2+}	3.62	16.31	19.93	20.73	0.80
Hg^{2+}	3.28	17.11	20.39	21.15	0.76

METAL ION-AADH-ASPARTIC ACID SYSTEMS

Metal ion	$\log\beta_{1100}$ (A)	$\log\beta_{1012}$ (B)	C = A+B	$\log\beta_{1112}$ (D)	Δlog K = D-C
Ca^{2+}	3.59	14.41	18.00	17.64	-0.36
Mg^{2+}	2.90	15.27	18.17	18.09	-0.08
Pb^{2+}	3.62	15.61	19.23	19.38	0.15
Hg^{2+}	3.28	14.93	18.21	18.32	0.11
Cd^{2+}	3.02	14.87	17.89	18.18	0.29

Table 6.7: ΔLog K values for the formation of **$MLXH_3$** species

METAL ION-SADH-HISTIDINE SYSTEMS

Metal ion	$\log\beta_{1101}$ (A)	$\log\beta_{1012}$ (B)	C = A+B	$\log\beta_{1113}$ (D)	Δlog K = D-C
Ca^{2+}	6.87	17.68	24.55	24.48	-0.07
Mg^{2+}	6.19	17.76	23.95	23.81	-0.14
Pb^{2+}	6.60	16.31	22.91	23.49	0.58
Hg^{2+}	6.51	17.11	23.62	23.90	0.28

METAL ION-SADH-ASPARTIC ACID SYSTEMS

Metal ion	$\log\beta_{1101}$ (A)	$\log\beta_{1012}$ (B)	C = A+B	$\log\beta_{1113}$ (D)	Δlog K = D-C
Ca^{2+}	6.87	14.41	21.28	21.55	0.27
Mg^{2+}	6.19	15.27	21.46	21.56	0.10
Pb^{2+}	6.60	15.61	22.21	22.25	0.04
Hg^{2+}	6.51	14.93	21.44	21.72	0.28
Cd^{2+}	6.28	14.87	21.15	21.28	0.13

METAL ION-AADH-HISTIDINE SYSTEMS

Metal ion	$\log\beta_{1101}$ (A)	$\log\beta_{1012}$ (B)	C = A+B	$\log\beta_{1113}$ (D)	Δlog K = D-C
Ca^{2+}	7.02	17.68	24.70	24.40	-0.30
Mg^{2+}	6.52	17.76	24.28	23.63	-0.65
Pb^{2+}	6.99	16.31	23.30	23.51	0.21
Hg^{2+}	6.60	17.11	23.71	24.08	0.37

METAL ION-AADH-ASPARTIC ACID SYSTEMS

Metal ion	$\log\beta_{1101}$ (A)	$\log\beta_{1012}$ (B)	C = A+B	$\log\beta_{1113}$ (D)	Δlog K = D-C
Ca^{2+}	7.02	14.41	21.43	21.28	-0.15
Mg^{2+}	6.52	15.27	21.79	21.31	-0.48
Pb^{2+}	6.99	15.61	22.6	22.65	0.05
Hg^{2+}	6.60	14.93	21.53	21.78	0.25
Cd^{2+}	6.52	14.87	21.39	21.33	-0.06

Table 6.8: ΔLog K values for the formation of **MLX_2H** species

METAL ION-SADH-GLYCINE SYSTEMS

Metal ion	$\log\beta_{1100}$ (A)	$\log\beta_{1021}$ (B)	C = A+B	$\log\beta_{1121}$ (D)	Δlog K = D-C
Ca^{2+}	3.31	13.88	17.19	17.32	0.13
Mg^{2+}	2.64	14.23	16.87	17.33	0.46
Hg^{2+}	3.19	16.90	20.09	19.37	-0.72
Cd^{2+}	2.80	16.90	19.70	18.31	1.39

METAL ION-SADH-HISTIDINE SYSTEMS

Metal ion	$\log\beta_{1100}$ (A)	$\log\beta_{1021}$ (B)	C = A+B	$\log\beta_{1121}$ (D)	Δlog K = D-C
Ca^{2+}	3.31	14.73	18.04	18.78	0.74
Mg^{2+}	2.64	14.82	17.46	17.63	0.17
Pb^{2+}	3.39	18.27	21.66	21.57	-0.09
Hg^{2+}	3.19	19.02	22.21	22.36	0.15
Cd^{2+}	2.80	16.97	19.77	19.58	-0.19

METAL ION-SADH-ASPARTIC ACID SYSTEMS

Metal ion	$\log\beta_{1100}$ (A)	$\log\beta_{1021}$ (B)	C = A+B	$\log\beta_{1121}$ (D)	Δlog K = D-C
Ca^{2+}	3.31	13.88	17.19	16.96	-0.23
Mg^{2+}	2.64	14.23	16.87	17.41	0.54
Pb^{2+}	3.39	17.33	20.72	21.31	0.59
Hg^{2+}	3.19	16.90	20.09	20.23	0.14
Cd^{2+}	2.80	16.90	19.70	19.13	-0.57

METAL ION-AADH-GLYCINE SYSTEMS

Metal ion	$\log\beta_{1100}$ (A)	$\log\beta_{1021}$ (B)	C = A+B	$\log\beta_{1121}$ (D)	Δlog K = D-C
Ca^{2+}	3.59	13.88	17.47	17.38	-0.09
Mg^{2+}	2.90	14.23	17.13	17.34	0.21
Pb^{2+}	3.62	17.33	20.95	21.32	0.37
Hg^{2+}	3.28	16.90	20.18	20.59	0.41
Cd^{2+}	3.02	16.90	19.92	19.40	-0.52

METAL ION-AADH-HISTIDINE SYSTEMS

Metal ion	$\log\beta_{1100}$ (A)	$\log\beta_{1021}$ (B)	C = A+B	$\log\beta_{1121}$ (D)	Δlog K = D-C
Ca^{2+}	3.59	14.73	18.32	18.69	0.37
Mg^{2+}	2.90	14.82	17.72	18.13	0.41
Pb^{2+}	3.62	18.27	21.89	21.14	-0.75
Hg^{2+}	3.28	19.02	22.30	22.87	0.57
Cd^{2+}	3.02	16.97	19.99	20.00	0.01

METAL ION-AADH-ASPARTIC ACID SYSTEMS

Metal ion	$\log\beta_{1100}$ (A)	$\log\beta_{1021}$ (B)	C = A+B	$\log\beta_{1121}$ (D)	Δlog K = D-C
Ca^{2+}	3.59	13.88	17.47	17.87	0.40
Mg^{2+}	2.90	14.23	17.13	17.88	0.75
Pb^{2+}	3.62	17.33	20.95	21.52	0.57
Hg^{2+}	3.28	16.90	20.18	20.22	0.04
Cd^{2+}	3.02	16.90	19.92	19.48	-0.44

Table 6.9: ΔLog K values for the formation of $\mathbf{MLX_2H_2}$ species

METAL ION-SADH-GLYCINE SYSTEMS

Metal ion	$\log\beta_{1100}$ (A)	$\log\beta_{1022}$ (B)	C = A+B	$\log\beta_{1122}$ (D)	Δlog K = D-C
Ca^{2+}	3.31	22.30	25.61	26.04	0.43
Mg^{2+}	2.64	22.58	25.22	25.80	0.58
Pb^{2+}	3.39	22.55	25.94	26.29	0.35
Hg^{2+}	3.19	23.32	26.51	25.83	-0.68
Cd^{2+}	2.80	23.16	25.96	25.50	-0.46

METAL ION-SADH-HISTIDINE SYSTEMS

Metal ion	$\log\beta_{1100}$ (A)	$\log\beta_{1022}$ (B)	C = A+B	$\log\beta_{1122}$ (D)	$\Delta\log K$ = D-C
Ca^{2+}	3.31	23.47	26.78	26.92	0.14
Mg^{2+}	2.64	23.56	26.20	26.39	0.19
Pb^{2+}	3.39	24.04	27.43	27.25	-0.18
Hg^{2+}	3.19	24.04	27.23	27.29	0.06
Cd^{2+}	2.80	22.48	25.28	25.43	0.15

METAL ION-SADH-ASPARTIC ACID SYSTEMS

Metal ion	$\log\beta_{1100}$ (A)	$\log\beta_{1022}$ (B)	C = A+B	$\log\beta_{1122}$ (D)	$\Delta\log K$ = D-C
Ca^{2+}	3.31	22.73	26.04	25.96	-0.08
Mg^{2+}	2.64	23.03	25.67	26.28	0.61
Pb^{2+}	3.39	23.56	26.95	27.57	0.62
Hg^{2+}	3.19	23.71	26.90	26.43	-0.47
Cd^{2+}	2.80	23.33	26.13	26.30	0.17

METAL ION-AADH-GLYCINE SYSTEMS

Metal ion	$\log\beta_{1100}$ (A)	$\log\beta_{1022}$ (B)	C = A+B	$\log\beta_{1122}$ (D)	$\Delta\log K$ = D-C
Ca^{2+}	3.59	22.30	25.89	26.10	0.21
Mg^{2+}	2.90	22.58	25.48	26.01	0.53
Pb^{2+}	3.62	22.55	26.17	26.85	0.68
Hg^{2+}	3.28	23.32	26.60	26.27	-0.33
Cd^{2+}	3.02	23.16	26.18	26.06	-0.12

METAL ION-AADH-HISTIDINE SYSTEMS

Metal ion	$\log\beta_{1100}$ (A)	$\log\beta_{1022}$ (B)	C = A+B	$\log\beta_{1122}$ (D)	$\Delta\log K$ = D-C
Ca^{2+}	3.59	23.47	27.06	26.51	-0.55
Mg^{2+}	2.90	23.56	26.46	26.14	-0.32
Pb^{2+}	3.62	24.04	27.66	27.07	-0.59
Cd^{2+}	3.02	22.48	25.50	25.82	0.32

METAL ION-AADH-ASPARTIC ACID SYSTEMS

Metal ion	$\log\beta_{1100}$ (A)	$\log\beta_{1022}$ (B)	C = A+B	$\log\beta_{1122}$ (D)	$\Delta\log K$ = D-C
Ca^{2+}	3.59	22.73	26.32	26.39	0.07
Mg^{2+}	2.90	23.03	25.93	26.30	0.37
Pb^{2+}	3.62	23.56	27.18	27.87	0.69
Hg^{2+}	3.28	23.71	26.99	26.35	-0.64
Cd^{2+}	3.02	23.33	26.35	26.46	0.11

Table 6.10: ΔLog K values for the formation of $\mathbf{MLX_2H_3}$ species

METAL ION-SADH-GLYCINE SYSTEMS

Metal ion	$\log\beta_{1101}$ (A)	$\log\beta_{1022}$ (B)	C = A+B	$\log\beta_{1123}$ (D)	Δlog K = D-C
Ca^{2+}	6.87	22.30	29.17	29.58	0.41
Mg^{2+}	6.19	22.58	28.77	28.93	0.16
Pb^{2+}	6.60	22.55	29.15	29.80	0.65
Hg^{2+}	6.51	23.32	29.83	28.92	-0.91
Cd^{2+}	6.28	23.16	29.44	28.83	-0.61

METAL ION-SADH-HISTIDINE SYSTEMS

Metal ion	$\log\beta_{1100}$ (A)	$\log\beta_{1023}$ (B)	C = A+B	$\log\beta_{1123}$ (D)	Δlog K = D-C
Ca^{2+}	3.31	29.52	32.83	32.97	0.14
Mg^{2+}	2.64	29.61	32.25	32.42	0.17
Pb^{2+}	3.39	29.59	32.98	33.25	0.27
Hg^{2+}	3.19	30.02	33.21	33.33	0.12
Cd^{2+}	2.80	28.22	31.02	31.34	0.32

METAL ION-AADH-GLYCINE SYSTEMS

Metal ion	$\log\beta_{1101}$ (A)	$\log\beta_{1022}$ (B)	C = A+B	$\log\beta_{1123}$ (D)	Δlog K = D-C
Ca^{2+}	7.02	22.30	29.32	29.63	0.31
Mg^{2+}	6.52	22.58	29.10	29.12	0.02
Pb^{2+}	6.99	22.55	29.54	29.93	0.39
Hg^{2+}	6.60	23.32	29.92	29.06	-0.86
Cd^{2+}	6.52	23.16	29.68	28.83	-0.85

METAL ION-AADH-HISTIDINE SYSTEMS

Metal ion	$\log\beta_{1100}$ (A)	$\log\beta_{1023}$ (B)	C = A+B	$\log\beta_{1123}$ (D)	Δlog K = D-C
Ca^{2+}	3.59	29.52	33.11	32.54	-0.57
Mg^{2+}	2.90	29.61	32.51	32.04	-0.47
Pb^{2+}	3.62	29.59	33.21	33.09	-0.12
Hg^{2+}	3.28	30.02	33.30	33.78	0.48
Cd^{2+}	3.02	28.22	31.24	31.88	0.64

Table 6.11: ΔLog K values for the formation of $\mathbf{M_2LXH}$ species

METAL ION-SADH-GLYCINE SYSTEMS

Metal ion	$\log\beta_{2100}$ (A)	$\log\beta_{1011}$ (B)	C = A+B	$\log\beta_{2111}$ (D)	Δlog K = D-C
Ca^{2+}	5.16	10.90	16.06	16.10	0.04
Mg^{2+}	4.60	11.25	15.85	16.02	0.17
Pb^{2+}	5.57	11.70	17.27	16.93	-0.34
Hg^{2+}	5.27	10.53	15.80	16.36	0.56
Cd^{2+}	4.54	10.84	15.38	16.24	0.86

METAL ION-SADH-HISTIDINE SYSTEMS

Metal ion	$Log\beta_{2100}$ (A)	$log\beta_{1011}$ (B)	C = A+B	$log\beta_{2111}$ (D)	Δlog K = D-C
Ca^{2+}	5.16	11.79	16.95	17.16	0.21
Mg^{2+}	4.60	11.90	16.50	16.11	-0.39
Pb^{2+}	5.57	11.21	16.78	16.46	-0.32
Cd^{2+}	4.54	10.88	15.42	15.70	0.28

METAL ION-SADH-ASPARTIC ACID SYSTEMS

Metal ion	$Log\beta_{2100}$ (A)	$log\beta_{1011}$ (B)	C = A+B	$log\beta_{2111}$ (D)	Δlog K = D-C
Ca^{2+}	5.16	11.12	16.28	16.16	-0.12
Mg^{2+}	4.60	11.56	16.16	16.23	0.07
Pb^{2+}	5.57	12.01	17.58	17.59	0.01
Hg^{2+}	5.27	11.23	16.50	16.87	0.37
Cd^{2+}	4.54	11.17	15.71	16.39	0.68

METAL ION-AADH-GLYCINE SYSTEMS

Metal ion	$log\beta_{2100}$ (A)	$log\beta_{1011}$ (B)	C = A+B	$log\beta_{2111}$ (D)	Δlog K = D-C
Ca^{2+}	5.52	10.90	16.42	16.85	0.43
Mg^{2+}	4.93	11.25	16.18	16.74	0.56
Pb^{2+}	5.84	11.70	17.54	17.46	-0.08
Hg^{2+}	5.38	10.53	15.91	16.58	0.67
Cd^{2+}	4.88	10.84	15.72	16.38	0.66

METAL ION-AADH-HISTIDINE SYSTEMS

Metal ion	$Log\beta_{2100}$ (A)	$log\beta_{1011}$ (B)	C = A+B	$log\beta_{2111}$ (D)	Δlog K = D-C
Ca^{2+}	5.52	11.79	17.31	17.45	0.14
Mg^{2+}	4.93	11.90	16.83	16.19	-0.64
Pb^{2+}	5.84	11.21	17.05	17.36	0.31
Cd^{2+}	4.88	10.88	15.76	16.45	0.69

METAL ION-AADH-ASPARTIC ACID SYSTEMS

Metal ion	$Log\beta_{2100}$ (A)	$log\beta_{1011}$ (B)	C = A+B	$log\beta_{2111}$ (D)	Δlog K = D-C
Ca^{2+}	5.52	11.12	16.64	16.46	-0.18
Mg^{2+}	4.93	11.56	16.49	16.98	0.49
Pb^{2+}	5.84	12.01	17.85	17.76	-0.09
Hg^{2+}	5.38	11.23	16.61	17.08	0.47
Cd^{2+}	4.88	11.17	16.05	16.89	0.84

Table 6.12: ΔLog K values for the formation of $\mathbf{M_2LX_2H}$ species

METAL ION-SADH-GLYCINE SYSTEMS

Metal ion	$\log\beta_{2100}$ (A)	$\log\beta_{1011}+\log\beta_{1010}$ (B)	C = A+B	$\log\beta_{2121}$ (D)	Δlog K = D-C
Ca^{2+}	5.16	12.86	18.02	19.11	1.09
Mg^{2+}	4.60	13.44	18.04	18.77	0.73
Cd^{2+}	4.54	15.05	19.59	20.66	1.07

METAL ION-SADH-HISTIDINE SYSTEMS

Metal ion	$\log\beta_{2100}$ (A)	$\log\beta_{1011}+\log\beta_{1010}$ (B)	C = A+B	$\log\beta_{2121}$ (D)	Δlog K = D-C
Ca^{2+}	5.16	14.71	19.87	20.17	0.30
Mg^{2+}	4.60	14.97	19.57	20.02	0.45
Cd^{2+}	4.54	16.26	20.80	21.53	0.73

METAL ION-SADH-ASPARTIC ACID SYSTEMS

Metal ion	$\log\beta_{2100}$ (A)	$\log\beta_{1011}+\log\beta_{1010}$ (B)	C = A+B	$\log\beta_{2121}$ (D)	Δlog K = D-C
Ca^{2+}	5.16	13.28	18.44	19.56	1.12
Mg^{2+}	4.60	14.04	18.64	18.96	0.32
Hg^{2+}	5.27	16.10	21.37	22.81	1.44
Cd^{2+}	4.54	15.51	20.05	20.74	0.69

METAL ION-AADH-GLYCINE SYSTEMS

Metal ion	$\log\beta_{2100}$ (A)	$\log\beta_{1011}+\log\beta_{1010}$ (B)	C = A+B	$\log\beta_{2121}$ (D)	Δlog K = D-C
Ca^{2+}	5.52	12.86	18.38	19.65	1.27
Mg^{2+}	4.93	13.44	18.37	19.37	1.00
Hg^{2+}	5.38	14.95	20.33	22.43	2.10

METAL ION-AADH-HISTIDINE SYSTEMS

Metal ion	$\log\beta_{2100}$ (A)	$\log\beta_{1011}+\log\beta_{1010}$ (B)	C = A+B	$\log\beta_{2121}$ (D)	Δlog K = D-C
Ca^{2+}	5.52	14.71	20.23	20.36	0.13
Mg^{2+}	4.93	14.97	19.90	20.14	0.24
Pb^{2+}	5.84	17.11	22.95	23.90	0.95
Hg^{2+}	5.38	18.69	24.07	23.96	-0.11
Cd^{2+}	4.88	16.26	21.14	22.23	1.09

METAL ION-AADH-ASPARTIC ACID SYSTEMS

Metal ion	$\log\beta_{2100}$ (A)	$\log\beta_{1011}$+ $\log\beta_{1010}$ (B)	C = A+B	$\log\beta_{2121}$ (D)	Δlog K = D-C
Ca^{2+}	5.52	13.28	18.80	19.63	0.83
Mg^{2+}	4.93	14.04	18.97	19.25	0.28
Pb^{2+}	5.84	17.84	23.68	23.34	-0.34
Hg^{2+}	5.38	16.10	21.48	22.70	1.22
Cd^{2+}	4.88	15.51	20.39	21.40	1.01

Table 6.13: ΔLog K values for the formation of $\mathbf{M_2LX_2H_2}$ species

METAL ION-SADH-GLYCINE SYSTEMS

Metal ion	$\log\beta_{2100}$ (A)	$2x\log\beta_{1011}$ (B)	C = A+B	$\log\beta_{2122}$ (D)	Δlog K = D-C
Ca^{2+}	5.16	21.80	26.96	28.40	1.44
Mg^{2+}	4.60	22.50	27.10	27.70	0.60
Pb^{2+}	5.57	23.40	28.97	28.57	-0.40
Hg^{2+}	5.27	21.06	26.33	28.44	2.11
Cd^{2+}	4.54	21.68	26.22	27.83	1.61

METAL ION-SADH-HISTIDINE SYSTEMS

Metal ion	$\log\beta_{2100}$ (A)	$2x\log\beta_{1011}$ (B)	C = A+B	$\log\beta_{2122}$ (D)	Δlog K = D-C
Ca^{2+}	5.16	23.58	28.74	27.99	-0.75
Mg^{2+}	4.60	23.80	28.40	27.97	-0.43
Pb^{2+}	5.57	22.42	27.99	29.40	1.41
Hg^{2+}	5.27	24.18	29.45	29.50	0.05
Cd^{2+}	4.54	21.76	26.30	27.45	1.15

METAL ION-SADH-ASPARTIC ACID SYSTEMS

Metal ion	$\log\beta_{2100}$ (A)	$2x\log\beta_{1011}$ (B)	C = A+B	$\log\beta_{2122}$ (D)	Δlog K = D-C
Ca^{2+}	5.16	22.24	27.40	28.56	1.16
Mg^{2+}	4.60	23.12	27.72	27.79	0.07
Pb^{2+}	5.57	24.02	29.59	28.76	-0.83
Hg^{2+}	5.27	22.46	27.73	29.07	1.34
Cd^{2+}	4.54	22.34	26.88	28.27	1.39

METAL ION-AADH-GLYCINE SYSTEMS

Metal ion	$\log\beta_{2100}$ (A)	$2x\log\beta_{1011}$ (B)	C = A+B	$\log\beta_{2122}$ (D)	Δlog K = D-C
Ca^{2+}	5.52	21.80	27.32	28.53	1.21
Mg^{2+}	4.93	22.50	27.43	28.37	0.94
Pb^{2+}	5.84	23.40	29.24	28.69	-0.55
Hg^{2+}	5.38	21.06	26.44	28.58	2.14
Cd^{2+}	4.88	21.68	26.56	27.85	1.29

METAL ION-AADH-HISTIDINE SYSTEMS

Metal ion	$\log\beta_{2100}$ (A)	$2x\log\beta_{1011}$ (B)	C = A+B	$\log\beta_{2122}$ (D)	Δlog K = D-C
Ca^{2+}	5.52	23.58	29.10	28.53	-0.57
Mg^{2+}	4.93	23.80	28.73	28.17	-0.56

METAL ION-AADH-ASPARTIC ACID SYSTEMS

Metal ion	$\log\beta_{2100}$ (A)	$2x\log\beta_{1011}$ (B)	C = A+B	$\log\beta_{2122}$ (D)	Δlog K = D-C
Ca^{2+}	5.52	22.24	27.76	28.61	0.85
Mg^{2+}	4.93	23.12	28.05	27.99	-0.06
Pb^{2+}	5.84	24.02	29.86	29.45	-0.41
Hg^{2+}	5.38	22.46	27.84	28.82	0.98
Cd^{2+}	4.88	22.34	27.22	28.21	0.99

It may be concluded that in general ternary complexes were found to be relatively more stable compared to binary. This observed stability may be attributed to the interaction between the ligands including hydrogen bonding (which is common for amino acids and amines) in addition to other factors that favour the formation of mixed ligand species. The Δlog K values in general do not follow[31] any of the sequences proposed for overall or step-wise formation constants by different theories such as Irving and Williams order[32], HSAB theory of Pearson[23, 33] and other theories based on the thermodynamic, electronegativity and other factors[34], although these are followed by the overall stability constants of the mixed ligand complexes.

6.3 REFERENCES

1. H. Sigel (Ed), In "Metal ions in Biological Systems", Vol.2, Chapter 2, Marcel Deckker, New York, (1973).
2. H. Sigel, "Coordination Chemistry", Pergamon Press, Oxford 20 (1980).
3. H. Sigel, P. R. Huber, R. Griesser, and B. Prijs, "Ternary complexes in solution. XV: Mixed-ligand copper (II) complexes with 2,2'-bipyridyl or 1,10-phenanthroline and pyrocatecholate or derivatives thereof", *Inorg. Chem.* 12 (1973) pp.1198-1200.
4. R. B. Martin and R. Prados, "Some factors influencing mixed complex formation", *J. Inorg. Nucl. Chem.*, 36 (*1974*) pp 1665-1670.
5. I. Sorago and A. Gergely, "Effects of steric factors on the equilibrium and thermodynamic conditions of mixed ligand complexes of the copper (II) ion with diamines", *Inorg. Chim. Acta.* 20 (1976) pp 27-32.
6. Sigel, H. "Ternary Cu^{2+} complex: stability, structure and reactivity", *Angew. Chem. Int. Ed. Engl.* 14 (1975) pp 394–402.
7. R. Griesser, and H. Sigel, "Ternary complexes in solution. VIII. Complex formation between the copper (II)-2, 2'-bipyridyl 1:1 complex and ligands containing oxygen and/or nitrogen donor atoms", *Inorg. Chem.*, 9 (1970) pp 1238-1243.
8. H. Sigel (Editor). "Metal ions in biological systems, Vol. 13 (1981), Marcel Dekker, Inc., New York.
9. N. Ernanuel and P. K. Bhattacharya. *Indian J. Chem.* 24A (1985) p 498
10. P. Chaudhari and H. Sigel, "Ternary complexes in solution. 26. Stacking interactions in the mixed ligand complexes formed by adenosine or inosine 5'-triphosphate, 2,2'-bipyridyl, and cobalt(II), nickel(II), copper (II), or zinc (II). Evidence for phosphate-protonated complexes", *J. Am. Chem. Soc.* 99, (1977) pp 3142-3150.
11. J. I. Watters and R. Dewitt, "The complexes of Nickel (II) Ion in aqueous solution containing Oxalate Ion and Ethylenediamine", *J. Amer. Chem. Soc.* 82 (1960) pp 1333-1339.

12. Y. Kamemura and J. I. Watters, "Acidimetric studies of cadmium and zinc complexes with ethylene diamine, oxalate, and their mixtures using the glass electrode", *J. Inorg. Nucl. Chem.,* 29 (1967) pp 1701-1709.
13. J. Bjerrum, "Metal-ammine formation in aqueous solution", Haase and son, Copenhagen (1941).
14. V. S. Sharma and Jack Schubert, "Statistical factor in the formation and stability of ternary and mixed complexes", *J. Chem. Educ.*, 46 (1969) p 506.
15. S. Kida, *Bull. Chem. Soc. Japan,* 29 (1956) p1805; 34 (1961) p 962.
16. Y. Marcus and I. Eliazer, "Mercury (II) halide mixed complexes in solution. V. Comparison of calculated and experimental stability constants", *J. Phys. Chem.*, 66 (1962) pp 1661-1663.
17. F. Gaizer and M. T. Beck, "Formation of mixed ligand complexes in the MA_3 + MB_3 system the interaction between $BiCl_3$ and BiI_3 in dioxane", *J. Inorg. Nucl. Chem.*, 28 (1966) pp 503-510.
18. Y. Marcus, "Mercury (II) halide mixed complexes in solution. III. The uncharged mixed complexes", *Acta. Chem. Scand.*, 11(1957) pp 610-618.
19. I. Nagypal, A. Gergely and E. Fankas, "Thermodynamic study of the parent and mixed complexes of aspartic acid, glutamic acid and glycine with copper (II)", *J. Inorg. Nucl. Chem.*, 36 (1974) pp 699-706.
20. R. P. Martin and R. A. Paris, *C.R. Acad. Sci., Paris*, 258 (1964) p 3038.
21. M. Calvin and K.W. Wilson, *J. Amer. Chem. Soc.*, 67 (1945) 2003; J. Bjerrum, Chem. Revs. 46 (1950) 381; A. E. Martell and M. Calvin, "Chemistry of Metal Chelate Compounds", Prentice-Hall, (1952); H. Irving and H. Rossotti, *Acta. Chem. Scand.*, 10 (1956) p 72.
22. A. Mohan, K. Radha, M. Mohan and Srinivas, *Orient. J. Chem.*, 13(2) (1997) p 105.
23. R. G. Pearson, "Hard and soft acids and bases, HSAB, part II: Underlying theories", *J. Chem. Educ.*, 45 (1968) p 643; *J. Am. Chem. Soc.*, 85 (1963) p.3533; Science 151(1966) p.172.
24. Y. D. Fridmann, *Proc. Symp. Coord. Chem.*, 3 (1971) p 77 edited by M.T. Beck.
25. D. L. Leusing and D.L. Shultz, *J. Amer. Chem. Soc.*, 86 (1964) p 4847
26. D. L. Leusing and E. M. Hanna, "Metal ion catalysis in transamination III. Nickel (II) and zinc (II) mixed complexes involving pyruvate and various substituted aliphatic amino acids", *J. Amer. Chem. Soc.*, 88 (1966) pp 693-696.

27. D. L. Leusing and K. S. Bai, "N-Salicylideneglycinato complexes. Comparison with pyridoxal", *Anal. Chem.,* 40 (1968) pp 575-581.
28. H. Sigel, *Chimca,* 21 (1967) p 489.
29. H. Sigel, B. E. Fischer and B. Pijs, "Ternary complexes in solution. 27. Biological implications from the stability of ternary complexes in solution. Mixed-ligand complexes with manganese (II) and other 3d ions", *J. Am. Chem. Soc.* 99 (1977) pp 4489-4496.
30. H. Sigel and C. F. Naumann, "Ternary complexes in solution. XXIV. Metal ion bridging of stacked purine-iodine adducts. The mixed-ligand complexes of adenosine 5'-triphosphate, tryptophan, and manganese (II), copper (II), or zinc (II) ", *J. Am. Chem. Soc.* 98(1976) pp 730-739.
31. H. Sigel, "Metal ions in Biological systems" Vol.2 (Mixed-Ligand Complexes) ed. H. Sigel, Marcel Dekker, INC, New York, (1973) p 97.
32. H. Irving and R. J. P. Williams, "The stability of transition-metal complexes", *J. Chem. Soc*., (1953) pp 3192-3210.
33. Adam Jacobs, "Understanding Organic reaction Mechanisms", Cambridge University Press, UK, (1997), Digital Print, (2003) p.50.
34. J.D. Hoeschele, J.E. Turner and M. W. England, "Inorganic concepts relevant to metal binding activity and toxicity in a biological system", *Sci. Total Environ.*, 109/110 (19791) pp.477-492.

CONCLUSIONS

Studies of the interaction of metal ions with ditopic ligands, sometimes in the presence of an additional ligand are of recent interest due to the special properties exhibited by the species formed, such as formation of well-ordered extended complexes containing different cations, synergistic bimetallic catalysis, mimicking metalloproteins, unusual magnetic properties, etc. The properties of the bound metal ions are highly dependent on the nature of the species formed. Therefore, chemical speciation is critical for understanding the forms of metal ions or chemicals of interest in natural, biological, industrial and analytical systems. It is essential in assessing the bioavailability of for example, a toxic metal ion and ultimately its fate, transport and risk to humans and ecosystems. The information expected from such a study includes, (i) the number and nature of the species in which a metal ion is present in solution, (ii) the extent of formation of each species as a function of pH and (iii) various forms of the ligand (or drug) present at a given temperature, ionic strength and pH. Chemical speciation is generally determined through analytical methods that measure free metal ion or hydrogen ion, in conjunction with thermodynamically based models. The reliability of the models obtained depends on the procedures followed in data acquisition and analysis. The potentiometric method using Calvin-Wilson titration technique for data acquisition, coupled with analysis using the SOPHD and MINIQUAD-75 programs was found to be successful to generate information about the chemical speciation.

The author had taken up a speciation study on the interaction of some ditopic ligands and amino acids with selected essential/ toxic metal ions. The ditopic ligands chosen were aliphatic dihydrazides derived from succinic and adipic acids. The metal ions were Ca^{2+}, Mg^{2+}, Pb^{2+}, Hg^{2+} and Cd^{2+}. The preferred amino acids were,

(i) Glycine, the simplest (ii) L-Histidine, (basic side chain) and (iii) L-Aspartic acid, (acidic side chain). The following conclusions were drawn based on the author's experimental results of the speciation study.

PROTON-LIGAND EQUILIBRIA OF SUCCINIC AND ADIPIC ACID DIHYDRAZIDES, GLYCINE, L-HISTIDINE AND L-ASPARTIC ACID:

- Succinic (SADH) and Adipic acid dihydrazides (AADH) are ditopic ligands containing two hydrazide coordinating units connected by $-CH_2-$ bridges of varying length.

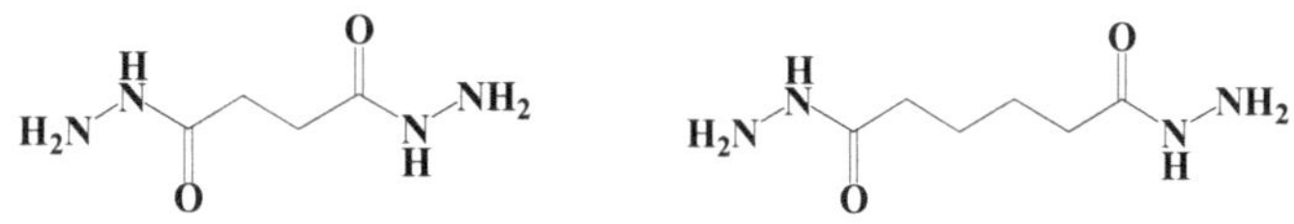

SADH AADH

- The proton-ligand equilibria of both SADH (L) and AADH (L) were studied in aqueous medium at 30.0^{0}C and ionic strength 0.1 mol dm^{-3}. The best-fit models obtained contained three formation constants β_{011}, β_{012} and β_{01-1} corresponding to the formation of LH^+, LH_2^{2+} and LH_{-1} species in solution. The protonation is at the two terminal amino groups. The deprotonation is from one of the enolic groups.

L(enol) LH$_{-1}$

The dissociation of the second enolic group may be out of the pH region of the study. The protonated species exist below a pH of ~6.0 and deprotonated form above ~9.0 pH. Between pH 6.0 and 9.0 both SADH and AADH exist totally in neutral unprotonated (L) form.

- The protonation constants of AADH are higher when compared to that of SADH. This is due to the increase in the length of the aliphatic chain between the two hydrazide groups which leads to an increase in the basicity of the $-NH_2$ groups.
- The ligands may be bound to metal ions in different states of protonation, thus enabling the properties of their complexes to be modulated by the degree of deprotonation. The extent of such modulation will be increased in systems where more than one ligand unit is present.
- The protonation constants of the amino acids glycine, L-histidine and L-aspartic acid were determined under the identical experimental conditions of ionic strength and temperature used to study the binary and the ternary systems. The formation constants obtained are in good agreement with the values reported in literature, allowing for variation in the experimental conditions.
- In solution glycine (XH) depending on the pH exists in protonated (XH_2^+), Zwitter ionic (XH) and deprotonated anionic (X^-) forms. The association and dissociation equilibria are widely separated on pH scale.
- L-histidine (XH) possesses a polar side chain and has three potential donor sites. The first centre to protonate in fully ionized histidinate anion (X^-) is the α-amino-nitrogen followed by the pyridine-like imidazole-nitrogen. The last centre to protonate is the α-carboxylate group. The ligand, depending on the pH, exists in XH_3^{2+}, XH_2^+, XH and X^- forms in the solution.
- L-aspartic acid (XH_2) possesses an acidic side chain containing an additional -COOH group. The first centre to protonate in the most anionic form of aspartic acid (X^{2-}) is the α-amino group followed by the side chain

carboxylate and α-carboxylate groups. The molecule possesses three potential donor atoms and exists in solution in different protonated forms, XH_3^+, XH_2, XH^- and X^{2-}.

- The species distribution diagrams generated indicate a spread of various protonated forms of glycine, histidine and aspartic acid over a wide pH region. Therefore, depending on the pH and composition of the solution, these amino acids may form a variety of metal ion complexes in protonated and unprotonated forms.

SPECIATION STUDIES OF METAL ION-DIHYDRAZIDE AND METAL ION-AMINO ACID BINARY SYSTEMS:

The results of the chemical speciation study on binary metal ion-dihydrazide and metal ion-amino acid systems using potentiometric methods of data acquisition followed by modern methods of computation are summarized as follows:-

- Succinic and Adipic acid dihydrazides are non-toxic ditopic ligands that contain two identical coordinating hydrazide groups separated by a flexible bridging part of the molecule. The microbial, chemical and industrial properties of dihydrazides are uniquely attributed to the structure of these ligands in which two identical units in a molecule attach to metal ions symmetrically or asymmetrically leading to better coordinating and synergistic catalytic properties than those of ligands with only one coordinating unit.
- The majority of the studies reported in the literature on metal complexes of dihydrazides were aimed at the preparation and elucidation of their structures by physicochemical methods. Studies on the solution equilibria of their metal complexes are scanty. Therefore, it is worthwhile to study their complexing properties in solution phase with some essential and toxic metal ions.

- Chemical speciation study is a prerequisite to understand the bioavailability, toxicity, distribution, fate and transport of various species. It gives the required information regarding the nature and extent of formation of various species as a function of pH.
- Both Succinic and Adipic acid dihydrazides (L), depending on the pH are found to exist in various protonated and deprotonated forms in the solution. The results of the author's study of proton-ligand equilibria indicate the formation of LH_2^{2+}, LH^+, L and LH_{-1} type of species in solution. Hence, there is a possibility of formation of a variety of coexisting mononuclear and binuclear species in protonated, unprotonated and deprotonated forms, enabling their properties to be modulated by the degree of deprotonation.
- The metal-ligand equilibria of both SADH and AADH were studied in aqueous medium at 30.0 ±0.1^{0}C and ionic strength 0.1 mole dm^{-3}. The metal ions selected were Ca^{2+}, Mg^{2+}, Pb^{2+}, Hg^{2+} and Cd^{2+}. Calvin-Wilson potentiometric titrations were conducted in 1:1, 1:2 and 2:1 metal ion to dihydrazide molar concentration ratios. The data were first subjected to analysis by classical methods to get initial estimates of the formation constants of the simple complexes for refinement by the Miniquad-75 program along with other chemically plausible species. The stoichiometry and stability constants of the complexes formed were determined by trying various possible composition models. The models selected gave the best statistical fit and were chemically consistent with the titration data without giving any systematic drifts in the magnitudes of various residuals, as described in Chapter-2 of the thesis.

- The best-fit models for all the M^{2+}-SADH and M^{2+}-AADH (1:1) mole ratio systems indicate the formation of MLH, ML and MLH_{-1} type of species. The formation of MLH_{-1} type of species may be due to the deprotonation of enolic group or hydrolysis of the corresponding species.
- The best-fit models obtained for 1:2 (M: L) molar composition indicate the formation of ML_2H_2, ML_2H, ML_2, ML_2H_{-1} and ML_2H_{-2} species. In each species the metal ion is bonded to two dihydrazide molecules. In ML_2H_2 species probably, only one of the hydrazide groups of each of the ligands is involved in bonding with the metal ion as a bidentate bonding through carbonyl oxygen and terminal nitrogen, while the other is left free and protonated. These species with increase in pH of the solution successively lose protons and are converted to ML_2H and ML_2.
- As Succinic and Adipic acid dihydrazide molecules possess two coordinating hydrazide units, there is a possibility of formation of binuclear complexes. Therefore, potentiometric titrations were conducted keeping 2:1 metal to ligand molar concentration ratio for all the selected metal ions. The best-fit models obtained indicate the formation of homo binuclear M_2L, M_2LH_{-1} and M_2LH_{-2} type of species, where SADH and AADH act as ditopic ligands. The ligand in each type of species is attached to two metal ions either in neutral or deprotonated enolic form. The ligand seems to act as bis bidentate, coordinating through terminal $-NH_2$ groups and carbonyl or enolic oxygens, forming five membered rings on both sides. Although solution phase studies of speciation cannot give the structures of the species, the probable general bonding nature of the dihydrazides in binuclear complexes inferred from the speciation results and supported by the solid state studies was shown.

- Species distribution diagrams were generated for all the systems using the HYSS program. The extent of formation of the symmetric M_2L type of species ranges from 64-80% of total metal for different metal ions in the pH range of study. Beyond this range deprotonation of M_2L takes place for all the systems, leading to the formation of M_2LH_{-1} and M_2LH_{-2} type of species.
- The coordination of a metal ion by one unit of the ligand may affect the coordination at the other unit. This was observed in the formation of M_2L from ML. The step-wise formation constant for ML to M_2L differs largely from that of ML, although both units of coordination are identical and separate.
- Formation constants of Ca^{2+} complexes with both SADH and AADH are found to be greater than those of Mg^{2+}. Both the metal ions are hard acids, not easily polarized, favour oxygen donors and show predominately electrostatic bonding in complexes. Ca^{2+} ion has relatively large size, low charge density and low affinity for inner sphere water molecules. The formation of a bond requires the breakage of metal ion-solvent bond and it is more difficult in the case of Mg^{2+} due to high charge density compared to Ca^{2+}. Each hydrazide group of a dihydrazide acts as a bidentate bonding through neutral oxygen and amino nitrogen, leading to the formation of five membered rings. Neutral oxygen donors prefer large metal ions. Small metal ions prefer six membered rings while large metal ions prefer five membered rings. All these factors cumulatively lead to higher stabilities of Ca^{2+} complexes relative to those of Mg^{2+}.
- In the case of heavy metal ion (Pb^{2+}, Hg^{2+} and Cd^{2+}) –dihydrazide complexes of both SADH and AADH, the relative stabilities were found to be in the order

$Pb^{2+} > Hg^{2+} > Cd^{2+}$. This may be explained on the basis of (i) HSAB theory and (ii) ionic sizes.

- According to Pearson's HSAB theory, Hg^{2+} and Cd^{2+} are soft Lewis acids while Pb^{2+} belongs to borderline category. On the other hand SADH and AADH provide hard oxygen and borderline $-NH_2$ donors. Hard acids prefer binding to the hard bases to give ionic complexes, whereas the soft acids prefer binding to soft bases to give covalent complexes. Metal ions of borderline category can behave as either hard or soft acid, depending on the solvent, stereochemical and electronic structural factors. Therefore, the HSAB principle accounts well for the decreased affinity of SADH and AADH towards metal ions, from Pb^{2+} (borderline) to Hg^{2+} (soft) and Cd^{2+} (soft).
- The ionic sizes of the metal ions are in the order, Pb^{2+} (0.118 nm) > Hg^{2+} (0.102 nm) > Cd^{2+} (0.095 nm). It has been proved by many investigators that neutral oxygen donors have higher affinity towards larger metal ions. This leads to an increase in the stabilities of complexes with large metal ions relative to small ions. Also, ligands that form 5- membered chelate rings are better pre-organized for coordinating with large metal ions. All these factors contribute to the observed relative stabilities of the complexes.
- An extensive chemical speciation study of the amino acid-metal ion (Ca^{2+}, Mg^{2+}, Pb^{2+}, Hg^{2+} and Cd^{2+}) binary systems of glycine, L- histidine and L-aspartic acid was carried out under the same experimental conditions to that of ternary systems. This is required as these amino acids were used as secondary ligands in the ternary systems. Also, the literature survey indicated a wide spread in the formation constants of both proton-ligand and metal-ligand complexes.

- The best-fit models obtained for metal ion- glycine systems indicate the formation of MXH, MX, MXH_{-1}, MX_2H_2, MX_2H, MX_2 and MX_2H_{-1} species. The formation of MXH_{-1} and MX_2H_{-1} type of species may be due to the hydroxylation. The ligand seems to act as a monodentate in protonated complexes bonding through only carboxylate oxygen while amino group is protonated and non-bonding. In MX and MX_2 type of complexes glycine may be acting as a bidentate bonding through carboxylate oxygen and α-amino group. The formation constants obtained are in good agreement with the literature values allowing for changes in the experimental conditions.
- The stability constants of Mg^{2+} complexes of amino acids are found to be generally greater than those of Ca^{2+}. Due to the high charge density, Mg^{2+} is expected to form a relatively strong electrostatic bond compared to Ca^{2+} with the anionic carboxylate group of amino acid.
- According to HSAB theory, Pb^{2+} belongs to borderline category, while Hg^{2+} and Cd^{2+} are soft acids. Soft acids prefer to bond with soft bases and hard acids prefer to bond with hard bases. The border line Pb^{2+} can interact with both hard and soft bases. Therefore, it forms stronger bonds with glycine relative to soft Hg^{2+} and Cd^{2+}. This is reflected in the observed order of stabilities $Pb^{2+} > Hg^{2+} > Cd^{2+}$.
- Keeping in view of the various protonation forms of histidine (XH) and its coordination modes, chemical models containing all the plausible species were submitted for analysis to the Miniquad-75 program. In the case of 1:1 metal to ligand composition, all the metal ion systems exhibited the formation of MXH_2, MXH, MX and MXH_{-1} type of species. In solutions containing 1:2 (M:L) molar ratio, species detected progressively with increasing pH are

MX_2H_4, MX_2H_3, MX_2H_2, MX_2H, MX_2 and MX_2H_{-1}. The higher formation constants of MX and MX_2 type of species, except for PbX_2, compared to those of glycine (bidentate) indicate tridentate behaviour of histidine bonding through imidazole nitrogen, carboxylate oxygen and amino nitrogen.

- The ambidentate nature of the histidine i.e. the ability to coordinate histamine-like, imidazole propionic acid-like and glycine-like modes in different species was indicated from the results obtained.
- Histidine in MX type of complexes behaves as a tri-dentate, bonding through carboxylate oxygen (O^-), N-imidazole and N-amino and is therefore a NNO donor. Hg^{2+} and Cd^{2+} are soft acids, while Pb^{2+} is of borderline category. Although nitrogen is classified as a class '**a**' or hard donor atom, it is considered to be more suitable than oxygen for soft acids. Its lower electronegativity (3.0) as compared to oxygen (3.5) and its neutral character in the studied ligands make it more suitable than oxygen for complexation with softer acids. On the other hand, both oxygen and nitrogen donors bond well with the large Hg^{2+} ion (ionic radius 102 pm) compared to Cd^{2+} (ionic radius 95 pm). This explains the relative stability order, $Pb^{2+} < Hg^{2+} > Cd^{2+}$ for histidine complexes.
- Aspartic acid with three potential complex-forming functional groups ($-COO^-$, $-NH_2$ and $-COO^-$ of the side chain) behaves as an ambidentate ligand and can bind the metal ions in different ways.
- The best-fit models obtained for L-aspartic acid- metal ion systems indicate the presence of MXH_2, MXH, MX and MXH_{-1} type of species in 1:1 (M: X) molar ratio systems and MX_2H_4, MX_2H_3, MX_2H_2, MX_2H, MX_2 and MX_2H_{-1} type of species in 1:2 systems.

- The relative order of stabilities of the metal ion complexes of L-Aspartic acid was found to be, $Mg^{2+} > Ca^{2+}$ and $Pb^{2+} > Hg^{2+} > Cd^{2+}$.
- The higher stability of the complex, PbX of aspartic acid, relative to that of glycine clearly indicates the tridentate nature of aspartate. The low value of the formation constant of PbX_2 generally observed for tridentate ligands was attributed to the tetrahedral stereochemistry around Pb^{2+} which arrests further bonding when three of the four positions are occupied.
- Hg^{2+} and Cd^{2+} are soft Lewis acids and therefore may have weak interaction with carboxylate oxygens of aspartic acid. Therefore a negligible interaction with the carboxylate group of the side chain is expected that may lead to lower stabilities.

CHEMICAL MODELLING STUDIES OF THE ESSENTIAL/ TOXIC METAL ION-DIHYDRAZIDE –AMINO ACID TERNARY SYSTEMS

- Mixed chelation occurs commonly in biological fluids as millions of potential ligands are likely to compete for metal ions *in vivo*. Ternary chelation creates specific structures and has been implicated in the storage and transport of active substances through biological membranes.
- Dihydrazides are ditopic ligands possessing two coordinating units separated by a carbon-carbon linker. Depending on the degree of flexibility of the molecule between the two coordination sites there is a possibility of formation of coordination polymers with supramolecular architecture. Two metal centres fixed at a certain distance often allow the binding and thus the recognition and/or activation of a substrate molecule. Therefore, they can be used to mimic metalloproteins and to understand the structure- reactivity relationships.

- A study of the ternary systems containing a metal ion, dihydrazide and amino acid throws light on the nature, stability of the specific structures and synergistic catalytic effects of the two metal centres separated by the carbon-carbon linker.
- To identify the species formed under different concentration conditions, Calvin-Wilson potentiometric titrations were conducted in 1:1:1, 1:1:2, 2:1:1 and 2:1:2 metal ion-dihydrazide-amino acid molar concentration ratios and the data were subjected to analysis by the Miniquad-75 program.
- Both Succinic (SADH) and Adipic (AADH) acid dihydrazides exhibited the formation of a variety of ternary species depending on the metal ion and amino acid.
- The species formed in 1:1:1 (metal ion (M) –dihydrazide (L) - glycine (XH)) systems of both Succinic and Adipic acid hydrazides are $MLXH_2$, MLXH, MLX, and $MLXH_{-1}$ where, M= Ca^{2+}, Mg^{2+}, Pb^{2+}, Hg^{2+} and Cd^{2+} and L= SADH or AADH and XH= glycine. In 1:1:2 systems with glycine as secondary ligand, the species converged include MLX_2H_3, MLX_2H_2, MLX_2H, MLX_2 and MLX_2H_{-1}. The step-wise deprotonation constants and the pH region of existence of various species indicate the probable binding sites of both the ligands. In all the above species metal ion is bonded to only one of the coordination pockets of the dihydrazide, while the other is in either protonated or unprotonated state depending on the species. In $MLXH_2$ and MLXH species glycine is bonded to the metal ion as a monodentate bonding through carboxylate group while α-amino group is protonated and nonbonding. In MLX type of species, it acts as a bidentate bonding through both carboxylate and amino groups.

- Symmetric and asymmetric binuclear species of the type M_2LXH, M_2LX, M_2LXH_{-1} and $M_2LX_2H_2$, M_2LX_2H, M_2LX_2, $M_2LX_2H_{-1}$ were observed, respectively for systems of 2:1:1 and 2:1:2 (M:L:X) concentration ratios. In all these species, dihydrazide acts as a ditopic ligand binding two metal ions, at the two hydrazide groups on either side of the molecule. The addition of glycine results in the formation of versatile species with one or two molecules of amino acid entering in coordination as monodentates or bidentates. Formation of deprotonated species may be due to the hydroxylation or deprotonation of the enolic protons of the dihydrazide. Species distribution diagrams, giving the extent of formation of each species against pH are included.
- Both histidine and aspartic acid possess side chains containing coordinating groups. L-histidine (XH) possesses a polar side chain and has three potential donor sites. Aspartic acid (XH_2) possesses a side chain containing a carboxylic acid group in addition to glycine like coordination groups. Ternary systems containing different concentration ratios of metal ion, dihydrazide and histidine/ aspartic acid indicated the formation of 1. $MLXH_3$, $MLXH_2$, MLXH, MLX and $MLXH_{-1}$ type of species for 1:1:1 (M:L:X) systems, 2. MLX_2H_5, MLX_2H_4, MLX_2H_3, MLX_2H_2, MLX_2H and MLX_2 type of species for 1:1:2 composition, 3. M_2LXH_2, M_2LXH, M_2LX, M_2LXH_{-1} and M_2LXH_{-2} for 2:1:1 systems and 4. $M_2LX_2H_4$, $M_2LX_2H_3$, $M_2LX_2H_2$, M_2LX_2H, M_2LX_2, $M_2LX_2H_{-1}$ and $M_2LX_2H_{-2}$ type of species for 2:1:2 composition. In 1:1:1 and 1:1:2 systems only one of the coordination units of dihydrazide is involved in bonding. Depending on the step-wise deprotonation constants and comparing

with the formation constants of ternary glycine systems, probable bonding sites of the ligands are proposed.

- Relative stabilities of ternary complexes compared to binary species are evaluated quantitatively using $\Delta \log K$ formulation. The factors that affect mixed ligand complex formation include (i) thermodynamic, (ii) statistical, (iii) electrostatic (iv) nature of the two ligands and (iv) interaction between the ligands. The $\Delta \log K$ values obtained for most of the species are on the positive side of the statistically allowed values indicating the stabilization of ternary systems compared to binary. The extra stability of the species may be attributed to stacking or side chain or other interactions. The negative values of $\Delta \log K$ compared to statistically allowed values, however, do not preclude the formation of ternary species in solution.

The work may be extended to solid state studies of the species identified in solution by physico-chemical methods to have a better knowledge on the mode of bonding and structure. However, all the species identified in a solution cannot be isolated as the very method of isolation may change the nature of the species.

* * *

www.ingramcontent.com/pod-product-compliance
Lightning Source LLC
LaVergne TN
LVHW080022210926
848481LV00011B/3088
* 9 7 9 8 2 3 1 9 8 8 0 9 9 *